A COMPANION & GUIDE TO

THE WARS OF THE

ROSES

Edward IV encourages his troops and leads them into battle, British Library, Harley 7353, Life of Edward IV.

A COMPANION & GUIDE TO
THE WARS OF THE ROSES

PETER BRAMLEY

First published by Sutton Publishing Limited, 2007
This edition published by The History Press, 2011

The History Press
The Mill, Brimscombe Port
Stroud, Gloucestershire, GL5 2QG
www.thehistorypress.co.uk

© Peter Bramley, 2007, 2011

Peter Bramley has asserted the moral right to be identified as the author
of this work.

British Library Cataloguing in Publication Data.
A catalogue record for this book is available from the British Library.

ISBN 978 0 7524 6336 0

Printed in India
Manufacturing managed by Jellyfish Print Solutions Ltd

For Racer

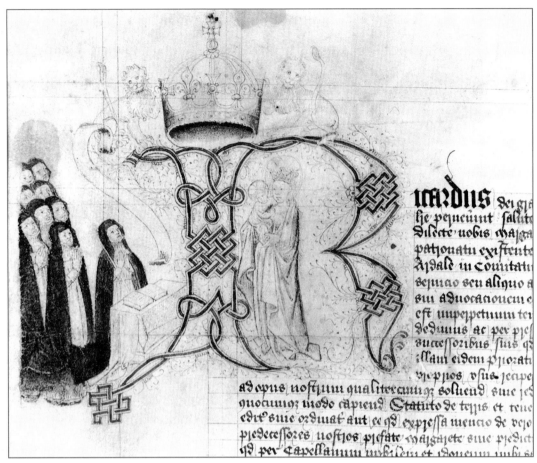

Detail of an initial letter 'R' which encloses a drawing of the Virgin and Child, surmounted by the royal crown and Yorkist white lion supporters. From the Esholt Priory Charter granted to Margaret Clifford, widow of Lord John, killed at Ferrybridge in 1461.

CONTENTS

PREFACE

This guide stems from a long-held belief that the understanding and enjoyment of history can be enhanced from visiting the actual sites of key historical events and monuments/ memorials to people involved in those events. Such visits can complement conventional reading through providing a memorable focus for further study. It has been immensely encouraging to see that in recent years TV documentaries on history now follow the same type of approach, using on-location shots of historic sites associated with the programme's subject matter.

Researching and writing the guide over the past five years has been a 'labour of love'. However, I would not have completed the task without the continuing support of my extended family. Everyone has contributed in their differing ways – from lending antiquarian books and advising on matters publishing to explaining the mysteries of digital photography and even joining me on visits. Special thanks must go, however, to my wife, who has provided much-needed encouragement at crucial times.

Many thanks to Rachel, with whom it has been a great pleasure to work again. I must also thank all the vicars, rectors and churchwardens who have kindly shown me round their churches.

PICTURE CREDITS

There are two sets of colour plates: Plates I are found between pp. 82 and 83; Plates II are found between pp. 178 and 179.

All images are from my own collection unless otherwise credited. I am grateful to the following organisations for permission to reproduce images in their collections.

All maps have been drawn by Derek Stone.

Bibliothèque Nationale
pp. 35, 173

British Library
pp. ii, 4, 33, 40

British Museum
p. 60

College of Arms
Plates I: 2 (top)

Dean and Chapter of Westminster
Plates I: 7 (bottom)

Geoffrey Wheeler
pp. vi, 10, 12, 13, 14 (left), 24, 29, 32, 42, 46, 47, 48, 50, 52, 64, 66, 68, 84, 136, 144, 150, 173, 208, 240, 247; Plates I: pp. 1, 2, 3 (bottom left and right), 4 (bottom left), 5 (top left), 7 (top), 8; Plates II: 2 (bottom), 5 (top right), 6 (bottom right), 7 (bottom), 8 (top left)

Glasgow City Council (Museums)
p. 15 (left)

National Archives
Plates I: p. 6 (top)

National Portrait Gallery
pp. 30, 51

Royal Collection
p. 41

Wallace Collection
pp. 14 (right), 15 (right)

MOST REWARDING PLACES TO VISIT

This guidebook recommends 260 historic sites and battlefields in England and Wales connected in some way with the Wars of the Roses. I have adopted a rating system (explained on pp. 61–2) to assist readers in selecting places to visit. The ratings reflect not only the historical importance of a site or battlefield but also its extent or attractiveness. The ratings given are based on my opinions alone.

TOP-RATED SITES

*****

Canterbury
Fotheringhay
St George's Chapel, Windsor
The Tower of London
Westminster Abbey

****

Beverley
Britford
Burghfield
Cambridge
Clarendon
Coldridge
Coventry
Gainsborough
Gipping
Leicester
Long Melford
Ludlow

Middleham
Ormskirk
Salisbury
Stony Stratford
Tewkesbury Abbey
Thetford
Warwick
Winchester
Wingfield

TOP-RATED BATTLEFIELDS

+++++
Bosworth
Tewkesbury
Towton

++++
First St Albans
Wakefield

ONE

INTRODUCTION TO THE GUIDE

My interest in the Wars of the Roses goes back many years but really developed following the upsurge in research and books published for the 500th anniversary of the Battle of Bosworth in 1985. Over the years my reading has highlighted that the Wars are incredibly rich in survivals of battle sites, houses, castles, plaques and church monuments. The objective of this guide is to introduce the reader to the best of these by providing for each such surviving site:

- A short description of what there is to see.
- A brief account of any events in the Wars of the Roses that occurred there and/or biography of the person(s) commemorated, covering his/her role in the Wars. Few battlefields and fewer churches contain any detailed information on this either in a leaflet or with a display notice, but there are exceptions. This guide fills the gap.
- Summary directions on how to find the site and other entry details. These directions are designed to complement modern road atlases.
- A broad-brush 'star' rating.

The guide covers the 260 sites in England and Wales which I consider to be the most interesting and important for the Wars of the Roses. They occur in virtually every county of England and Wales, showing that although the battles were confined to the central and northern heartlands of England, the conflict was a truly national one. I have visited more than 600 such sites over the last five years, selecting those to visit by consulting recent historical literature (see Bibliography), including the Pevsner and Arthur Mee county guides. My criteria for including sites in the guide are:

- There must be *something memorable to see* to act as a focus of interest. So churches where someone is known to have been buried but where no memorial has survived have been excluded. All the major battles of the Wars are included.

- Castles only rarely featured actively in the Wars, except in Northumberland and Wales. However, they still served as the military and domestic headquarters of the aristocracy. Where a castle or manor house was built or substantially rebuilt by a participant in the Wars, it has been included in the guide as a memorial to that person (e.g. Herstmonceux Castle), in addition to any castles that did see major action (e.g. Harlech Castle).
- Last, but not least, each site must be accessible to the public.

I have visited all the sites selected for the guide at least once. From the human angle, I have included sites as memorials to people if they fought at least one battle in the Wars or if they were royal or government officials. The biographies of participants have been built up from the same literature, but significantly enhanced by consulting J.C. Wedgwood's parliamentary biographies and Cokayne's *The Complete Peerage*, together with W.E. Hampton's *Memorials of the Wars of the Roses: A Biographical Guide* for church memorials.

A real bonus from this exercise is that the 260 selected sites include some of the most beautiful buildings in England and Wales. The fifteenth century saw the flowering of Perpendicular architecture in churches, while brick was just beginning to be used in fortified manor houses and castles. The sites themselves are often in beautiful country as well – although some are definitely not! It is worth noting that there are many more sites connected with participants from the final phase of the Wars, between 1483 and 1487. This is probably because of increasing prosperity in the early Tudor years.

The guide also includes a summary of the key dates, the causes and key features of the Wars, together with profiles of their main participants, designed to provide the reader with background for site visits.

Finally a perspective. The main attraction of the Wars of the Roses as a period for historical study is the political and military drama involved. The late Professor Ross wrote, 'The two years from June 1469–May 1471 form a period of political instability without parallel in English history since 1066.' However, do not expect to find a full and coherent explanation of all these events in the literature. The Wars took place just before the printed word became widely available, there are few contemporary sources (some of which are written with clear bias) and many later sources were influenced by the Tudor 'spin machine'. The mystery of the Princes in the Tower is well known, but there are others. That is the other attraction of the period – it is a crossword with some key clues still missing.

TWO

THE BACKGROUND TO THE WARS

ENGLAND IN 1450

- Total Population: 2–2.5 million, down from over 4 million in 1300 as a result of the ravages of the Black Death and successive plagues.
- Still predominantly a rural economy, with 80–90 per cent of the population employed in agriculture.
- Nearly one-third of the land area was held by monasteries. Abbots sat in the House of Lords.
- Government of the country was in the hands of the landed aristocracy, including clerics (who regularly held key positions) plus some burgesses/merchants.
- Society was highly stratified. The landed aristocracy was divided into gentry (around 10,000), peers (about 70) and magnates (a handful of great peers). Gentry sat with burgesses and merchants in the House of Commons as MPs; peers, magnates, abbots and bishops sitting in the Lords. Aristocracy tended to marry from the same stratum and usually as a 'property transaction'. The manor was the bedrock of this property system.
- Eldest sons inherited lands, although strict 'tail male' was rare. When there were no sons, daughters usually shared the inheritance. The marriage market was therefore lively and largely a matter of business.
- English had been spoken universally among the aristocracy for only around fifty years.
- Do not expect to read much in this guide about the lower levels of society. Few church monuments survive below the aristocratic level and history rarely mentions the lower orders.
- At the bottom of society, serfdom still existed although the lot of the working man was improving following the appalling loss of life in the Black Death.
- The country was in the grip of a severe agricultural depression which only eased in the 1480s.
- The north and south of the country were still largely separate, divided by the River Trent. English dialects were so different that communication across the north–south divide could be difficult.
- An army could move at maximum 30 miles per day, so the country was far-flung.

3

KINGS OF ENGLAND 1327–1509

Monarch	Ruled	Comments
Edward III	1327–77	Died
Richard II	1377–99	Deposed and later murdered
Henry IV	1399–1413	Died
Henry V	1413–22	Died on campaign
Henry VI	1422–61 and 1470–1	Deposed twice
	Readeption	Murdered
Edward IV	1461–83 (less 1470–1)	Died
Edward V	1483 (April–June)	Deposed and later disappeared, presumed murdered
Richard III	1483–5	Killed in battle
Henry VII	1485–1509	Died

DEFINITIONS

The term '**Wars of the Roses**' refers to the series of linked civil wars in England and Wales spread over a generation in the second half of the fifteenth

John of Gaunt from the Golden Book of St Alban's.

century. These politico-military conflicts were dynastic in nature, during which the throne of England was disputed by rival branches of the ruling Plantagenet family. The throne changed hands violently on five occasions during this time. King Edward III had five surviving sons. The rival branches (or houses) in the Wars took their names from the third and fourth sons – John of Gaunt, Duke of Lancaster, and Edmund of Langley, Duke of York. However, the descent of the Dukes of York from the second son, Lionel, Duke of Clarence, through the female line was to be key.

The description 'Wars of the Roses' was not contemporary. It was first coined in the nineteenth century by Sir Walter Scott. Prior to that, the term the 'Cousins' Wars' had been used, because a large number of the principal protagonists were cousins. The term 'Roses' has the major advantage of conveying the sense of dynastic rivalry between two royal houses. However the roses themselves were not widely used as military emblems in the Wars. The white rose became the personal emblem of Elizabeth of York (she was Edward IV's daughter and became Henry Tudor's queen). Henry was able to call on an old Lancastrian emblem, the red rose, so as to create the Tudor Rose after his accession in 1485, to signify the union of the two rival houses.

The disadvantage of the Roses title is that it implies a degree of continuity of support or 'party' to each side over the full duration of the Wars. In fact, support was very much determined by the individual leader. The Yorkist supporters of Edward IV at the Battle of Towton in 1461 were not necessarily from the same political faction as those who fought for Richard III at the Battle of Bosworth (1485).

In some ways, 'Cousins' Wars' gives the better flavour of the civil wars by not implying two fixed 'parties' and focusing more on the role of the leaders. However, the term is nothing like as memorable.

Timing: If a war is defined by its set-piece battles, then the Wars stretched from 1455 (First Battle of St Albans) to 1487 (the Battle of Stoke Field, which marks the first and last time King Henry VII's throne was seriously challenged). If a war is defined by the start and end of serious political or military conflict, then 1450 is a better start date, when London and the south were aflame with Jack Cade's Rebellion, which challenged King Henry VI's hold on the throne.

The Wars were not continuous. There were periods of little or no military activity, e.g. in the 1470s. The Wars are best understood in four distinct but linked **phases**:

1. The **Descent into War**, 1450–9, during which King Henry VI suffered at least two mental breakdowns, Queen Margaret and Richard, Duke of York established themselves as the principal protagonists, the Nevilles added much-needed bite to York's cause, and the two sides flirted with war at the First Battle of St Albans in 1455.

2. The **Wars of Succession**, 1460–5, in which York's leadership of the Yorkist cause was eclipsed by Richard Neville, Earl of Warwick, Edward IV was established as king at the Battle of Towton (1461) and the Nevilles finished off lingering Lancastrian resistance in Wales and Northumberland. Henry VI was eventually imprisoned.

3. The **Destruction of the Nevilles and of Lancaster**, 1469–71. Repeatedly goaded by Edward IV, Warwick rebelled in conjunction with the Duke of Clarence, Edward's brother, and then changed sides and allied with Queen Margaret. Fortunes fluctuated wildly until the two sides met at the Battle of Barnet and the Nevilles were killed – Clarence having changed sides yet again. The exiled Lancastrian leadership seized the opportunity to challenge again for the throne. At the Battle of Tewkesbury, just a few weeks later, the Lancastrians were destroyed. Henry VI was murdered in the Tower and Queen Margaret captured. The Lancastrian cause seemingly died.

4. The **Rise of Henry Tudor**, 1483–7, in which Edward IV died young, his son Edward V was deposed and murdered, probably by his uncle Richard III, and then Richard in turn was challenged by Henry Tudor as the Lancastrian candidate, who had promised to marry Edward IV's daughter Elizabeth of York. At the Battle of Bosworth, Richard's support evaporated and he was killed. Henry Tudor took the vacant throne and beat off an attempted Yorkist challenge at the Battle of Stoke Field.

CAUSES OF THE WARS OF THE ROSES

The Inadequacy of Henry VI as King

It is one of English history's supreme ironies that Henry V, arguably the most effective medieval king in both war and peace, was succeeded in 1422 by his infant son, Henry VI, who grew up to be the least effective king of England of any era.

From an early age Henry VI performed the ceremonial duties of monarchy. After the death of John, Duke of Bedford, Henry V's brother, in 1435 he began to take over the reigns of executive government. He was to prove a complete failure in this most exacting of roles, at a time when the government of the country revolved completely around the person of the king. Intellectually unable to grapple with the complexity of policy, and emotionally disinclined to undertake the essential power-brokering with the nobility, Henry failed to stamp his personal mark on the events of the reign. It is rarely possible to discern the King's individual will. There was always someone else driving events forward (Cardinal Beaufort, the Dukes of Suffolk and Somerset). At the centre of power, therefore, a vacuum developed. This had a number of consequences.

Inevitably, other, more dynamic and ruthless members of the higher nobility sought to fill this power vacuum. Partisan politics developed out of debates on the conduct of the French war – Beaufort led a peace 'party', Duke Humphrey, Henry V's youngest brother, the pro-war 'party'. During the 1440s these roles were passed on to Suffolk and Richard, Duke of York. The inept and almost pell-mell retreat from France after 1445, pushed through by Suffolk, meant that, by 1450, opposition between the two groups was at boiling point and the country in chaos.

Corruption flourished throughout government. The medieval polity needed a strong king to combat this perennial evil, not a vacuum.

Expenditure on the French wars, plus this corruption in high places, led to disastrous decline in the government finances. Taxes for the French war were very reluctantly granted by parliament and the Lancastrian regime was probably technically bankrupt. Henry V would have prevented this situation from happening; his son was clueless.

In the Middle Ages, the king was the linchpin in the process of maintaining law and order. Without a strong king to enforce the system, civil order (never at high levels anyway) tended to break down,

notably in the north, East Anglia and the south-west. Aristocratic violence became even more common-place than usual.

A crucial role for a medieval king was to lead the military machine of his realm at home and abroad. Henry V represents the role model. His son, by contrast, was a man of peace and would not/could not fight. He was the only medieval English king never to lead an army overseas in battle. In fact, he was present with his army at five battles in the Wars of the Roses but never fought, let alone took command. This was a serious shortcoming for a monarch in such a militaristic society.

Henry's Mental Collapse

During 1452/3, after the fall of Lancastrian France, Henry seemed to be making a determined effort to be more involved in the detail of government. Unfortunately, in August 1453, catastrophe struck. Triggered either by the news that Gascony, the last English colony in France, had fallen with the death of John Talbot, Earl of Shrewsbury at the Battle of Chatillon, or even by the discovery that Queen Margaret was pregnant, or both, Henry suffered a major nervous breakdown (probably caused by catatonic schizophrenia), after which he was incapable of communication for nearly eighteen months. This tragedy had two effects.

First, despite Queen Margaret's demands to be regent, from February 1454 Richard, Duke of York became Lord Protector, with power to govern through the Council. This gave the opposition party of York and the Nevilles (Earls of Salisbury and Warwick) a taste of real power for the first time.

Second, Henry suffered a second breakdown after being injured in the neck by an arrow at the First Battle of St Albans in May 1455. His mental state worsened and from then on he was severely mentally incapacitated and a mere cipher in his own kingdom. England's power vacuum was filled with the competing claims of Henry's Queen Margaret and Henry, 3rd Duke of Somerset on the one side, and Richard, Duke of York and the Neville earls on the other. Henry's future as king, and indeed his life, were now completely at the mercy of others.

The Plantagenet Dynastic Position

In fact Henry's position as king was much worse than this. His grandfather, King Henry IV's, title to the throne, enunciated at the 1399 usurpation, contained a potentially fatal flaw. The usurped King Richard II had had no children. His heir presumptive had been

THE ROYAL HOUSES OF LANCASTER AND YORK

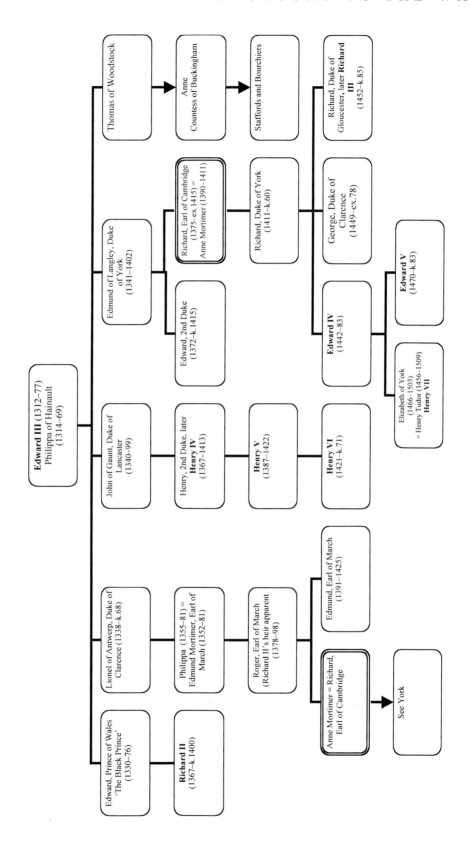

Edward III (1312–77)
Philippa of Hainault
(1314–69)

Edward, Prince of Wales
'The Black Prince'
(1330–76)

Richard II
(1367–k.1400)

Lionel of Antwerp, Duke of
Clarence (1338–k.68)

Philippa (1355–81) =
Edmund Mortimer, Earl of
March (1352–81)

Roger, Earl of March
(Richard II's heir apparent
(1378–98)

Edmund, Earl of March
(1391–1425)

Anne Mortimer = Richard,
Earl of Cambridge

See York

John of Gaunt, Duke of
Lancaster
(1340–99)

Henry, 2nd Duke, later
Henry IV
(1367–1413)

Henry V
(1387–1422)

Henry VI
(1421–k.71)

Edmund of Langley, Duke
of York
(1341–1402)

Edward, 2nd Duke
(1372–k.1415)

Richard, Earl of Cambridge
(1375–ex.1415) =
Anne Mortimer (1390–1411)

Richard, Duke of York
(1411–k.60)

Edward IV
(1442–83)

Elizabeth of York
(1466–1503)
= Henry Tudor (1456–1509)
Henry VII

Edward V
(1470–k.83)

George, Duke of
Clarence
(1449–ex.78)

Thomas of Woodstock

Anne
Countess of Buckingham

Staffords and Bourchiers

Richard, Duke of
Gloucester, later Richard
III
(1452–k.85)

Roger Mortimer (killed in Ireland in 1398). The Mortimers were descended from Lionel, Duke of Clarence the *second* surviving son of Edward III through his daughter Philippa, who married Edmund Mortimer, Roger's father. In England it was unclear at this time whether Salic law applied to the succession of the monarchy (i.e. the crown could only pass through males, as in France), because since the Plantagenet succession in 1135, the crown had passed directly through the male line for 250 years. If succession through the female line was possible in England then Edmund Mortimer (Roger's 7-year-old son) was heir presumptive at Richard II's deposition.

Henry Bolingbroke, Duke of Lancaster swept to power in 1399 as Henry IV on a wave of widespread support from the nobility, who were thoroughly disenchanted with Richard II's attempts to place himself and his homosexual favourites on a pedestal above the rest of the nobility. Henry represented a monarchy that would be more likely to rule in the interests of the nobles. His formal claim to the throne was based on an alternative descent from Edmund, brother to Edward I, that avoided comparison with Lionel, Duke of Clarence or Edmund Mortimer. In the excitement of usurpation, this rival claim was overlooked. Edmund, in fact, proved a thoroughly loyal supporter of the Lancastrian kings, even 'cooperating' to the extent of having no children, and died in 1425.

However, even more extraordinarily, Henry IV allowed Edmund's sister Anne Mortimer to marry Richard, Earl of Cambridge, the second son of Edmund, 1st Duke of York. In 1411 Anne gave birth to a son, also Richard. In 1415 Richard, Earl of Cambridge was executed by Henry V in 1415 for his part in the Southampton Plot, and his elder brother, Edward, 2nd Duke of York (who was childless) was killed at the Battle of Agincourt, 'young' Richard becoming 3rd Duke of York as heir to his uncle. In 1425 on the death of Edmund Mortimer, Richard, Duke of York not only inherited the huge Mortimer estates in the Welsh Marches and in Ireland but also the rival Mortimer claim to the throne of England, which he was to put forward in dramatic fashion many years later, in October 1460. It is unclear at which exact point Richard decided to bid for the throne but certainly by 1450, during Jack Cade's Revolt, the eponymous leader was styling himself 'Mortimer' – an indication that others, at least, saw Richard of York as a candidate for the throne.

The Lancastrian monarchy was safe so long as its kings were effective and popular. By 1422, at Henry V's death, the regime was thoroughly established, both Henry IV and Henry V proving very effective kings. In fact the glories of the Agincourt campaign, the subsequent conquest of Normandy by Henry V and the naming of Henry as heir to the throne of France by Charles added a lustre to the Lancastrian ruling house that enabled Henry's younger brothers John, Duke of Bedford and Humphrey, Duke of Gloucester, together with Cardinal Beaufort, to maintain its popularity until Bedford's death in 1435. Thereafter, events went downhill in France and Henry VI's complete ineffectiveness was to change everything. Nevertheless there was no overt mention of a Yorkist claim to the throne between 1415 and 1450.

The Small Size of the Lancastrian Royal Family

When he died in 1413, Henry IV would have been confident that not only was his throne in the secure hands of his eldest son but that the future of his dynasty was assured. Although Henry V was not yet married at 25, this should not be a problem because he had three healthy brothers to support his regime and to provide future heirs if needed. In the event, the four brothers produced just one legitimate child between them – Henry V's son, Henry VI. While John, Duke of Bedford and Humphrey, Duke of Gloucester provided splendid support to Henry VI in their lifetimes, there was no one else to follow on. The only other members of the Lancastrian royal family in addition to Henry in 1450 were

- Henry Holland, Duke of Exeter, who was descended from Henry IV's sister Elizabeth.
- Edmund and Jasper Tudor. These were the offspring of the probably illegal marriage between Owen Tudor, a Welsh courtier, and Catherine of Valois, Henry V's widow. Out of respect for his mother, Henry VI co-opted these stepbrothers into the royal family, making them Earls of Richmond and Pembroke respectively in 1452. Edmund became the father of Henry Tudor (later Henry VII), while Jasper was to provide huge support to his nephew's later bid for the throne.
- The Beauforts. John of Gaunt and his mistress, Katherine Swynford, produced four illegitimate children between 1372 and 1379. They married in 1396 and the children were legitimated by Richard II and by the pope. Although probably barred from the throne by an amendment to an Act of Parliament inserted by Henry IV in 1407,

this talented family provided the support to Henry VI through his step-uncle Cardinal Beaufort and his step-cousins Edmund and Henry Beaufort, Dukes of Somerset. Unfortunately only the primary branch of the family were significant landowners, in the person of Lady Margaret Beaufort after 1444. Although key members of the Court party, the Beauforts therefore brought little wealth and military might to the table.

The Alienation of Richard, Duke of York from the Lancastrian Regime

Richard had been made Lieutenant of Normandy in 1439 and took a long time in actually crossing over to Rouen. His performance there was indifferent, but he seemed naturally to ally with the pro-war opposition party led by Duke Humphrey of Gloucester. He formed a particular dislike of Edmund Beaufort, 1st Duke of Somerset, a leading member of the Court party. In many ways, Richard should have been Henry VI's natural 'chief minister' after Humphrey's death in 1447. Instead, by 1450 he was positioned as the champion of reform, with good support in the House of Commons. It is unclear when Richard first decided to claim the throne but his behaviour in the 1440s and 50s is clearly consistent with his subsequent formal claim in October 1460.

The Appearance of Warwick the Kingmaker

Richard, Duke of York's first attempts at armed opposition to the Lancastrian monarchy lacked decisiveness and ruthlessness. The confrontation with the King and Court party at Dartford was a fiasco for Richard. After Henry's mental collapse in 1453, however, more dynamic and ruthless characters entered the power vacuum around the King. The Neville Earls Salisbury and Warwick (father and son) were by 1454 in serious conflict in Yorkshire with the Percys over land. By the First Protectorate in 1455 they had allied themselves with Richard, Duke of York. Warwick in particular brought a new edge to York's cause – great intelligence, dynamism, bombast and a disregard for the rule of law, as well as great wealth and military might. This edge was to sweep the Yorkists to power in 1460/1, but also led to the death of York himself. The term 'Warwick the Kingmaker' appeared later, but fits the bill. He was the epitome of the overmighty subject who, through marriage, had accumulated such wealth that he could challenge the military might of the Crown.

Queen Margaret of Anjou as Regent

In similar fashion, after 1453 Queen Margaret comes to the fore. A strong, intelligent, determined and emotional woman, she sought to protect the dynastic interests of her infant son, Prince Edward. Disregarding precedent in England, she demanded to be regent while Henry was ill. Formally, this did not happen but, after the death of Edmund Beaufort, Duke of Somerset at the first Battle of St Albans in 1455 and York's Second Protectorate in 1455, she in effect ruled England from 1456 to 1460. From 1458, she was determined on war with York, even if King Henry was not.

Other background causes of the Wars were:

* Bastard feudalism. By the fifteenth century, knights could be retained by a lord, not just through the feudal system but by cash payment, enabling the lord to build up a much stronger retinue. Money was even more closely linked to power.
* In 1450, England was in the grip of deep agricultural depression, exacerbated by the chaos at the end of the French wars, which squeezed aristocratic rents. The depression did not really begin to lift until the early 1480s. The increasing prosperity of the early Tudor years is reflected in the large increase in the number of brasses and tomb-chests found in churches round the country for this period.

KEY FEATURES OF THE WARS OF THE ROSES

The Wars were more about power than principle – the power resulting from possessing the crown of England. The aristrocracy's choice of which side to support depended largely on potential personal gain and on intra-family loyalties. The only important principle involved was whether to stay loyal to an anointed king, a principle that was broken five times in the Wars. Some families remained dedicated to one side, especially Lancastrians (e.g. Hungerford and de Vere), but others changed sides with changing circumstances (e.g. Audley). The political composition of the armies of Lancaster and York thus varied considerably through the thirty-year period; for example, the Yorkist army of Richard III at Bosworth in 1485 did not have the same composition as that of his brother Edward IV at Towton twenty-four years earlier.

Prince of Wales feathers badges, on choir stall, Ludlow church, Shropshire.

The Wars were not territorial or economic, except in Northumberland and Wales. Outside these areas, sieges of castles and towns were extremely rare (but did occur, e.g. Bodiam Castle briefly in 1483).

The Wars therefore revolved around sixteen battles or skirmishes fought between the leaders of the Houses of Lancaster and York and their supporters. The battles are spread through a large part of England and Wales but are mainly in central, western and northern England. The armies involved usually had a local flavour but were very much national in context. Often the main objective of a battle was to target a small number of magnates and to kill them in battle or shortly afterwards (e.g. the First Battle of St Albans, Northampton, Wakefield and Bosworth). In effect, the battlefields gave a thin veil of 'legitimacy' to political assassination, for example the death of Richard, Duke of York at the Battle of Wakefield in December 1460, and to vendetta.

The Wars were not a geographic contest between Lancashire and Yorkshire. The House of York held few lands in Yorkshire, which, at the beginning of the Wars, was actually a Lancastrian stronghold. In fact members of the aristocracy from all counties of England and Wales were involved in the Wars at some time or another.

Since personal gain (usually in the form of extra land) was often the main motivator for the aristocracy then treachery before or on the field of

Weeper on the fifteenth-century tomb of the Fitzherberts of Norbury, Derbyshire, who were Yorkist supporters.

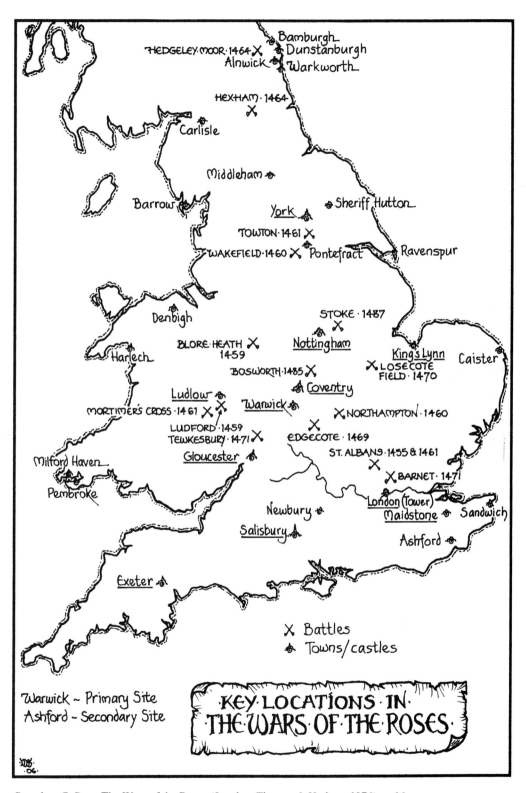

Bamburgh
Dunstanburgh
HEDGELEY·MOOR·1464 X
Alnwick
Warkworth

HEXHAM·1464
X

Carlisle

Middleham

Barrow

York

Sheriff Hutton

TOWTON·1461 X

WAKEFIELD·1460 X
Pontefract
Ravenspur

Denbigh

STOKE·1487
X

BLORE·HEATH X
1459
Nottingham

King's Lynn
Caister

Harlech
LOSECOTE
X FIELD·1470

BOSWORTH·1485 X

Ludlow
Coventry

Warwick

MORTIMER'S CROSS·1461 X
X NORTHAMPTON·1460

LUDFORD·1459
EDGECOTE·1469

TEWKESBURY·1471 X
ST·ALBANS·1455 & 1461
X

Gloucester
X BARNET·1471

Milford Haven

Pembroke
London (Tower)

Newbury
Maidstone
Sandwich

Salisbury
Ashford

Exeter

X Battles
Towns/castles

Warwick ~ Primary Site
Ashford ~ Secondary Site

KEY·LOCATIONS·IN·
THE·WARS·OF·THE·ROSES·

Based on C. Ross, The Wars of the Roses (London, Thames & Hudson, 1976), p. 16.

Margaret of Anjou, drawing of a stained glass portrait once in the church of the Cordeliers, Angers, where she was buried.

Edmund, Lord Grey and his wife Katherine – his treachery was decisive at the Battle of Northampton.

battle was common; in fact there was treachery or hints of it at most of the battles. Nowhere was the practice more openly admitted or more effective than at the Battle of Northampton in July 1460, when Lord Grey of Ruthin switched to the Yorkists at the last minute. The battle lasted twenty minutes and ended in a Lancastrian rout.

All non-clergy members of the aristocracy were trained in the use of arms and other military matters from a young age. Medieval England was a militaristic society which needed to protect its borders with Wales and Scotland and had, over the last hundred years, sent expeditionary forces to France. There was no significant national standing army. The aristocracy provided the trained manpower in the form of their own household men or paid retainers, i.e. their retinue, and typically led and participated in the fighting themselves. The knight in armour was the aristocratic core of the fifteenth-century army. Ownership of land determined the size of retinue and therefore the power an aristocrat wielded.

Perhaps surprisingly, virtually all the battles in the Wars were fought on foot. Since the fourteenth century, the deadly effectiveness of large numbers of English archers had revolutionised warfare, much reducing the effectiveness of cavalry. Each army would comprise three or more times as many archers as knights in armour. Body armour had evolved from chain mail to plate to counter archers, but the

protection of horses was less effective and very expensive. English knights had learned in France to dismount on the battlefield and tether their horses at the rear in the horse-park. Very often, commanders preferred to dig into a prepared position, protected by steep natural slopes and rivers, so that if the line broke, the ensuing rout was catastrophic for the beaten side as knights attempted to lumber back to the horse-park.

Artillery was in its infancy and only impinged fitfully as at Losecote Field and Tewkesbury. Handguns were just being introduced.

Tactical options in battle were therefore limited. Battles were 'chaotic, noisy and murderous' hand-to-hand clashes which, in the case of the Battle of Towton, lasted all day. The easy route to success was, in fact, treachery. Otherwise the key to success in a Wars of the Roses battle was strategy, i.e. maximum mobilisation of fully loyal supporters and rapid concentration of forces at the point of battle (the First Battle of St Albans is a great example of this). Edward IV excelled as a general in all these areas (e.g. his awesome performance at the battles of Barnet and Tewkesbury in 1471). Deception on the battlefield could also play its part (e.g. the Earl of Salisbury at the Battle of Blore Heath in 1459).

This was a civil war very much influenced by our European neighbours. The French kings gave support to Henry VI, Warwick and Henry Tudor, the Duke of Burgundy to Edward. The Scots lent their support to Queen Margaret of Anjou in the early

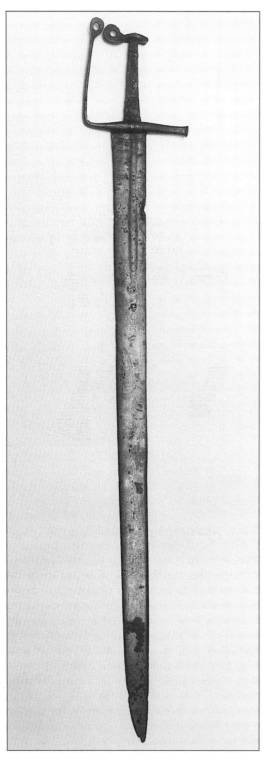

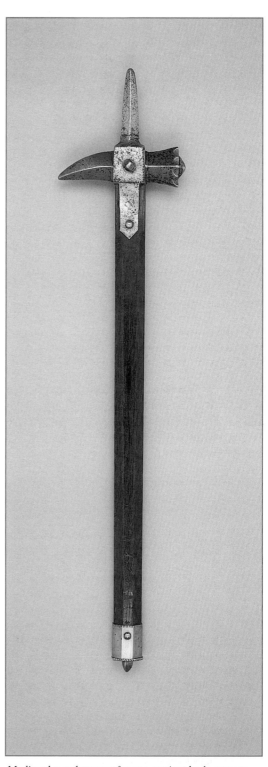

The Wakefield Sword, excavated from the site of the Battle of Wakefield.

Medieval war hammer for use against body armour.

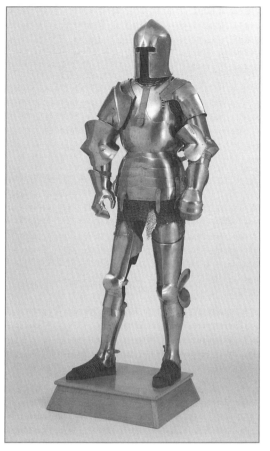

Milanese Avant armour, c. 1450. Most armour worn by wealthy aristocrats was made abroad.

South German armour for horse and rider, c. 1480.

1460s and Ireland was also involved, especially in Lambert Simnel's rising.

Naval engagements and seaborne invasions therefore play a surprisingly large part in the Wars. Since the Kingmaker was Captain of Calais and something of a naval man, he and Edward as Earl of March were able to use Calais as a base to invade Kent (Sandwich) in 1460, prior to the Battle of Northampton. Furthermore, when Edward IV returned from Burgundy to end the Readeption in 1471, his small flotilla, including Burgundian troops, eventually landed at Ravenspur in the East Riding. Henry Tudor similarly brought over his French troops and other supporters to Dale Bay in Pembrokeshire in 1485. The Earl of Lincoln and Lambert Simnel landed near Barrow-in-Furness with their mixed German/Irish force in 1487, prior to the Battle of Stoke Field.

THE EFFECTS OF THE WARS

The short term

Although long-lasting, the Wars of the Roses did not involve total war. The battles were relatively short and often involved low casualties among the commons. The Battle of Towton (1461) was the exception. There were long periods with only limited conflict, e.g. 1464–8 and 1471–83 and there were very few sieges or sackings or laying waste of the countryside. The exception was December 1460–March 1461 during the Lancastrian drive to St Albans, when Yorkist towns were attacked along the Great North Road.

Overall casualties thus had a limited impact on the country, with the important exception of the murderous casualty rate among the magnates. Although many families continued in the male line because peers had already fathered sons, between 1469 and 1471 the Beauforts and the Nevilles were eliminated in the male line.

Where the Wars had a really significant impact was in the breakdown of law and order within the aristocracy as a whole. Aristocratic violence usually occurred during property disputes and had long been endemic in medieval England. Levels of violence flared up in the 1440s and 50s because of Henry VI's ineffectiveness and the increasing tension between Yorkists and Lancastrians. The subsequent warfare and chaos exacerbated matters greatly, giving a free hand to the aristocracy to resolve disputes violently, especially in the 1469–71 phase, when the last private battle in England was fought, at Nibley Green in 1470 between Lord Berkeley and Viscount Lisle. Areas of the country bordered on the ungovernable, such as East Anglia, Derbyshire and the north. In the 1470s and 80s Edward IV managed to get some grip on aristocratic lawlessness.

The place of the Wars in history

In the short term the Wars contained drama a-plenty both on and off the battlefield, but what impact did they have on England and Wales from the longer-term perspective?

The Wars were dynastic in concept. Unquestionably their most significant impact was the climactic seizure of the throne of England by Henry Tudor at the Battle of Bosworth (1485). Under no other circumstances than those created by the Wars from 1455–85 is it likely that the 'outsider' Henry Tudor would have become King of England and founded our most celebrated dynasty. The Tudors were an intelligent, forward-looking and proactive dynasty which oversaw the seismic events of the Tudor Revolution and the Reformation. England began the journey towards the modern world.

The murderous loss of life in the Wars among the magnates had by 1485 created a situation where, temporarily at least, the power of the magnates as a group was reduced by death, minority and demotion. The de Vere Earls of Oxford and the Stanley Earls of Derby remained very strong but were pillars of the Tudor regime. The weakness of the other big families, especially after 1490, gave Henry a unique opportunity to establish his dynasty. This he took. Although there were rebellions in the 1490s (e.g. Sir William Stanley's), they never seriously threatened. The 'overmighty' subject did not raise his head again. By the reign Henry VIII, the Tudors and the Crown itself were supreme.

The Tudors were helped in this process by the steady improvement in the agricultural economy which took place from the 1480s onwards – a peace dividend?

Many exam syllabuses assume 1485 as the end of the medieval period. It was more the beginning of the end. The medieval world lasted until the Reformation, in the 1530s.

KEY DATES OF THE WARS OF THE ROSES AND THE BUILD-UP TO THEM

Background

1399	**August**	Deposition of Richard II by the Lancastrian King Henry IV. Mortimer claim to the throne ignored.
1420	**May**	Treaty of Troyes between Henry V and Charles VI of France.
	June	Henry V marries Charles's daughter, Catherine of Valois.
1421	**December**	Catherine gives birth to Henry of Windsor.
1422	**August**	Death of Henry V and accession of Henry VI, aged 9 months
	October	Death of Charles VI. Henry VI accedes to dual monarchy of England and France.
1435	**September**	Death of John, Duke of Bedford, Regent of France.
1441	**June**	Richard, Duke of York takes up appointment as Lieutenant-General of Normandy.
1443	**March**	John Beaufort, Duke of Somerset appointed Captain-General of France and Gascony.

1444	May	Treaty of Tours between Henry VI and Charles VII of France. Suicide of Somerset.
1445	April	Henry VI marries Margaret of Anjou at Titchfield, Hants under terms of Treaty of Tours.
	December	Secret agreement to surrender Maine to the French.
1447	February	Death of Henry's uncle, Humphrey, Duke of Gloucester.
	March	Death of Cardinal Beaufort.
	December	York 'exiled' as Lieutenant of Ireland.
1448	March	Surrender of Le Mans.
	Spring	Henry VI confers dukedoms on William de la Pole (Suffolk) and Edmund Beaufort (Somerset). Richard, Duke of York begins to use surname Plantagenet to emphasise his royal blood.
1449	July	Richard Neville junior succeeds to Earldom of Warwick through his wife Anne Beauchamp after the failure of her brother's line.
	October	Surrender of Rouen. Loss of Normandy.

The Descent into War

1450	January	Bishop Moleyns murdered in Portsmouth.
	May	Duke of Suffolk murdered on the Thames.
	June–July	Cade's Rebellion. Henry flees London for Midlands. Bishop Ayscough murdered in Wiltshire.
	August	Surrender of Cherbourg.
1451	June	Surrender of Bordeaux.
	August	Surrender of Bayonne in Gascony.
1452	March	York takes up arms but eventually submits to the King and the Duke of Somerset at the Dartford fiasco.
	October	Recovery of Bordeaux by English under John Talbot, Earl of Shrewsbury.
1453	July	French victory at Castillon near Bordeaux. Shrewsbury killed. All Henry V's French possessions except Calais permanently lost.
	August	First mental collapse of Henry VI at Clarendon. Neville–Percy clash at Heworth Moor, York.
	October	Prince Edward born to Queen Margaret.
1454	March	York appointed Protector and Defender of England. Richard Neville, Earl of Salisbury becomes Lord Chancellor. Somerset imprisoned in the Tower.
	October	Neville–Percy clash at Stamford Bridge, Yorkshire.
	25 December	Henry recovers his wits.
1455	March	York, Salisbury and others dismissed from government by Henry VI.
	May	First Battle of St Albans. Somerset and Earl of Northumberland killed. Yorkists (York, Salisbury, Warwick) escort Henry back to London. Second mental collapse of Henry.

	November	York reappointed Protector.
1456	February	York resigns as Protector.
	August	Henry VI (i.e., Queen Margaret) moves the Court to Coventry.
1458	March	Love Day held as public reconciliation of the opposing factions in St Paul's Cathedral.
1459	September	Victory for Salisbury over Lord Audley at Battle of Blore Heath on the way to join York and Warwick at Ludlow.
1459	October	Rout of Ludford Bridge. Yorkists flee to Ireland (York and Rutland) and Calais (March, Warwick and Salisbury).
	November	Parliament of Devils attaints Yorkist leaders.
1460	June	Calais Earls land at Sandwich. The gates of Canterbury are opened to them.
	July	Quick advance first to London and then on to Northampton. Battle of Northampton. Yorkists capture King Henry, Buckingham killed. Queen Margaret flees to Wales. Warwick runs country.
	September	York returns from Ireland.

The War of Succession

	October	York unsuccessfully claims the throne, refused but recognised as Henry's heir in the Act of Accord. York's Third Protectorate.
	December	York killed at Battle of Wakefield, Salisbury executed next day at Pontefract.
1461	January	Warwick runs country from London.
	February	Edward, Duke of York defeats Lancastrians at Battle of Mortimer's Cross. Lancastrian force heads south for London. Sacks Yorkist towns on Great North Road, including Stamford. Warwick defeated by Somerset at Second Battle of St Albans. Queen Margaret passes up opportunity to enter London and returns to Yorkshire.
	March	Edward IV proclaimed King in London. Yorkists achieve decisive victory at Battle of Towton on Palm Sunday.
1462	February	Execution of Oxford and eldest son for treason.
	December	Queen Margaret lands in Northumberland.
1463	December	Somerset reneges on Edward's pardon and joins Lancastrians in Northumberland.
1464	April	Yorkist victory at Battle of Hedgeley Moor.
	May	Secret wedding of Edward IV to Elizabeth Woodville at Grafton Regis. Somerset defeated at Battle of Hexham and executed. Lancastrian residence in England ended.
	September	Announcement of Edward's wedding at Council meeting at Reading.
1465	July	Henry VI captured at Clitheroe.

The Destruction of the Nevilles and of Lancaster

1467	**June**	Lord Chancellor, George Neville dismissed.
1468	**August**	Harlech Castle besieged by Lord Herbert. Surrender marks end of Lancastrian resistance in England and Wales.
	September	Herbert made Earl of Pembroke.
1469	**June**	'Robin of Redesdale' rebellion in Yorkshire.
	July	George, Duke of Clarence marries Isobel, Warwick's daughter in Calais. Yorkists defeated by 'Redesdale' at Battle of Edgcote. Pembroke executed. Edward IV 'arrested' at Olney, Bucks, by the Nevilles.
	August	Edward imprisoned by Warwick at Middleham Castle, Yorks. Warwick runs country.
	September	Sir Humphrey Neville rebels. Warwick forced to release Edward to quell rebellion.
	October	Edward re-enters London and regains control.
1470	**March**	Rebellion of Sir Robert Welles in Lincs in support of Clarence and Warwick, but defeated by Edward at Battle of Losecote Field.
	April	Clarence and Warwick flee to France from the West Country.
	July	Warwick and Clarence change sides and ally with Queen Margaret of Anjou.
	September	Warwick invades England through West Country.
	October	Edward IV confronted by Marquis Montagu, deserts his kingdom via King's Lynn to Burgundy with a small band. Readeption of Henry VI, with the country in practice ruled by Warwick. Queen Margaret and Prince Edward stay in France.
	November	Birth of Prince Edward (later Edward V) to Queen Elizabeth Woodville in sanctuary.
1471	**March**	Edward lands at Ravenspur to recover his kingdom.
	April	Clarence declares for Edward. Warwick besieged by Yorkists at Coventry. Edward regains control of London and his kingdom. Battle of Barnet. The brothers Warwick and Montagu killed. Queen Margaret returns to England.
	May	Yorkists defeat Lancastrian army at Tewkesbury. Somerset executed. Prince Edward killed. Queen Margaret captured. Henry VI murdered in the Tower. Bastard of Fauconberg rebels in Kent and besieges London. Rebellion put down. Henry Tudor flees to France with his uncle, Jasper.
1473		The Earl of Oxford occupies St Michael's Mount.
1474		Oxford surrenders and imprisoned in Hammes Castle, Calais.

1475	**July**	Edward embarks on French expedition but makes peace with Louis XI through Treaty of Picquigny. Collects pension.
1478	**February**	Clarence arraigned for treason and executed. Prince Richard of York (aged 4) marries Anne Mowbray, heiress of dukedom of Norfolk.
1481	**November**	Anne Mowbray dies. Prince Richard retains lands and title of Norfolk. John Howard disinherited.

The Rise of Henry Tudor

1483	**April**	Death of Edward IV. Accession of King Edward V. Gloucester's and Buckingham's first coup at Stony Stratford. Edward imprisoned.
	June	Gloucester's second coup. Execution of Hastings. Edward V deposed. Gloucester proclaimed king and crowned Richard III.
	Summer	Disappearance of Princes in the Tower.
	October	Buckingham's Revolt in south and west of England. Abortive landing by Henry Tudor but he emerges as serious contender for throne.
	November	Execution of Buckingham at Salisbury.
	December	In France, exiled Henry Tudor proclaims intention to marry Edward IV's daughter Elizabeth of York, which would bring two warring factions together.
1484	**April**	Death of Richard III's only son, Prince Edward.
1485	**August**	Henry Tudor lands polyglot force at Milford Haven and marches through Wales to Atherstone, Warwickshire. Richard III killed at Battle of Bosworth, deserted at the last minute by Lord Stanley. Henry VII proclaimed king.
1486		Lovell and Staffords lead unsuccessful uprisings against Henry.
1487		Yorkist army lands near Barrow-in-Furness, marches south and crosses River Trent near Newark. Battle of Stoke Field. Yorkists defeated and Earl of Lincoln (Richard III's heir) killed.
1489		Tax rebellion in Yorkshire. Earl of Northumberland killed.
1495	**February**	Sir William Stanley executed for involvement in Perkin Warbeck conspiracy.
	July–October	Unsuccessful landings in England and Ireland by Warbeck, who surrenders.
1499	**November**	Warbeck and Earl of Warwick (Clarence's son) executed.
1503		Death of Queen Elizabeth of York.
1509	**April**	Death of Henry VII.
	June	Death of his mother, Lady Margaret Beaufort.

THREE

THE MAIN PROTAGONISTS

Key players in the Wars of the Roses are introduced by a sub-heading in bold letters. Other important participants are introduced by underlining. Sites associated with a protagonist are introduced in bold.

THE HOUSE OF YORK

Richard, 3rd Duke of York (1411–k.60)

'Richard of York gained battles in vain' appropriately summarises Richard's overambitious career. The younger child of Richard, Earl of Cambridge and Anne Mortimer, Richard the younger was an orphan by the age of 4. He was brought up in the household of Ralph Neville, Earl of Westmorland and his second wife, Joan Beaufort. Life soon began to improve. In 1425 he came into the dukedom of York from his paternal uncle and also inherited the vast Mortimer estates in the Welsh Marches from Edmund Mortimer, his maternal uncle. He was now the richest man in England, below the King. From Edmund he also inherited the Mortimer claim to the throne of England, which had been ignored when Henry IV deposed Richard II in 1399. To complete the good fortune, Richard was married to Cecily Neville, Ralph and Joan's youngest daughter.

In his early years, Richard followed a conventional career of a senior royal, supportive of Henry VI. He was Governor of Normandy, where he served without real personal distinction. During his time there, he developed a particular dislike of the Beaufort brothers, John and Edmund. In the bipartisan political atmosphere that developed around France in the 1440s, York sided with the pro-war party of Humphrey, Duke of Gloucester against the Beauforts and the King.

Fetterlock and falcon emblem of the York family in Fotheringhay church.

The ignominious exit from Normany in 1450 boiled over into Cade's Rebellion in southern England. Rumours abounded that the Duke of York's agents were behind it. One of Jack Cade's pseudonyms was Mortimer, and York became seen as the voice of reform. York first took up arms against Henry VI at the Dartford fiasco in 1452. There was no fighting, and York was tricked and taken prisoner. This instigated eight years of opposition to the Court party led by Queen Margaret of Anjou and Edmund Beaufort, Duke of Somerset. Initially helped by King Henry's mental breakdown, York (and his Neville allies) tasted real power as

21

THE HOUSE OF YORK

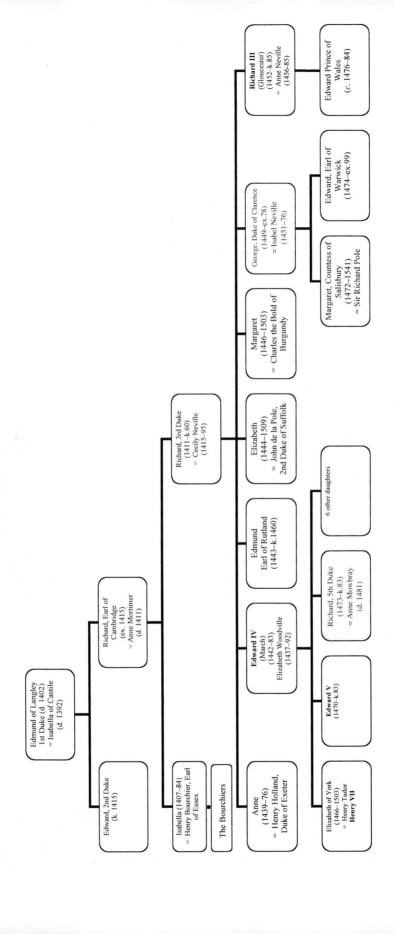

Royal Franchises in England and Wales

PRINCIPAL ESTATES OF THE PEERAGE AND CROWN c.1461

Cecily Neville, Duchess of York. Detail from the frontispiece miniature of The Luton Guild Book.

Lord Protector in the First Protectorate in 1454. Armed conflict with the Lancastrian Court party broke out at the First Battle of St Albans in 1455. Another protectorate followed, with a third in 1460. Richard governed competently enough although, not surprisingly, with a degree of partisanship in favour of his own supporters.

From the rout of Ludford Bridge in October 1459, however, the tide was running against York personally. He stayed in exile in Ireland too long in 1460, allowing the initiative to pass to the earls of Salisbury and Warwick. His attempt to claim the throne in **Westminster Hall** in October 1460 was another fiasco and a huge mistake that cost him his life. The compromise Act of Accord kept Henry as king but made York heir, with Henry's son, Edward, Prince of Wales, dispossessed. York felt it necessary to leave London with the Earl of Salisbury and a modest force in December, and headed north to defend his Yorkshire estates against the massing Lancastrians. Unbelievably, these two experienced soldiers fell into a trap at the Battle of Wakefield, in which York and his second son, Edmund, Earl of Rutland, were killed and Salisbury beheaded the next day at Pontefract, where both were buried. Richard and Edmund were reburied at **Fotheringhay** after a long delay in 1476 with much pomp by his sons. His estates lay in Northamptonshire, Suffolk and the Welsh Marches, with a relatively small area in Yorkshire. His other principal seat was **Ludlow Castle**.

Cecily Neville (1415–95)
Cecily was the youngest daughter of Ralph Neville, Earl of Westmorland and his second wife, Joan Beaufort. She was born at Raby Castle. She was beautiful (she was known as the Rose of Raby) and spirited. She married Richard, Duke of York in 1424 and from 1441 produced seven surviving children. When the Yorkists fled from the rout of Ludford Bridge in ignominy in October 1459, Cecily was left to protect her two young sons, George and Richard, and stood defiantly alone in Ludlow marketplace with them. They were unharmed and together they were sent to live with her sister, Anne, Duchess of Buckingham. A year later, however, she was able to meet her husband at Hereford and accompany him to Westminster to claim the throne of England (but fail).

When her son Edward became king she styled herself 'Queen of Right'. She could not bring herself to accept Elizabeth Woodville as queen. One explanation of the delay until 1476 in reburying the Duke of York is that Cecily would not accept royal protocol at a funeral at which the Queen was present. In the end Cecily did not attend! During Warwick and Clarence's rebellions in 1469/70, Edward IV became so concerned about his mother's involvement in intrigue that he moved her out of London to **Berkhamsted Castle**. In later life, Cecily

Yorkist suns-and-roses collar from the effigy of Sir Humphrey Blount at Kinlet.

was renowned for her piety. She died in 1495 at Berkhamsted, where she had lived the life of a nun.

One big question for Cecily is, of course, was Edward IV illegitimate? On learning of Edward's marriage to Elizabeth Woodville, in desperation Cecily is said to have announced that Edward was not her legitimate son but the result of an adulterous liaison. News of such dynamite proportions was to rebound on her when Richard III attempted to use this argument to disinherit Edward V. Cecily is buried at **Fotheringhay**.

Edward IV (1442–83, King 1461–70 and 1471–83)

Edward of Rouen was born on 28 April 1442, while his father, Richard, 3rd Duke of York, was serving as Lieutenant-General of Normandy during the French wars. He was the eldest surviving son of Richard and Cecily Neville. An elder brother, Henry, died young. Edward was born with many advantages: he was aristocratic and of the royal blood, he was intelligent

and affable and the chroniclers tell us he was good-looking. Exceptionally for medieval times he grew to 6ft 4in tall. Edward looked every inch a king. Yet as a boy, he cannot have expected to be king, with his Lancastrian cousin Henry VI installed on the throne for more than twenty years. Edward was styled Earl of March in the 1440s and became 4th Duke of York on the assassination of his father at the Battle of Wakefield in December 1460.

In early 1461 Edward fought his way to the throne of England at the age of only 18 through emphatic victories over the Lancastrians at Mortimer's Cross and at Towton. He was acclaimed king in London before Towton courtesy of Warwick the Kingmaker. By the time Edward had reclaimed his throne from Henry VI and Warwick in spring 1471, with awesome victories at Barnet and Tewkesbury during the third phase of the War, he had notched up five straight victories as commander, a military record which stands comparison with any medieval English king.

Edward's strength was in his bold and decisive action, particularly in pre-battlefield strategy. By 1471 he was much feared by his opponents as a general.

On the wider canvas, Edward was an energetic and conscientious king who, above all else, brought peace and stability to the realm after 1471. In very difficult times he achieved much:

- He transformed the royal finances; he was one of the few medieval kings to die solvent. He even made money in business. Parliament was hardly called between 1471 and 1483.
- He eschewed expensive and wasteful foreign wars without creating internal dissension and conflict.
- He gave every opportunity to rebellious subjects to be pardoned, including Henry Beaufort, Duke of Somerset, who had commanded the Lancastrian army at Towton and Wakefield.
- He promoted many members of the gentry to positions in the household and in the Church on ability, rather than preferring nobility. In many ways Edward seemed to prefer the company of gentry to that of the nobility.
- It can be said that Edward's approach to kingship foreshadowed what J.R. Green called the 'New Monarchy', which reached fruition under Henry VII.
- He died in his own bed at home – no mean feat for a medieval king.

These constitute a lot of positives, but there is a big negative. As Charles Ross has pointed out, 'Edward remains the only king in English history since 1066 in active possession of his throne who failed to secure the safe succession of his son. His lack of political foresight is largely to blame for the unhappy aftermath of his death.' How can we explain the disaster of his son's deposition? Edward comes across the centuries as the most human of kings: his obvious charisma, his popularity, his love of ceremony, his great interest in commerce, his love of women; and because he did make mistakes – mistakes which very much shaped the political climate after his death. With the benefit of hindsight, we can pick out a number of Edward's actions that clearly contributed to the disaster:

- He married Elizabeth Woodville. The Woodvilles were seen as parvenus. They had a large extended family, which Edward, once married to Elizabeth, chose to promote on the marriage market in order to build up an affinity separate from that of the Nevilles. In the process, the Woodvilles 'stole' many of the good marriage catches in the nobility and became seen as grasping and overly ambitious. They were never popular.
- His son, Edward, Prince of Wales, was allowed to be brought up by and associated with the unpopular Woodvilles far too closely through the Council of Wales, based at Ludlow in the Marches. When the crisis came on Edward's death in April 1483, the Woodville faction was unable to raise support in the Marches or in London sufficient to counter the moves of Gloucester as his first coup unfolded. They had neither the landed wealth nor the popular support to achieve this.
- During his reign Edward rode roughshod over the established laws of inheritance on a number of occasions in order to reap financial/landed gain for the Yorkist family themselves, or for the Woodvilles, especially with the Mowbray, Duke of Norfolk inheritance. Although Acts of Parliament were obtained to support these, a build-up of aristocratic resentment occurred, stemming from fear of possible Woodville domination of Edward V later. Deprived of his Mowbray inheritance, the energetic and powerful John, Lord Howard was driven 'offside'.
- Aristocratic estates had for many years been consolidating into larger groupings leading to the strengthening of the magnates' position vis-à-vis the smaller nobility. By 1483 a small group of magnates, Buckingham, Gloucester (the King's brother), Stanley, Howard (later Duke of Norfolk), and the Woodvilles had come to dominate the Council. Gloucester (aided by the Earl of Northumberland) became dominant in the north-east, Stanley in the north-west, Howard in East Anglia, Woodvilles in the Marches/Wales (but with few estates) and Buckingham in the south and Midlands (but less dominant). This process gave Gloucester in particular access to a huge affinity in the north, which he was able to mobilise in support of his coups in 1483.

Although totally loyal to his brother Edward while the latter was alive, Richard of Gloucester clearly showed him no loyalty at all once he was dead. The York family seem to have been dysfunctional. The destruction of his other brother, George, Duke of Clarence, in 1478 remains a blot on Edward's reputation. The contrast with the Lancastrian family working together after the death of Henry V in 1422 is stark.

Michael Jones has recently reopened the debate about whether Edward was in fact illegitimate. He was conceived at a time (summer 1441) when, although both his parents were in Normandy, his father was on campaign at Pontoise. Evidence is inevitably scarce and we should bear in mind that, to the medieval mind, being born abroad was always suspect. Nevertheless such a situation would certainly explain the disloyal behaviour of both Clarence and Gloucester.

Edward died at Westminster after a brief, unexplained illness on 9 April 1483, just short of his 41st birthday. He may have gone fishing and caught a chill, he may have had a stroke. He had grown corpulent in recent years, not helped by his love of the good life. He was buried at **St George's Chapel, Windsor** which was being rebuilt by him for that purpose.

He was comforted on his deathbed by John Morton, Bishop of Ely, the man who, as a brilliant young lawyer, had drafted the Lancastrian bill of attainder against Edward in 1459 and who subsequently became Henry VII's Lord Chancellor! There were rumours of poison, but there is no evidence.

Queen Elizabeth Woodville (1437–92)

In the 1450s Dame Elizabeth Grey was a lady-in-waiting to Queen Margaret of Anjou. She may well have dreamed of becoming queen herself one day but she cannot have expected to do so. Her father had been but a chamberlain to John, Duke of Bedford. He had married well to Bedford's widow but Elizabeth was herself now married to Sir John Grey, who would inherit a relatively minor barony.

Husband John was killed fighting for the Lancastrians at the Second Battle of St Albans in 1461. In 1464 Elizabeth petitioned Edward IV to resolve a family property dispute (with a little help from Lord Hastings) and love/lust did the rest. Elizabeth was crowned Edward's queen consort in May 1465. With Elizabeth came a large extended family, particularly of sisters. Edward used these to good effect in the marriage market in order to build up a network of related supporters who were not dependent on the Nevilles. With this background, the upstart Queen Elizabeth was never going to be popular especially with the nobility. However, Elizabeth may have been somewhat overzealous in insisting on the strictest court etiquette, even within the royal family. She herself produced a big family of eight surviving children, including the two Princes in the Tower.

In 1469 her father and brother were executed by Warwick while Edward was imprisoned in Middleham Castle. In 1470, when Edward quit the kingdom, Queen Elizabeth took sanctuary in Westminster Abbey, where she gave birth to Prince Edward. With Edward IV's premature death in 1483, Queen Elizabeth took centre stage. Terrified of what might happen once Richard, Duke of Gloucester appeared on the scene, the Dowager Queen once again took sanctuary with Richard, Duke of York, her second son. With great reluctance and after much counsel by the Archbishop of Canterbury, she eventually gave up Richard so that he could join his brother Edward V in the Tower to prepare for Edward's forthcoming coronation. The boys were never seen again.

When it appeared that the Princes were indeed dead, Elizabeth intrigued with Lady Margaret Beaufort to bring about the marriage of her daughter Elizabeth of York with Henry Tudor. Elizabeth was to see her daughter married to Henry in January 1486 and she stood godmother to Prince Arthur, born later that year. Seemingly reconciled to the new regime, Elizabeth nevertheless managed to fall out with Henry and by 1487 she exchanged her possessions for a pension and entered the convent at Bermondsey.

Queen Elizabeth is buried next to Edward at **Windsor**.

The Princes in the Tower

Prince Edward (b. 1470, in 1483 King Edward V) and Prince Richard (b. 1473) did not exert independent influence on the Wars of the Roses. At his accession, Edward was only 12 years old and his two-month reign was dominated by his uncle Richard, Duke of Gloucester, acting as Lord Protector. At his father's death in April 1483, Edward was at Ludlow. Accompanied by his maternal uncle Anthony, Earl Rivers, he was intercepted by Gloucester and the Duke of Buckingham at **Stony Stratford** and escorted straight to the **Tower** (then having royal apartments as well as a prison), from which he never emerged.

Prince Richard was made Duke of York in 1474, thus beginning the tradition that the second son of a sovereign is given that title. In 1478 Richard, aged 4, was married to Anne Mowbray, heiress to the dukedom of Norfolk (she was 5 years old). Anne died in 1481 but Edward IV insisted Richard retain the dukedom and lands. For the events of 1483 see Queen Elizabeth Woodville above. The Princes' alleged remains reside in **Westminster Abbey**.

Queen Elizabeth of York (1466–1503)

The eldest child of Edward IV and Queen Elizabeth Woodville, she came into her own after the disappearance of her brothers, the Princes in the Tower. In the summer of 1483 Dowager Queen Elizabeth Woodville and Lady Margaret Beaufort reached agreement that Princess Elizabeth would marry Henry Tudor, currently in exile in France. Buckingham's Revolt in that autumn confirmed Henry as a serious contender for the crown. At Christmas 1483 Henry swore a solemn oath at Rennes Cathedral, Brittany to marry Elizabeth to unite the two royal houses of York and Lancaster.

After the death of his wife, Anne Neville, in March 1485, even Richard III showed interest in marrying his niece but was firmly told by his advisers that the north would not accept this (presumably because of the Woodville connection.) In January 1486 Henry and Elizabeth were married and quickly produced an heir. Her coronation had to wait until after the Battle of Stoke Field (1487), though Elizabeth seems to have been an exemplary royal wife to Henry VII. They produced four surviving children, including of course the future Henry VIII. There was never a hint of her involvement with Yorkist plots (despite a wobble or two by her mother). In fact, Elizabeth left the politics to Henry; that side of their marriage was already 'crowded' with his mother, Lady Margaret Beaufort's, heavy involvement. Elizabeth died in childbirth in 1503 and is buried in **Westminster Abbey**.

George, Duke of Clarence (1449–78)

At Edward IV's accession in 1461 Clarence became heir apparent. Although showered with honours and lands by Edward, George somehow managed to take offence. No doubt flattered by the Earl of Warwick, he decided he wanted to marry Isabel, Warwick's elder daughter. The King refused the match, so Warwick and Clarence combined in rebellion in 1469. Together they crossed to Calais, where Clarence and Isabel were married. When they returned to England, Edward's armies were defeated and Edward imprisoned – but not for long, because he managed to regain his throne quickly enough. Rebellion was repeated in 1470, but unsuccessfully, in Lincolnshire.

When Edward invaded England after the Readeption in 1471, Clarence famously changed sides at a late hour, declaring for Edward near Coventry. Shakespeare captured the spirit as 'False, Fleeting, Perjur'd Clarence'. Clarence brought much-needed reinforcement and fought for Edward at the subsequent battles of Barnet and Tewkesbury, where the three brothers combined in harmony (a rare occurrence indeed) and destroyed not only Warwick and his brother Montagu, but also the Lancastrian cause. Clarence had not been given a top command at these battles, perhaps not being completely trusted by Edward.

Clarence and Richard, Duke of Gloucester then squabbled over the Warwick inheritance. Clarence could not resist dabbling in intrigue again with John de Vere, Earl of Oxford. He grew increasingly erratic in his behaviour as he became alienated from Edward. He went too far in the Annette Twyno affair in 1477, where he packed a jury in Warwick to ensure a guilty verdict against a servant accused of poisoning his wife. In so doing, he had ignored the King's judicial system.

In 1478 Clarence was brought to trial for treason by Edward, who personally led the prosecution. The verdict was a foregone conclusion and Clarence was executed privately in the **Tower**, traditionally in a butt of Malmsey wine – his own choice. His daughter, Margaret is said to have worn a bracelet with a barrel on it. Perhaps inevitably, the Woodvilles have been blamed for Clarence's downfall. Clarence and Isabel are buried at **Tewkesbury Abbey**.

Clarence's principal seats were at **Warwick** and Tutbury castles. He was attainted and his children lost their rights to the succession. Nevertheless, when Henry Tudor claimed the throne, George's son, Edward, Earl of Warwick, was imprisoned in the Tower, where he remained until 1499, when he was executed on **Tower Hill** to impress the Spanish envoys sent to reconnoitre Prince Arthur's forthcoming wedding to Catherine of Aragon. Edward, who was probably feeble-minded, was buried at Bisham Abbey but nothing remains.

Margaret, Countess of Salisbury was George's elder child. She married Sir Richard Pole and had a large family, one of whom became Archbishop of Canterbury under Queen Mary. This connection had already caused problems during the Reformation. Henry VIII, who initially had a particular liking for Margaret, turned nasty and executed her with great brutality in 1541. (See **Christchurch**.)

Richard III (1452–85, King 1483–5)

Henry Tudor had no credible claim to the throne of England. It has been calculated that there were twenty-nine other people with a better claim at the time. But the Tudors were intelligent monarchs and masters of spin. It was therefore essential that

Portrait of George, Duke of Clarence, 1595, from a set of the 'Constables of Queenborough Castle', Brocklet Hall.

the defeated Yorkist dynasty should be denigrated. Edward IV could not be targeted too hard, since his daughter had married Henry as part of the post-Bosworth political settlement and was now queen. In historical terms, therefore, Richard III's reputation never stood a chance. He took the full fury of the Tudor propaganda machine. At one time or another he has been accused of most of the political murders between 1460–85. On the other hand he had left the spin-doctors some marvellous material to work with.

Richard was the youngest son of Richard, 3rd Duke of York and Cecily Neville. He was made Duke of Gloucester by his brother Edward in 1461 and was brought up in the household of Richard Neville, Earl of Warwick at Middleham Castle, where he first met Anne Neville, Warwick's

daughter. In the crises of 1469–71 he stayed totally loyal to Edward and fought with great distinction in the thick of the mêlée at the battles of Barnet and Tewkesbury. He was given command of the favoured left flank at Tewkesbury. In 1472 he married Anne and consolidated his position in Yorkshire and the north with the lands and properties once owned by Warwick. He stood up to Clarence over the split of the Warwick inheritance and became the model younger royal. He was rarely at Court and probably not well known to Edward's children.

Edward's premature death changed everything. Richard moved decisively to secure the person of the new king and execute the Woodvilles, even before he had been confirmed as Lord Protector by the Council. His Second Coup, in June 1483,

Portrait of Richard III by an unknown artist.

magnates of the period. He had been a 'model' Duke of Gloucester. The ruthlessness and illegality of his coup did not really single him out significantly from contemporaries. The murder of the boy princes was something different.

During his short reign, Richard did not really have time to make much of a mark on the realm largely because he was too busy defending it. He held only one parliament. In 1484 he made a serious error when reacting to the failed revolt of the Duke of Buckingham the previous year. He brought in considerable numbers of loyal gentry from his northern heartlands to 'police' the disaffected southern counties. This was much resented and drove the southern gentry into the hands of Henry Tudor.

Richard was ready for Henry Tudor's invasion in the summer of 1485, and based himself at Nottingham Castle. On paper, the Battle of Bosworth should have been a comfortable victory for Richard's much larger army. However, battles in the Wars of the Roses were rarely about comparisons on paper. They were much more often about double-cross and treachery. In this department the Stanleys excelled. All the sources point to Richard's dying a hero's death, fighting to the last, declining to flee and deserted by many of his men. He was buried in the **Greyfriars, Leicester**, but his remains and grave site are lost to posterity.

Queen Anne Neville (1456–85)

Anne was the younger daughter of Richard Neville, Earl of Warwick (the Kingmaker). When Warwick changed sides in 1470, it was agreed with the Lancastrians that Anne should marry the 16-year-old Edward, Prince of Wales (somewhat against Queen Margaret of Anjou's better judgement). The marriage took place at Angers in France in December 1470. Prince Edward was killed at the Battle of Tewkesbury in 1471. In 1472 Anne married Richard, Duke of Gloucester, who now possessed the northern half of her father's estates.

In 1473 Anne gave birth to Edward, subsequently created Earl of Salisbury and, after Richard's usurpation of the throne, Prince of Wales. Prince Edward died on 9 April 1484, a year to the day after the death of his uncle Edward IV. He is buried at **Sheriff Hutton**. Never a strong person, Anne herself died in March 1485 and is buried in **Westminster Abbey**.

Richard Neville, Earl of Salisbury (c. 1400–60)

Richard Neville was the eldest son of Ralph Neville, Earl of Westmorland and his second wife, Joan

was equally ruthless and illegal. The precipitate execution of his lifelong colleague Lord Hastings was shocking, but the real difference in 1483 was that Richard's usurpation was not backed by strong support from the aristocracy in the south of England, as was the case in both 1399 (Henry IV) and 1461 (Edward IV). Richard's coup was instead backed by the presence of a strong northern army. Richard III remains the only king of England to secure the throne from a power base in the north.

Exactly what followed Richard's coronation we shall probably never know. After the summer of 1483 the Princes were never seen again. By September, rumours were flying around about their deaths on Richard's orders. Even to contemporaries, with all the horror of the previous thirty years, this crime of murdering children was seen as completely unacceptable. There is no evidence that Richard ordered their deaths, and Henry Tudor had equally strong motives for their murder later. Richard remains the chief culprit, if only because he held the top job, responsible for their 'safety' at the time. If he did the deed, then it is really this one heinous act that distinguishes Richard from other kings and

THE NEVILLES (JUNIOR BRANCH)

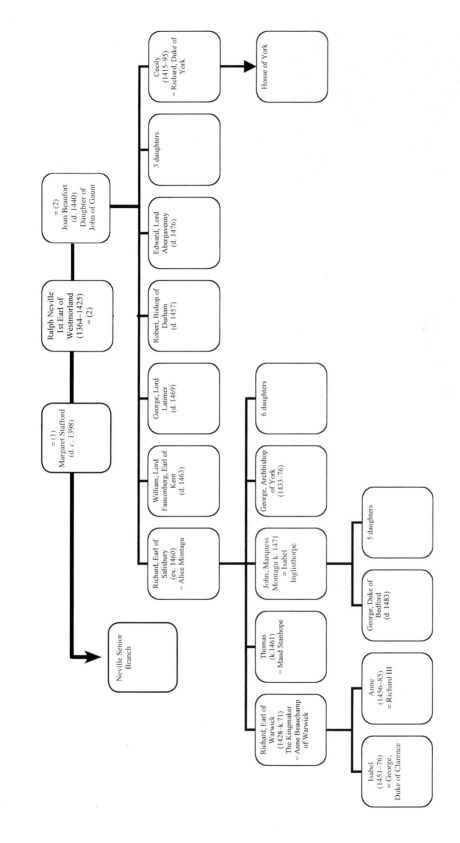

Ralph Neville
1st Earl of
Westmorland
(1364–1425)
= (2)

= (1)
Margaret Stafford
(d. 1398)

= (2)
Joan Beaufort
(d. 1440)
Daughter of
John of Gaunt

Neville Senior
Branch

Richard, Earl of
Salisbury
(ex. 1460)
= Alice Montagu

William, Lord
Fauconberg, Earl of
Kent
(d. 1463)

George, Lord
Latimer
(d. 1469)

Robert, Bishop of
Durham
(d. 1457)

Edward, Lord
Abergavenny
(d. 1476)

3 daughters

Cecily
(1415–95)
= Richard, Duke of
York

House of York

Richard, Earl of
Warwick
(1428–k.71)
The Kingmaker
= Anne Beauchamp
of Warwick

Thomas
(k.1461)
= Maud Stanhope

John, Marquess
Montagu k. 1471
= Isabel
Inglisthorpe

George, Archbishop
of York
(1433–76)

6 daughters

Isabel
(1451–76)
= George,
Duke of Clarence

Anne
(1456–85)
= Richard III

George, Duke of
Bedford
(d. 1483)

5 daughters

Beaufort (daughter of John of Gaunt). He thus came of impeccable Lancastrian credentials and royal blood flowed in his veins. In all, Ralph Neville had twenty-two children by two wives. In the struggle between the two halves of the family, it was the Beaufort junior branch that was favoured. Richard inherited the great lordships of Middleham, Sheriff Hutton and Penrith, although the dispute with the Raby branch dragged on until 1443. Richard became a great landowner in the north. He was Warden of the West March for most of his adult life. In addition, in 1429 he married Alice Montagu, heiress to the earldom of Salisbury with large properties in the south of England. He served in France in the 1430s and became a royal councillor.

Salisbury's ambitions in the north inevitably led to clashes with the Percys, the traditional dominant power, particularly on the East March. 'Private battles' between the families ensued at Heworth Moor (1453) and Stamford Bridge (1454), both in Yorkshire. During York's First Protectorate, Salisbury became Lord Chancellor of England, but was replaced at the end of it. Until now, Salisbury had backed the King in his differences with the Duke of York. However, the Percy disputes, plus a similar wrangle of his eldest son the Earl of Warwick with the Duke of Somerset over Glamorgan, led to an alliance of interest with York which culminated in the First Battle of St Albans.

The Nevilles' wealth, ambition and drive transformed York's challenge to Henry VI, although from now on it was Warwick, rather than Salisbury, who tended to be the driving force. Salisbury fought a very clever battle at Blore Heath (1459) after being intercepted by Lord Audley on his way to rendezvous with York and Warwick at Ludford Bridge, Shropshire. After the Ludford debacle, Salisbury escaped with Warwick and Edward, Earl of March to Calais and shared the fate of attainder. The three Calais earls returned in triumph to London in July 1460.

Crucially Salisbury was quoted by Warwick as being against the Duke of York's bid for the throne in October 1460. After the Act of Accord, which confirmed York as Henry VI's heir, Salisbury accompanied York northwards to confront the Lancastrians, who were harrying their estates in Yorkshire. After York's death at the Battle of Wakefield in December 1460, Salisbury was initially taken prisoner for ransom. However, next day he was seized from gaol in Pontefract and beheaded. Salisbury was initially buried at Pontefract and then reinterred at the family mausoleum at Bisham Abbey in 1463 with much ceremony (but see **Burghfield**).

Richard Neville, Earl of Warwick (1428–k.71)

History has dubbed him 'the Kingmaker', but for someone who is a household name, surprisingly little

Seal of Richard Neville, Earl of Salisbury.

is known about him personally; there is no known visual likeness. All we have is a 'weeper' on the tomb of his father-in-law at **Warwick**. He was the eldest son of the Earl of Salisbury above and, at the age of 8, married Anne Beauchamp, daughter of Richard Beauchamp, Earl of Warwick in a 'bride swap' involving also his sister, Cecily Neville, and Anne's brother Henry Beauchamp. With massive good fortune for Richard, both Henry and his infant daughter by Cecily died young, leaving him to inherit the huge Beauchamp estates and title in 1449/50 through his wife. At a stroke he became both the premier earl in England and the second-wealthiest subject behind the Duke of York.

Richard worked in harmony with his father; the Nevilles were a family who pulled together. By 1454 they were in dispute over property with the Percys in Yorkshire. Originally solid supporters of the Lancastrian kings, the Nevilles switched their support to the Duke of York and enjoyed positions in government during York's protectorates. It was

Warwick's decisive thrust through back gardens that swung the First Battle of St Albans (1455). Warwick was something of a nautical man and put this to good use as Captain of Calais. In fact Warwick was a politician first and military man second (his handling of the Second Battle of St Albans appears downright sloppy). By 1460 Warwick had become the dominant figure in the Yorkist camp, eclipsing the Duke of York, with Salisbury happy to fit in with his son. At the Battle of Northampton, Warwick captured Henry VI and for four months ruled the country in Henry's name.

For the next eleven years, Warwick vied with Edward IV as the central character in the Wars of the Roses. Unfortunately the country was not big enough for both of them. After the Lancastrians were ejected from Northumberland, Edward IV made a whole string of decisions that underlined his independence from his older cousin. Warwick was driven to rebellion in 1469 with Edward's brother, the Duke of Clarence. August and September of that year were in many ways Warwick's finest hour. He governed the

Bear badge of Richard Neville, Earl of Warwick, from Fenn's Book of Badges, *BL Add MS 40742.*

country with not just one but two kings of England in prison – Henry VI in the Tower, and Edward at Middleham Castle. But it did not last.

Warwick could never be king, but by marrying his two daughters to the right men he could again be the power behind the throne. Isabel had married Clarence, and Anne then married the Lancastrian Edward, Prince of Wales in the deal in 1470 that saw Warwick change sides again. After Edward IV's flight to the Low Countries in 1470, Warwick governed the country during the Readeption of Henry VI. Let down by his Lancastrian allies and continually out-thought and out-generalled by Edward, Warwick's nemesis came at the Battle of Barnet (1471). He was buried at Bisham Abbey but nothing survives.

Warwick was an arch-plotter, energetic, highly intelligent and a good administrator, but could be also utterly ruthless on and off the battlefield. He had family loyalty but probably not many friends. His principal seats were **Middleham** and **Warwick Castles**.

Sir Thomas Neville (*c*. 1429–k.60) was the second son of the Earl of Salisbury, Sir Thomas married Maud Stanhope, co-heir to Lord Cromwell, at the latter's seat at **Tattershall Castle** in 1453. After the Battle of Blore Heath (1459), Thomas and brother John were taken prisoner by the Lancastrians at Tarporley, Cheshire and held in Chester Castle. During the acrimonious discussions held at Westminster between the Duke of York and Warwick in October 1460, after York's claim to the throne, Thomas acted as go-between the two parties. He accompanied his father, Salisbury, and York on their fateful mission into Yorkshire in December 1460. Thomas was killed in the Battle of Wakefield. His remains were reburied alongside those of his father at Bisham Abbey in 1473.

John Neville, Marquis Montagu (*c*. 1430–k.71)

John was the third son of the Earl of Salisbury. He was the soldier of the family and remains one of the unsung heroes of the Wars. He married relatively modestly to Isabel Inglisthorpe, who was a gentry heiress but with substantial lands. John fought for his father at the Battle of Blore Heath (1459) and, with his brother, was captured by the Lancastrians after the battle. He was ennobled in early 1461 by Warwick, as Lord Montagu. He fought for Warwick at the Second Battle of St Albans (1461) and took the brunt of the Lancastrian attack on Bernard's Heath while his brother skulked on No Man's Land nearby. Lord John was again captured in the defeat, but not executed (a charmed life indeed). He was held in York Castle during the Battle of Towton, but released in the

panic as the Lancastrian leadership departed in a hurry after the defeat.

After Towton, Edward IV still needed to achieve control of Northumberland, where die-hard Lancastrians had congregated and fortified the border castles. Warwick and Lord John were given command. John was the constant presence with his base at **Warkworth Castle**; Warwick made visits. The task took three years, with castles regularly changing hands, but John achieved decisive success in 1464 with two overwhelming victories at the battles of Hedgeley Moor and Hexham. Later in the year, Edward rewarded John with the earldom of Northumberland, which was removed from the Percys, attainted after Towton.

As a result, in 1469, when Warwick rebelled against Edward, John stayed loyal to his king and put down the Robin of Holderness revolt of that year. In November 1469, Edward, in a desperate bid to retain his loyalty (and as a peace offering to Warwick), offered his daughter, Elizabeth (aged 3), in marriage to John's son George and elevated George to Duke of Bedford. However, as the conflict with Warwick progressed, Edward felt it necessary in 1470 to restore the earldom of Northumberland to Henry Percy (4th Earl) to guarantee support in the north. John was recompensed with elevation to marquis and lands in the West Country. Later in the year, Edward's army was camped around Doncaster when news arrived that Montagu had just declared for Warwick and was heading straight for them. He had memorably dismissed Edward's compensatory package for the loss of the Northumberland earldom as a 'magpie's nest'. Edward was so alarmed that he turned tail and fled into exile via King's Lynn.

In fact, Montagu was treated with great suspicion by most Lancastrians during the Readeption. Edward's gamble proved astute, because as he moved down through Yorkshire after landing at Ravenspur in 1471, Northumberland's and Montagu's forces cancelled each other out. John Neville stuck with his brother and found himself commanding the van at the Battle of Barnet, where he was killed in the mêlée. If ever a man found himself 'between a rock and hard place' – loyalty to his family or to his King – it was Montagu. Edward is said to have regretted Montagu's death (unlike Warwick's). Both were buried at Bisham Abbey.

John and Isobel had five daughters and George. In 1478 George was degraded from duke on the grounds of insufficient income. He died childless in May 1483, aged 26, and was buried at **Sheriff Hutton**.

George Neville, Archbishop of York (*c.* 1432–76) was the youngest of Salisbury's sons was destined for the church and became the archetypal magnate-churchman. He was educated at Oxford and elected to its chancellorship at only 21 years old. In 1455, when the Yorkists were in power, he was given the see of Exeter. He became a patron of humanism and was described as 'stately and eloquent'. George was much more than that, though. He enjoyed power and high living. In the autumn of 1460 Warwick appointed George as Lord Chancellor. He took the leading clerical role in the acclamation of Edward IV as king in London in March 1461. In 1464 he was elevated to Archbishop of York, holding a huge banquet in celebration in September1465 at his **Cawood Palace**.

Unfortunately, George's chosen path in politics was too closely allied to the Kingmaker's. Unlike the Yorks, the Nevilles had family loyalty. In 1467 Edward IV discovered that George was intriguing to obtain papal dispensation for the Duke of Clarence's marriage to Isabel Neville, the Kingmaker's daughter, a match the King had expressly forbidden. George lost his job as Lord Chancellor. Undeterred, he joined his brother and niece in Calais and officiated at the wedding of Isabel to Clarence. George was closely involved in the rebellions of 1469–70 and the Readeption of 1470/1. In a nice touch, he was sent by Warwick to arrest King Edward at Olney after the Battle of Edgecote. George was left in charge of London in 1471, but on King Edward's unwelcome arrival at the city gates, George vacillated, guaranteed his own safety by letting Edward enter but helped to condemn his brothers to defeat on the battlefield of Barnet.

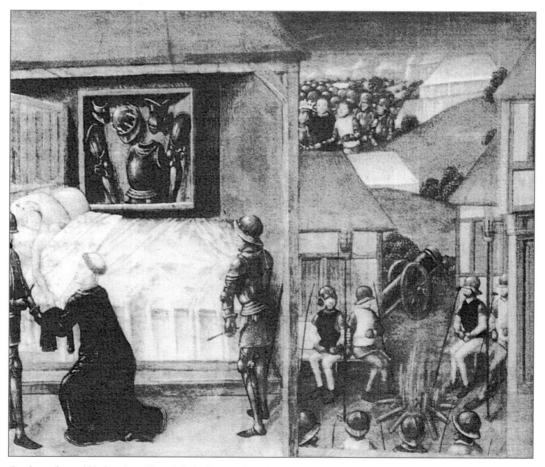

On the orders of his brother, Warwick the Kingmaker, George Neville, Archbishop of Canterbury, 'arrests' Edward IV at Olney, Buckinghamshire.

In 1472 George was accused of further intrigue and imprisoned by Edward IV in Hammes Castle in Calais. Richard, Duke of Gloucester obtained his release in 1474 but George had been broken by the experience. He never recovered, and died in 1476. His official London residence was the Moor in Hertfordshire.

William Neville, Lord Fauconberg (c. 1402–63) was the next-youngest brother after Richard, Earl of Salisbury, William was a small and fierce man who was probably one of the unsung heroes of the early part of the Wars. He had been a field commander in France, where he had been captured and ransomed. In 1455 he found himself on the Lancastrian side at the First Battle of St Albans but was not penalised afterwards. In 1459 he gave solid support to his nephew Warwick. He 'managed the shop' in Calais while Warwick was away at Ludford Bridge in 1459. He commanded the van at the Battle of Northampton (1460) and led the flanking march via Castleford that secured the crossing at the Battle of Ferrybridge the day before Towton. It may have been his military expertise that carried the day for the Yorkists at the Battle of Towton itself (1461). Afterwards he was elevated to the earldom of Kent by King Edward. His natural son Thomas, the Bastard of Fauconberg, unsuccessfully besieged the city of London in a last-gasp attempt to keep alive the Warwick cause in 1471.

The Woodvilles

Tradition tells us that Edward IV married Elizabeth Grey, née Woodville, for love or lust, or both. He may have done, but Edward was too much of a thinking king for it to have been that simple. Elizabeth's parents, Richard Woodville, 1st Lord Rivers (1416–69) and Jacquetta of Luxembourg, had a large family of fourteen, including eight daughters. Richard also had a distinguished war record in France in John, Duke of Bedford's retinue, and a solid but less distinguished record supporting Henry VI in the 1450s from Cade's Rebellion to the Second Battle of St Albans and Towton (1461). Lord Richard was no Yorkist but he and his brother Anthony were relatively quickly pardoned by Edward after Towton.

After his marriage, Edward consistently promoted the interests of his new in-laws, especially in the marriage market. Elizabeth's sisters scooped six prime aristocrats (one duke, two earls, one viscount and two mere lords). Scandalously, her brother John also married Catherine Neville, the 67-year-old Dowager Duchess of Norfolk. The Woodvilles came from modest gentry stock, with lands in Northampton-shire and Kent. Richard Woodville had risen socially largely because of his marriage (Jacquetta was the widow of John, Duke of Bedford and the daughter of the Count of St Pol). With a second step up from Elizabeth's marriage to Edward, the family became widely unpopular and resented. They were certainly never liked by the rest of the Yorkist royal family.

Edward was in fact building a power base which was independent of the Kingmaker (whose Neville family had done so much to establish Edward on the throne). The triumph of this policy was Edward's 1471 military campaign to recover his kingdom, in which he was supported by the 2nd Earl Rivers, plus the husbands of five of the Woodville sisters, together with Thomas Grey, Marquis of Dorset, Elizabeth's son by her first marriage.

During the 1470s the Woodvilles prospered. Anthony, 2nd Earl Rivers (1440–83) was made governor to Edward IV's sons at Ludlow, presiding over the Council of Wales and becoming a power in the principality. However, Edward was not so supportive with grants of extra lands to the Woodville men. The family lacked land, income and sizeable retinue, and therefore real power. When it came to Richard, Duke of Gloucester's coups in 1483, the Woodvilles offered little effective resistance. Anthony, 2nd Earl was tricked and captured at Northampton in April 1483 and executed in June at Pontefract. When it came to the crunch, there was little support for the Woodvilles from the rest of the peerage.

The other elements in the Woodville 'affinity' are the Greys, the family of Elizabeth Woodville by her first husband Sir John Grey, heir to Lord Grey of Groby. Sir Richard, the second son, was executed at Pontefract in 1483 with Earl Rivers after Richard of Gloucester's coup d'état. Thomas the elder (1455–1501) was made Marquis of Dorset in 1475 by Edward IV. He was a great womaniser, competing in this field with King Edward and Lord Hastings. He fought at the Battle of Tewkesbury (1471) for Edward and was one of the leaders of Buckingham's Revolt in the West Country in 1483. His second marriage was to Cecily Bonville, who is buried at **Astley**.

The Woodville family seats were Grafton Regis (Northants) and The Mote, Maidstone. The Marquis of Dorset also held lands in Devon, around Torrington.

The Bourchiers

This family was descended in the maternal line from Thomas of Woodstock, youngest son of Edward III. His daughter, Anne, Countess of Buckingham, widowed twice in succession by the

THE WOODVILLES

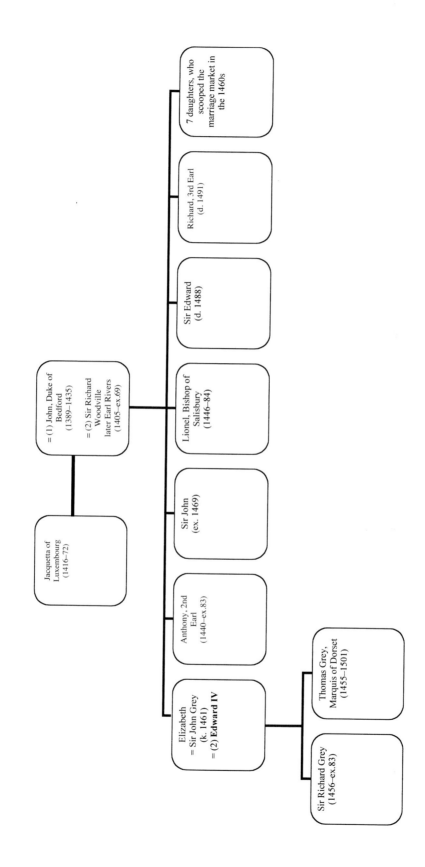

Jacquetta of Luxembourg (1416–72)

= (1) John, Duke of Bedford (1389–1435)

= (2) Sir Richard Woodville later Earl Rivers (1405–ex.69)

Elizabeth
= Sir John Grey (k. 1461)
= (2) **Edward IV**

Anthony, 2nd Earl (1440–ex.83)

Sir John (ex. 1469)

Lionel, Bishop of Salisbury (1446–84)

Sir Edward (d. 1488)

Richard, 3rd Earl (d. 1491)

7 daughters, who scooped the marriage market in the 1460s

Sir Richard Grey (1456–ex.83)

Thomas Grey, Marquis of Dorset (1455–1501)

THE BOURCHIERS

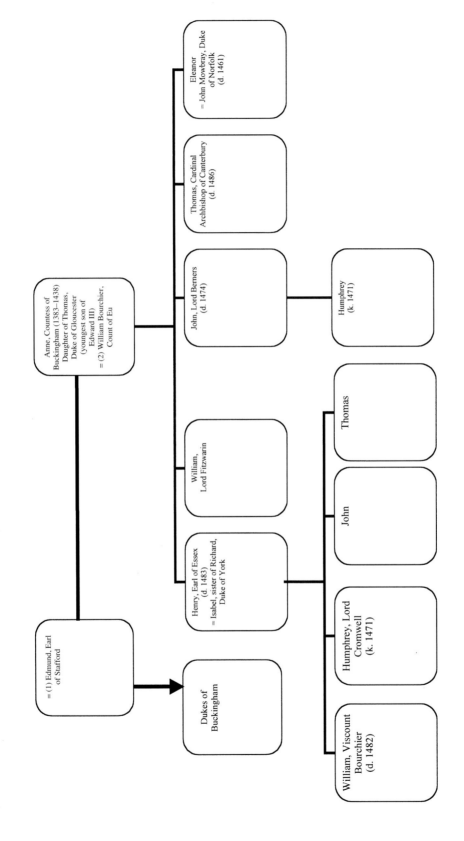

Stafford brothers, married William Bourchier, Earl of Eu, who was much in favour with Henry V after outstanding war service in France. This maternal connection to the Stafford family was to prove important in the Wars of the Roses fifty years later. William and Anne had four sons, two of whom rose to the highest level in government – Henry, who became Lord High Treasurer under Edward IV in 1461–2 and 1471–83 and Earl of Essex (d. 1483) and Thomas, who was Archbishop of Canterbury see from 1454 to 1486, a record thirty-two years. He was therefore close to all the really important events of the Wars of the Roses; in particular, he crowned three sovereigns – Edward IV, Richard III and Henry VII. In addition, he crowned Elizabeth Woodville in 1465 and recrowned Edward in April 1471 before the Battle of Barnet. Not long before his death, he married Henry VII and Elizabeth of York, an event of great political significance in the uniting of the two Roses.

Thomas was appointed as Bishop of Worcester at the young age of 22 and Archbishop at 24. Despite his clear Yorkist connections, Bourchier initially took a neutral political stance. He was made Lord Chancellor in the 1455 political reshuffle after York's First Protectorate. By June 1459, however, he was not attending the Great Council and in May 1460 he was at Sandwich to welcome the Calais earls (Warwick, Salisbury and March) and accompany them through London to confront King Henry's army at Northampton. Bourchier may have been involved in negotiations with Henry VI before battle was joined.

Bourchier played a leading part in two of the most dramatic events in the Wars. In October 1460, he had to deal with Richard, Duke of York when the latter put his hand on the throne and laid claim to it in St Stephen's Hall, Westminster. The crushing silence from the assembled Lords which greeted this act was subsequently explained away by Warwick as being due to Bourchier's opposition because of the previous oaths of allegiance sworn to Henry VI by all present. Bourchier calmly asked York if he had come to see the King!

Secondly, during Richard III's Second Coup in June 1483, Bourchier found himself in the unenviable position of having to persuade Dowager Queen Elizabeth Woodville to release her second son Richard, Duke of York from sanctuary in Westminster Abbey so that he could join his brother Edward V, for the latter's coronation. Bourchier died in 1486 and is buried in the chancel of **Canterbury Cathedral**.

The Bourchiers were natural Yorkists because Henry had married Isabella Plantagenet (1409–84), elder sister of Richard, Duke of York. They gave support to York's son Edward in the war of succession at the Second Battle of St Albans (John, Lord Berners) and at Towton (Henry and Humphrey, his youngest son). Eleanor, Henry's sister, had married John Mowbray, Duke of Norfolk, whose late intervention at Towton on Edward's side proved decisive.

Once again in the crisis of 1471, the Bouchiers turned out for Edward in force. At the Battle of Barnet they were involved in the thick of the fighting, and both Humphrey, Lord Cromwell and Sir Humphrey Bourchier, Berners' son, were killed and buried in **Westminster Abbey**. The principal seat was **Little Easton** in Essex, where Henry and Isabella are buried.

The Mowbrays (Dukes of Norfolk)

An old-established family but one which suffered money problems in the first half of the fifteenth century caused by dower commitments. John, 3rd Duke (1415–61) supported York at Dartford in 1452 but did not take part in the First Protectorate in 1454 because of ill health. Ill health dogged him again at Towton (1461) and his forces were nearly late for the battle. Their timely arrival in the afternoon, however, swung that battle for Edward IV. The Duke died later that same year. His son, John, 4th Duke (1444–76) has been described as an 'inept, irresponsible thug' who had big problems with members of the lively East Anglian gentry, e.g. the Wingfields of Letheringham and the Pastons of Caister Castle fame. He even had to spend time in the Tower! Duke John fought at the Battle of Tewkesbury and, as Constable, presided alongside Richard of Gloucester at the trial of Edmund Beaufort, Duke of Somerset immediately afterwards. Their principal seat was Framlingham Castle in Suffolk. They were buried at **Thetford Priory**.

The Howards (Dukes of Norfolk)

John Howard (k. 1483) was originally from modest gentry stock in Stoke-by-Nayland, Suffolk becoming JP and MP in the 1450s. He was on the Duke of Norfolk's Council and may have led his Yorkist retinue at the Battle of Towton when Norfolk was ill. Howard was knighted after the battle and ennobled in 1470. He and his son Thomas fought for Edward IV at the Battle of Barnet. Howard, something of a naval expert, became one of Edward's inner circle. However, when John Mowbray, the

Eagle badge and motto of Thomas Bourchier, Archbishop of Canterbury from Fenn's Book of Badges, *BL Add MS 40742.*

4th Duke, died in 1476, things started to go down-hill. In 1478 Edward married his son, Prince Richard, Duke of York to the <u>Mowbray heiress, Anne</u>, when both were still infants. Anne died in 1481 and Edward retained the Mowbray lands for his younger son, thereby disinheriting Howard, whose mother was Margaret Mowbray, now sole heiress of the dukedom. One of Edward's greatest mistakes in matters of state, this act made Howard a natural ally of Richard of Gloucester when the latter made his move for the crown. Another schism in the Yorkist 'party' had opened up. Once described as 'as wild as a bullock' Howard (and his son) played a big part in Richard's Second Coup in June

1483. Howard was indeed made duke by Richard and died on the battlefield at Bosworth, fighting for him, in 1485.

Howard's son, <u>Thomas, Earl of Surrey</u> (1443–1524), was, if anything, an even more impressive operator than his father. At Bosworth, after Richard's death, he was captured but his life spared. He was imprisoned and deprived of his dukedom. Thomas, as Earl of Surrey, went on to great things under the Tudors. He was the victor over the Scots at the Battle of Flodden Field (1513) and subsequently recovered the dukedom under Henry VIII. The Fitzalan-Howard dukes are still with us. Father and son were originally buried at **Thetford Priory**.

Portrait of John Howard, 1st Duke of Norfolk by an unknown artist. (The Royal Collection © 2006, Her Majesty Queen Elizabeth II)

Thomas Howard, Earl of Surrey. Engraving of his lost memorial brass, once at Lambeth.

The de la Poles (Dukes of Suffolk)

This family came to prominence in the fourteenth century as successful, wealthy merchants and financiers from Hull. William, 1st Duke (1396–1450) inherited in 1415 when his father and elder brother were killed in France. He had a very successful career himself in France under the Duke of Bedford. From 1433 onwards, however, he was converted to peace and helped Cardinal Beaufort and King Henry pursue that goal. He became the King's chief councillor in the 1440s and effectively isolated Henry from any conflicting counsel. Unfortunately the pursuit of peace in France led to rapid defeat with dishonour. Suffolk became widely unpopular by the late 1440s, being seen as also shamelessly 'feathering his own nest' while in office. He was impeached in parliament in early 1450 but Henry intervened and sent him into exile instead. En route to the Continent, he was beheaded in a boat by seamen in Dover Roads.

The de la Pole seat was at **Wingfield** in Suffolk. At the height of his power, William ran the whole of East

Graffiti is not a new phenomenon! John de la Pole, Duke of Suffolk and his wife Princess Elizabeth, sister to Edward IV, at Wingfield.

Anglia like a fiefdom. He had married <u>Alice Chaucer</u>, granddaughter of the poet and heiress to her father, Thomas, based at Ewelme, Oxfordshire. Suffolk moved his principal seat to **Ewelme**.

His son, <u>2nd Duke John</u> (1442–91) was a minor when he inherited and the estates were managed by the Dowager Duchess Alice, a formidable woman in her own right. She dominated her son into adulthood. John married <u>Princess Elizabeth</u> (1444–1503), the second daughter of Richard, Duke of York and sister to Edward IV and Richard III before 1460. John was present at the Second Battle of St Albans (1461) and at Towton (1461). He was an active supporter of his brother-in-law Edward IV in 1469–71 and probably fought at the Battle of Losecote Field. All in all, though, here was a leading magnate who did not really punch his weight during the Wars – he may have been subject to bouts of illness. The couple were buried in **Wingfield Church**. Duke John's eldest son was <u>John, Earl of Lincoln</u> (1464–87). After the death of his son Prince Edward of Middleham, Richard III groomed Lincoln to be his heir. He was appointed President of the Council of the North in 1483 and Lieutenant of Ireland in 1484. He may have supported Richard III at the

Battle of Bosworth. Initially he seemed to accept Henry Tudor as king and was pardoned. However, in 1486 he fled the country and openly plotted against Henry. He was a leading light in the Lambert Simnel conspiracy, which climaxed in the Battle of Stoke in July 1487, where Lincoln was killed. Henry was said to be very annoyed because he had ordered that Lincoln should be taken alive for subsequent interrogation. Lincoln had married Margaret Fitzalan, daughter of the Yorkist Earl of Arundel and had five surviving brothers. They kept the Yorkist flag flying well into the reign of Henry VIII, but with little effect.

William, Lord Hastings (*c.* 1431–83)

William Hastings came from substantial gentry stock with lands in Yorkshire and Leicestershire. Both he and his father had been members of the retinue of Richard, Duke of York. Hastings joined Edward, Duke of York on the road from Mortimer's Cross to London in February 1461 and was knighted on the field of Towton in March. Thereafter Hastings was Edward's constant companion, becoming his friend and confidant and even sharing the same mistress. Hastings was appointed Lord Chamberlain of the

Household and member of the Council and gradually acquired estates in the 1460s, mainly in the Midlands. Hastings married Warwick's sister, Katherine, and thus received Warwick's support.

Hastings shared with Edward all the vicissitudes of the second phase of the Wars from 1469–71. He and Gloucester were with Edward at Olney in 1469, when George Neville, Warwick's brother, arrived to 'arrest' him. He and Gloucester fled with Edward from Doncaster via King's Lynn in September 1470 and went into exile in Burgundy. On Edward's return to England in March 1471, Hastings met him at Leicester with almost 3,000 men. This shows that through a combination of large estates and recognition of his influence at court Hastings had become a major power in the Midlands. Hastings commanded a wing of Edward's army at each of the victories of Barnet and Tewkesbury.

During the 1470s Hastings fell out with the grasping Woodvilles, particularly the Queen's son, the Marquis of Dorset. He himself is usually seen as an honourable man. Because of this, on the death of Edward in April 1483, Hastings supported Gloucester's First Coup from London to establish Gloucester as Protector. However, he clearly had not read Gloucester's true intentions. Hastings was a man who, because of his close friendship with Edward IV, above all wanted his son Edward V to succeed to the throne. At the Council meeting on Friday 13 June 1483 in the Tower, Gloucester suddenly announced that there was a traitor in their midst and that this was Hastings. He was accused of plotting with the Woodvilles against the Protector. Hastings was hauled from the room and without delay executed on a makeshift block on **Tower Green**.

With Hastings dead, the way was clear for Richard to claim the crown two weeks later and depose Edward V. Hastings was never attainted by Richard, who 'generously' allowed his wife, Katherine, to have custody of Hastings' estates during the minority of their son Edward and to keep two valuable wardships. Richard also allowed Hastings' request to be buried in his chantry next to Edward IV in **St George's Chapel, Windsor**. Hastings was a castle-builder at **Kirby Muxloe** and **Ashby de la Zouch, Leicestershire**.

THE HOUSE OF LANCASTER

Henry VI (1421–71, King 1422–61 and 1470–1)
When Henry V died in 1422 hopes were no doubt high that the infant king would grow to emulate his illustrious father as England entered the longest minority in its history. Henry V's surviving brothers, John, Duke of Bedford and Humphrey, Duke of Gloucester, together with his uncle, Cardinal Henry Beaufort, were intelligent and active, if tempestuous, characters who ensured that Henry V's legacy in France was maintained through to 1437 when Henry VI came of age. Bedford was regent in France, and Gloucester Protector in England. Working with the aristocratic Council, they did a remarkably good job to hold the two kingdoms together. But the hopes were in vain.

Henry VI has strong claims to being England's most ineffective king since the Conquest; certainly his reign is seen 'as the most calamitous'. The forty years of his rule saw the loss of all Henry's V's possessions in France except Calais by 1453, the descent into civil war from 1450 onwards, his deposition by Edward IV not once but twice, and huge debts run up by the Crown as Henry gave lands and titles away to his favourites. Intellectually, Henry seemed neither capable of grappling with the complexities of affairs of state nor interested in the twists and turns of the power-brokering essential for a medieval monarch. He was not entirely 'hands-off', though, and often dabbled in issues.

The overriding objective of Henry's kingship seems to have been a desire to maintain peace, particularly in France. Henry never actively led an army. He rode with Lancastrian armies in the Wars of the Roses but stood aloof by his standard in the battles. He was the first monarch since the Conquest not to lead an army on foreign soil. Linked to this desire for peace was Henry's piety. He was obsessed with religious observance and standards of morality. Henry would never travel on a Sunday and missed the Battle of Towton because it was fought on Palm Sunday. He thought nothing as a young man of upbraiding elderly bishops on their personal behaviour. This religious obsession, however, found its flowering in the most wonderful manner. Advised by Bishop Waynflete, Henry planned and constructed the twin foundations of **Eton College** and **King's College**, Cambridge from 1440. It is one of the supreme ironies of English history that this most ineffective of monarchs should have bequeathed such outstanding legacies to the nation.

In 1445, as agreed in the Treaty of Tours with the French king, Henry married Margaret of Anjou, daughter of Duke René, at **Titchfield Abbey**, Hampshire. Although he was at no time an effective king, matters became dramatically worse when he

HOUSES OF LANCASTER AND TUDOR

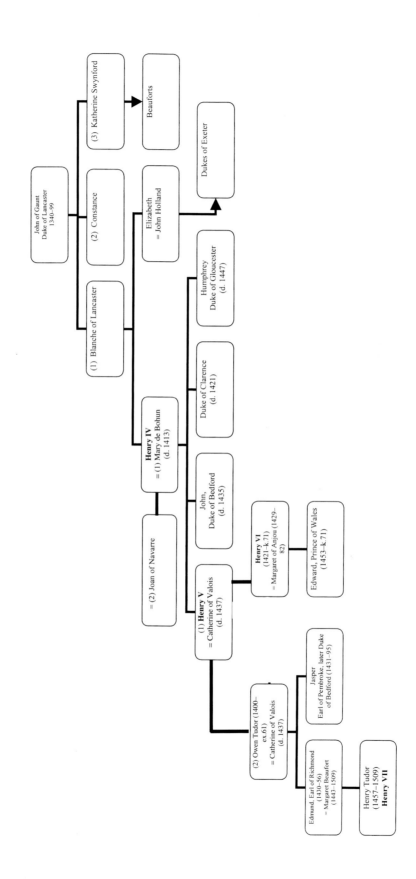

suffered a major nervous breakdown at Clarendon Palace in July 1453. Probably brought on by the loss of his father's French conquests, culminating in Gascony, the breakdown was to last seventeen months and thrust Richard, Duke of York into power as Lord Protector. For much of this time, Henry could not communicate, could not stand unaided and even showed no interest when his newly born son Prince Edward was presented to him.

Only six months after his recovery, in late 1454, Henry was injured in the neck while standing beside the Lancastrian standard at the First Battle of St Albans in May 1455 and watching many of his household cut down by the Yorkists. Within two weeks he was ill again. From now on he was really only a 'puppet' king, his faction driven along by Queen Margaret.

Deposed by Edward IV after the Battle of Towton in March 1461, Henry and Queen Margaret escaped to Scotland with the Duke of Somerset and a small band of followers. Henry was on the run for the next four years until he was captured in July 1465 near Clitheroe in Lancashire. He was then imprisoned in the Tower. When Edward fled the country in September 1470, Henry was produced from the Tower by the Earl of Warwick as once again the rightful king – his readeption. He was by now a mere cipher. It was not to last: Edward IV re-entered London in April 1471 and Henry was back in prison. With Warwick killed at Barnet and Prince Edward and Somerset killed at Tewkesbury, Henry was put to death in the **Tower** on the night of Edward's return to London on 21 May 1471.

He was buried at Chertsey Abbey in Surrey and rapidly became a martyr. A steady stream of pilgrims prayed at his tomb, many from the north of England, where Lancastrian sympathies were still strong. In 1484 Richard III ordered his reburial in **St George's Chapel**, Windsor. Henry VII and Lady Margaret Beaufort campaigned unsuccessfully with the pope to have Henry canonised.

Dowager Queen Catherine of Valois (1405–37)

By the Treaty of Troyes (1420) Henry V was recognised as heir to the French throne of Charles VI and obtained the hand of his daughter Catherine in marriage. Charles's son, the Dauphin, was disinherited. Henry and Catherine were married at Troyes, France in June 1420. Catherine was 19 years old. In December 1421 she gave birth to a boy, named Henry of Windsor. Tragedy struck in 1422 when Henry V died on campaign at Vincennes in France, probably from dysentery. Henry V's brothers now ruled the

two countries. There were concerns that Catherine was likely to be unduly influenced by potential suitors such as Edmund Beaufort, Earl of Somerset, so in 1428 an Act of Parliament was passed to regulate the remarriage of dowager queens.

Nevertheless, around this time Catherine formed a liaison with one of the members of her household, Owen Tudor, from gentry stock in Anglesey. They had four children, two of whom were to prove the saviours of the Lancastrian dynasty – Edmund and Jasper. Edmund became the father of Henry VII, but died young. It is probable that Henry VI inherited his mental condition through Catherine from her father, King Charles of France, who had a number of bouts of madness during his reign.

Catherine died in 1437, following a long illness, after which Owen Tudor was imprisoned for his 'illegal' liaison with her. Catherine is buried in **Westminster Abbey**.

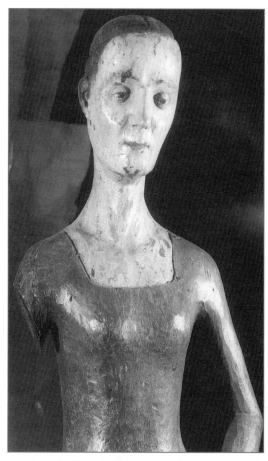

The funeral effigy of Henry VI's mother, Catherine of Valois – later wife to Owen Tudor.

Queen Margaret of Anjou (1429–82)

Margaret was the younger daughter of King René, Duke of Anjou, Bar and Lorraine and King of Sicily, etc. As part of the Treaty of Tours (1444), which gave Henry VI the peace he craved, it was agreed that Margaret would marry King Henry. She was attractive, vivacious and determined, in sharp contrast to Henry's more withdrawn personality. The ceremony was held in April 1445 at **Titchfield Abbey**. Margaret had had a difficult sea crossing and the wedding had been postponed because of her seasickness (more likely because she had just met Henry!). The Lancastrian dynasty desperately needed offspring but none was forthcoming until 1453, when Prince Edward was born. The timing unfortunately coincided with Henry VI's first mental breakdown. There were no further children.

During Henry's prolonged illness, Queen Margaret demanded to have the powers of regent, a step without precedent in England for a woman. The Council preferred Richard, Duke of York as Lord Protector, a man for whom Queen Margaret had developed a strong dislike. After Edmund Beaufort, Duke of Somerset was killed at the First Battle of St Albans (1455), Queen Margaret took over the full reins of Lancastrian government in 1456 (the King being by now largely incapable). She moved Henry, Prince Edward and the Court to **Coventry**, where they were based until 1460. By 1458 Margaret was ready to move against the Duke of York and his allies. During the War of Succession, she was of course not on the battlefield but was sometimes nearby (e.g. the Battle of Blore Heath). After the victory at the Second Battle of St Albans in February 1461, it was her fateful decision not to force an entry into London but to return northwards, which led to catastrophe for Lancaster. Within a week, the Yorkists 'broke the paradigm', slipped into London and declared the 18-year-old Earl of March, King Edward IV.

After the disaster of Towton, Margaret tried unsuccessfully to wage war against the Yorkists in Northumberland with the help of Scottish and French forces. She then retired to France, where she set up a court in exile at Koeur in France with Prince Edward. From 1465, King Henry meanwhile languished in prison in the Tower of London. In 1470 Warwick the Kingmaker and George, Duke of Clarence were driven out of England and headed for France. Here at Angers on 22 June 1470 occurred one of the more bizarre moments in the Wars. Queen Margaret became the ally of one of her greatest enemies, the Earl of

Portrait of Margaret of Anjou, Queen to Henry VI on a medal dated 1463.

Warwick. At their first meeting, she is said to have kept him waiting for a full fifteen minutes on his knees. Actually she never really trusted him and only returned to England the following April on the day Warwick was killed at the Battle of Barnet (1471). Defeat at the Battle of Tewkesbury three weeks later was the end for Margaret. Her son was killed in the battle, she was captured nearby – probably at **Little Malvern Priory** – and King Henry was murdered in the Tower.

She was imprisoned in Wallingford Castle, where her old friend Alice, Dowager Duchess of Suffolk, was Constable, and then repatriated to France as part of the Treaty of Picquigny in 1475. She died penniless in 1482 and is buried in Angers Cathedral in France.

Edward, Prince of Wales (1453–71)

Edward was born to Queen Margaret of Anjou in October 1453 but was not even 'recognised' by his father, Henry VI who was mentally ill at the time. Henry supposedly lacked interest in sex and so rumours had developed that Edmund, Duke of Somerset was the father. Queen Margaret clearly decided that Edward should have a conventionally tough upbringing. Edward is alleged to have been allowed to give the order to execute Lord Bonville and Sir Thomas Kyriell as traitors after the Second Battle of St Albans (1461), at the age of 7 years. After the Battle of Towton (1461), Edward fled with his mother to Scotland and then, in 1464, to France, where Margaret established a Court at Bar. Edward was tutored by none other than Sir John Fortescue, former Lord Chief Justice. Sir John wrote one of the first textbooks on English Law for Prince Edward.

Prince Edward and his mother returned to England in April 1471. At the Battle of Tewkesbury, Prince Edward commanded the centre with John, Lord Wenlock, an experienced soldier. Their division failed to support the attack launched by Edmund, Duke of Somerset. In the ensuing rout, Prince Edward was killed either on the field of battle or, having been captured by Sir Richard Croft, at the hands of the York royal family. Queen Margaret was captured a few days later. The Lancastrian cause was finished, and the spotlight moved to the Tudors. Prince Edward was buried in **Tewkesbury Abbey**.

Silver swan and ostrich feathers emblem of Edward, Lancastrian Prince of Wales.

The Tudors

Henry Tudor, the founder of the illustrious royal house, was descended, on his father's side, from gentry stock from Anglesey. In the 1420s his grandfather, Owen Tudor (1400–61) found himself in the service of Queen Catherine, Henry V's widow. He may have managed her estates in Wales or been keeper of her household. A relationship started and they were probably married around 1430 (no evidence exists), a move much complicated by a recent statute governing the remarriage of dowager queens and by Henry IV's statutes against Welshmen. Owen was given the status of an Englishman to counter these. When Queen Catherine died in 1437, Owen was imprisoned for violating the statutes. Owen fought at the Battle of Mortimer's Cross for Lancaster with son, Jasper. He was executed after the battle in Hereford marketplace on the orders of Edward, Duke of York.

Owen and Catherine had three surviving children, two of whom, Edmund and Jasper, were taken under his wing by their stepbrother, King Henry VI, in the 1440s. The Lancastrian royal family was by then dangerously small. In 1452 the two brothers were elevated to the rank of Earl of Richmond (Edmund) and Earl of Pembroke (Jasper) and given lands accordingly. In October 1455 the elder Edmund Tudor (*c*. 1430–56) married Lady Margaret Beaufort (1443–1509), heiress of John, 1st Duke of Somerset and thus related to Henry VI in her own right. Edmund was relatively inactive in state affairs until, in 1455, he was sent as the King's representative to Wales in order to quell the power of the rebel Gruffyd ap Nicholas. Edmund captured **Carmarthen Castle** in 1456, but then was himself captured when a Yorkist force led by Sir William Herbert seized the castle. Although released, Edmund died of the plague at Carmarthen in November 1456. His 13-year-old wife Lady Margaret gave birth to a son Henry in January 1457 in Pembroke Castle. Edmund's tomb can be seen at **St David's Cathedral**.

Jasper, Earl of Pembroke (1431–95)

Jasper seems to have been the more dynamic of the brothers. He was involved throughout the Wars, even if he was not consistently successful. He fought at the First Battle of St Albans (1455) on the losing side, at the Battle of Mortimer's Cross, where he commanded the beaten army, and at the battles of Towton, Bosworth and Stoke Field. Jasper's speciality was escaping when beaten and 'living to fight another day'. In the 1460s he kept the Lancastrian cause alive

Tomb-chest of Edmund Tudor, father of Henry VII, in St David's Cathedral.

in Wales. After Tewkesbury in 1471 (where he was not present), he escaped to France from Tenby with his nephew, Henry Tudor, to whom he gave unstinting support in exile in the 1470s. After Bosworth, Jasper was made Duke of Bedford and given extra lands by a grateful nephew and king.

Henry VII (1457–1509, King 1485–1509)

Henry Tudor was the great winner of the Wars of the Roses. At the Battle of Bosworth in 1485 he scooped the big prize – the crown of England – when Richard III was killed. Until this time Henry was a relatively obscure figure in English politics, living in exile in France. It has been calculated that at this time there were twenty-nine other members of the aristocracy with better theoretical claims to the throne. Henry triumphed for three main reasons.

Any claim to the throne came from his mother, Lady Margaret Beaufort, the sole heiress to the primary line of this illustrious family, the legitimated descendants of John of Gaunt and his mistress, Katherine Swynford. However, Henry IV had seemingly barred the Beauforts from the crown itself

in 1407. Henry Tudor's paternal grandfather, Owen, had 'married' Henry V's widow Catherine of Valois, but this, of course, did not generate a claim to the throne – merely membership of Henry VI's small royal family. Henry Tudor was an unusual admix of Welsh, French and English blood. On the execution of Henry, Duke of Buckingham in 1483, Henry became the prime Lancastrian claimant. Henry VI in earlier years is said to have shown much favour to his namesake and his mother and to have predicted his eventual accession to the throne.

In the summer of 1483 Lady Margaret Beaufort negotiated a deal with the Dowager Queen Elizabeth Woodville, in which Henry would marry Elizabeth's eldest daughter, Elizabeth of York, on becoming king. This move bolstered Henry's weak claim to the throne because Elizabeth was now Edward IV's true heir, following the death of the Princes in the Tower. It secured the support of many of Edward IV's former household members in the south and thus split the Yorkist party.

'Who dares wins.' Henry Tudor was not a fighting man in the traditional sense but, with his mother's

Crown Hill, the birth place of the Tudor dynasty at the end of the Battle of Bosworth. Henry Tudor is crowned by the Stanleys.

and the Stanleys' covert backing in England, he was prepared to invade with a small force, very much against the odds – at least on paper. His force was composed largely of French troops whose support he had finally secured from the French king, Charles VII, who preferred to see Henry as the surviving son of Henry VI! After he had acquired the throne under such difficult and tenuous circumstances, Henry's performance in the role of monarch no doubt confounded his critics. A naturally cautious but highly intelligent man, Henry secured his dynasty and built on the good work of Edward IV by transforming the finances of the Crown – England's greatest accountant-king?

In all this, he was supported by his mother, Lady Margaret Beaufort (the true heir to the Lancastrian throne), who remained his close confidante throughout his reign. There was therefore little place for his wife, Elizabeth of York, politically (or for other members of the Yorkists), although their marriage is said to have been loving. Elizabeth's greatest achievement was of course to produce 'an heir and one to spare'. The latter was needed and succeeded his father as Henry VIII in 1509. This awesome monarch is both the biological and political legacy of the union of Lancaster/Tudor with York. Henry VII and Elizabeth are buried in **Westminster Abbey**.

Portrait of Henry VII by an unknown artist.

The Beauforts
In 1396 John of Gaunt finally married his third wife, Katherine Swynford (née Röet) in **Lincoln Cathedral**. They already had four children, all of whom had been therefore illegitimate. That same year they were legitimated by Richard II and the pope. This illustrious family was given the name Beaufort, probably after one of Gaunt's castles in France. John Beaufort the eldest (1st Earl of Somerset) became a pillar of Henry IV's regime. (See **Canterbury**.)

The senior Beaufort line then passed to John's second son, John Beaufort the younger (1st Duke of Somerset) who was unfortunately captured at the Battle of Baugé (1421) against the French. He was not released until 1438. Although suffering from spells of illness, he was elevated to duke but in 1443 led a disastrous expedition to France. Here he clashed with Richard, Duke of York, who was Lieutenant-General of Normandy. Beaufort's military intervention in Brittany and apparent financial irregularities left deep resentment in York's mind against the Beauforts – even Henry VI was enraged. He died in 1444, perhaps by his own hand. John was buried in **Wimborne Minster**, near the family seat of Corfe Castle.

Lady Margaret Beaufort (1443–1509)
Lady Margaret was one of the greatest heiresses of the age, with large estates, particularly in the West Country. At the age of 7, she was married to John de la Pole, the son of the Duke of Suffolk, but after the latter's fall from power this was annulled and she married Edmund Tudor, Henry VI's stepbrother, in 1455. King Henry seems to have had a genuine desire that this match should go ahead. He was keen to widen and strengthen the now-so-narrow Lancastrian royal family. In January 1457 Margaret, aged 13, gave birth to a boy, Henry. Unfortunately the birth was difficult, so Margaret was unable to have further children. Even worse, Edmund had died of the plague in Carmarthen three months earlier.

Another husband was quickly found for Margaret and in January 1458 she married Sir Henry Stafford, second son of Humphrey, 1st Duke of Buckingham and securing for her much needed stability. Stafford was pardoned after the Battle of Towton (1461) and made peace with the Yorkist regime. Unfortunately this meant long separations for Margaret from her small child, Henry Tudor, who became the ward of William, Lord Herbert and lived at **Raglan Castle**.

Portrait of Lady Margaret Beaufort, mother and champion of Henry VII, by Maynard Waynwyk.

John Beaufort, Duke of Somerset, and maternal grandfather of Henry Tudor. He is wearing a Lancastrian SS collar.

that Henry Tudor would marry Elizabeth of York, Edward IV's eldest daughter. This agreement enabled many Yorkists to support Henry Tudor, especially in the south.

After Bosworth, Lady Margaret quickly became her son's closest confidante. Not surprisingly, she is said to have shed tears of joy at his coronation. She played a leading part in the campaign to have Henry VI made into a saint, but without success. She died in June 1509, just two months after her beloved son and is buried in **Westminster Abbey**.

The secondary Beaufort line derived from Duke John's younger brother, **Edmund, 2nd Duke of Somerset** (1406–55), who inherited the title but not the lands. These Beauforts were totally loyal courtiers for Lancaster but never had sufficient landed wealth to be fully effective. Only their status qualified them to command armies. Edmund became Richard, Duke of York's implacable opponent after his role in the debacle of England's departure from France in 1449–50. Edmund outsmarted York at Dartford in 1452 but was imprisoned during York's Protectorate in 1454. Somerset's name was linked to Queen Margaret of Anjou when it was announced that she was pregnant in 1453. The feud between the two men came to a head at the Battle of **St Albans** (1455), where Edmund was killed. Edmund had married Eleanor Beauchamp, daughter of the Earl of Warwick (d. 1439), and they produced a large family.

His son, **Henry, 3rd Duke** inherited the dukedom, and was appointed Captain of Calais in 1459. He challenged Warwick there but with little success. He went on to command the Lancastrian armies in late 1460–1, initially with great success at the Battle of Wakefield and Second Battle of St Albans. He and his adviser Andrew Trollope are credited with bringing a more dynamic approach to the battlefield. However, even this was not enough at the Battle of Towton, where the Lancastrians were so decisively beaten. Henry escaped and set about opposing the Yorkists in Northumberland. He was captured at Christmas 1462, and in a quite extraordinary blunder pardoned by Edward IV and taken into his own chamber. A year later, Henry reneged on his pardon and rejoined his old comrades in Northumberland. However, his army was caught in camp by John Neville, Lord Montagu in May 1464 at Hexham. Duke Henry was captured and executed in Hexham marketplace on the same or the next day.

When the Lancastrians returned to power during the Readeption in 1470/1, Henry's younger brother **Edmund** was now **4th Duke of Somerset**. In April

Stafford fought for Edward IV at the Battle of Barnet (1471) but died later that same year from wounds he received there. Within the year Lady Margaret married for a fourth time, to Thomas, Lord Stanley, the supreme 'trimmer' of the Wars of the Roses. This was to be the great political marriage of the Wars whose supreme achievement was the conspiracy behind the Battle of Bosworth. Son Henry Tudor meantime fled with Jasper, to France and exile.

Lady Margaret and Lord Thomas maintained a low profile for the rest of Edward IV's reign. However, after his death, Margaret played a central role in plotting opposition to Richard III. In particular she established contact with Dowager Queen Elizabeth Woodville, who was in sanctuary in Westminster Abbey. After it was clear that the Princes in the Tower were dead, a rapprochement was achieved by agreement between the two women

THE BEAUFORTS

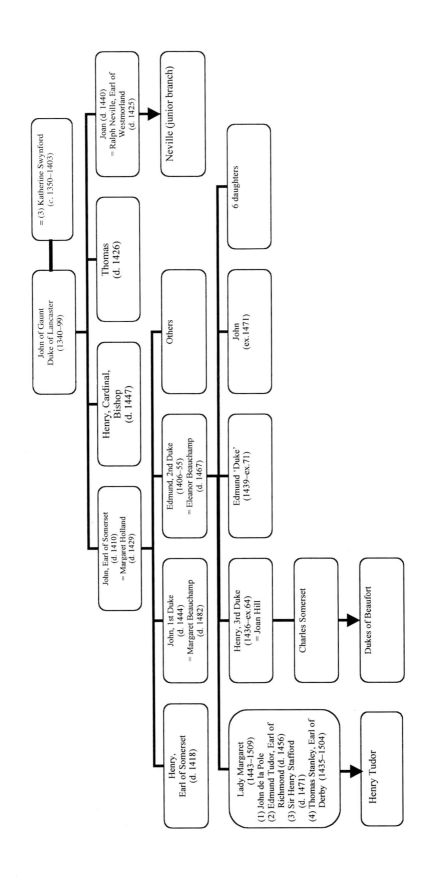

John of Gaunt
Duke of Lancaster
(1340–99)

= (3) Katherine Swynford
(c. 1350–1403)

Joan (d. 1440)
= Ralph Neville, Earl of
Westmorland
(d. 1425)

Neville (junior branch)

Thomas
(d. 1426)

Henry, Cardinal,
Bishop
(d. 1447)

John, Earl of Somerset
(d. 1410)
= Margaret Holland
(d. 1429)

Henry,
Earl of Somerset
(d. 1418)

John, 1st Duke
(d. 1444)
= Margaret Beauchamp
(d. 1482)

Edmund, 2nd Duke
(1406–55)
= Eleanor Beauchamp
(d. 1467)

Others

6 daughters

John
(ex.1471)

Edmund 'Duke'
(1439–ex.71)

Henry, 3rd Duke
(1436–ex.64)
= Joan Hill

Lady Margaret
(1443–1509)
(1) John de la Pole
(2) Edmund Tudor, Earl of
Richmond (d. 1456)
(3) Sir Henry Stafford
(d. 1471)
(4) Thomas Stanley, Earl of
Derby (1435–1504)

Charles Somerset

Dukes of Beaufort

Henry Tudor

54

1470 Edmund spurned the opportunity of fighting alongside the Earl of Warwick, leaving London before the Battle of Barnet in order to greet Queen Margaret when she landed in the West Country. Edmund had previous military experience in Italy and so took command of Margaret's forces at the Battle of Tewkesbury. Perhaps double-crossed by Lord Wenlock, Somerset's army was defeated in detail by Edward IV. Somerset was captured, executed in **Tewkesbury** marketplace and buried in the abbey.

The Staffords

The Staffords owned vast estates through the Midlands and Wales. In total income, they ranked alongside the Earls of Warwick. Through Anne, Countess of Stafford, daughter of Thomas of Woodstock (Edward III's youngest son), they possessed royal blood and they were related to most other magnate families. The family had a long tradition of royal service, which <u>Humphrey Stafford, 1st Duke of Buckingham</u> (1402–60) followed, serving in France under John, Duke of Bedford. He was elevated to duke in 1444 with precedence over all non-royal dukes. Humphrey was a conciliator by nature. He fought for Henry VI at the First Battle of St Albans only because he was king, not because he was fervent for the King's party. However, by 1460 the time for moderation had passed. At the Battle of Northampton, Duke Humphrey's faction was destroyed by the Yorkists led by Warwick and Edward of York, and the Duke cut down outside his tent.

Duke Humphrey's eldest son, <u>Sir Humphrey</u>, had died from wounds sustained at the First Battle of St Albans, so the dukedom passed to his grandson, **Henry, 2nd Duke**, at an early age. Duke Humphrey's second son, <u>Sir Henry</u> (d. 1471), married Lady Margaret Beaufort, mother of Henry Tudor. (See Beaufort.)

Henry Stafford, 2nd Duke of Buckingham (*c*. 1457–83)

The new duke was married to a sister of Elizabeth Woodville. He felt he should have been given more respect and more power under Edward IV than he received (perhaps because Edward did not trust him in view of the family's Lancastrian background). Henry's influence was constrained by Hastings in the Midlands and by his Woodville kinsmen in Wales (he was excluded from the Council of Wales). On Edward's death, Buckingham was thus very ready to fall in with Richard, Duke of Gloucester and provide him with invaluable support in the coups of April–June

1483 that made Richard king. He was with Richard when they took over custody of Edward V at **Stony Stratford**. As a result, Buckingham received yet more lands and honours, ending up as constable of fifty-three castles in the Marches – an unprecedented delegation of royal authority by a medieval king.

After he had achieved everything he could have dreamed of, in one of those spectacular U-turns for which the Wars of the Roses are notorious, Buckingham then decided, soon after Richard III's coronation in July 1483, to rebel against him. Was it when he realised that Richard intended to kill the two Princes or already had done so? Was it because he secretly wanted the crown for himself? It is not clear. Buckingham has in fact long been a suspect himself for these murders. We do know, however, that the arch-plotter and ally of Lady Margaret Beaufort, Bishop Morton of Ely, had been sent by Richard under house arrest to Buckingham in Brecon Castle after Richard's Second Coup in 1483. It appears that the two men discussed the idea of a revolt against Richard. Stafford wrote to Henry Tudor, inviting him to join the revolt. This crystallised into the so-called Buckingham Revolt of October 1483, an ill-coordinated affair which was literally a 'damp squib' (heavy rains severely hampered communications). After the failure of the rebellion, Buckingham was captured and beheaded in **Salisbury marketplace** on 2 November 1483, in front of his former co-conspirator, Richard III. His tomb can be seen at nearby **Britford**.

The family held lands in many counties – in the Midlands, the Marches, Wales and Kent. Their principal residences were Brecon Castle, **Penshurst Place**, Tonbridge Castle (Kent) and Maxstoke Castle (Warwickshire).

The Hollands

The Hollands were another aristocratic family with serious pretensions to royalty. They were descended from Joan, the Fair Maid of Kent (who married the Black Prince) by her first husband Sir Thomas Holland. Their son John Holland married Elizabeth, daughter of John of Gaunt and elder sister of Henry IV. During the chaos of the Wars of the Roses John's grandson <u>Henry Holland</u> (1430–75), 4th Duke of Exeter, even had aspirations for the throne. Before 1447 he married Anne Plantagenet, the eldest child of Richard, Duke of York and Cecily Neville. York is reputed to have paid the largest dowry of the age for this match. Whether he was disappointed later, we do not know, but Duke Henry turned out a die-hard and unpleasant Lancastrian. He fought at the battles

THE STAFFORDS AND THE HOLLANDS

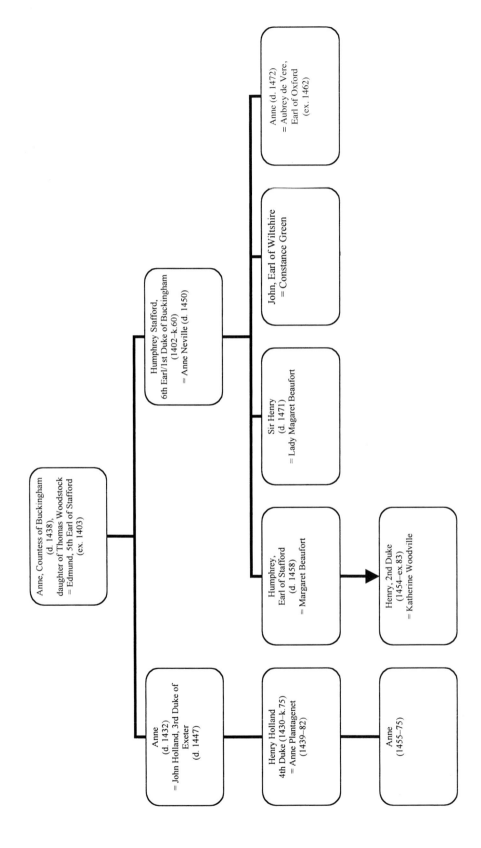

Anne, Countess of Buckingham (d. 1438), daughter of Thomas Woodstock = Edmund, 5th Earl of Stafford (ex. 1403)

Humphrey Stafford, 6th Earl/1st Duke of Buckingham (1402–k.60) = Anne Neville (d. 1450)

Anne (d. 1432) = John Holland, 3rd Duke of Exeter (d. 1447)

Anne (d. 1472) = Aubrey de Vere, Earl of Oxford (ex. 1462)

John, Earl of Wiltshire = Constance Green

Sir Henry (d. 1471) = Lady Magaret Beaufort

Humphrey, Earl of Stafford (d. 1458) = Margaret Beaufort

Henry, 2nd Duke (1454–ex.83) = Katherine Woodville

Henry Holland 4th Duke (1430–k.75) = Anne Plantagenet (1439–82)

Anne (1455–75)

of Wakefield, Second St Albans, Towton and Barnet, where he was left for dead but recovered.

In 1472 he and Anne were divorced, Anne marrying her lover, Sir Thomas St Leger. In 1475 Henry accompanied Edward IV on his French expedition but did not return. On the voyage back Duke Henry was drowned, probably having been thrown overboard on the orders of Edward. The Hollands built the splendid medieval house at Dartington in Devon, which survives.

The Percys

The Percys were traditionally the most powerful family east of the Pennines, being Wardens of the East March, protecting the Scottish borders. Their heartland was eastern Yorkshire but they also held extensive estates in Northumberland. The family's prestige began to wane when they rebelled against Henry IV in 1403. (The famous Hotspur was killed at the Battle of Shrewsbury.) Ralph Neville, Earl of Westmorland and his family, also with wide estates in the north, replaced them as favourites with the Lancastrian monarchs. Nevertheless the Percys supported Lancaster during the first phase of the War. The 2nd Earl of Northumberland Henry (1394–1455), commanding a division, was killed by the Yorkists at the First Battle of St Albans, while his son, another Henry, 3rd Earl, suffered the same fate at Towton (1461), being blamed for the Lancastrian defeat because his left wing was slow to move forward in support of the Lancastrian right. Henry's younger brother Thomas, Lord Egremont (1422–60) was a Lancastrian 'hothead' who was executed outside his tent at the Battle of Northampton (1460) on the orders of Warwick.

Another Henry, 4th Earl (c. 1446–89) was only 15 years old when he succeeded. He was imprisoned in the Tower by Edward IV, and his estates and titles given to John Neville, the Kingmaker's brother, in 1464. However, in 1470, in an effort to shore up his support in the north, Edward IV dramatically returned the earldom to Henry Percy. John Neville was unimpressed with Edward's compensatory lands in the West Country and eventually declared for his brother, Warwick. Nevertheless, Edward got his reward, because on his return to England in March 1471, Percy's support in Yorkshire was sufficient to cancel out Neville's threat – not that Percy did anything constructive! During May 1471, while Edward was engrossed in the Tewkesbury campaign, Percy secured the north for the Yorkists, ensuring that no rebellions took hold.

During the 1470s Percy achieved an accommodation with Richard, Duke of Gloucester and accepted the latter's hegemony. He assisted Richard as king to suppress Buckingham's Revolt in October 1483. He commanded the rear for Richard at Bosworth but is generally regarded as being inactive during the fighting. He was imprisoned by Henry VII but later released. Tradition has it that he was murdered at his Topcliffe manor (near Thirsk) in 1489, trying to put down a tax revolt. Northern supporters of Richard III may have been looking for revenge for his inactivity at Bosworth – it is said his own retainers stood by and did nothing. He was buried in **Beverley Minster**.

The Percys had seats at **Alnwick Castle** and **Warkworth Castle** in Northumberland and Spofforth and Wressle castles, plus Topcliffe, **Leconfield** and Healaugh manors in Yorkshire.

The Stanleys

This was a family which had the singular advantage of dominating their locality of western Lancashire. Thomas, 2nd Lord Stanley (1435–1504) was the eldest son of Sir Thomas Stanley (d. 1459), who was created first Lord Stanley in 1455. Sir Thomas was a prominent member of Henry VI's household, including a spell as Lieutenant of Ireland. The family lived at Lathom and Knowsley in south Lancashire and held many estates in Cheshire and north Wales. In 1454 Thomas junior married Eleanor Neville, sister of the Kingmaker. In 1459 he succeeded his father to the barony. Within seven months he was to show he was more independently minded. Perhaps piqued at not being given command of the overall army, he refused to fight for the Lancastrians at Blore Heath, preferring to keep his troops a few miles off. In fact he allowed his brother Sir William Stanley to join the Yorkist force under the Earl of Salisbury and congratulated the latter when victory was secured! A few months later, the Commons tried to impeach Stanley but Henry VI overruled them.

This then was the nature of the man – prepared to sit on the fence and regularly changing sides, not to be trusted, probably not liked. In short, a 'trimmer', but astute and successful. He fought for York at Towton, supported the Readeption in 1470/1, and let his brother Sir William do the fighting at Barnet/Tewkesbury in 1471. In 1472 he married Lady Margaret Beaufort and re-established himself with Edward IV. It was, of course, the last minute defection of the Stanleys (especially Sir William's) that was decisive at Bosworth. Thomas is said to have placed the crown on Tudor's head at **Stoke Golding**.

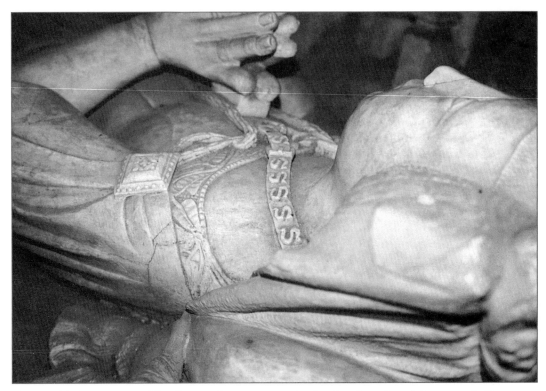

An example of a Lancastrian SS collar worn by a woman in the church at Broughton. It is most probably Elizabeth Wykeham.

Thomas was well rewarded for his efforts by Henry VII. Created Earl of Derby in 1485, he became Constable of England and Chief Steward of the Duchy of Lancaster. He survived his brother's execution for treason in 1495 by carefully staying neutral. The family's success continues today. There have been nineteen earls of Derby, one of whom was prime minister in the nineteenth century. Thomas was buried at **Ormskirk**.

Sir William Stanley was Thomas's younger brother. Although coordinating their efforts, Sir William became a military force in his own right during the Wars. As a result, he became the wealthiest commoner in the country. William was a fighting man, being present at the battles of Blore Heath, Towton, Barnet, Tewkesbury and, most famously, at Bosworth, where his late intervention against Richard III was crucial for Henry Tudor. In many ways, he did brother Thomas's fighting for him. Surprisingly, Sir William was exposed as part of the Perkin Warbeck conspiracy in 1495 and executed by Henry VII on **Tower Hill**. His principal seat was Holt Castle, Denbighshire.

The de Veres (Earls of Oxford)

In the fifteenth century the de Vere earls possessed the oldest noble title but were not particularly wealthy. They held lands mainly in Essex and Suffolk. John, 12th Earl, avoided commitment in the 1450s but was a Yorkist sympathiser. In early 1462, however, he became embroiled in a plot to depose Edward IV, which was quickly unmasked. He and his elder son, Aubrey, were hanged, drawn and quartered on **Tower Hill**. Not surprisingly, this act seems to have driven John, 13th Earl (*c*. 1443–1513) to be an unregenerate Lancastrian. John came under similar suspicion in 1468 when Edward IV was very nervous about Warwick-induced plots. He was sent to the Tower but turned King's evidence.

John married the Kingmaker's sister, Margaret Neville, and attended the wedding of George, Duke of Clarence to the Kingmaker's daughter, Isabel, in July 1469. He seems to have become a Clarence supporter in his fight against Edward. After exile with Warwick and Clarence, Earl John returned to England during the Readeption and fought alongside

Stoke Golding village signpost depicting the crowning of Henry Tudor.

the Kingmaker at Barnet, where his wing swept Lord Hastings on the Yorkist left from the field. Escaping to Scotland after the battle, Oxford remained opposed to Edward, staging raids at St Osyth near Colchester and occupying **St Michael's Mount** with John, Viscount Beaumont in 1473. Trapped, he managed to negotiate his life for imprisonment in Hammes Castle, Calais. De Vere escaped from this castle in 1484 and returned triumphantly with Henry Tudor in 1485. He played a decisive part at the Battle of Bosworth against his East Anglian rival John Howard, Duke of Norfolk and again at the Battle of Stoke Field in 1487.

John became a mainstay of the Tudor regime as Great Chamberlain, Steward and High Admiral of England. He was seen as a kindly man. He looked after his old companion in arms Viscount Beaumont when the latter lost his mind in 1487. The de Vere principal seat was **Castle Hedingham**.

Archbishop John Morton (*c.* 1420–1500)

John Morton came from gentry stock in Dorset and developed into one of the most formidable bishop-politicians of his age. He obtained a doctorate in law from Balliol College, Oxford and then practised as a lawyer in London, where his abilities were spotted by Archbishop Bourchier. By 1459 he was assisting in drafting the attainders of the York and Neville families for Queen Margaret for use at the Parliament of Devils of that year. Morton was most likely present at the Battle of Towton in March 1461 as a Lancastrian observer. Trying to flee the country afterwards, he was arrested and imprisoned in the Tower but managed to escaped from that fortress in late 1461. He was present at the siege and surrender of Dunstanburgh Castle in Northumberland in December 1462. Then exiled, he joined Queen Margaret's Court-in-waiting in France. In 1464 he was attainted in his absence.

After the Battle of Tewkesbury in May 1471, he was captured, but by July he had received a general pardon from Edward IV. Allegedly converted to the Yorkist cause, he served Edward IV 'faithfully'. By March 1472 he was already Master of the Rolls and became a Privy Councillor and diplomat. In 1478 he was appointed Bishop of Ely. By April 1483, he was even comforting Edward IV on his deathbed. There were rumours of poisoning.

He was present at the Council meeting on Friday 13 June 1483, when Richard of Gloucester staged his Second Coup by beheading Hastings. Morton was again imprisoned but then very surprisingly sent 'under house arrest' to the Duke of Buckingham's castle at Brecon. Here, Morton pulled off his greatest coup – he managed to persuade Buckingham not only to join the largely gentry revolt in the south of England, but also to invite Henry Tudor to lead it.

After the collapse of Buckingham's Revolt, Morton hid in the Fens and then escaped to Flanders, where he remained in exile until after Bosworth in 1485. Here, he kept very much in contact with both Henry Tudor and Lady Margaret Beaufort at the very centre of conspiracy. He officiated at Henry VII's coronation later that year. In 1486 Morton reached the very top of his profession, being appointed Lord Chancellor and Archbishop of Canterbury. He was also Chancellor of Oxford University. He is, of course, best remembered for 'Morton's Fork', the approach later used to ensure that the aristocracy paid their full due in taxes to Henry VII. Morton's canopied tomb-chest lies in the crypt of **Canterbury Cathedral**. He is also commemorated by Morton's Tower in Lambeth Palace, built by him from 1490.

HENRICVS DEI GRÃ REX ANGLIE ·

Henry VIII, aged 53, by Cornelis Massys. This awesome monarch was the end product of the Wars of the Roses – Henry VIII represents both their biological and political legacy. His father, Henry Tudor, was the victor at Bosworth, his mother, Elizabeth of York, was the eldest daughter of the impressive Yorkist monarch Edward IV.

FOUR

THE GUIDE BY REGION

VISITING THE SITES

- It is better to go in summer – houses and castles are often closed to the public in winter. Even churches are more likely to be open in the summer months.
- Afternoons are best, until 4.30 p.m.
- Access to churches can be difficult, even in summer, because of problems of theft and vandalism. Parish churches in urban or semi-urban environments are often likely to be locked. Churches in very isolated rural environments may also be locked. Cathedrals and large town churches are usually open with supervision. A phone call or letter before your visit is the best idea. Alternatively, a phone number is usually given on the board in the churchyard or in the church porch, or a key is sometimes available locally.
- Phoning clergy and parish offices in the morning is better.
- Church brasses are often under carpets.
- Most cathedrals ask for visitors' donations.
- All of the sites in this guide are open to the public.
- Directions are given to each site, and are designed for use with modern motoring atlases. Where there is more than one church in a town (tower) or (spire) is indicated.

RATING SYSTEM FOR SITES

*	Standard monument. Person involved in battle or royal official.
**	More detail known of involvement or some architectural interest.
***	A significant participant in the Wars.
****	Outstanding historical interest.
*****	Truly national importance.

RATING SYSTEM FOR BATTLEFIELDS

+   Site known but little survives.
++   Site known and some interesting survivals.
+++   Plenty to see or key battle with some survivals.
++++   Key battle with much to see.
+++++ Decisive battles with plenty to see.

POUND SYMBOL

£   Entrance fee charged.
££   Higher entrance fee charged.

ABBREVIATIONS

NT   National Trust property
EH   English Heritage property
Cadw   Welsh Historic Monuments
KAL   Key to church available locally (check porch/board)
PO   Parish office phone number

UNDERLINING

<u>Underlining</u> is used to highlight the person(s) involved in the Wars of the Roses who is being celebrated at a particular site.

BOLD TYPE

Bold type is used in site descriptions in three ways:
1. To highlight locations in a building, e.g. **chancel**.
2. To indicate a secondary site, e.g. **Pickworth**.
3. To highlight a memorial at a site to a person who features in Chapter 3, 'Main Protagonists', where biographical information is given, e.g. **<u>Lady Margaret Beaufort</u>**.

SITE CATEGORIES

Sites are split into primary sites (220) and secondary sites (40). Secondary sites are conveniently close to primary sites but do not necessarily warrant a long-distance visit on their own merit. They are 'whilst you are in the area do also visit' sites. Full directions are not necessarily given for secondary sites.

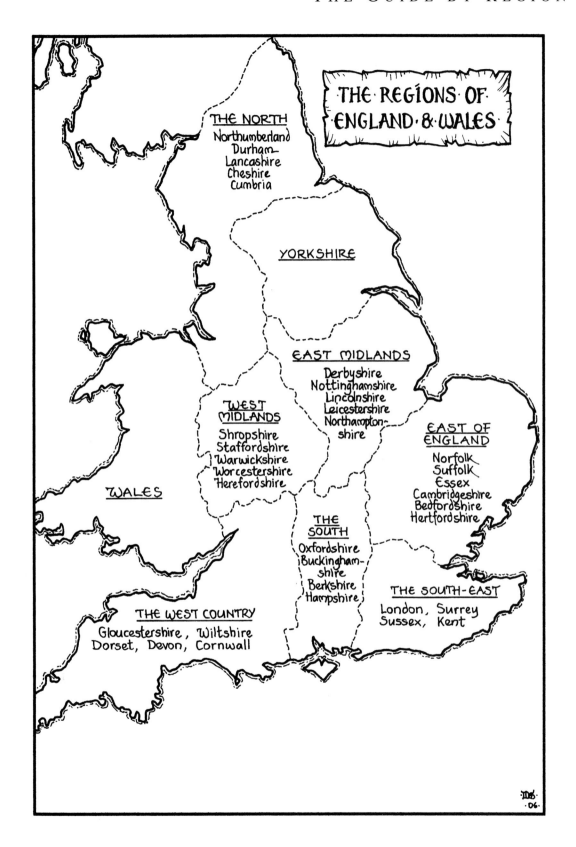

THE REGIONS OF ENGLAND & WALES

THE NORTH
Northumberland
Durham
Lancashire
Cheshire
Cumbria

YORKSHIRE

EAST MIDLANDS
Derbyshire
Nottinghamshire
Lincolnshire
Leicestershire
Northampton-
shire

WEST MIDLANDS
Shropshire
Staffordshire
Warwickshire
Worcestershire
Herefordshire

EAST OF ENGLAND
Norfolk
Suffolk
Essex
Cambridgeshire
Bedfordshire
Hertfordshire

WALES

THE SOUTH
Oxfordshire
Buckingham-
shire
Berkshire
Hampshire

THE SOUTH-EAST
London, Surrey
Sussex, Kent

THE WEST COUNTRY
Gloucestershire, Wiltshire
Dorset, Devon, Cornwall

LONDON AND THE SOUTH EAST

ARUNDEL, Castle *** ££

*Close to the town centre, the **Fitzalan Chapel** of*
St Nicholas Church contains a fine collection of Fitzalan and
Howard monuments. Note that the chapel can now only be
reached from the castle grounds.

Our interest is in the superb chantry-tombs of William
Fitzalan, 9th Earl and his son Thomas, 10th Earl in the
Fitzalan Chapel.

William Fitzalan (1418–88) married Joan Neville,
the Kingmaker's sister, and thus became Edward IV's
and Richard III's cousin by marriage. He fought in
the French wars and was involved in suppressing
Cade's Rebellion in 1450. He had early Yorkist
sympathies in the 1450s but may have been present
at the rout of Ludford Bridge (1459) on the Lancastrian side. He fought for the Yorkists at the Second
Battle of St Albans (1461) and, probably, Losecote
Field (1470). He became a member of Edward IV's

Effigy of William Fitzalan, 9th Earl of Arundel in the
Fitzalan Chapel, Arundel Castle.

close circle, accompanying him to George Neville's
lodgings in 1467 to recover the Great Seal – an
event of great political significance at the time, as it
signified Edward's break with the Nevilles. Arundel
also was in the party that accompanied Edward in
October 1469 on his re-entry into London following
his release from captivity by Warwick. Arundel
was involved in suppressing the Fauconberg risings
of May 1471 and was Constable of Dover Castle
and Warden of the Cinque Ports. He appears to
have supported Richard III in October 1483 but not
to have been involved, probably owing to old age.
Although they were thoroughly involved in the Wars
the Fitzalans do not seem to have really 'punched
their weight'.

Thomas Fitzalan (earl from 1488, died 1524)
married Margaret Woodville (Queen Elizabeth's
sister) in 1464. He was created Lord Maltravers
in the 1460s by Edward IV, and Knight of the Bath
at Elizabeth's coronation. He supported Richard III
during his reign and patrolled the Channel on his
behalf. He fought for him at Bosworth. Thomas lived
and died at Downley Park hunting lodge, Singleton.
Two empty tombs can still be seen in **Singleton
parish church** – one for Thomas and one for his son,
also Thomas, 11th Earl. Both were probably buried in
Singleton to start with and moved to Arundel at the
end of the sixteenth century when the Singleton lands
were lost to the earldom.

ASH-BY-SANDWICH, St Nicholas Church **

2 miles west of Sandwich, in village centre now bypassed
by A257.

In the **chancel** are alabaster effigies on a tomb-
chest of John de Septvans (d. 1458) and his widow,
Katherine. Round his neck is the 'SS' collar of the
House of Lancaster. He was pardoned for taking part
in Jack Cade's Rebellion in 1450 against Henry VI's
government, one of a substantial number of wealthy
people involved in that dangerous uprising. (See
Cade Street.)

ASHFORD (Kent), St Mary's Church ***

Town centre, within pedestrian precinct (tower).

In the **chancel** are a tomb-chest with brass (only
the head remains) and the tilting helmet of Sir John
Fogge (c. 1418–90). Sir John is one of the very few
people to have been involved throughout the Wars.
He is said to have served Henry VI and helped put
down Jack Cade's Revolt of 1450. However, along

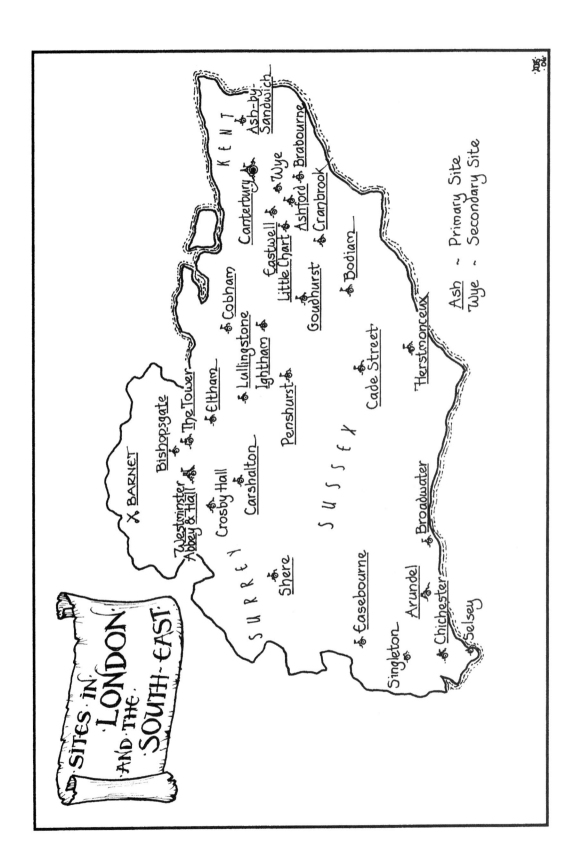

SITES IN LONDON AND THE SOUTH-EAST

KENT

SUSSEX

SURREY

Ash-by-Sandwich
Canterbury
Wye
Brabourne
Eastwell
Ashford
Little Chart
Cranbrook
Goudhurst
Bodiam
Cobham
Lullingstone
Ightham
Penshurst
Herstmonceux
Cade Street
Eltham
The Tower
Bishopsgate
Westminster Abbey & Hall
Crosby Hall
Carshalton
BARNET
Shere
Broadwater
Easebourne
Arundel
Singleton
Chichester
Selsey

Ash ~ Primary Site
Wye ~ Secondary Site

Monumental brass remains and inscription from the tomb-chest of Sir John Fogge in Ashford church.

with Sir John Scott, he threw open the gates of Canterbury to the Calais earls (March, Salisbury and Warwick) in July 1460 and joined the Yorkists. He fought at the battles of Northampton, Second St Albans and Towton. He married Alice Haute, a cousin of Elizabeth Woodville and related to Sir Richard Haute, and was a hunting companion of Edward IV in the mid-1460s.

Fogge became a prominent courtier under Edward as King's Knight and Treasurer of the King's Household 1461–7, as well as administrator of the Duchy of Lancaster for the Prince of Wales, later Edward V. He was specifically named in Warwick's and Clarence's manifesto for their 1469 rebellion against Edward IV as one of the 'persons giving covetous rule and guiding' to the King. In the summer of 1471 he was involved in the subjugation of the last pockets of resistance following the Bastard of Fauconberg's revolt. Fogge was prominent in the Kent risings during Buckingham's Revolt in October 1483, having been absent from Richard III's coronation. He was attainted for his part in it but then surprisingly pardoned by Richard. Sir John helped rebuild this church, including building the existing tower between 1470 and 1490.

THE BATTLE OF BARNET (14 April 1471) +++
Strategic Background and the Campaign
Relations between Edward IV and Richard Neville, Earl of Warwick (the 'Kingmaker') deteriorated steadily through the late 1460s. Warwick was driven to rebellion with Edward's brother George, Duke of Clarence in both 1469 and 1470, both ultimately unsuccessful. After the Lincolnshire rebels' defeat at the Battle of Losecote Field (12 March 1470) Warwick realised he was never going to succeed in placing Clarence on the throne of England. By April, Warwick and Clarence were forced into exile in France. Here Warwick immediately declared for Henry VI and enlisted the help of King Louis XI of France to reinstate Henry to the throne of England. A reconciliation of sorts with Queen Margaret was achieved (although she kept Warwick on his knees for a full fifteen minutes before the interview) and Warwick's younger daughter Anne Neville was betrothed to Henry's son, Prince Edward, now nearly 17 years old. By early September 1470, Warwick was ready. His invasion fleet landed near Exeter and Warwick was able to regain entry to London unopposed on 6 October, because Edward had been lured to the north by rebellion and then suddenly and treacherously abandoned at Doncaster by his long-standing supporter John Neville, Marquis Montagu (Warwick's brother). Potentially caught between two 'rebel' armies, Edward chose flight to King's Lynn with just a few companions, including Richard of Gloucester, his brother and Lord Hastings, and on 2 October departed by ship to the Low Countries and the protection of his brother-in-law, Duke Charles of Burgundy. The Readeption of Henry VI, with Warwick again in power, had begun (Queen Margaret and Prince Edward remained behind in France until England was fully safe).

By early March, Edward was to ready to return to England to reclaim the throne he had so dramatically vacated. A fleet of thirty-six ships containing Burgundian mercenaries set sail on 2 March from Flushing harbour. An abortive attempt was made to land at Cromer in Norfolk, but the area was too well guarded by Lancastrians. The fleet continued up the east coast but was hit by storms and scattered. Eventually the ships reunited at Ravenspur (near Spurn Point), at the mouth of the Humber. Edward bluffed his way through traditionally Lancastrian country by claiming he was coming to regain only his dukedom of York and by playing off Marquis Montagu, watching, undecided, from Pontefract Castle, against Henry Percy, Earl of Northumberland, whose title had only recently been restored by Edward. To begin with, support for Edward was very slow in joining his army but, after Doncaster, support grew steadily as he moved south.

At Nottingham, Edward learned that Lancastrian forces led by John de Vere, Earl of Oxford, Henry Holland, Duke of Exeter and Lord Beaumont had arrived at Newark in strength. With typical daring, Edward immediately turned to meet them but they declined to fight and wheeled south to link up with Warwick the Kingmaker, who was now in the Midlands raising troops. On 25 March at Leicester, Edward was joined by 3,000 men-at-arms, retainers of Hastings led in by Sir William Norris. Edward moved to Coventry, where he found the Kingmaker already in residence behind the city walls. Montagu had at last left Pontefract and moved south to join his brother, clearly now siding with Warwick's cause. Warwick had been inactive up until now because he had been advised by Clarence to wait until he, Clarence, could provide reinforcements. Clarence was now at Burford, Oxfordshire with his retainers. In fact, through his mother and sisters, Clarence had been kept in touch with Edward. Under the Readeption Clarence had become a marginal and disillusioned figure at Court and was now only heir to the crown if the Lancastrian line failed. On 3 April, therefore, the three York brothers with their armies were dramatically reunited on the road between Banbury and Coventry and Clarence reconciled to Edward's cause. Apparently Clarence and Richard of Gloucester had a quiet word together at the end. Clarence tried to mediate between his father-in-law, Warwick, and his brother, Edward, but Warwick would have none of it. Edward again offered battle but Warwick refused as he was still waiting for Montagu's arrival.

On 5 April, Edward suddenly decided to leave Coventry and march on London. The Lancastrian leaders, Edmund Beaufort, Duke of Somerset and Sir John Courtney, heir to the Earl of Devon, had already left town to meet Queen Margaret of Anjou in the West Country, where she was expected at any time. Warwick's youngest brother, George Neville, Archbishop of York, and the veteran Lord Sudeley were left to try and organise resistance to Edward's army. Henry VI was paraded in the streets to try and rally troops but he looked so pathetic in his blue gown that this did more harm than good. The mayor received orders from both Edward and from Warwick, and was so put out that he took to his bed and refused to continue in his job. Eventually the citizens agreed not to oppose Edward, and the vacillating George Neville sent a message to Edward agreeing to surrender Henry VI on his entry. On 11 April Edward entered London, Henry VI was returned to the Tower and Edward was reunited with Queen Elizabeth Woodville in Westminster Abbey, where she had been living in sanctuary through the Readeption, which was now over.

Meanwhile Warwick's army, reinforced by Montagu, reached St Albans on 12 April. Edward reacted quickly and on 13 April led out his force on the Great North Road. Late in the evening as they approached Barnet, they encountered Warwick's army drawn up on the plateaued ridge of high ground north of the town. In fading light, Edward forced Warwick's scouts out of the town itself and pushed on north to the open ground. Here they encamped very close to the Lancastrians. Warwick could not avoid battle this time.

The Battle

Both sides advanced to the attack just after 4.00 a.m. on Sunday 14 April (Easter Sunday). It was still very dark and there was apparently thick mist. On engaging, it became clear that the two battle lines were misaligned (which was not surprising, given the conditions) – the Lancastrians extended further west and the Yorkists further east. This had two effects. First, the Earl of Oxford took full effect of his overlap and quickly drove Hastings' left wing into retreat through Barnet and down the slope towards London, some men even reaching the capital and announcing a Yorkist defeat. It is worth noting that the same manoeuvre occurred at the Battle of Mortimer's Cross in 1461, when the Earl of Wiltshire initially routed Sir Walter Devereux's force on the Yorkist right.

Second, Gloucester turned the flank of Exeter's left wing in similar fashion, probably after negotiating a dip in the plateau. The gently rising ground at this point, coupled with Warwick's quick reinforcement from his reserve, did not lead to the same precipitous collapse on the Lancastrian left. Gloucester's and Exeter's divisions engaged in a savage mêlée, which led to heavy casualties on both sides. The net result was that the battle lines skewed on to a north-west–south-east, or even north–south, alignment. The position in the centre was evenly balanced, with the Lancastrians reinforced by Warwick slowly pushing back Edward's force.

Meanwhile Oxford's men were drawn into looting and took a long time to regroup. Eventually Oxford led a force of some 800 men back on to the battlefield. However, at this point, disaster is said to have struck. Because of the heavy mist, Oxford actually attacked Montagu's force on his own side. Montagu, for his part mistaking Oxford's star and streams emblem for Edward's sun and streams, ordered his archers to open fire. Cries of treason were heard before Oxford and Beaumont rapidly fled the field with many of their men (and did not stop until they reached Scotland). Edward spurred his men on to push harder on Montagu's distracted troops.

At this time, Warwick learned that Exeter was dead and his left wing had broken and fled (in fact he was only badly wounded, and later recovered). The battle was not looking good – Oxford flown, Exeter 'dead' and Montagu still possibly suspect.

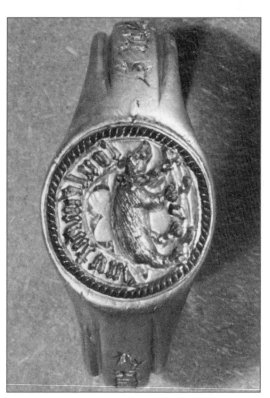

Ring believed to have been taken from Warwick the Kingmaker's body after Barnet in 1471. It shows the bear and ragged staff badge of Richard Neville.

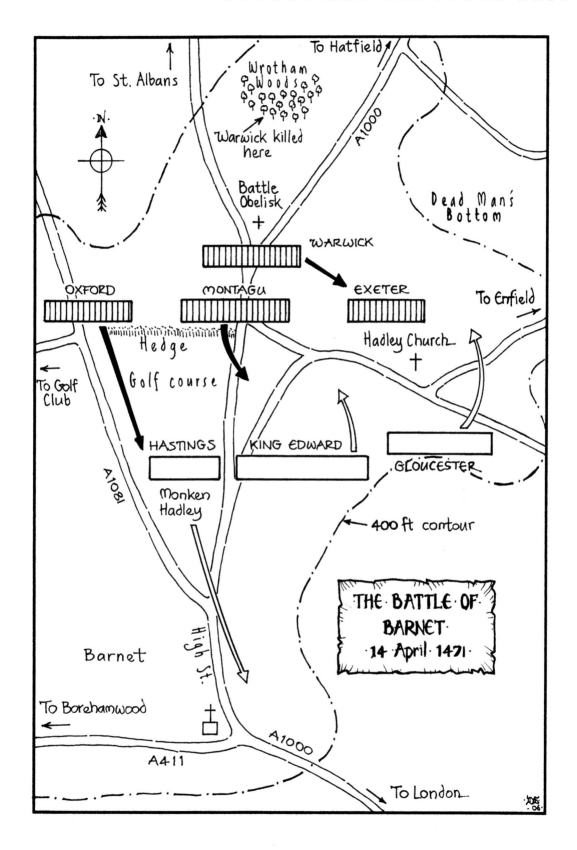

To St. Albans

To Hatfield

Wrotham Woods

Warwick killed here

Battle Obelisk

A1000

Dead Man's Bottom

WARWICK

OXFORD

MONTAGU

EXETER

To Enfield

Hadley Church

Hedge

Golf course

To Golf Club

HASTINGS

KING EDWARD

GLOUCESTER

A1081

Monken Hadley

400 ft contour

High St.

THE BATTLE OF BARNET 14 April 1471

Barnet

To Borehamwood

To London

A411

A1000

Then came the news that Montagu was dead, killed from behind by one of Oxford's men as a traitor. By tradition, Montagu is said to have implored Warwick before the battle to remain on foot during the battle in order to inspire his army. Warwick now looked to save his own life with disaster crowding round him, and he waddled back to the Lancastrian horse-park. He may or may not have reached his horse but, in any event, he could not find a way out of Wrotham Wood. He was recognised by Yorkist foot soldiers, wrestled to the ground and done to death with a knife prised through his visor and into an eye. He died in the vicinity of the modern **battle obelisk**.

Aftermath and Commentary

Edward had won a stunning victory. It may have been particularly chaotic, but although the 'smart money' had been on Warwick, it was Edward who triumphed. With the death of Warwick and Montagu, the junior branch of the Nevilles was all but exterminated.

Edward was not going to make the same mistake as Henry IV and execute an Archbishop of York, so the third brother, George, lived on. However, quite suddenly in April 1472, Edward had him arrested and sent to Hammes Castle, near Calais, perhaps for plotting with the Earl of Oxford and/or Clarence. Imprisonment broke George Neville and he died in June 1476. Clarence and Richard of Gloucester shared the massive Warwick inheritance after much squabbling. In due course, Richard married the widowed Anne Neville and thus, posthumously, Warwick achieved one of his principal ambitions when she became Queen of England in 1483. Edward did allow Warwick and Montagu to be buried at Bisham Abbey.

On the very evening of 14 April, Queen Margaret and Prince Edward arrived from France at Weymouth, Dorset to be met by the Duke of Somerset and Earl of Devon. The Nevilles may be dead but Edward still had a job to do.

Participants and Casualties

Yorkists (~12,000)
Kind Edward IV
George, Duke of Clarence
Richard, Duke of Gloucester
William, Lord Hastings
Anthony Woodville, Earl Rivers
Henry Bourchier, Earl of Essex
Thomas, Lord Stanley
Walter Blount, Lord Mountjoy
Lord Berners
Humphrey Bourchier, Lord Cromwell
Walter Devereux, Lord Ferrers
William Fiennes, Lord Saye and Sele
Sir Ralph Hastings
John, Lord Howard
Sir William Parr
Sir Humphrey Bourchier
Sir William Stanley
Sir Robert Chamberlain
Sir Gilbert Debenham
King Henry VI was present on the Yorkist side.

Lancastrians (~15,000)
Richard Neville, Earl of Warwick
John Neville
Marquis Montagu
John de Vere, Earl of Oxford
Henry Holland, Duke of Exeter
William, Viscount Beaumont
Sir John Marney
Sir John Paston
Sir William Tyrell
Sir George and Sir Thomas de Vere

Casualties: A combined total of 3,000 dead, with casualties heavy on both sides

Note: Inspection of the list of participants in this battle reveals it to be one of the most extraordinary in British history, in the sense that so many of the commanders were interrelated. King Edward and his two brothers were fighting their two maternal cousins, the Neville brothers. Edward was assisted by the Bourchiers, who were his paternal cousins. Hastings, however, was the Nevilles' brother-in-law. Rivers was Edward's brother-in-law. The Nevilles were assisted by Oxford, their brother-in-law, and Exeter, the York brothers' brother-in-law. Given the times, this was a recipe for treachery at some point.

Obelisk erected near the spot where Warwick the Kingmaker was killed during the Battle of Barnet.

Location and What to See

- The battle was fought on open ground near what is now called **Monken Hadley**, to the north of High Barnet between the A1081 St Albans, A1000 Potters Bar and Hadley Wood roads.
- The battlefield **obelisk** stands alongside the A1000 in the triangle formed with Kitt's End Road, 1½ miles north of High Barnet.

- A battle **information board** is situated at the south end of Hadley Common, close to the initial position of Richard of Gloucester's right wing.
- Hadley Church (built only in 1494) is the approximate location of Exeter's left wing.
- Between the A1081 and A1000 there is now a golf course. Glimpses can be obtained of the **hedge** behind which the Lancastrian forces

sheltered before the battle. Oxford's extreme right wing position can be viewed from the footpath crossing the golf course from the A1081, 1½ miles north of Barnet.

- Much of the slaughter occurring as Exeter's left wing collapsed late in the battle took place at the aptly named **Dead Man's Bottom**. Turn right off the A1081, 2½ miles north of Barnet Church, down Wagon Road. Deadman's Bottom is immediately right before Ganwick Farm.

BODIAM, Castle *** £

Bodiam lies a mile east of the B2244, between Hastings and Hawkhurst. The castle is just south of the village. NT. 01580 830436.

This wonderful late-fourteenth-century castle was in the hands of the Lewkenor family at the time of the Wars. During Buckingham's October 1483 rebellion Thomas Lewkenor held the castle for the rebels (see Salisbury). Thomas's mother was from the Lancastrian Camoys family of West Sussex. However, his uncle, Richard Lewkenor, was dispatched with the Yorkist government forces under Thomas Howard, Earl of Surrey to take the castle. A siege, a rare event in England in the Wars, ensued, but was probably brief before Thomnas Lewkenor surrendered. A great place to visit and to picnic.

BRABOURNE, St Mary's Church **

A delightful rural spot east of Ashford in Kent. Turn left off the old A20, 3 miles south-east of town, through Smeeth and Brabourne Lees, reaching Brabourne hamlet after another 2 miles north.

A lovely church containing a tomb-chest of Sir John Scott (d. October 1485). Sir John was a prominent courtier during Edward IV's reign, as Privy Councillor, Lord Warden of the Cinque Ports, MP and Controller of the King's Household. He had joined the Yorkists in June 1460 when he and Sir John Fogge threw open in dramatic fashion the gates of Canterbury to the Calais earls (March, Warwick and Salisbury) after their invasion at Sandwich. He fought for Edward IV at Towton (1461). He may have shared Edward's exile to Burgundy in 1470/1 and certainly fought at Barnet. He also played a major role in suppressing the 1471 risings in Kent orchestrated by the Bastard of Fauconberg. Sir John was implicated in the Kent risings of Buckingham's Revolt (October 1483) against Richard III but escaped attainder afterwards.

There is a floor brass to Sir William Scott (d. 1524), son of Sir John, above. He accompanied Thomas Howard, Earl of Surrey, Lord Cobham and other Yorkists in beseiging Bodiam Castle, which had been occupied by Thomas Lewkenor and other rebels against Richard III during Buckingham's Revolt in October/November 1483.

BROADWATER, Parish Church *

2 miles north of Worthing on A24, ½ mile south of the A27 junction (tower). PO: 01903 823916.

Canopied tomb-chest to Thomas West, 8th Lord de la Warr (1457–1524), who died at nearby Offingham Hall. The family held lands and influence in Sussex, Hampshire and Kent. His father, Richard West, fought for Lancaster and married Catherine, daughter of Robert, Lord Hungerford, a prominent Lancastrian. In 1464 Richard was also implicated in the Bastard of Fauconberg's rising in 1471.

Thomas himself took part in the 1483 Buckingham Revolt against Richard III (see Salisbury) and was removed from the bench but not attainted. After Henry VII's accession, Thomas was created Knight of the Bath and supported him during the 1489 northern tax revolt.

CADE STREET, near Heathfield **

On the B2096, 3 miles east of Heathfield on the road to Battle.

On the **roadside** in the middle of the village on the opposite side of the road to the Half Moon pub, there is a monument to Jack Cade, leader of the eponymous rebellion against Henry VI of June 1450. It marks the spot where Alexander Iden, Sheriff of Kent, mortally wounded and captured Cade after the collapse of the rebellion. Cade died while the party was en route to London. His body was stripped naked and placed in a cart. Once in London, the corpse was beheaded and quartered. The head was placed on London Bridge, the quarters displayed in various towns in the south-east.

Jack Cade's origins are obscure; he may have been an Irishman or from Kent. He styled himself 'Dr Aylmer', 'John Amend-all' and 'John Mortimer' and claimed to be a cousin of the Duke of York. In fact he was probably from the lower ranks of society. Nevertheless the rebels did include significant numbers of respectable members of society – esquires (including former sheriffs), gentlemen and yeomen. The king's negotiators (Archbishops Stafford

This monument in Cade Street is said to mark the spot where Jack Cade was mortally wounded in 1450.

and Kemp and the Duke of Buckingham) found Cade 'courageous, well-spoken and of transparent intelligence'. His rising has been described by R.A. Griffiths as 'the first popular rising in English history to produce a coherent programme of grievances, requests and remedies in the form of written, published manifestos'.

The rebellion started around Ashford in Kent and shook Henry VI's regime to the core. The rebels broke into the City of London and Lord Saye, one of Henry's counsellors, was beheaded. A frightened king fled London for Kenilworth. Eventually, order was restored by Lord Scales and a general pardon offered to the rebels. Although the Duke of York remained in Ireland throughout, it was widely believed he was behind the rebellion. By 1451 the government attitude hardened and many rebels were hanged in the infamous 'harvest of heads'.

Note: There is a view that Iden actually cornered Cade at Hothfield, near Ashford in Kent (a more likely location), and certainly Shakespeare has it this way. Perhaps Cade Street stole the location in a later century?

CANTERBURY, Cathedral *****
City centre, within pedestrian precinct.

In the **Trinity Chapel**, there are effigies and a tomb-chest for Henry IV (1367–1413, King from 1399). Henry of Bolingbroke was the son of John Gaunt by his first wife, Blanche of Lancaster (through whom he became Duke of Lancaster). He was one of the Lords Appellant who clashed with Richard II in 1385–6. A state of conflict between the two persisted in an on-and-off fashion until Richard deprived Henry of his rightful inheritance from Gaunt when the latter died in 1397. This action led directly to Richard's deposition by Henry in September 1399. Henry received strong support in the country – he was everything Richard was not: a crusader, a jouster, chivalrous.

Richard was forced to abdicate, upon which Henry claimed the literally empty throne, but based on descent from Edmund of Lancaster, brother to Edward I. Archbishop Arundel preached a sermon which rejected not only Richard's claim but also that of Edmund Mortimer, Earl of March, a boy aged 8. Mortimer's claim derived from Edward III's second son Lionel, Duke of Clarence through his daughter, Philippa, who married an earlier Edmund Mortimer. England had not adopted Salic law, so it was unclear at that time if the throne could be inherited through the female line. It does not appear that this was an important issue in 1399 – Henry was everyone's clear choice – but it was to prove the Lancastrian Achilles heel. The Mortimer claim reappeared as early as 1403, and again in 1415, but after the successes in France it was not to resurface until the 1450s. Eventually, however, it exactly formed the basis of the Yorkist challenge to Henry VI in 1460.

Henry IV's main achievement was to lay the foundations of the Lancastrian dynasty on which his son, Henry V, dazzled Europe. Henry produced four sons by his first wife, Mary de Bohun, two of whom (Henry V and John, Duke of Bedford) rank very highly in any list of English historical achievers. Henry is buried with his second wife, Joan of Navarre (1370–1437), whom he married in 1403. There was no issue from this marriage.

Below the royal tombs, nearly all of the places of honour in the cathedral **chancel** are occupied by the canopied tomb-chests of the archbishops of Canterbury. In the fifteenth century the archbishop was an automatic member of the King's Council. All were regular attenders and, as such, played important roles in the affairs of state.

Henry Chichele (d. 1443) is important for the Wars of the Roses because he baptised Henry VI in December 1421. He is remembered by history as the co-founder with Henry VI of All Souls College, Oxford in 1438. He died aged 81 in 1443.

John Kemp (d. 1454) was born around 1375. He came of 'ordinary' parents from Wye in Kent but, through his ability and application, worked himself to the top of his profession. He proceeded via Merton, Oxford and service under Chichele to become Archbishop of York by 1425. He was very much the politician – diplomat and was Chancellor of Normandy and England. Latterly, he was converted to Cardinal Beaufort's peace policy. At the age of 70, he was brought back as chancellor to replace John Stafford in 1450, and in 1452 was appointed to Canterbury on Stafford's death. As a Kentishman, Kemp was involved in the mediation with the Cade rebels in 1450 alongside Stafford. However, his major contribution to the Wars of the Roses was through his death in March 1454. Until this time there had been no official mention of Henry VI's mental breakdown. Now, however, the great seals were unusable; a successor must be appointed by Henry himself. A delegation of Lords spiritual and temporal attended Henry at Windsor at the end of the month, with the Bishop of Chester as their spokesman. They received no response to their questions, so, within two days, Richard, Duke of York was appointed Protector for the first time.

Kemp is also remembered in his home village, **Wye**. He founded the college (now part of the University of London), of which part of the original building remains. He rebuilt the parish church and he is commemorated there by stained glass from the nineteenth century.

Cardinal Thomas Bourchier (1411–86) was Archbishop of Canterbury from 1454 to 1486. He was therefore close to all the really important events of the Wars of the Roses. In particular, he crowned three sovereigns – Edward IV, Richard III and Henry VII. Not long before his death, he married Henry VII and Elizabeth of York, an event of great political significance in the final uniting of the two Roses.

In the **crypt** is the tomb of **Cardinal John Morton** (c. 1420–1500). He had an extremely long and colourful involvement in the Wars, was a major figure in the final phase and survived to be Henry VII's Chancellor.

Although rather overwhelmed by 'modern' military paraphernalia **St Michael's Chapel (south-west transept)** contains a most interesting

triple tomb-chest to Lady Margaret Holland (early 1380s –1439) and her two husbands, John Beaufort, Earl of Somerset and Prince Thomas, Duke of Clarence. Margaret herself had royal blood from both her parents. Her paternal grandparents were Joan, the Fair Maid of Kent, descended from Edward I and his second wife Margaret, and Sir Thomas Holland. (Joan's second husband was, of course, the Black Prince.) In 1397 Margaret married John Beaufort, Earl of Somerset (1372–1410). He was the eldest of the four highly talented offspring of the adulterous union of John of Gaunt with Katherine Swynford who were later legitimated by both the pope and Richard II. John was Henry VII's maternal great-grandfather. In 1407 John Beaufort petitioned Henry IV to obtain clarification of the legitimation. Henry confirmed the original letters but added the words '*excepta dignitate regali*' on the patents roll. This represented a refinement of the original act but was not binding on his successors because it was not incorporated in an Act of Parliament. So it was never fully clear whether the Beauforts could qualify for the throne. They were certainly treated very much as members of the royal family by Henry VI, but it is noticeable that in 1485 Henry Tudor did *not* in fact use his Beaufort lineage as justification to claim the crown.

John Beaufort provided Henry IV with exceptional service both as a councillor/diplomat and through military commands. John's financial position was transformed in 1408 when his wife, Margaret, became co-heiress of the Holland earldom of Kent. This inheritance ensured that, in her turn, Lady Margaret Beaufort, as John's granddaughter, became a rich heiress in 1444 on the death of her father, John Junior. John shared Henry IV's devotion to St Thomas of Canterbury and ensured that St Michael's Chapel became something of a family shrine.

Thomas, Duke of Clarence (1388–1421): Margaret's second husband was Henry IV's second son, whom she married 1411/12. An experienced soldier, he was killed leading the English army at the Battle of Baugé in March 1421. Thomas was renowned for his headlong charges on the battlefield, when he seemed to be trying to emulate his famous, but more prudent, elder brother. This is exactly what happened at Baugé; the English archers even got left behind. There are suggestions that the battle plan was hatched by Thomas 'in his cups' the night before. The resulting defeat led to the capture and ransom of a number of English knights, including Thomas's half-cousin John

Beaufort junior, who was to spend the next seventeen years in captivity.

In the north-west transept (high up) is the **Edward IV window**. This beautiful stained-glass window is dated to 1482 and includes all the members of Edward's **family**. One of the daughters died later in 1482. Unfortunately it is not easy to view the window with the naked eye because it is so high. It is poignant to realise that within a year Edward and the two boys would all be dead, while the eldest daughter, Elizabeth, would already be talked about as a future queen by both Henry Tudor and Richard III.

CARSHALTON, All Saints' Church **
Just west of town centre, on south side of A232 Sutton–Croydon road (tower). Rectory behind churchyard.

The church contains a very nice tomb-chest of Nicholas Gaynesford (1422–97) and wife. Nicholas was a squire of the body to Edward IV, and his hunting companion in the mid-1460s. He performed a number of roles in the King's household – servitor and usher of the chamber. He transferred to Queen Elizabeth Woodville's household as usher of the chamber; his wife, Margeret Sidney, also served the Queen. He became receiver of the Queen's Duchy in the south and attended Edward's funeral in April 1483. Nicholas and his half-brother, John Gaynesford (d. 1491), were both 'fighting' solicitors and together were involved in Buckingham's Revolt in 1483 in Kent and Surrey. Nicholas was attainted but fought for Henry Tudor at Bosworth Field. He was appointed Sheriff of Surrey in 1485 and again became a squire of the body to Henry VII. Both he and his wife attended Elizabeth of York at her coronation in 1486.

CHICHESTER, Cathedral *
City centre.

There is a picture of Adam Moleyns (bishop 1440–50) in the **north transept**, part of a large wooden panel painted in *c*. 1520, showing the bishops of Chichester. Moleyns, more of a politician than a churchman, was a prominent member of the Court party in the 1440s and ally of both Beaufort and Suffolk. In 1445 he unsuccessfully accused the Duke of York in parliament of corruption in Normandy. However, in December 1449 he resigned his position as Lord Privy Seal, accusing Suffolk of malpractice. He was murdered by sailors in Portsmouth a month later in January 1450, as he tried to explain Suffolk's abuses.

This murder set the tone for the rest of 1450, such a catastrophic year for Henry VI.

While in Chichester, why not visit **St Peter's Church, Selsey** and view the marvellous stained glass in the south porch depicting **Henry Tudor** finding the crown of England at Bosworth. It is twentieth-century Pre-Raphaelite school.

COBHAM (KENT), St Mary's Church *
Village centre. 1 mile south of M2, west of Rochester on B2009 to Sole Street.

The church houses a superb collection of brasses of the Cobham family. We are interested in **brass number 9**, to Sir John Brooke, 5th Lord Cobham (d. 1511) and his wife, Lady Margaret Neville, daughter of Edward, Lord Abergavenny (d. 1503). Unfortunately the brass of Sir John himself is missing. There is also a brass of his son, Sir Thomas, and wife. From an early date the Cobhams were committed Yorkists. Lord Edward, John's father (d. 1464), was present at the Dartford fiasco and was involved in the siege of the Tower in July 1460 with the Earl of Salisbury.

Lord John himself fought at the Battle of Tewkesbury in 1471 and played a prominent part in suppressing the 1483 revolt against Richard III in Kent and Surrey, alongside the Duke of Norfolk and the Earl of Surrey. As a result, he was rewarded by Richard III with additional lands in Devon, Cornwall and Kent.

CRANBROOK, St Dunstan's Church ***
Town centre. Park north of church.

An original sixteenth-century **window** commemorating Sir Richard Guldeford (1450–1506), who lived at East Guldeford, near Rye. Sir Richard came to prominence during Buckingham's Revolt, which was backed by his father, Sir John. He was one of the leaders of the revolt in the south-east. Afterwards, he was attainted and fled to join Henry Tudor in Brittany. His father was captured and imprisoned but at least escaped with his life.

Sir Richard was an engineer and a specialist in ordnance, a role which he fulfilled at Bosworth Field. He was knighted by Henry Tudor on landing at Milford Haven. On Henry's accession, Sir Richard was made a knight of the body and performed a number of important roles in the household – Master of Ordnance, Chamberlain of the Exchequer and Controller of the Household. He was very much one of Henry's inner circle and was one of the most frequent attenders of Council. He was made Knight of the Garter. He resigned in disgrace in the early 1500s for allegedly corrupt activity and then went on pilgrimage to Jerusalem in 1506. He died while there in September of that year and was buried on Mount Zion. Sir Richard's first marriage was to Anne de Pympe, with whom he had six children; his second wife was Jane Vaux. He was freeholder of the thirteenth-century **George Hotel** opposite the church, so drink a toast to him there before you leave Cranbrook.

EASEBOURNE, Priory Church **

On bend in A272, 1 mile north of Midhurst on Petworth road.

The church contains an alabaster effigy of Welshman Sir David Owen (1459–1535), bastard son of Owen Tudor, Henry VII's grandfather. He was therefore half-brother to Edmund and Jasper Tudor, and Henry's 'half-uncle'. David Owen was in exile in France with Henry, and in 1485 was part of his invasion force. He was knighted with others by Henry after the landing at Dale Bay and fought at Bosworth. No doubt, as family and as a valued early supporter, Owen was found a suitably wealthy bride by Henry.

He married Mary de Bohun, the Cowdray heiress, and constructed **Cowdray House** in the late fifteenth century (the ruins lie at the north end of Midhurst). He was also granted the Northamptonshire lands of the executed William Catesby.

EASTWELL, St Mary's Church (remains) *

3 miles north of Ashford (Kent) at north end of lake.
Turn left off A251 Faversham road on right-hand bend,
signposted to Westwell. After 1 mile, take unmarked right
down hill to lake.

This is one for the connoisseur. The roof of St Mary's collapsed in 1951 and the church is all but a ruin; the tower still stands. The remains stand in a beautiful spot beside a large lake and adjacent to the former manor house at the end of a 'no through road'. In the **graveyard** around the church there is a derelict stone tomb reputed to be that of Richard Plantagenet (d. 1550). This name occurs in the Eastwell parish register of that year. The story tells that Sir Thomas Moyle, who lived in Eastwell in the sixteenth century, was intrigued that his chief bricklayer not only liked reading but could read Latin. On cross-questioning the man turned out to be a bastard son of Richard III born in 1469, who had met up with his father, the

The outdoor tomb-chest of Richard III's natural son in Eastwell churchyard.

King, on the eve of Bosworth. After Richard's defeat, he kept his identity secret for obvious reasons. Moyle gave Richard the use of a cottage on the estate for the rest of his life, on the site of which there still stands a Plantagenet Cottage. Some have even claimed that Richard Plantagenet was really Richard, Duke of York the younger Prince in the Tower.

Richard III had other known bastards: John of Gloucester (*c*. 1470–99?), who was Captain of Calais; Katherine, who married William Herbert, Earl of Huntingdon (*c*. 1455–91); and Stephen Hawes. It was acceptable in medieval society for a young royal to father bastards, and even for churchmen to do this. It certainly did not stop Richard as king from moralising about the lifestyles of his brother Edward IV and William, Lord Hastings.

GOUDHURST, St Mary's Church **

Village centre by A262, on hilltop.

This interesting church contains rare wooden effigies of 'Ould' Sir Alexander Culpepper (d. 1537) and one of his two wives (nave, south side). The full colouring makes the effigies a splendid sight. Sir Alexander joined Buckingham's Revolt in 1483 and was attainted (see Salisbury). The Bedgebury chapel contains brasses of Sir Alexander's ancestors and detailed genealogical information.

HERSTMONCEUX, All Saints' Church ***

Not in the village centre but signposted, 1 mile south at the end of long 'no through road'.

This is a church where we get two for the price of one. The main monument is the spectacular tomb-chest with panelled arch of Thomas Fiennes, 8th Lord Dacre of the South (1470–1533) and to his son, Sir Thomas, who predeceased him. Thomas the elder was a squire of the body to Edward IV. He joined Buckingham's Revolt against Richard III in 1483 and, with his brother, intrigued again in 1484 at Winchelsea, for which he was pardoned. He fought at Bosworth. Thomas married Anne Bourchier.

His father, Richard Fiennes, had married Joan Dacre, granddaughter of Thomas Dacre and niece of Humphrey, Lord Dacre of Gilsland (killed at Towton), and had been created 7th Baron Dacre in 1459. Richard was very much a member of Edward IV's inner circle, being named by Warwick and Clarence in their 1469 rebel manifesto and then accompanying Edward back into London in October 1469 after his release by Warwick. Richard was a councillor and

became Queen Elizabeth's chamberlain. He died in 1484 and is buried in the church, but there is no monument. Richard's eldest son, John, predeceased him in 1483.

Lying on top of the Dacre tomb-chests in the church are two recumbent effigies. These have attached the arms of the Hoo family and are of an earlier date. They are thought to represent Thomas, Lord Hoo and Hastings (*c*. 1396–1455) and his half-brother, Sir Thomas Hoo, who succeeded him and who died 1486. The effigies came to Herstmonceux from Battle Abbey at the Dissolution, perhaps being reused by an impoverished Dacre family? Lord Hoo had the misfortune to be Chancellor of Normandy at the time of its reconquest by the French in 1450. He was thus one of the main targets of the defeated and disgruntled soldiers returning to London and the south-east. He was ridiculed by Cade's rebels and named alongside Somerset and Dudley in parliament's demand for removal from the King's side in late 1450. He subsequently had to leave London in a hurry in December 1450. He was also the subject of an embezzlement inquiry in 1451/2 related to his time in Normandy.

Also buried in the church, but with no monument, is Sir Roger Fiennes (1384–1449) father of Richard above. Sir Roger was Treasurer of Henry VI's household, and it was he who made all the family money. His monument is **Herstmonceux Castle** (£), next door to the church, but a 3-mile signposted car journey. Be sure to take your picnic to the castle grounds and take in the magnificent brick building and moat begun in the early 1440s. Herstmonceux is one of the oldest surviving brick buildings of note in the country. However, as the brochure says, it is more stylish country house than military fortress. Sir Roger was elder brother to James Fiennes, who became Lord Saye and Sele. The castle is now an educational institution and its interior reflects this.

IGHTHAM, Mote ***

4 miles east of Sevenoaks, south of A25; 1 mile south of Ivy Hatch. Signposted from A25. NT. 01732 810378.

This house is an absolute gem. Built in two phases, in 1330–40 and 1470–1510, the house retains a real feel of the fourteenth and fifteenth centuries. The second round of building was started by Richard Haute, who lived in the house from 1462 until his death in 1487. He rebelled against Richard III in October 1483 in Buckingham's Revolt and was attainted. He fought for Henry Tudor at Bosworth. Richard was a younger son of Sir William Haute (1390–1482), who lived in the house before him. Sir William fought in France and supported Jack Cade and his rebels in 1450. The Hautes were a powerful family in Kent, with other properties near Maidstone and links to the Woodvilles. Sir Richard Haute, a kinsman, was a prominent courtier to Edward IV and Edward V who was executed at Pontefract Castle with Earl Rivers in June 1483, as part of Richard III's Second Coup.

LITTLE CHART, St Mary's Church **

4 miles north-west of Ashford (Kent). Turn off the old A20 for Hothfield and continue another 2 miles north-west to Little Chart. Contact Charing Church.

The church is modern, having been built in 1955 to replace the medieval one destroyed by a 'doodlebug' during the last war. It had been the mausoleum of the Darell family from nearby Calehill House. Most of the medieval monuments were lost, but fortunately the alabaster effigy and helmet of Sir John Darell (1446–1509) were saved from the old church. The effigy displays the Lancastrian 'SS' collar. The Darells were powerful retainers of the Staffords in Kent. Sir John was attainted for his leading role in

the 1483 Buckingham Revolt in Kent and fled to join Henry Tudor in Brittany. He may have been present at Bosworth and became esquire of the body to Henry VII. He was knighted in 1497. So here is a man who has seen front-line action in major conflicts in both life and in death. Also visit the remains of the **old church** 1 mile to the north-west. The Darell lion rampant can be seen at the west end. Nearby Calehill Heath was a rallying point for Cade's Rebellion in 1450.

LONDON, BISHOPSGATE, St Helen's Church ** £

Towards south end of street, set back through modern arch on east side. Access through church office. EH. 020 8294 2548.

A fine tomb-chest and effigies of Sir John Crosby (d. 1475) and first wife Agnes (d. 1460). Sir John was a great benefactor of this church. He was knighted in May 1471 by Edward IV immediately on the King's return to London in triumph from the Battle of Tewkesbury. John was one of the sheriffs of London for 1470/1 and had been part of the group of citizens which on 12 May repulsed the attacks on nearby Aldgate by the Bastard of Fauconberg's

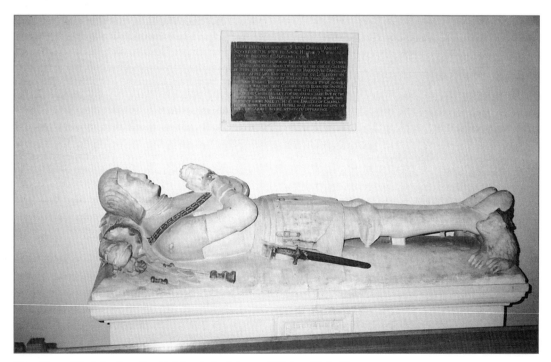

The effigy of Sir John Darell, which has led a 'charmed life', at Little Chart.

Effigies of Sir John Crosby and his wife Agnes in St Helen's Church, Bishopsgate.

Lancastrian forces, which were trying to gain entry to London. The Yorkist force was led by the Mayor, John Stockton, and Thomas Urswick (see Dagenham) who were also knighted by Edward. Sir John had recently constructed a splendid city dwelling called **Crosby Hall**. <u>**Richard III**</u> lived there in 1483 before he usurped the throne in June. Sir Thomas More also lived there. The building was moved stone by stone to Cheyne Walk, Chelsea (close to Danvers Street). Unfortunately the building is currently closed for major restoration.

LONDON, ELTHAM, Palace **
½ mile off Eltham High Street (A210), west of Court Road (A208) to Mottingham. Take Tilt Yard.

A favourite palace of both <u>**Henry VI**</u> and <u>**Edward IV**</u>. Both spent lavishly on it and Edward constructed a new hall with superb hammer-beam roof, which survives. The palace had been a favourite of queens since the early fourteenth century. <u>**Queen Margaret of Anjou**</u> stayed here just prior to her coronation in Westminster Abbey in 1445. Henry VI is said to have loved the palace and kept a library here. Unfortunately the palace was very badly damaged in 1450 after being struck by lightning – an *annus horribilis* for Henry. Between 1475 and 1483, Edward IV rebuilt the hall and roof. Note the Yorkist badges in stained glass.

This site gives you the added bonus of viewing the art deco interior of the house, installed by the Courtaulds before the last war.

LONDON, THE TOWER ***** ££
Tower Hill tube.

Not just a fortress in medieval times: the king and royal family had apartments here. On a number of occasions the Tower was involved in conflict during the Wars. What remain to be seen today are:

The Bloody Tower, at the Tower of London, by tradition the location of the murders of the two Princes, the sons of Edward IV.

Wakefield Tower

In the **upper chamber** is a small chapel with painted timber screen in which, by tradition, **Henry VI** was murdered on the night of 21 May 1471, almost certainly on the orders of Edward IV, who had just returned in triumph from victory over the Lancastrians at the Battle of Tewkesbury. As Constable of the Tower, Richard, Duke of Gloucester (later Richard III) may have ensured that the order was carried out. In the space of three weeks, the Lancastrians' cause had been all but extinguished, with the death of Henry's son Prince Edward at Tewkesbury, the capture of his queen, Margaret of Anjou, a day or two afterwards and now the death of Henry.

Bloody Tower

This is said to be the part of the fortress where the two **Princes in the Tower** were murdered some time after June 1483. No evidence exists. The building houses a good exhibition and provides an opportunity to vote on who you think killed them – a nice democratic touch. Richard III led Henry VII by 60:40 at the time of the author's visit.

The boy king **Edward V** had been placed under house arrest in the Tower by his uncle and Lord Protector, Richard, Duke of Gloucester, soon after his accession. Richard had pressurised Edward's mother, Dowager Queen Elizabeth Woodville, into releasing Edward's younger brother, **Richard, Duke of York**, from sanctuary to join Edward in the Tower to prepare for the latter's coronation. The coronation never happened: Richard of Gloucester seized the throne and Edward V was deposed. The boys remained in the Tower, were seen less and less and finally disappeared. No solid evidence of their deaths or the identity of their killers has ever been found. Richard III's motive is obvious, but Henry Tudor, as Henry VII, had equal incentive. Other suspects have been Henry, 2nd Duke of Buckingham and John Howard, Duke of Norfolk. Most historians on balance plump for Richard – his behaviour during his 1483 coup was demonstrably ruthless. Remember to vote!

White Tower

Just **before** you enter the tower, note the **plaque** indicating that the remains of the **Princes** were found in the staircase here in 1674. This keep houses the Tower's armoury.

Tower Green

A **plaque** marks the spot where **William, Lord Hastings** was executed by Richard, Duke of Gloucester (at the time Lord Protector) in June 1483 in what was the first act in Richard's second *coup d'état*. In many ways a sensational event. By that time, Richard and Hastings were the leaders of the Yorkists on behalf of Edward V. They had twice held commands in battle alongside each other in 1471. Hastings was the close friend of Edward IV, Richard's brother, and Richard had known Hastings most of his life. Hastings was dragged out of the Council chamber and, with indecent haste, a handy log found and Hastings executed. The fatal tendency of the Yorkists towards schism had reared itself once again.

Tower Hill

Just before you enter the tube station on your return, look back at the Tower of London. Slightly to your left, on the **inner curtain wall**, you will see the **Bowyer Tower**, not open to the public. By tradition, **George, Duke of Clarence** (the middle brother of Edward IV and Richard III) was privately executed here after being tried and found guilty of treason in 1478. Again by tradition, the method of execution was drowning in a butt of Malmsey wine (chosen by George himself). George's daughter subsequently Margaret wore a bracelet displaying a barrel of wine.

Adjacent to the tube station on the **west** side are **Trinity Square Gardens**, which contain large war memorials. On the far west side, towards All Hallows Church, is a low-lying memorial marking the spot where the gallows on Tower Hill used to be erected. **Plaques** record people who were executed here, including **John de Vere, 12th Earl of Oxford** and his son Aubrey (1462), John Tiptoft, Earl of Worcester (1470, see Ely) and **Sir William Stanley** (1495). It is gruesome stuff but the memorial is understated and nicely done.

LONDON, WESTMINSTER ABBEY, *** £**

If you want to know who won the Wars of the Roses, this is the place to come. You can just concentrate on the Sanctuary/Confessor's Chapel, the surrounding chapels and ambulatories and **Henry VII**'s magnificent chapel. As at Windsor, there is a strange mixture of memorials to the great and good and to 'ordinary' gentry of the fifteenth century. Public entrance to the abbey is via the north transept. The Wars of the Roses entries follow the normal route through the abbey. The Sanctuary is described separately:

North ambulatory

As you turn left into the ambulatory, on the left is a tomb-chest with brass effigy of John Esteney, Abbot

The Bowyer Tower, at the Tower of London, traditionally the location of the execution of George, Duke of Clarence.

of Westminster. Esteney had the guardianship of **Dowager Queen Elizabeth Woodville** in May/June 1483 when she took sanctuary in the Abbey from Richard, Duke of Gloucester firstly as Lord Protector then as King. It was here in the abbey complex that the Dowager Queen was 'persuaded' by Archbishop Bourchier to yield up custody of the younger of the Princes, Richard. Esteney was the patron of Caxton, whose press was set up in the precincts of the abbey.

The memorial plaque to those executed at Tower Hill over the centuries.

Opposite the entrances to the Chapel of St John the Baptist and the Islip Chapel is a **stone coffin** said to belong to <u>Thomas Millyng, Abbot of Westminster</u> (1469–74). Millyng was the guardian of **Queen Elizabeth Woodville** when she took sanctuary in the abbey (the Abbot's House) for the first time during the Readeption of Henry VI in 1470/1, when her husband Edward IV vacated his throne. Their son, later Edward V, was born here in November 1470.

Chapel of St John the Baptist
Go through the small chapel of **Our Lady of the Pew** and you will find on the left a tomb-chest with brass of <u>Sir Thomas Vaughan</u> (ex. 1483). His origins are obscure and he should not be confused with Sir Thomas Vaughan of Tretower. He was close to the Woodvilles and became Treasurer of the Chamber 1465–83. As such, he was sent with Sir William Parr to take possession of the treasure of George Neville, Archbishop of York, after his fall in 1467, and became Chamberlain of Prince Edward, spending much time at Ludlow with the two Princes. After the death of Edward IV in 1483, he accompanied the new King Edward V from Ludlow to London. At Stony Stratford the whole party was intercepted by Richard,

Duke of Gloucester and the Duke of Buckingham and Vaughan arrested. He was sent with the Woodville Earl Rivers and Richard Haute to Pontefract Castle, where they were executed after a trial in front of Henry Percy, Earl of Northumberland on 24 June 1483.

Chapel of St Paul
In the **centre of the chapel** is a tomb-chest with effigies of <u>Giles, Lord Daubeny</u> (1451–1508) and his wife <u>Elizabeth Arundel</u>, surrounded by an iron grille. Daubeny was one of those who did well out of the Wars of the Roses. He was the son of plain William Daubeny. He accompanied Edward IV to France in 1475 and was esquire of the body two years later. He was knighted in 1478. He had powerful local presence in the south-west and joined Buckingham's Revolt in October 1483 at Salisbury. He was attainted by Richard III, so fled to join Henry Tudor in France. He fought at the Battle of Bosworth and obviously impressed Henry. In 1486 he was ennobled and made Master of the Mint and Lieutenant of Calais. By the 1490s, he was attending Council meetings. His epitaph, penned by the poet laureate, reads 'a good man, prudent, just, honest and loved by all'.

Memorial brass of Sir Thomas Vaughan in Westminster Abbey.

Henry VII Chapel

This one speaks for itself. It is a celebration of the Tudor triumph – look for all the badges/emblems including the Yorkist falcon and fetterlock (used by Richard, 3rd Duke of York) and the Tudor crown in thorn bush (from Bosworth). In clockwise order do not miss:

- The small **sarcophagus** at the end of the **north aisle** containing the bones found in 1674 in the Tower of London, allegedly of the **Princes in the Tower** (Edward V and his brother Richard, Duke of York, who disappeared in the summer of 1483).
- In the **north-eastern chapel**, near Queen Anne of Denmark, is buried poor Anne née Mowbray, Duchess of York (d. 1481, aged 9). Anne was married in 1478 to Richard, Duke of York, the younger of Edward IV's sons. She was an important person in the history of the Wars. There is no monument, but there should be. (See **Howard, Dukes of Norfolk**.)
- The centrepiece of this chapel (and for us of the whole abbey) is the **magnificent tomb** and effigies of **Henry VII** (1457–1509) and his wife **Elizabeth of York** (1466–1502), eldest daughter of Edward IV. The tomb was produced by Torrigiano and symbolises the union of the rival Houses of York and Lancaster. The union had its origins in the agreement between Lady Margaret Beaufort and Dowager Queen Elizabeth Woodville that Lady Margaret's son Henry would marry Queen Elizabeth's daughter, also Elizabeth, if he could seize the throne of England. Elizabeth died after childbirth in the Tower in 1503. Henry spent lavishly on her funeral. He was not a natural spender, so this is taken as a sign of his true feelings for her.
- In the south aisle is the most splendid effigy in this guide – that of Henry VII's mother, **Lady Margaret Beaufort** (1443–1509), described in the guidebook as 'Torrigiano's masterpiece'. Lady Margaret kept the Lancastrian cause afloat in the dark years of 1471–83 and then, with Bishop John Morton and others, plotted the downfall of the Yorkists. A formidable woman in her own right who in a different age could have been queen.

Chapel of St Nicholas

At the **front left** can be seen a floor brass to Sir Humphrey Stanley (d. 1505). He was the second son of Sir John Stanley (d. 1486) of Elford. He began as a Hastings retainer but in 1485 fought for Henry Tudor at the Battle of Bosworth, where he was knighted. He was made a knight of the body and fought at the Battle of Stoke Field, where he was dubbed knight banneret. He rose to command the royal attack at the Battle of Blackheath against the Cornish rebels in 1497.

Chapel of St Edmund

On the far side of the chapel, on the right, there is a low tomb-chest with remains of a **brass** to Sir Humphrey Bourchier (k. 1471). He was the son of John Bourchier, Lord Berners, and both were members of the powerful Yorkist family headed by Henry, Earl of Essex. Hampton tells us he was chief carver to Queen Elizabeth Woodville. He was killed in the intense fighting at the Battle of Barnet (1471), fighting for Edward IV. His widow Elizabeth, née Tilney, married Thomas Howard, later Duke of Norfolk. She is celebrated in the stained glass at Long Melford.

Sir Humphrey's cousin, Humphrey Bourchier, Lord Cromwell, was also killed at Barnet and is buried in the abbey. There is no monument.

South Ambulatory

Towards the **end** of the ambulatory, near the recess and tomb of King Sebert (d. 616), is a modern bronze **tablet** of **Queen Anne Neville** (1456–85), wife of Richard III and younger daughter of Warwick the Kingmaker.

Sanctuary/Confessor's Chapel

The route round the ambulatories takes you past the pantheon of the medieval kings of England. Do note (clockwise):

- The tomb of Henry V (ruled 1413–22). Henry V was the victor of the Battle of Agincourt and the conqueror of France. He was the model medieval king, and everything his son, Henry VI was not.
- **Queen Catherine of Valois** (1401–37). As part of the Treaty of Troyes (1421), Henry V married Catherine, daughter of King Charles VI of France. Catherine was the mother of Henry VI, the infant king who succeeded his father in 1422. After Henry's death, Catherine married **Owen Tudor**, by whom she had two boys, **Edmund** and **Jasper**. Edmund was the father of Henry Tudor. Catherine's funeral effigy has survived and is in the Undercroft Museum (see below).
- The tombs of Edward III (ruled 1327–77) and his first wife, Queen Philippa of Hainault. Dynastically, Edward and Philippa laid the foundations of the Wars of the Roses by having five surviving sons. Three of them are represented by the lovely weepers on Edward's tomb, from left to right: (1) the Black Prince, his eldest son, who predeceased his father; (2) Lionel, Duke of Clarence, second son, through whom the House of York eventually made its claim to the throne in 1460; (3) Edmund, Duke of York, fourth son.

- The tomb of Richard II (ruled 1377–99). The son of the Black Prince, Richard succeeded to the throne at the age of 10. His pretensions and his favourites alienated the peerage, enabling Henry Bolingbroke, Duke of Lancaster, his cousin (the son of John of Gaunt, Edward III's third son), to seize the throne in 1399 in a relatively bloodless coup. Richard was probably starved to death in Pontefract Castle in 1400.

Undercroft Museum

Here are displayed the funeral effigies of **Henry VII**, **Queen Elizabeth of York** and **Queen Catherine of Valois**. There is also a relief bust of Sir Thomas Lovell (d. 1524). Lovell took part in Buckingham's Revolt at Exeter (he was a client of Thomas Grey, Marquis of Dorset). He was attainted and joined Henry Tudor in exile. He fought at Bosworth (1485) and Stoke Field (1487), where he was knighted. Under Henry VII, he became Chancellor of the Exchequer and esquire of the body. He also served Henry VIII.

LONDON, WESTMINSTER, Great Hall * £**

Part of the Houses of Parliament complex. Access only through Parliament tour.

This wonderful old building, originally the Great Hall of the King's Palace in Westminster, was the scene of one of the most dramatic 'non-events' in English history. On 10 October 1460, **Richard, 3rd Duke of York** strode into the hall from exile in Ireland and laid his hand on the empty throne (the enfeebled Henry VI being elsewhere in the palace). Instead of acclamation from the assembled lords, however, his action was met with silence, in spite of the fact that most of the lords were Yorkist. The Earl of Warwick, in charge of the government since the Battle of Northampton in June, blamed opposition from, variously, Thomas Bourchier the Archbishop of Canterbury and his own father, the Earl of Salisbury. A furious row broke out among the Yorkist leaders. York persisted and was rewarded with the Act of Accord later that month, which reaffirmed Henry VI as king but made York (and his sons) his heir even though York was ten years older than Henry. Prince Edward, Queen Margaret's son, was disinherited. The War of Succession and York's death at the Battle of Wakefield were the result. Westminster Hall in medieval times housed the Courts of King's Bench and Common Pleas and was the hub of the kingdom's judicial system.

To see the hall you will have to join a tour party for the **Houses of Parliament**. Pay special attention, because on the tour the Houses in fact contain a fair amount of interest for the Wars of the Roses enthusiast. The House of Lords is festooned with Tudor badges (the Tudor Rose, the Beaufort portcullis, etc.). The emblem adopted by the House of Commons is the Beaufort portcullis and is everywhere. The Peers' Lobby has two modern stained-glass windows with medieval coats of arms. The East Corridor, off the Central Lobby, houses the well-known painting of York and Lancaster plucking roses in the Temple Gardens.

LULLINGSTONE, Castle, St Botolph's Church **

Signposted off west side of A225 Farhingham–Otford road. 1½ miles south of Eynsford. In castle grounds. Summer only. 01322 862114.

In the **chancel** there is a floor brass (under the carpet) to Sir William Pecche (d. 1487). He was an early Yorkist, being present at the Dartford fiasco and joining them when the Calais earls landed at Sandwich in 1460. In 1462, during the war in Northumberland, he relieved the Earl of Warwick (the Kingmaker) under siege at Warkworth Castle, the Yorkist base. From 1462 to 1485 he held the prestigious position of King's Carver. Next to his brass is one of Sir William's daughter, Elizabeth,

Lady Cobham (d. 1544), wife of George Brooke, 7th Lord Cobham. There is an unusual effigy of his son Sir John (d. 1522) in the north chapel. Sir John assisted in the rounding-up of survivors from Perkin Warbeck's revolt in 1495. Note also the fine **gatehouse** to the castle, built in 1497, said to be one of the earliest brick gatehouses in England.

PENSHURST PLACE, near Tonbridge ** £

4½ miles south-west of Tonbridge. Take B2027 south-west off B245 Tonbridge–Hildenborough road to Leigh. Signposted south on B2176. 01892 870307.

During the fifteenth century, this was one of the principal seats of the Stafford dukes of Buckingham and said to be one of their favourites. Earlier in the century the house had been owned by John, Duke of Bedford, to whom the building of the second hall, known as the Buckingham Building, is attributed around 1430. On Bedford's death in 1435, the house became the property of his younger brother, Humphrey, Duke of Gloucester. Presumably on the latter's death in 1447 the property went to **Humphrey Stafford, 1st Duke of Buckingham** and was held by the family until the execution of the 3rd Duke in 1521. But the real reason for coming to Penshurst is the fabulous fourteenth-century

The late fifteenth-century gatehouse at Lullingstone Castle.

main hall, built in the 1340s and still very much in period.

SHERE, St James's Church ***
In village centre, ½ mile south of A25.

Here can be seen a delightful **floor brass** to John Touchet, Lord Audley (d. 1490). Audley was a member of a family thoroughly involved in the Wars over a long period. The family held Shere Manor together with lands in the Midlands. John's father, James, commanded Henry VI's army at the Battle of Blore Heath, Shropshire in September 1459 but was defeated and killed there. John himself initially adopted the Lancastrian colours and may have been present at the rout of Ludford Bridge in the following month. However, while serving the King in Calais in 1460, Audley was captured by Warwick and Edward of York. He then seems to have undergone a conversion to the Yorkist cause. In this guise, Audley was present at the battles of Northampton (1460), Mortimer's Cross (1461) and Towton (1461).

There followed a lifetime of service to the Yorkist kings. In fact, Audley had the distinction of being one of the 'grasping favourites' of Edward singled out in Warwick and Clarence's rebel manifesto of 1469. Audley was a member of the inner circle which accompanied Edward on his re-entry into London following his release by Warwick after the collapse of the 1469 rebellion. Audley was also implicated in the Buckingham Revolt against Richard III in the autumn of 1483, because of his son's involvement with the Dorset rebels, but was pardoned along with his son. In December 1484 John was appointed Richard III's Lord High Treasurer. He probably failed to make Bosworth Field in time.

John sold Shere Manor to Lancastrian stalwart Reginald Bray in 1487. The Brays hold the living today (although there was a long interruption). Look out for their family crest (a hemp bray, for separating fibres). See Windsor.

Floor brass to John Touchet, Lord Audley in Shere church.

SOUTH

BROUGHTON (Oxfordshire) *** £
½ mile west of village just off B4035 Banbury–Shipston road, 2 miles south-west of Banbury. Signposted off B4035. Church open with castle. 01295 722547.

A magnificent house, moat, park, church and rectory grouping.

St Mary's Church
The church contains an interesting collection of memorials, some of difficult attribution. In the **chancel** there is something special. At first sight it looks like a husband and wife tomb-chest with effigies, the former with Yorkist collar, the latter with Lancastrian. Given the nature of the conflict, this is highly unlikely (although Lady Margaret Beaufort and Lord Stanley did maintain this fiction under Richard III). Further inspection reveals that the effigies were originally separate, and then put together. In addition, the 'wife's' effigy is much earlier. It is now thought that she represents Elizabeth Wykeham (née Wilcotes) wife of Sir Thomas Wykeham, heir of the William of Wykeham

who founded New College, Oxford. William bought Broughton Castle in 1377. Elizabeth's granddaughter, Margaret, married William Fiennes, second Lord Saye and Sele, who is thought to be represented by the male effigy. William's father, James Fiennes, was ennobled in 1447 after a distinguished career in France. (He was brother to Sir Roger Fiennes; see Herstmonceux.) He became Lord High Treasurer to Henry VI in 1449/50 but was unfortunately executed by the London mob during Cade's Rebellion of 1450. During the French wars, his son William fought to defend Calais; he then became an early Yorkist and was present at the Battle of Northampton (1460). He accompanied Edward IV in exile to Holland in 1470 but was killed fighting for him at the Battle of Barnet (1471).

Castle
A later Richard Fiennes and his son remodelled the 'castle' (really a fortified manor house) during the sixteenth century, but Pevsner describes this as 'little more than veneer'. For him, Broughton represents the 'finest and most complete medieval house in the county'. Do not miss it. The Fiennes family still own Broughton today.

Effigy of William Fiennes, Lord Saye and Sele in Broughton church.

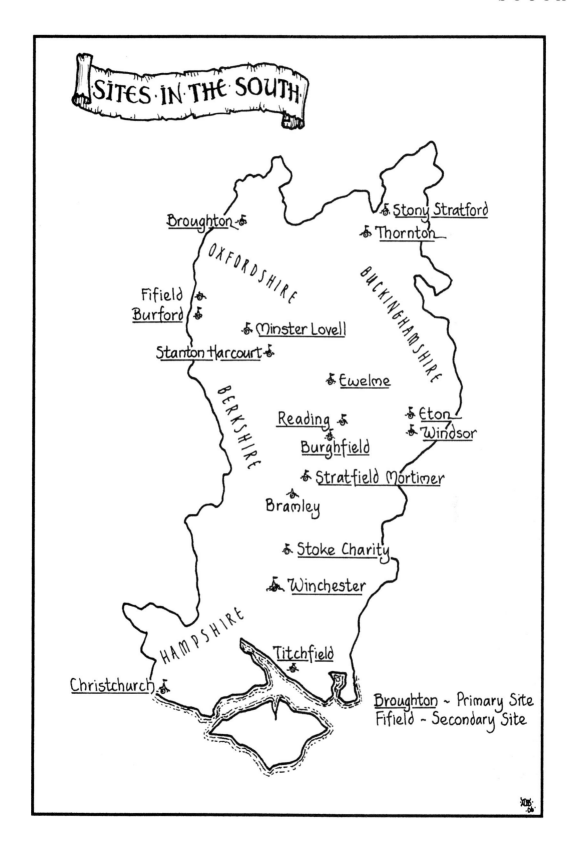

SITES·IN·THE·SOUTH

Broughton

OXFORDSHIRE

Stony Stratford

Thornton

BUCKINGHAMSHIRE

Fifield
Burford

Minster Lovell

Stanton Harcourt

Ewelme

BERKSHIRE

Reading

Eton
Windsor

Burghfield

Stratfield Mortimer

Bramley

Stoke Charity

Winchester

HAMPSHIRE

Titchfield

Christchurch

Broughton ~ Primary Site
Fifield ~ Secondary Site

BURFORD, The Great Almhouses *
Off western end of High Street, north side, by St John's Church.

A **plaque** declares, 'These almshouses were founded by **Richard Neville, Earl of Warwick** in the year 1457.' They were rebuilt in 1828, but according to Pevsner the outside 'front differs little from drawings made before this date'. This is fortunate because so little else survives of the Earl. Burford was a Warwick manor and borough. It may have been here that the Earl and Edward, Duke of York met up with their respective armies in February 1461, after Warwick's defeat at the Second Battle of St Albans. The sources are unclear, quoting Burford or Chipping Norton (Edward was en route from Hereford to London). As a substantial Warwick manor, Burford would have been a natural choice. Whichever it was, on 22 February 1461 the two men must have hatched (or confirmed) their daring plot to march on London, despite the presence of a victorious Lancastrian army, and declare Edward king. 'A paradigm was broken' and England had two kings for the first time since before the Norman Conquest. Do visit the nearby church as well – the porch is wonderful.

While in Burford, take in the lovely fifteenth-century stained glass at **Fifield, St John's Church**, 5 miles north on the east side of the A424 to Stow on the Wold. The simple church is delightful; the glass includes a Yorkist sun in splendour and a Tudor crown in thorn bush commemorating Bosworth.

BURGHFIELD, St Mary's Church ****
5 miles south-west of Reading. 1½ miles south of the M4 services exit, junction 11 (A33 south) and then turn right on minor road at Three Mile Cross. Turn right again to Burghfield Common. Proceed under railway and turn right to Burghfield. Follow twisting road to far end of village (north). Church is on right.

This is indeed a humble resting place for a former Lord Chancellor of England, and at his death the third-most-powerful man in the country. The **porch** of this church by tradition contains the effigies of **Richard Neville, Earl of Salisbury**, who was the father of Warwick the Kingmaker and a prominent Yorkist, and his wife, <u>Alice née Montagu</u>, through whom he inherited his illustrious title. Salisbury was captured at the Battle of Wakefield (1460), and beheaded the next day outside Pontefract Castle. He was originally buried in that town but, with great ceremony, Warwick organised a reburial at

Worn effigy of Richard Neville, Earl of Salisbury, father to Warwick the Kingmaker, in Burghfield church.

the Montagu family mausoleum of Bisham Abbey in 1463. At the Dissolution of the Monasteries, all the tombs at Bisham were destroyed (including the Kingmaker's). Tradition has it that the Salisbury effigies were rescued from this fate and brought by 'speeding horses' to Burghfield. They represent the only survivals from Salisbury's powerful brood.

CHRISTCHURCH, Priory ***
½ mile south of town centre. Car park next door.

This splendid former abbey church contains four items of interest. The first is the fabulous **Chantry Chapel**, built in 1529 by **Margaret Pole, Countess of Salisbury** for herself and her son, Cardinal Reginald Pole, but never used. The wonderful fan vaulting includes Yorkist roses. Margaret was, in fact, very much of the royal blood, being the elder child of **George, Duke of Clarence**. Margaret was born in 1473 and was only 5 years old when her father was judicially murdered by Edward IV and attainted.

Thus, Margaret could only secure a relatively lowly marriage to Sir Richard Pole (in 1494) who had served Edward IV at Ludlow and fought at Bosworth for Henry Tudor. Richard died in 1504. They had five children, four of whom were boys.

Henry VIII took a liking to his great-aunt Margaret and so, in 1519, she was restored to her father's lands and title. As Henry's reign unfolded, however, her family remained staunchly Catholic, and Reginald went abroad (later he became Archbishop of Canterbury in Queen Mary's reign). In the 1530s Reginald published a treatise that was very critical of Henry's actions. As a result, Henry hounded the rest of his family in England. One son, Geoffrey, was broken on the rack and betrayed other family members. Margaret was imprisoned in the Tower in 1539, attainted for treason and in 1541, at the age of 69, beheaded with great brutality. The executioner required a number of blows to complete his task. It appears either he was inexperienced or Margaret refused to kneel down. In the nineteenth century, Margaret was beatified. It is not entirely clear whether she was executed for purely religious reasons or because Henry was now anxious to eliminate the last of the Plantagenets, especially Margaret, who was arguably the true heir of Richard, Duke of York.

The origins of the **Berkeley Chantry** (1486) are obscure, but it was probably built by Sir William Berkeley of Beverstone (d. 1485), who held lands in south-west Hampshire. Sir William was a prominent figure in Southampton and an esquire of the body of Edward IV. He attended Edward's funeral in 1483. Knighted at the coronation of Richard III, he nevertheless took part in Buckingham's Revolt at the Salisbury muster-point and then fled the country to join Henry Tudor in France. He also fought at Bosworth but died within weeks, possibly from wounds received there. Note the separate red and white roses on the walls and ceiling.

In the Great Quire can be found a misericord installed in 1515, depicting **Richard III**.

The priory also boasts a tomb-chest and effigies of Sir John Chidiock (d. 1449) and wife. He is depicted in armour and has the double 'SS' chain of the Lancastrians.

ETON, College and Chapel ** £
Town centre, east side of High Street.

It is one of the supreme ironies of English monarchy that a king as feeble as **Henry VI** should have left so rich a legacy. In 1440 Eton College was founded as the first stage of two linked educational establishments modelled on the lines of Winchester College and New College, Oxford. King's College, Cambridge also founded by Henry, was to follow in 1441.

Henry was 'advised' by William of Waynflete, later Bishop of Winchester (see Winchester). Work had got under way by 1443. The chapel went up quickly but Henry's deposition stopped work for eight years. It was finished in 1475 and remains one of the great Late Perpendicular buildings in England. The school buildings are in brick; Cloister Court and Lupton's Range are particularly good. Appropriately enough, there is a statue of Henry in the ante-chapel and one in School Yard, both of the eighteenth century. Together with King's, this enduring institution surely represents as fine a memorial as any in this guide.

EWELME, St Mary's Church **
Village centre, ½ mile south of B4009 Watlington–Benson road. Close to RAF Benson.

Set in lovely countryside, the charitable gifts of the **church**, **almshouses** and the **school** together form a magnificent and indeed unique monument to both **William de la Pole, Duke of Suffolk** (k. 1450) and his wife, **Alice née Chaucer** (1404–75). Unfortunately nothing remains of their palace. The fifteenth-century school buildings are still in use as a primary school, a truly enduring legacy.

St John's Chapel in the church contains two splendid tomb-chests and brass for Thomas Chaucer (1367–1434) and his wife, Matilda Burghesh. Thomas was the son of the great Geoffrey Chaucer. He was Constable of Wallingford Castle, Speaker eight times and a member of Henry VI's Council in the 1420s. Thomas's mother was Philippa Roet, sister of Katherine Swynford, who was the mother of the Beauforts by John of Gaunt. Matilda had inherited the manor of Ewelme from her father.

The main attraction for the Wars of the Roses here is a magnificent canopied **tomb-chest** and **effigy** of Alice, only daughter of Sir Thomas. Alice's first husband was Thomas Montagu, Earl of Salisbury, who was killed at the siege of Orléans, where Joan of Arc's divine inspiration rallied the French. She then married William de la Pole, who rose to be the most powerful man in England during the 1440s, was made a duke in 1448, but became unpopular and was murdered during the year of turmoil, 1450. Alice herself was a very grand lady in her own right. She was a member of the party which accompanied Margaret of Anjou when she came to England for her wedding in 1445. They became friends. Margaret was captured after the Battle of Tewkesbury in 1471. Edward IV in a compassionate gesture agreed to move her from the Tower to Wallingford Castle, where Alice was now Constable. Alice was a member of the Order of the Garter. Her son John became 2nd Duke of Suffolk and married Princess Elizabeth, sister to Edward IV and Richard III. But Alice could also 'mix it' with the best of the feuding landowners of East Anglia, the Mowbrays and the Wingfields. She was a formidable woman.

MINSTER LOVELL, Hall and St Kenelm's Church ***

Signposted north-east off the Witney–Burford road (B4047), 2 miles west of Witney.

Delightfully situated next to the River Windrush, this group forms a splendid memorial to both William, 7th Lord Lovell (1397–1455) and his grandson, Francis, 9th Lord Lovell (1456–87). The Lovells were among the wealthiest of the peers below the

level of earl. They held over eighty manors, as well as mineral and mining rights. William fought in France and settled here in 1431. Over the next twenty years he rebuilt both church and hall. In 1450 he was active in resisting Cade's Rebellion on behalf of Henry VI. His tomb-chest and effigy stand in the church.

His son, John, remained Lancastrian but died in 1468. John's son, Francis, was still only a minor and became the ward of Richard Neville, Earl of Warwick. He thus grew up at Middleham Castle with Prince Richard of Gloucester and they became firm friends. On Richard's seizure of the throne, Francis was elevated to viscount and appointed as Chief Butler of England, Chamberlain of the Household and Constable of Wallingford Castle. He became one of the inner circle.

Francis fought for Richard at Bosworth but escaped to Flanders via sanctuary at St John's Abbey, Colchester. He returned to England and in spring 1486 led a force near York which nearly captured Henry VII. He was one of the Yorkist commanders at the Battle of Stoke Field (1487), after which he was not seen again. He may have perished in the

The ruins of Minster Lovell House where Francis, Lord Lovell may have starved to death.

battle but was reported as being seen crossing the River Trent on his horse at Fiskerton. He may have drowned. An alternative story is that he hid in one of the cellars of Minster Lovell. Only one servant knew his whereabouts, but this servant was captured and Francis starved to death. In 1708 a skeleton was discovered in one of the cellars. Whatever the truth of the matter, it is a great story. Francis built the south-west tower of the hall, next to the river. Henry Tudor gave Minster Lovell to his uncle Jasper. Both Henry and Richard III stayed here – no doubt captivated by its beauty.

READING, Abbey (remains) **

Situated just east of the town centre beside Forbury Gardens and the Crown Court, originally no doubt a beautiful south-facing location between the Kennet and Thames. The remains are sparse but do not miss the gatehouse adjacent to the Crown Court, which was restored in 1869 by Scott. Car parking is difficult, so Sunday is a good day to visit; otherwise use the Queens Road multi-storey.

Founded by Henry I in 1121, this monastery was an important medieval institution. It was here at a Great Council in mid-September 1464 that **Edward IV**, under pressure from Warwick to marry a French princess, revealed to an astonished assembly that he was already married to **Elizabeth Grey (née Woodville)**. On 29 September 1464 Elizabeth was then presented to Court by Warwick and Clarence at a service in the abbey chapel. This event was of major political significance at the time and definitely changed the course of history. Since the Conquest, no <u>reigning</u> monarch had married an English bride, let alone one from the lower echelons of the nobility (her father was Richard, Earl Rivers, whose title had only been achieved through marriage). In addition, the Woodvilles were Lancastrian; Elizabeth was also a widow, whose husband, Sir John Grey, had been killed fighting for Lancaster at the Second Battle of St Albans in 1461, and she had two children by him. This move was entirely consistent with Edward's policy of promoting close courtiers from the ranks of the gentry and lower nobility (e.g. Sir William Hastings, Sir William Herbert), rather than relying on traditional magnate support.

Edward had been expected to marry a foreign princess, which Warwick had been trying to arrange. His move clearly upset the upper nobility (including his mother, Cecily, and brother, Clarence) but not

sufficiently to prevent both Warwick and Clarence playing a major part in the 29 September service. Nevertheless this event really denotes the beginning of the split between Edward and Warwick, which ended with Warwick's death at the Battle of Barnet in 1471. Throughout his reign, Edward consistently chose to promote the Woodville family, which was large, ambitious and grasping and thus deeply unpopular in the country, particularly with the nobility. Initially successful as a counterbalance to the Nevilles, this policy was to reach its nemesis after his death in 1483 with the deposition and death of his Woodville-dominated son, Edward V, at the hands of Richard III.

STANTON HARCOURT, St Michael's Church **

3 miles south-east of Witney, just off B4449 Hardwick–Eynsham road in village centre.

This site, comprising church, remains of the medieval manor and Pope's Tower is a gem. The **Harcourt chapel** in the church was built in 1470 and houses two splendid tomb-chests/effigies to Sir Robert Harcourt (1410–70) and his wife, Margaret Byron, and to his grandson, also Sir Robert (d. 1509). Sir Robert senior was in fact murdered on 14 November 1470 by the Bastard of Grafton (son of Sir Humphrey Stafford of Grafton) and 150 retainers as a result of an extraordinarily long-running feud between the Harcourts and the Staffords. By the 1440s aristocratic violence and lawlessness was endemic throughout England because of Henry VI's weak and arbitrary government. This particular family feud serves as a very good example of the nature of these conflicts, which, often unchecked, provided the environment in which the Wars of the Roses could start and thrive.

The feud started in May 1448, when Sir Robert and his armed retainers clashed with Sir Humphrey and his party in Coventry. A mêlée developed, in which Sir Humphrey was injured but, worse, his son Richard was killed. Unfortunately for the Harcourts, Sir Humphrey was part of the large and powerful Stafford clan headed by the Duke of Buckingham. Sir Robert was arrested and incarcerated in Chester Castle. However, he managed to evade justice, probably because he was 'protected' by William de la Pole, Duke of Suffolk, who had a principal seat at nearby Ewelme. Sir Robert had been a member of Suffolk's party who went to France in 1445 to accompany Margaret of Anjou on her journey to England to marry Henry VI.

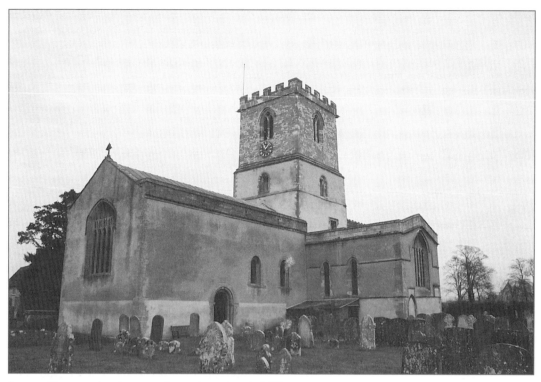

Stanton Harcourt church, scene of a vendetta siege in 1450.

Suffolk himself was murdered on 2 May 1450. On the very same day, Sir Humphrey led a force of retainers overnight to Stanton Harcourt. Sir Robert Harcourt managed to barricade himself in this church tower and so began 'the siege of Stanton Harcourt church', as R.L. Storey has called it. There cannot have been too many church sieges in British history. The room below the tower was torched and the siege lasted six hours, but Sir Robert survived. Within two months, Sir Humphrey Stafford himself was dead, killed in an ambush between Sevenoaks and Tonbridge by Jack Cade's rebels (but there is no suggestion the Harcourts were involved).

Sir Robert now looked for Yorkist protection and became the Earl of Warwick's estate steward. In 1462 he was involved in the siege of Alnwick Castle. In 1463 he was made Knight of the Garter by Edward IV but was present with Warwick at the Duke of Clarence's wedding in Calais in 1469. Just one month after Edward IV had fled the country to Holland in September 1470, Sir Robert was set upon by the Bastard of Grafton and killed, once again deprived of his protector. The family feuding,

however, did not stop until Humphrey Stafford (brother of the Richard above) was beheaded at Tyburn in 1486.

Sir Robert's son John was initially a retainer of the Duke of Clarence and then of Lord Hastings. In October 1483 he joined Buckingham's Revolt against Richard III, mustering at Newbury. He was attainted and fled into exile with Henry Tudor but died in Brittany in 1484. His son, Robert, fought at the Battle of Bosworth for Henry and is said to have been a standard-bearer. He became a member of Lord Stanley's affinity and may have been present at the Battle of Stoke Field (1487).

STOKE CHARITY, St Mary's and St Michael's Church *
In Dever Valley on minor road linking Sutton Scotney (A34) and Micheldever (A33), 2½ miles east of Sutton Scotney.

There can scarcely be a more charming village church in Britain than this one at Stoke Charity. Set in rural tranquillity north of Winchester, this church should not be missed. In the **Hampton Chapel** there is some fine Yorkist **glass** featuring radiant suns and perhaps dating from 1471/2 after the Battle of Tewkesbury. The glass was sponsored by Thomas Hampton (d. 1483), whose tomb-chest is nearby. Note also a tomb-chest to John Waller (d. 1526) and brass to Thomas Wayte (d. 1482).

STONY STRATFORD, 16–28 High Street ****
Town centre (southern end).

The **plaque** on this house (hiding the former medieval Rose and Crown) commemorates the event that started the final phase of the Wars. It defines the spot where **Richard, Duke of Gloucester** carried out his first *coup d'état* on the morning of 30 April 1483. Following the death of his father three weeks earlier, the new king, **Edward V**, was making his way from his castle at Ludlow to the capital for the first time. Accompanied by his maternal uncle, **Earl Rivers** and half brother, Sir Richard Grey, plus Sir Thomas Vaughan and Sir Richard Haute, they had arranged to meet Richard of Gloucester and the **Duke of Buckingham** in Northampton the day before. Instead, on that day the party went on to Stony Stratford. Edward remained there while Rivers and Grey then rode back to Northampton to meet Gloucester. A convivial evening was spent there by the four men. However, in the early morning, Gloucester and Buckingham arrested Rivers and Grey and rode at full gallop on to Stony Stratford (14 miles). They caught up with Edward and party at this house just as they were about to depart for London. Gloucester, as Lord Protector, denounced Edward's Woodville courtiers, arrested Vaughan and Haute and in effect took control of the King's person, escorting Edward himself into

London. All these actions were technically illegal, since the Council had not yet approved Richard's position as Protector. Worse was to follow: Rivers, Vaughan, Grey and Haute were all beheaded in June 1483.

STRATFIELD MORTIMER, St Mary's Church **
7 miles south-west of Reading. From junction 11 on M4 proceed south for ½ mile on A33. Turn right to Three Mile Cross. Follow signs to Mortimer, cross railway and reach church on left after station. PO: 0118 933 3704.

Tucked away behind the **organ**, there is a collection of reconstructed medieval glass, one pane of which contains the arms of the royal family and Mortimer, celebrating the marriage in 1406 or 1408 of Richard, Earl of Cambridge and Anne Mortimer, sister of Edmund Mortimer, Earl of March. This marriage is of the utmost importance to our story, because Edmund and Anne were the children of Roger Mortimer, who had been designated heir presumptive by Richard II in recognition of his descent through the female line from Lionel, Duke of Clarence, the second son of Edward III. Henry IV's usurpation of the throne from Richard II in 1399 ignored the potentially superior claim of Edmund, who was a child. It was this claim that Richard, Duke of York was to reassert in October 1460 as the only son of this marriage, Edmund having died childless in 1425. Anne is buried in King's Langley church. There was also a daughter, Isabel, who married Henry Bourchier, Earl of Essex. Anne is buried with her father-in-law, Edmund, 1st Duke of York (see King's Langley).

Nearby **Bramley parish church** also contains good Yorkist glass with sunbursts, perhaps installed after the Battle of Tewkesbury (1471).

The plaque in Stony Stratford that marks the start of Richard of Gloucester's first coup in 1483.

This charming memorial brass in Thornton church includes the whole family of Robert Ingylton.

THORNTON (Bucks), St Michael and All Angels Church *

3 miles north-east of Buckingham, ½ mile south of A422 road to Stony Stratford. Turn right off A422 over river bridge. Church is in the grounds of Roman Catholic college. Key from reception.

The lovely interior contains a splendid tomb-chest and brass to Robert Ingylton (d. 1482) and his three wives. Robert was Chancellor of the Exchequer in the reign of Edward IV from 1465 to 1469. At that time, the role dealt with the King's household, not with the national 'canvas' as today. That was handled by the Lord Treasurer. Robert was lord of the manor of Thornton from 1464 until his death. Note also the effigies of John Barton (d. 1434) and wife, Isabella (d. 1457). He is clad in armour and wears round his neck a pendant of the White Lion of March. This is rare and indicates he was in the service of either Edmund Mortimer, Earl of March (d. 1425) or Richard, Duke of York (d. 1460), or both.

TITCHFIELD, Abbey (remains) *

½ mile north of village centre between A27 and M27 on minor road just west of the River Meon. 01329 842133.

The abbey was the scene of the wedding of **Henry VI** to **Margaret of Anjou** on 23 April 1445, conducted by William Ayscough, Bishop of Salisbury, who was Henry's confessor (see Edington). The marriage had been brokered by William de la Pole, Duke of Suffolk with King Charles of France and Duke René of Anjou, Margaret's father. It was part of a peace package centring on the Treaty of Tours (1444), which included the secret ceding of Maine and Anjou by Henry to the French. When news of the full package leaked out after the wedding, there was a storm of protest in both England and the French provinces, led by Humphrey, Duke of Gloucester. Nevertheless, withdrawal eventually took place in 1447, but only after Gloucester's death earlier that year. In a way, then, this marriage marks the beginning of the descent into civil war. On the day, Margaret was apparently unwell, having had a dreadfully rough Channel crossing some days before – or was it he prospect of marrying Henry which had generated this condition? Henry had apparently been so eager to see his wife that he disguised himself as a squire and took her a letter written by the King of England so that he could get a good sight of her. Margaret was so engrossed in the letter she did not notice the squire and kept him on his knees.

It was not an auspicious start to a marriage. The most pressing strategic need for the Lancastrian dynasty in 1445 was for the couple to produce a male heir quickly, but one did not arrive until late 1453. Bishop Ayscough's advice to Henry cannot have helped though. He advised against self-indulgence and not to 'come nigh her any more than was necessary to create heirs'. Ayscough was subsequently blamed for the lack of an heir.

The surviving abbey gatehouse presents a fine spectacle, but unfortunately was built in early Tudor times. The scant remains of the **old abbey** lie to the right of the gatehouse.

WINCHESTER, Cathedral ****
City centre.

As one of the richest bishoprics in England it is not surprising that this cathedral contains monuments to some of the most eminent churchmen of the fifteenth century.

The **chantry chapel** for Cardinal Henry Beaufort (*c.* 1376–1447) is in the **retrochoir**. To quote L.P. Hartley in *The Go-Between*: 'The past is a foreign country: they do things differently there.' In the career of this most eminent of fifteenth-century bishop-politicians, we can see the aptness of this quotation. Henry Beaufort was of the royal blood, being the second illegitimate son of John of Gaunt and Katherine Swynford who was legitimated in 1397. As such a high-ranking aristocrat, he was made Bishop of Lincoln at the early age of 22. Subsequently, he held the bishopric of Winchester, with its huge incomes, for forty-three years.

But first and foremost, though, Henry was a politician. He served all three Lancastrian kings; he was Chancellor three times under Henry V and Henry VI. He was also a major financier to the Crown during the French Wars but, as befitted a churchman, without charging any interest. After the Duke of Bedford's death in 1435, he became the leader of the Court party and, in turn, the prime mover for peace in support of Henry VI's views. Beaufort often clashed with Humphrey, Duke of

Gloucester over policy but together they somehow managed to keep the Lancastrian 'show on the road' after Bedford's death. Contrast this approach to that of the Yorkist family forty years later. It was only their gradual withdrawal from public life in the 1440s and their deaths, both in 1447, that allowed more ruthless counsellors access to Henry VI (the Dukes of Suffolk and Somerset) and brought about the Lancastrian disaster of the late 1440s in France. Beaufort officiated at the trial and burning of Joan of Arc in Rouen in 1431, surely a day of true infamy in English history. He also fathered a bastard daughter, Jane – not a unique event among senior clerics in those days.

Although he died before the Wars of the Roses began, as leader of the Peace Party in the 1430s and 40s, Beaufort must take some of the blame for the calamitous results of the policy that led to the English being thrown out of France in the late 1440s and early 1450s in such chaos. This caused the regime's popularity to plummet from 1449 and created a political climate in which the Wars of the Roses could ignite in the next decade.

Also in the retrochoir is the **chantry chapel** for William of Waynflete (*c.* 1394–1486, bishop 1447–86). A pillar of the Lancastrian establishment, he was Henry VI's confessor and baptised Prince Edward in 1453. He was a member of the delegations negotiating with Cade's rebels in 1450 at Blackheath, and at Southwark with Richard, Duke of York at Dartford in 1452. His palace in Winchester was sacked in the aftermath of Cade's revolt. From 1456 to 1460 he was Chancellor of England and a member of the King's and Prince's Councils (the latter run by Queen Margaret). Waynflete accompanied King Henry's army to Northampton in July 1460. He became so alarmed by the size and menace of the Yorkist army that he fled before the battle, never to return to office. Waynflete was a giant of early education. He was variously headmaster of Winchester College, Provost of Eton and founder of Magdalen College, Oxford. He was closely involved with Henry VI's project which founded Eton and King's College, Cambridge. Wayneflete is credited with channelling Henry towards a solution that mirrored the establishment of Winchester and New College, Oxford by William of Wykeham sixty years earlier.

The **south-east chapel** contains a tomb-chest and brass indent of Thomas Langton (bishop 1493–1501). Langton was chaplain to Edward IV and to Richard III and a member of Richard's Council.

After Bosworth he was put into Bishop Courtenay's custody, but was rewarded with Winchester on Courtenay's death.

The nineteenth-century tomb-chest of Peter Courtenay (bishop 1486–92) is in the **chancel**. This is the most interesting monument in the cathedral from the Wars of the Roses viewpoint. Courtenay, as Bishop of Exeter in the early 1480s, was something of a 'fighting' bishop. He was a member of the Courtenay family of Powderham, who played a major part in the Buckingham Revolt against Richard III at Exeter in October 1483. Alongside his brother and cousin he participated in the revolt. He was attainted but fled to Brittany to join Henry Tudor. He was present at Bosworth with Tudor, being subsequently rewarded with the wealthy see of Winchester. He became Keeper of the Privy Seal. Courtenay had earlier been secretary to Henry VI during the 1470/1 Readeption, and to Edward IV in 1472–4.

Richard Fox (bishop 1501–28) is commemorated in a chantry chapel in the **chancel**, with cadaver. Fox joined Henry Tudor in exile while a student in Paris. He worked closely with Morton. He became secretary to Henry II as king, and Keeper of the Privy Seal from 1492. He developed into one of the most influential bureaucrats of the early Tudor period, retaining the latter position for the first seven years of Henry VIII's reign – no mean feat. He is seen as the true architect of 'Morton's Fork', the infamous money-raising technique used under Henry VII.

WINDSOR, St George's Chapel ***** ££

Town centre in castle grounds. Park north of castle near river. Entrance stops at 4 p.m.

This is one of the glories of English architecture. It was begun by **Edward IV** in 1475 and finished by Henry VII at a time when Henry was thinking of being buried here, rather than at Westminster. The monuments relevant to the Wars of the Roses are therefore a rather strange mixture of Yorkist grandees, Henry VI, and close, but not so important, supporters of Henry Tudor. The monuments are discussed in the order they are encountered round the chapel.

In the **nave** in the **south-west** or **Beaufort Chapel** are tomb-chests and two recumbent alabaster effigies relating to Charles Somerset, Earl of Worcester (c. 1460–1526). Charles was the natural son of Henry Beaufort, 2nd Duke of Somerset and Joan Hill. He probably joined Henry Tudor, his second cousin, in exile before Bosworth. He was knighted at the Milford Haven landing in 1485 and fought for Henry at the Battle of Bosworth and the Battle of Stoke (1487). His first marriage was to Elizabeth Herbert (1476–1510), daughter and heiress of William, Earl of Huntingdon, in turn son and heir of William, Earl of Pembroke, who had been Henry VII's guardian before his execution after the Battle of Edgcote in 1469. Charles later married Elizabeth West, daughter of Thomas, Lord de la Warr. Charles was created Earl of Worcester in 1514 by Henry VIII. The present dukes of Beaufort are descended from Charles and his first wife.

Christopher Urswick (d. 1523) was Henry VII's confessor and King's Almoner. He became Dean of York Minster and Master of King's Hall College, Cambridge. He had been very much involved in the plotting in 1483 as a go-between and diplomat for Lady Margaret Beaufort, John Morton and Henry Tudor. In the autumn he fled to Flanders to join Morton. While there, Morton learned of Richard III's machinations designed to lead to Henry Tudor's arrest in Brittany. Urswick was sent by Morton to warn Henry in Vannes and then to the French Court to ask for permission to enter France. This was given and Henry duly escaped. Urswick landed with the invasion party at Milford Haven in 1485 but did not participate at Bosworth Field.

In the **north transept**, the Rutland Chapel, in which there is a fine tomb-chest and alabaster effigies relating to Anne Manners, née St Leger, Baroness Ros (1476–1526) was the daughter of Thomas St Leger and Anne Plantagenet (see below). She married George Manners, 12th Baron Ros and had two children, Eleanor (d. 1547) and Thomas (d. 1543). Thomas became 1st Earl of Rutland, which title remains in the family to this day. George Manners (d. 1513) was the son of Sir Robert Manners, who in 1469 had married Eleanor Ros, heiress to the Ros baronetcy, whose Lancastrian father had been executed after the Battle of Hexham in 1464. Eleanor's brother, Edward, inherited the baronetcy in 1464 but died unmarried in 1508, leaving George to succeed to the title.

In the chapel there is also a brass to Princess Anne Plantagenet (1439–76) and her second husband, Sir Thomas St Leger (ex. 1483). Anne, born at Fotheringhay Castle, was the eldest surviving child of Richard, Duke of York and Cecily Neville, and Edward IV's favourite sibling. Before 1447 she had been married to Henry Holland, 4th Duke

The renovated tomb of Edward IV and Queen Elizabeth Woodville in St George's Chapel, Windsor.

The Tresilian Gates, which stand in front of Edward IV's tomb.

of Exeter, who was himself of the royal blood. In 1455 they had a daughter, another Anne (d. 1475). With the descent into civil war, Exeter had become a staunch Lancastrian. He fought at Towton and commanded the left wing at Barnet in Warwick's army, thus opposing three brothers-in-law. Left for dead on the battlefield, he recovered, but he and Anne were divorced in late 1472. Anne quickly married her lover, Thomas St Leger. In 1476 she produced a second girl, another Anne, but died in January that year, possibly in childbirth. This is the Anne, Baroness Ros in this chapel. Exeter had mysteriously drowned at sea in the Channel in 1475, the same year that his daughter died. The Holland inheritance passed first to Anne Plantagenet, and then to Baroness Ros.

Sir Thomas St Leger had family estates in both the south-west and Kent. He held Torrington and Barnstaple Castles. Thomas became a knight of the body to Edward IV, as well as Controller of the Royal Mint (from 1461) and Master of the Harthounds

(from 1478). He resisted Clarence and Warwick in 1469/70 and joined Edward in exile in 1470. After Edward's death in April 1483 he attended Richard III's coronation, but in July was dismissed from his posts. He had become aligned closely with Thomas Grey, Marquis of Dorset, of the Woodville clan. He was a leader of the Buckingham Revolt around Exeter along with his brother, Bartholomew, and held out against the royal forces at Bodmin Castle until mid-November. He was executed at Exeter Castle on 13 November 1483.

In the **north chancel aisle** is a chantry chapel dedicated to **William, Lord Hastings** (*c.* 1431–83), who in his will requested to be buried here, close to his friend and sovereign, Edward IV. Here is a man most famous for the manner of his execution by his close friend's brother, Richard III, during Richard's second coup on Friday 13 June 1483.

Also in the **north chancel aisle** is the wall-tomb of **King Edward IV** and **Queen Elizabeth Woodville**. The tomb was rebuilt in the seventeenth

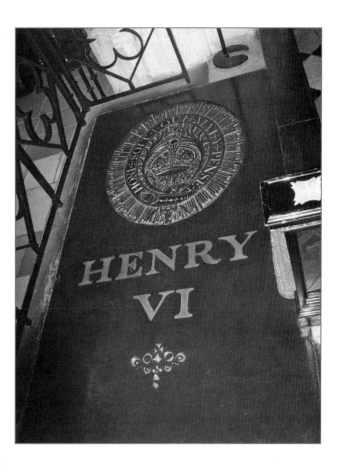

The final resting place of Henry VI in St George's Chapel, Windsor.

century after the original tomb was despoiled. In the **chancel** itself note the Tresilian gates, designed for Edward's tomb and, of course, the Knight of the Garter stalls and **plates**. As you turn left out of the chancel, note the misericord depicting the meeting between Edward and Louis XI of France on the bridge at Picquigny, which resulted in the eponymous treaty in 1475.

In the **south transept** is the Bray Chapel. Sir Reginald Bray (d. 1503), whose family emblem was a hemp knot, was a major benefactor to the chapel in the late fifteenth century. Bray, from the Worcester area, was an outstanding household administrator, particularly in financial matters. He began as receiver-general to Sir Henry Stafford, third husband to Lady Margaret Beaufort, Henry VII's mother. On Stafford's death, he remained in the household of Lady Margaret Beaufort. By 1478 he had become an MP. He was implicated in the 1483 Buckingham Revolt when he was used as go-between between Buckingham, Lady Margaret and Morton.

He fought at Bosworth and was knighted on the battlefield. He became very close to Henry VII and was appointed Chancellor of the Duchy of Lancaster. He was a highly valued member of this Council. At his death, Bray held lands of his own over a wide area.

Next in the **south chancel aisle** come portraits of four kings – **Edward III**, **Edward IV**, **Edward V** and **Henry VII**, painted *c*. 1495. The painting of Edward V is especially interesting, as his crown hovers above his head, indicating he was never crowned (see Coldridge). The portraits are part of Oliver King's **chantry**. King was secretary to Edward IV, Edward V and Henry VII. He held the last office from 1487 to 1496, so was obviously particularly well regarded by Henry. In 1483 he had been imprisoned by Richard III. Henry made him successively Bishop of Exeter, and then of Bath and Wells.

Last but not least, in the **same aisle** we come to the tomb of **King Henry VI**, moved here from Chertsey. The collecting box for pilgrims is nearby.

WEST COUNTRY

BRISTOL

St Mark's Church *

City centre, on opposite side of College Green from the cathedral (tower), 0117 929 4350.

A lovely fan-vaulted **chantry chapel** founded by Sir Robert Poyntz (d. 1520) of Iron Acton. The tomb-chest was destroyed, although remnants lie in the south aisle. During Edward IV's reign, Poyntz had been a squire of the body and he participated in Edward's funeral. One source describes Poyntz as the 'captain' of Buckingham's Revolt (see Salisbury). He was a member of the Duke of Buckingham's council and the son-in-law of the 2nd Earl Rivers, Anthony Woodville (his wife was Rivers' natural daughter). He rose against Richard III at Salisbury and, after the failure of the revolt, sought sanctuary in Beaulieu Abbey with Lionel Woodville. He fought for Tudor at the Battle of Bosworth and was knighted afterwards.

Note the fine tomb-chest and effigy in the chancel to Sir Maurice Berkeley (d. 1464) of Stoke Gifford and his wife, Ellen. He sports a Yorkist collar.

St Mary Redcliffe Church ***

On inner ring road south side, ½ mile west of Temple Meads station (tower).

You should visit this church whether you are interested in the Wars of the Roses or not, and then tell your friends about it. Queen Elizabeth I was correct in most things. After visiting this church, she described it as 'the goodliest, fairest and most famous parish church in England'. Beverley Minster and Tewkesbury Abbey might come close. The interior is stunning.

It has a splendid collection of fifteenth- and sixteenth-century brasses of former sheriffs, mayors and priests, and effigies of the Cannyng family, benefactors of the church. William Cannyng (1399–1474) has two monuments. He was a major shipowner who was MP for Bristol and very active.

Effigy of William Cannyng in St Mary Redcliffe Church, Bristol.

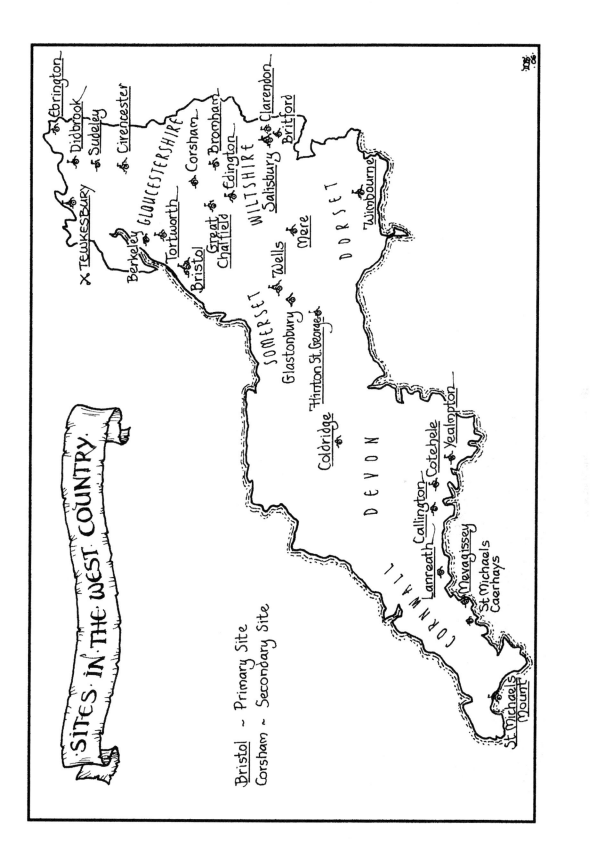

SITES IN THE WEST COUNTRY.

Bristol ~ Primary Site
Corsham ~ Secondary Site

In 1456/7 he held Bristol Castle for York against the Duke of Somerset, and in 1461 he sent an expedition into Wales against the Lancastrians. In the **north ambulatory** are double tomb-chests to Thomas Mede (d. 1491) and his wife, and to his brother Philip Mede (d. 1475). Philip's is in the eastern recess with a fine brass above it, probably of himself (or his son Richard) and two wives. Philip was sheriff and mayor of Bristol in the 1450s and 60s, and an MP. He is known to have fought at the Battle of Nibley Green in Gloucestershire in 1470, the last private battle fought in England, between Lord Berkeley and Viscount Lisle – a unique survival. Philip was father-in-law to Berkeley's younger brother Maurice (although the Medes were not considered by Berkeley to be of the right background for Maurice).

BRITFORD, St Peter's Church ****
2 miles south-east of Salisbury, left off the A338 Ringwood road. Church close to the River Avon.

Tomb-chest probably containing the remains of **Henry Stafford, 2nd Duke of Buckingham**,

executed in front of Richard III on 2 November 1483 in Salisbury marketplace (see Salisbury). The chest is believed to have come from the nearby Greyfriars Abbey at the Dissolution.

BROMHAM, St Nicholas's Church ***
In village centre on minor road joining A342 Chippenham–Devizes road to A3102 Melksham–Calne road.

The **Tocotes and Beauchamp Chapel** was built in 1492 and commemorates two leaders of the 1483 Buckingham Revolt in Berkshire and Wiltshire against Richard III: Sir Richard Beauchamp, styled Lord St Amand, and his stepfather, Sir Roger Tocotes (d. 1492). Within the chapel, there is a tomb-chest to Elizabeth, née Braybrooke (d. 1492), mother to Sir Richard by her first husband, William, Lord St Amand, and wife to Sir Roger (d. 1492). Unlike Elizabeth's first husband, Richard was not called to parliament as a lord. Sir Roger has a separate tomb-chest and fine alabaster effigy (complete with ancient graffiti). Sir Roger, a Yorkshireman, had a decidedly chequered Wars

Effigy of Sir Roger Tocotes in Bromham church.

of the Roses. He appears to have been an early Yorkist and became king's servant to Edward IV. By 1468, however, he had fallen in with George, Duke of Clarence. He was steward of Clarence's lands in Hampshire and his chief councillor. He joined Clarence's rebellion in 1470 (in Lincolnshire) against Edward IV but changed sides with Clarence in 1471 and fought at Barnet and Tewkesbury. He was created a knight banneret.

In April 1477 Sir Roger became embroiled in a murder trial orchestrated by Clarence which was to lead to Clarence's eventual execution by his brother Edward IV in February 1478. Two Clarence servants, Ankarette Twynho and John Thursby were accused by Clarence of poisoning his wife, Isabel, and his baby son and Sir Roger of aiding, abetting and harbouring them. Twynho and Thursby were forcibly removed to Warwick by Clarence, where a cowed jury found them guilty and they were executed within the day. Sir Roger 'miraculously' managed to escape.

Clarence was clearly acting above the law and this led to his downfall and death.

Tocotes joined Buckingham's Revolt against Richard III in 1483 and was attainted. Sir Roger fought for Henry Tudor at the Battle of Bosworth. Henry VII appointed him Sheriff that year. He seems to have joined Stanley's affinity at that time.

CALLINGTON, St Mary's Church **
On town centre crossroads.

In the chancel a fine tomb-chest and life-size effigy of Sir Robert Willoughby, Lord Willoughby de Broke (*c.* 1452–1502/3) Sir Robert's father, Sir John, held lands in Wiltshire and Cornwall and fought for Lancaster at Towton. He died in 1477. Robert married Blanche Champernowne, the heiress of Bere Ferrers, in Devon. The Willoughbys were retainers of the Dukes of Buckingham and, in 1470, Robert on two occasions attacked his near neighbour across the Tamar in

Effigy of Sir Robert Willoughby at Callington.

Cornwall, Richard Edgcumbe, who at that time was a supporter of George, Duke of Clarence. Fortunately the two were to fight on the same side at Bosworth and become friends.

In 1483 Sir Robert joined the Duke of Buckingham's Revolt in Exeter. He then fled to France to join Henry Tudor and became a key member of Henry's 'band of brothers'. He returned with Henry and fought at the Battle of Bosworth. He was now clearly a confidant of Henry's, for he was sent on the delicate mission after the entry into London to secure Edward, Earl of Warwick (Clarence's son, with a potential claim to the throne) from Sheriff Hutton castle near York. Under Henry, Sir Robert went from strength to strength. He was immediately made Controller of the Royal Household and was heavily involved in Henry's coronation. He was knight of the body and a king's councillor. He assisted Henry in pacifying the north in early 1486.

In 1488 he was called to parliament as the first Lord Willoughby de Broke, one of only three members of the 'band' to be so ennobled (Cheyney and Daubeny were the others). In 1489 he led a military expedition to Brittany in a vain attempt by Henry to prevent the French taking over the peninsula. He was also mayor of Callington, where he died on a visit to the town. His son, also Lord Robert, is commemorated by a tomb-chest in the splendidly sited church at Bere Ferrers by the River Tavy.

CIRENCESTER, St John the Baptist's Church ***
Town centre.

In the Trinity Chapel (north side) of this fine church in the east window is original stained glass depicting the head of **Richard, Duke of York** (1411–k.60), one of only two likenesses to survive. The chapel was founded in 1430 by two members of the Duke's household, Richard Dixton (d. 1438) and William Prelatte (d. 1462). They are both buried in the chapel and their respective brasses survive (both are depicted in armour). The chapel also commemorates the Weavers' Guild of the Holy Trinity, of which Dixton and Prelatte were members. Note the early Yorkist badge of falcon and fetterlock on the arches.

Pevsner describes the great south porch of this church, built in 1490, as 'the most splendid of all English church porches'. Also do not miss the wonderful fan vaulting in St Catherine's Chapel.

CLARENDON, Royal Palace (remains) ****
3 miles east of Salisbury. Approach only by long-range footpath called Clarendon Way from Milford suburb. Milford is just east of the Southampton–Salisbury railway line on east edge of Salisbury. Parking limited, walk last 1½ miles.

This is a gem. The remains of the royal hunting lodge rebuilt in the thirteenth century are visible and accessible from the Clarendon long-range footpath as it crests the north-sloping ridge of the downs along the medieval main route from Salisbury to Winchester. Because the Clarendon estate is now in private hands, this is a delightfully isolated spot with great views back down to the cathedral. Much clearance and excavation on the site has been undertaken in recent years.

Perhaps surprisingly, **Henry VI** was fond of hunting. It was while staying here in early August 1453 that he succumbed to what appears to have been a severe depressive stupor or, possibly, catatonic schizophrenia. Henry became incapable of conversation, of recognising his courtiers or even of standing. For the next seventeen months he was unable to carry out his kingly duties until, quite suddenly, he appears to have recovered, at Christmas 1454. The timing of the onset of the illness suggests it was triggered by news of the disastrous defeat of the English forces at Castillon, near Bordeaux, on 17 July 1453 and the death of the great John Talbot, Earl of Shrewsbury, together with the loss of Gascony. Henry had now lost all his father's conquests in France, except Calais. Perhaps inevitably, counter-rumours circulated that, in fact, the condition was triggered by Henry's learning that his wife's child-to-be was not his, but had been fathered by Edmund Beaufort, Duke of Somerset.

Today we would see a large genetic element to the illness. Henry's grandfather, Charles VI of France – his mother's Valois father – also suffered long periods of mental incapacity. Whatever the exact reason(s) for the illness, its onset had huge ramifications in the realm. If you want a single cause for the outbreak of the Wars of the Roses, this is it. Although the Queen and the Court tried to hide Henry's incapacity, eventually the death of Archbishop Kemp of Canterbury in March 1454 demanded the personal intervention of Henry to appoint a successor. A delegation of lords visited him in Windsor. Once they realised how bad his condition was, the Duke of York was made Protector of the Realm within two days. For the next nine months, York and the Nevilles were

Clarendon Palace, near Salisbury, where Henry VI had his breakdown.

given a first taste of power, but then unceremoniously dumped, on Henry's recovery. These events led directly to the first battle of St Albans in May 1455. In fact, within two weeks of St Albans, Henry was ill again. In the battle, Henry had become isolated; he suffered a neck wound as his household men were cut down around him. The shock may have been severe. It is unlikely that Henry ever really returned to full health again, his condition deteriorating over the years.

COLDRIDGE, St Matthew's Church ****
Village centre 1 mile north of B3220 Copplestone–Winkleigh road.

Coldridge may be in the depths of the north Devon countryside but, whatever you do, do not miss this one, for this little church contains one of the most fascinating survivals from our story. On the north side lies the **Evans chantry chapel**, which contains the effigy of John Evans, park keeper and yeoman of the crown, who died in the first twenty years of the sixteenth century. Evans held a lease on the manor, Coldridge Barton, which he acquired during the reign of Henry VII from Thomas Grey, 1st Marquis of Dorset. Evans was evidently Welsh (the name was not common in England at that time).

In the east window of the chantry is one of the few representations of **Edward V** as king found outside St George's Chapel, Windsor. What is more, Edward is represented with the crown of England suspended above him, showing that, although legitimate heir, he was never crowned (just as at Windsor). In addition, a small light in the window contains a particularly evil-looking representation of **Richard III**. The alignment of the Evans effigy is such that he is looking towards this window in perpetuity. Why such politically charged stained glass in a tiny Devon church? Literature in the church includes a splendid article from the *Journal of Stained Glass*, volume XXVI, by Cherry and Brooks, which really sets the mind racing with possibilities. The authors suggest that John Evans in fact attended the funeral of Henry VIII's first son, Henry, in 1511.

The Marquis of Dorset had been the leading figure in the October 1483 Buckingham Revolt in Devon and Cornwall. He raised the standard of revolt in Exeter and in Bodmin, but the rebellion quickly collapsed. In fact, Dorset was never really trusted by Henry VII. As the son of Elizabeth Woodville by her first marriage, he was a leading member of the Woodville faction.

So who was Evans? The authors suggest that he may have been in the service of Edward V but could he also have been a royal impostor discredited at Bodmin in Buckingham's Revolt? Could he have been the real thing?

Do not miss the 'medieval joke' behind the rood-screen (see church leaflet), evidence that someone had an ironic sense of humour in Coldridge.

Effigy of Sir John Evans at Coldridge – but who was he?

COTEHELE, House ** £

6 miles south-west of Tavistock, signposted south off
A390 Tavistock–Callington road at St Ann's Chapel.
NT. 01579 351346.

Cotehele provides a splendid half-day outing for the Wars of the Roses enthusiast and supplies us with another of the colourful 'tradition has it' stories. It was the home of Sir Richard Edgcumbe (d. 1489), who is commemorated in the **house chapel** by a painting of his tomb at Morlaix, Brittany (destroyed during the French Revolution). It is necessary to pay for house entrance to gain access to the chapel. The house itself is also a memorial to Sir Richard and to his son, Sir Piers, who died in 1539. Dating originally from the thirteenth and fourteenth centuries, the house was thoroughly remodelled by Sir Richard in the last four years of his life – he built the chapel and the gatehouse – while Sir Piers completed the great hall in the early sixteenth century.

Sir Richard first comes to notice in 1470 as a follower of George, Duke of Clarence. He was ambushed by his neighbour Robert Willoughby of Bere Ferrers, after which Cotehele was attacked, but little harm seems to have come of this spat. In October 1483 he joined Buckingham's Revolt. After its collapse in Exeter, Edgcumbe laid low at Cotehele. However, he was pursued here by that Yorkist ruffian Sir Henry (Trenowith of) Bodrugan. Bodrugan trapped Edgcumbe in the house and grounds, and posted sentries. 'Tradition has it' that Edgcumbe cut the throat of a sentry and sped down to the edge of the River Tamar. Taking off his cap, he primed it with a stone and dropped it into the river. His pursuers noticed the floating cap 'swimming' away and, assuming that Edgcumbe had been drowned, ceased their searching. Meanwhile, Edgcumbe remained hidden in the undergrowth and at an appropriate moment slipped away and escaped to Brittany. The story might be thought to contain a large amount of romantic embroidery, but it is worth walking down through the woods from the house to the river (go by car, if time presses, and walk the ½ mile along). There is still a lot of undergrowth but, more particularly, you will find a small **chapel** built by Edgcumbe on a cliff above the river in grateful memory of that day. It is clear that something must have happened there.

Cotehele House, remodelled by Sir Richard Edgcombe and his son.

On arrival in Brittany, Edgcumbe joined Henry Tudor's 'band of brothers' and was reacquainted with his neighbour Sir Robert Willoughby; they seem to have become firm friends. Both fought at the Battle of Bosworth. Under Henry VII, Sir Richard prospered, becoming Controller of the Royal Household and knight of the body. He was granted the lands of his old enemy, Sir Henry Bodrugan, and is said to have gained his revenge in the most appropriate manner (see Mevagissey). In 1488 he joined Sir Robert Willoughby's expedition to Brittany, during which he died.

DIDBROOK, St George's Church *
Village centre, south of B4077 Stow on the Wold–Broadway road, 2 miles north-east of Winchcombe.

This charming church was rebuilt in 1475 by Abbot Whitchurch of nearby Hailes Abbey. An inscription in the fifteenth-century stained glass in the east window celebrates this. The rebuilding was for a particular reason. In the rout after the Battle of Tewkesbury (1471), some Lancastrian soldiers sought sanctuary

in the old church. Their Yorkist pursuers violated sanctuary and massacred them. It is said that the holes in the west door were made by Yorkist gunmen trying to enter the church. The Bishop of Worcester declared the church desecrated and had it rebuilt.

EBRINGTON, St Eadburga's Church **
South-west side of village, 1 mile north of B4035 Chipping Campden–Shipston road.

A tomb-chest and unexpectedly larger-than-life effigy commemorate <u>Lord Chief Justice John Fortescue</u> (1390/4–1476), Lancastrian stalwart and legal heavyweight. He was made up to Chief Justice of the King's Bench in 1442, and by 1450 had become sufficiently unpopular to be named personally by Cade's rebels. Along with John Morton, he was much involved in drafting the 1459 Act of Attainder against York, Salisbury and Warwick. He was present at Towton but escaped with King Henry VI to Scotland. Thus began ten years away from his native land, during which he became Margaret of Anjou's 'Chancellor-in-exile' at her small court, which included Prince Edward, at Koeur in France. He was her chief adviser and, in that role, is credited with promoting Margaret's alliance with the Kingmaker in 1470. Fortescue returned with Queen Margaret in spring 1471 and was present at Tewkesbury. He was captured (by now he was about 80) after the battle, but his life was spared.

A condition of his pardon was that he repudiated some of his writings penned in exile. He became a member of Edward IV's Council. Those writings identify Fortescue as a major legal figure. Hicks sees him as the 'outstanding constitutional theorist of late medieval England'. He wrote *De Laudibus Legum Angliae* to ensure that Henry VI's son, Prince Edward, had sufficient understanding of English law. His *Governance of England* translated parts of this into English. It constitutes 'the earliest constitutional treatise in the English language'. But the work is not universally acclaimed. The historian G.R. Elton wrote, 'The alleged prominence of Sir John Fortescue in the fifteenth century is that of a mole-hill on a very flat plain.' Whatever the truth of that, Fortescue is surely one of the few men from the Wars of the Roses who have left a truly lasting legacy – along with his monarch, Henry VI.

EDINGTON, Priory Church **

½ mile north of B3098 Market Lavington–Wesbury road, at western end of village.

William Ayscough, Bishop of Salisbury and Henry VI's confessor, officiated at Henry's wedding to Margaret of Anjou in 1445 at Titchfield Abbey (see Titchfield). He was a prominent member of the Court party in the 1440s, a friend of the Duke of Suffolk and notoriously acquisitive. On 29 June 1450, in the midst of the Cade Rebellion, as he prepared to celebrate mass, Ayscough was dragged from this church's chancel by rebels to the nearby **hillock** and then hacked to death and his corpse stripped. The hillock is still there and accessible, but makes a chilling place for a picnic. That year also saw the murders of Bishop Moleyns and the Duke of Suffolk, and the Cade Rebellion – a true *annus horribilis* for Henry VI.

GREAT CHALFIELD, Manor **

On Broughton Common–Bradford Leigh minor road. Signposted from B3107 Melksham–Bradford on Avon road. Approx. 3 miles west of Melksham. NT. 01225 782239.

Pevsner describes this as 'one of the most perfect examples of the late medieval English manor house' –

reason enough to include it in this guide. Substantially rebuilt between 1465 and 1480 by Thomas Tropnell, the manor has fortunately seen little subsequent rebuilding. It therefore feels very 'in-period' and is a splendid place to visit.

Tropnell (*c.* 1405–88) was from a family of modest Wiltshire landowners but, in modern parlance, was 'upwardly mobile'. He became steward for Lord Hungerford, covering eighty-seven properties, including Farleigh Hungerford Castle over the border in Somerset. Tropnell was very much part of the lesser-gentry network in Wiltshire, which revolved around the Hungerfords, but he himself was probably not a fighting man. He became an MP and a member of Lincoln's Inn. He built a chapel in the adjoining Great Chalfield church in 1480, but is buried with his second wife in a large tomb-chest in **Corsham** church. At his death, he owned seven manors.

HINTON ST GEORGE, Church *

2 miles north-west of Crewkerne. Church at west end of village.

In the **Paulet Chapel** (requires special access) is a tomb-chest and effigies to Sir Amyas Paulet (d. 1537) and his wife. Sir Amyas was the son of Sir William, who in 1429 had married Elizabeth Denaband, the heiress of Sir John Denaband of Hinton. Sir Amyas joined Buckingham's Revolt in 1483 at Newbury. In 1485 he made his way all the way up to Bosworth to fight for Henry Tudor which he did again in 1487 at Stoke Field, where he was knighted. Hinton St George is a lovely village and boasts a good pub.

LANREATH, St Marnarch's Church *

Village centre lies ½ mile west of B3359 Looe–Bodmin road, 2 miles north-west of Pelynt.

This church contains a fine early sixteenth-century **rood screen** which at one time contained forty brightly painted images of saints. One of these represents **Henry VI** (with antelope and orb). They were associated with Henry VII's campaign to obtain sainthood for his Lancastrian predecessor from the pope, probably started by Henry's mother, Lady Margaret Beaufort, at the end of the fifteenth century.

MERE, St Michael's Church **

In village centre off A303.

Between the **south chapel** and chancel is a tomb-chest to a member of the Stourton family from the

Great Chalfield Manor, rebuilt by Thomas Tropnell.

fifteenth century. The guidebook suggests that it could be John I, 1st Lord Stourton (d. 1462) or John II, the 3rd lord (*c*. 1453–85), but is most likely the latter. John I served the households of both Henry V and Henry VI. He rose to be treasurer of the household and member of the royal Council and was ennobled by Henry VI in 1448. He was a member of Suffolk's faction but survived to be involved in the negotiations with the Duke of York on Henry's behalf in February 1452 at Dartford. He was also a member of the lords' delegation attending Henry at Windsor in March 1454, during Henry's spell of insanity, when he was unable to recognise anyone or speak at all. The Stourton family appears to have converted to the Yorkist cause in the 1460s. John, the 3rd Lord, came into his title in 1477/8 on the death of his father, William. John married Catherine Berkeley. He was implicated in Buckingham's Revolt of 1483 and sought a pardon, but was not attainted.

Note that the Stourtons lived at the nearby Stourhead estate, now boasting magnificent gardens. The church there contains a tomb-chest and effigies to the 6th Lord, Edward (b. *c*. 1462–1535), younger brother of the 3rd Lord.

MEVAGISSEY, Bodrugan's Leap ***

Coastal walk – see below.

Bodrugan's Leap is the name given to a small stretch of Cornish coastline now owned by the National Trust. Here, in late 1485/6, soon after Henry VII's accession, Sir Richard Edgcumbe moved to secure the lands and person of his great Cornish rival, the Yorkist Sir Henry Trenowith of Bodrugan. Edgcumbe was seeking revenge for Bodrugan's invasions of his property in 1483/4. Sir Henry lived at Bodrugan Barton, 1 mile south of Mevagissey, on high ground overlooking the dramatic coast. At the approach of Edgcumbe, tradition has it that Trenowith fled the ¼ mile to the sea, somewhere near to a spot now marked by the National Trust sign 'Bodrugan's Leap'. At this point tradition splits into a Yorkist version and a Tudor version.

The Yorkist story suggests that Sir Henry outwitted his pursuers by leaping, on his horse, down on to the beach (Colona Beach?) and then boarding a waiting ship, bound for France and exile. The Tudor version tells that Sir Henry, harassed by his pursuers, leapt to his death, no doubt a few hundred yards further south, over the cliffs towards Turbot Point. The truth of the matter is no longer relevant, but the story is very much in keeping with the colourful detail that adorns much of the Wars of the Roses history in the western parts of the country and in Wales.

Sir Henry Trenowith of Bodrugan (or just Sir Henry Bodrugan – he had married the heiress of Bodrugan Barton) was a Yorkist from the early 1460s onwards. Even in a riotous age, he was clearly even more wild than most. Described variously as a bandit, pirate and local party boss, Bodrugan was the subject of at least two commissions of inquiry. In October 1473 he was appointed by Edward IV to besiege St Michael's Mount, which had been occupied by John de Vere, Earl of Oxford and eighty men. A good deal of fraternising with the rebels appears to have gone on, so he was sacked by Edward in December 1473 and replaced by John Fortescue, Sheriff of Cornwall.

Bodrugan supported Richard III in 1483 and gained rebel lands after the failure of Buckingham's Revolt in October of that year. He led a force to Cotehele House (see Cotehele) to take possession of Richard Edgcumbe's property in late 1483/early 1484. He was present at the Battle of Bosworth joined the unsuccessful Lambert Simnel rebellion in 1487 and fought at the Battle of Stoke Field.

Do visit this marvellous stretch of **coastline**. It makes a great walk with a historical focus and provides a break from sunbathing. The walk can be extended to Gorran Haven. Head straight through Mevagissey (very narrow streets) and park in Portmellon (¾ mile south). Head southwards and upwards, but keeping left round the point to reach open country. Follow the path past Chapel Point to find Colona Beach and the National Trust sign. Continue along the clifftop path through splendidly wild scenery. On your return from Mevagissey, head south-west on minor roads to the delightful church of **St Michael Caerhays** (about 4 miles). There is nothing of relevance to the Wars of the Roses to see, but that is the point. Caerhays is a good example of why so many churches have to be locked today. The church brochure explains all.

Bodrugan's Leap, located on the Cornish coast.

ST MICHAEL'S MOUNT *** £

Take A394 to Marazion. Once there you cannot miss the
Mount. NB: accessible via the causeway for only 2 hours
each side of low tide, and by boat at other times in season.
NT. 01736 710507.

This is the perfect Wars of the Roses site for the
holidaymaker. A visit fits nicely into a day on the
superb beach at Marazion. On 30 September 1471
John de Vere, 13th Earl of Oxford, accompanied by
his two brothers and his faithful companion, <u>Viscount
Beaumont</u> (see Wivenhoe), sailed into Mount's Bay
with approximately eighty men and, by stealth, occupied the monastery and the Mount. Since the Battle
of Barnet, he had been ineffectually harassing Essex
and conducting some pirating on the side. Oxford proceeded to hold the Mount against Yorkist forces until
February 1474. Edward IV mobilised local Cornish
forces under Sir John Arundell, our friend <u>Sir Henry
Bodrugan</u> and John Fortescue. Regular clashes
occurred, but the Yorkists could not force the issue.
Fraternisation built up and Bodrugan was suspected
of making financial gains (the rebels were victualled).
Arundell was killed in one of the skirmishes and
in December Bodrugan was removed. Edward sent
four ships to provide a supporting naval blockade
and Fortescue was put in charge. His most powerful weapons were pardons given to him by Edward.
By February 1474 only eight or nine men remained
with Oxford. Despite having plenty of stores, he was
forced to surrender, having negotiated for his own and
Beaumont's life. Both were attainted and spent the
next ten years incarcerated in Calais prisons.

A visit to the Mount is a great experience. It is
steep but it has great views. Only the chapel (where
<u>Sir John Arundell</u> is buried with no memorial)
and the hall retain any fifteenth-century flavour
but the visitor really does get a sense of the
island's invulnerability. A few men could hold it
indefinitely against any number of assailants. But
the opposite also holds true. Once Oxford and his
men were ensconced on the Mount, they were, in
fact, imprisoned. After Edward laid down his naval
blockade, they were trapped and besieged. Why did
Oxford do it? One reason was perhaps that he had
anticipated an invasion of Cornwall by the French
king, Louis. One of his brothers sailed over to France
in November – perhaps to set this up – but it did
not happen. Alternatively, Oxford may at that time
have been in cahoots with George, Duke of Clarence,
who, since Tewkesbury, had become the largest
landowner in the West Country. Perhaps he was

expecting Clarence to raise the West Country against
his brother, Edward IV.

This ill-judged venture thus ended all 'Lancastrian'
opposition to Edward, and the country enjoyed nearly
ten years of peace.

SALISBURY

Marketplace ****

In city centre, with some parking.

Two **plaques** beside Debenham's front entrance
commemorate the execution of **Henry Stafford,
2nd Duke of Buckingham** in front of Richard III
on 2 November 1483 after the failure of the revolt
given his name. The unrest was widespread through
southern England in October 1483 and had its origins
in the Westminster sanctuary plots that occurred
among Woodville and former Lancastrian sympathisers from July 1483. In September, Dowager Queen
Elizabeth Woodville and Lady Margaret Beaufort
had reached agreement that Elizabeth of York should
marry Margaret's son, Henry Tudor, now that it was
clear that the two Princes were dead. This would
broaden the appeal of Henry's claim to the throne
very considerably.

At five centres – Maidstone in Kent, Guildford
in Surrey, Newbury in Berkshire, Salisbury in
Wiltshire and Exeter in Devon – large numbers of disenchanted gentry and yeomen took up arms against
Richard. This was no peasant revolt. Former members
of Edward IV's household were prominent in the
risings, having joined the cause as rumours of the
murder of the Princes grew through the summer of
1483. Buckingham was induced to join the revolt by
John Morton, who had been sent by Richard III to
Buckingham's castle at Brecon under 'house arrest'
following Richard's Second Coup in June 1483.
Morton persuaded Buckingham to acknowledge Henry
Tudor as heir to the Lancastrian faction and to invite
Henry to invade England from Brittany in concert with
the main risings.

Gales and torrential rains prevented Buckingham
from making progress beyond the Forest of Dean.
The rivers were unfordable and his tenants, many
unwilling Welshmen, slipped away. On the run,
Buckingham was betrayed by one of his tenants in
Shropshire. Meanwhile Sir Thomas Vaughan had
seized Brecon Castle for King Richard. The rest of
the risings were unfortunately not well coordinated
and Richard, through John Howard, Duke of Norfolk
and Lord Cobham, was able to snuff them out with

little real fighting. Henry Tudor's fleet was unable to land in the West Country because of the storms, and so the revolt petered out. Sir George Browne and St Thomas St Leger (Richard's brother-in-law) were also executed during the uprising. The result was more of an armed demonstration than an active rebellion.

However, crucially, it established Henry Tudor as the main rival to Richard III for the throne of England, appealing to unregenerate Lancastrians, Woodvilles and former adherents to Edward IV and Edward V. The widespread belief that the two Princes were now dead and Henry's pledge to marry Elizabeth of York underpinned this dramatic development.

Cathedral

½ mile south of marketplace.

In the **nave** there is the tomb-chest and effigy of Lord John Cheyne (d. 1501), a rarity in the Wars of the Roses – someone known to be a genuine hero. Cheney, a giant of a man in any era at 6ft 8in, was knocked out of the saddle by a blow from

Richard III himself at the climax of the Yorkist 'death ride' during the Battle of Bosworth in August 1485. His intervention almost certainly saved Henry Tudor's life, because Richard just failed to reach Henry himself. Cheyne had been a squire of the body to Edward IV. He was a prominent gentry leader in the 1483 Buckingham Revolt against Richard III, after which he joined Henry in exile. He was ennobled at the first parliament after Bosworth.

In the **nave** are two tomb-chests of the Hungerford family, prominent Lancastrians from Heytesbury, who have left their mark in many locations in Wiltshire and Somerset. Firstly, Walter, Lord Hungerford (d. 1449) was Lord High Treasurer to Henry VI. His son, Robert, who became 2nd Lord but died in 1459, is also here. Lord Robert's son, in turn another Robert (Lord Moleyns by marriage), had been captured by the French at the Battle of Castillon in 1453 and ransomed for a huge amount, no doubt reflecting the great wealth acquired by the Hungerford family under Henry VI. When Robert senior died, his wife, Margaret, née Botreaux, was left to carry on the fight to pay the ransom but preserve the Hungerford estates. She was not helped by the unregenerate Lancastrian

Effigy of Lord Cheyne, Salisbury cathedral.

sympathies of her son Lord Moleyns and his eldest son, Thomas.

Moleyns fought at Towton, was attainted but joined the Lancastrians in Northumberland. He was executed after the Battle of Hexham 1464. His son, Thomas, was executed by Edward IV for treason in January 1469 and is said also to be buried in the cathedral. Margaret died in 1478 and had her own chantry in the cathedral. Walter, Moleyns' second son, made his peace with Edward IV, joined Buckingham's Revolt in 1483 and regained the family estates after fighting at Bosworth.

In the **south aisle** the tomb-chest of Lionel Woodville, Bishop of Salisbury, brother of Queen Elizabeth Woodville. He was an active plotter against Richard III in 1483 but died in 1484. His tomb-chest is now thought more likely to be that of Dean Gilbert Kymer (1449–63). But there are other anonymous tombs in the nave so perhaps Lionel is here after all. Never mind, we get two for the price of one. A distinguished physician and dietitian, Gilbert Kymer accompanied Henry V to France and attended Humphrey, Duke of Gloucester. He was Dean of Salisbury from 1449 to 1463. On 5 June 1455 he was summoned to Windsor to attend Henry VI, who was once again ill, within a fortnight of the Battle of St Albans. Given the proximity of Clarendon to Salisbury, Kymer may also have been in attendance at Henry's first breakdown in August 1453. So here is one of the men who actually tried to help Henry during his illnesses.

Note also in the **nave** the tomb-chest of Richard Beauchamp, Bishop of Salisbury from 1450 to 1481, who supervised the building of St George's Chapel, Windsor on behalf of Edward IV.

The King's House in the cathedral close (now a museum). **Richard III** stayed here at the time of Buckingham's execution.

SUDELEY, Castle **

South-east of Winchcombe village, signposted.
01242 602308.

In the early 1440s Ralph Boteler (d. 1473), recently created Lord Sudeley by Henry VI, began building a fortified manor house on this site. A large portion of that house survives in the **Inner Court**, the **Gateway** to the **Outer Court**, **St Mary's Church** and the **Tithe Barn**.

Lord Ralph had had a good French war, including being appointed Captain of Calais. As a trusted member of the King's household, Ralph

was made Knight of the Garter and then Lord High Treasurer of England. (Treasurers under Henry VI were wealthy men.) The highlight of the house for the Wars of the Roses is the church, on whose frontage are two **statues**, of **King Henry** and **Queen Margaret of Anjou** (the figures are not original). There is also modern stained glass inside. Lord Ralph continued into the 1450s as a prominent courtier and king's councillor. Surprisingly, considering his age, he was present at the First Battle of St Albans for Lancaster and was slightly injured. Although reconciled to Edward IV in the 1460s, he declared early for the Readeption of Henry VI in 1470. He is famous for parading Henry through the streets of London with Archbishop George Neville (the Kingmaker's brother) in 1471 in an attempt to drum up support for the faltering Lancastrian cause ahead of the Battle of Barnet. It is said that George needed to hold the King's hand throughout the procession. The parade did more harm than good.

Lord Ralph's daughter-in-law, Eleanor, née Talbot (widow of his son Thomas), was the Eleanor Butler (d. 1468) with whom Edward IV was claimed by Richard, Duke of Gloucester in 1483 to have had a pre-contract to marriage before Edward married Queen Elizabeth Woodville. Richard used this argument to declare the Princes in the Tower illegitimate in 'Titulus Regulus' (Richard's 'usurping' act of parliament of 1483) and therefore to make himself king.

Lord Sudeley lost possession of the house in the late 1460s. Edward IV granted the castle to his brother **Richard, Duke of Gloucester**, who is said to have used it as a base prior to the Battle of Tewkesbury (1471). Richard built the splendid banqueting hall in the **Inner Court**, now ruined. In 1478 Richard swapped Sudeley for Richmond Castle in Yorkshire with his brother Edward, as he sought to consolidate his power base in Yorkshire. When he seized the throne in 1483, Richard got Sudeley back. After the Battle of Bosworth, Henry VII granted Sudeley to his uncle, Jasper Tudor, now Duke of Bedford.

TEWKESBURY, Abbey ****

At south end of town centre on A430 to Gloucester.

This splendid church is much associated with the nearby battle. In the **choir** there is a nineteenth-century floor **brass** commemorating **Edward, Prince of Wales**, son of Henry VI, who was killed at the

Statue of Henry VI, Sudeley Castle. The figure is not original.

Battle of Tewkesbury. His death, followed by the murder of his father in the Tower, marked the end of the House of Lancaster.

In the **ambulatory** behind the high altar the remains of **George, Duke of Clarence** (1449–k.71) and his wife, Isabel Neville, elder daughter of Warwick the Kingmaker, lie in a vault marked by a brass.

After the battle, in 1471, many of the defeated Lancastrians sought sanctuary in the abbey. Edward IV gave them short shrift. They were dragged out and many executed the next day in the marketplace. Their bodies, together with those slain in the battle, were buried in the **north transept** of the abbey, including Edmund Beaufort, 4th Duke of Somerset. There is no memorial. The **sacristy door** in the ambulatory is said to be made from plate armour picked up by monks from the battlefield and hammered flat. The inner roof of the **tower** is decorated with Yorkist badges added after the battle. Note also the Beauchamp Chantry (opposite the shop in north aisle), built around 1430 by Isabella le Despenser in memory of her first husband, Richard Beauchamp, Earl of Worcester. Her second husband was also a Richard Beauchamp, this time Earl of Warwick (see St Mary's, Warwick).

THE BATTLE OF TEWKESBURY
(4 May 1471) +++++
Strategic Background and the Campaign
King Edward IV had regained his throne and ended the six-month-long Readeption of King Henry VI in dramatic fashion at the Battle of Barnet on Easter Sunday, 14 April 1471. The Earl of Warwick and the rest of his Neville family were destroyed. King Henry found himself back in captivity in the Tower, while Edward was reunited with Queen Elizabeth Woodville and their new-born son, Prince Edward, in Westminster Abbey, where the Queen had been in sanctuary. However, on the very day of the Battle of Barnet, Henry's Queen, Margaret of Anjou, and his son, another Prince Edward, landed at Weymouth from exile in France and were met by Edmund Beaufort, Duke of Somerset and John Courtenay, Earl of Devon, leaders of the 'old' Lancastrian faction. Margaret, long the driving force behind the Lancastrians because of her husband's insanity, immediately set about raising forces in the West Country. Margaret based herself at Exeter, and the process proved very successful because of the area's deep Lancastrian roots. One source tells us, 'the whole might of Devon and Cornwall was behind her.

Meanwhile King Edward, now governing the country from London, heard about Margaret's landing within two days. In order to be master of his whole kingdom, Edward needed to confront Queen Margaret with all urgency before support for her cause increased markedly. Most of his victorious army from Barnet had been disbanded, so he had to start again by sending the usual commissions of array to fifteen counties. He called for his men to muster at Windsor, and by 24 April was on his way to Cirencester. Queen Margaret really had two strategic options:

- To make for the Welsh Marches, link up with Jasper Tudor's Welsh army and then head for the Lancastrian stronghold in the north of England.
- To march directly on London via Hampshire, Sussex and Kent.

It appears Edward guessed correctly that the first of these was her preferred plan (she was never popular in London). By 30 April he had moved so quickly that he reached Malmesbury and was, in fact, already in a position to cut off the Lancastrian army, now in Bristol, from the river crossings further up the River Severn. The Lancastrians would need to use these in order to link up with Jasper Tudor in Wales. Queen Margaret had stopped off in Bristol to refresh her troops and take in much-needed arms. By a neat piece of deception, Margaret persuaded Edward that the Lancastrians were going to give battle at Sodbury. The Yorkists in fact took up position on Sodbury Hill, but nothing happened.

Instead, Queen Margaret had ordered a night march along the banks of the Severn towards Gloucester and so slipped through Edward's net. Early on the morning of 3 May, Edward grasped the situation and set off in pursuit on the Portway, the ancient road high up on the western edge of the Cotswolds – the two armies now travelling northwards in parallel at top speed. Edward had sent a message to Sir Richard Beauchamp, governor of Gloucester town and castle, to prevent the Lancastrian army from entering the town and gaining access to the river crossing. Despite the strength of the Lancastrian army, Sir Richard achieved this (for which he was later rewarded by Edward) and they were forced to continue up the Severn towards the Tewkesbury crossing. The men-at-arms were by now exhausted from the effects of their night march. The Lancastrians arrived at Tewkesbury in the evening of 3 May, but a crossing of the Severn was now out of the question because of the proximity of Edward's force. They encamped for the night.

Edward's army had experienced similar problems caused by the long, rapid march – over 30 miles on 3 May. Their particular problem was the lack of water on the Cotswold plateau. It was not until Cheltenham that Edward allowed his army to eat and drink. Having ascertained that the Lancastrians had not been able to cross the Severn, Edward made camp at Tredington, 3 miles south of Tewkesbury.

The Battle
Very early in the morning of 4 May, Edward roused his army and moved up to Tewkesbury in order to prevent the Lancastrians eluding battle again. They crossed the River Swilgate and marched along the ridge to beyond Stonehouse Farm. The Yorkists were arrayed in three battles – the left led by Richard, Duke of Gloucester, the King in the centre with his other brother, George Duke of Clarence (where he could be kept an eye on), and the right led by William, Lord Hastings.

The Lancastrian position was somewhat protected by scrubland and deep lanes and dykes, and had the advantage of a small hill. Somerset commanded the right, Prince Edward and Lord John Wenlock the centre (he was a very experienced soldier – see Luton), and the Earl of Devon the left. The Yorkists had considerably more field guns and so Edward opened up with these and the usual archery barrage, targeting Somerset's division. Unable to reply to similar effect, Somerset was quickly forced to lead a charge down to the Yorkist guns. This may have been a prearranged move but it took the attack crashing diagonally into Edward's centre division not Richard's division on the Yorkist left. Perhaps it had been arranged that simultaneous support would be provided by the other Lancastrian commanders, Wenlock and Devon. As it was, none was forthcoming. It appears there had been dissension among the Lancastrian commanders in their battle-planning sessions. Somerset had been given overall command because of previous military experience and because of his royal blood, but he was an arrogant and forceful man. Somerset's division was now badly exposed to attack by Richard of Gloucester's men. On top of this, a plump of 200 mounted spearmen hidden by Edward in Tewkesbury Park chose this moment to attack from the wooded hill. The Lancastrian right were pushed back up their hill; then the line broke and they fled, many being killed in what became known as 'Bloody Meadow'.

Somerset managed to make his way back to the Lancastrian centre and is said to have confronted Wenlock, accused him of being a traitor to the cause and, without pausing, dashed out his brains with

a poleaxe. This has some credibility – Wenlock had fought for the Yorkists and, while he had been in the service of Queen Margaret in the 1450s, was really a confirmed Warwick supporter. The Lancastrians had hardly provided sterling support to Warwick at Barnet. Whatever the truth of the matter, the Lancastrian line now disintegrated. The Earl of Devon, Sir John Beaufort (Somerset's brother) and, most famously, Prince Edward were killed in the field, the latter probably as he fled towards the abbey. Many survivors took sanctuary in the abbey but Edward ruthlessly burst into the church under arms and forcibly removed them. A number were killed in the process, so that the abbey was considered so polluted that it had to be reconsecrated later in May by the Bishop of Worcester.

Aftermath and Commentary
Two days after the battle, the Lancastrian prisoners were tried by Richard, Duke of Gloucester in his capacity as Constable of England. Most were found guilty of treason and beheaded in Tewkesbury marketplace – Somerset, Sir John Langsbrother, Sir Gervase Clifton and nine others – but some were pardoned, among whom was Sir John Fortescue, Henry VI's Lord Chief Justice and Queen Margaret's long-time adviser. Margaret herself was captured the next day by Sir William Stanley at a nearby 'poor religious house', probably Little Malvern Priory. With her were Anne Neville, Princess of Wales and two other 'new' widows.

England was still troubled by risings in both the north and in Kent. After the battle, Edward headed straight for Coventry, where he met Henry Percy, Earl of Northumberland, who informed him that there was no need for the King to go north, because he himself had captured the leaders and the threat had disappeared. This left only the rising in Kent and London led by Thomas Neville, Bastard of Fauconberg (a natural son of Warwick's uncle, William, Lord Fauconberg). Stiff resistance in the city of London on 14 May ensured that this dangerous revolt was not a success.

On 21 May 1471 Edward returned to London in triumph with his army. The Duke of Gloucester led a procession containing four other dukes (including Clarence), six earls and sixteen barons, including Hastings. At the rear of the procession was a carriage containing the captured Queen Margaret. A solemn service of thanksgiving was held at St Paul's Cathedral. That night, King Henry VI was murdered in the Tower, undoubtedly on the orders of Edward IV, probably conveyed by Richard of Gloucester as

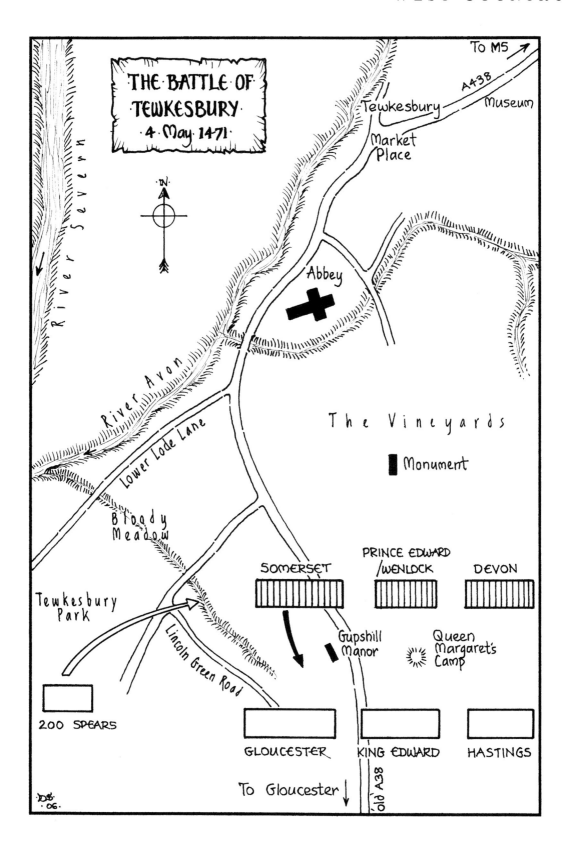

THE BATTLE OF TEWKESBURY · 4 · May · 1471

River Severn

River Avon

To M5

A438

Museum

Tewkesbury

Market Place

Abbey

Lower Lode Lane

The Vineyards

■ Monument

Bloody Meadow

Tewkesbury Park

Lincoln Green Road

SOMERSET

PRINCE EDWARD /WENLOCK

DEVON

Gupshill Manor

Queen Margaret's Camp

200 SPEARS

GLOUCESTER

KING EDWARD

HASTINGS

To Gloucester ↓

'old A38

DS · 06 ·

Constable of England. With King Henry and his son Prince Edward and Warwick dead, and the real Lancastrian mastermind, Queen Margaret, in custody, Edward was for the very first time in full command of his kingdom. Even Jasper Tudor, Henry VI's step-brother, went into exile in France, but taking with him his nephew, one Henry Tudor, Earl of Richmond by now aged 14. It was these two, together with Henry's redoubtable mother, Lady Margaret Beaufort,

who kept the Lancastrian cause alive for the next twelve years.

Edward had regained his kingdom through stunning victories at Barnet and now at Tewkesbury. While the detailed tactical picture in each battle remains somewhat confused, there is much to admire in Edward's awesome speed and decision in the manoeuvring preceding each battle. He was a general without peer in the Wars of the Roses.

Participants and Casualties
Yorkists (~5,000)
King Edward IV
George, Duke of Clarence
Richard, Duke of Gloucester
William, Lord Hastings
Thomas Grey, Marquis of Dorset
John Mowbray, Duke of Norfolk
John Butter, Earl of Ormonde
John Brook, Lord Cobham
George Neville, Lord Abergavenny
Sir Ralph and Richard Hastings
Sir Richard Croft
Sir John Savage
Sir John Stanley
Sir Henry Pierrepont
Sir Thomas Mongomery
Sir Thomas Vaughan
Sir Humphrey Blount
Sir James Tyrell

Lancastrians (~6,000)
Prince Edward of Wales
Edmund Beaufort, Duke of Somerset
John, Lord Wenlock
Sir John Beaufort
John Courtenay, Earl of Devon
Sir Robert Whittingham
Sir John Fortescue
Sir John Delves
Sir Hugh Courtenay
Sir John Lewkenor
Sir Gervase Clifton

Casualties: Lancastrian ~2,000 dead, Yorkist light

Location and What to See
The battle was fought astride the 'old A38' road ¾ mile south of Tewkesbury Abbey, in the area of Gupshill Manor and Queen Margaret's Camp. Tewkesbury is proud of its association with the battle and has done much to encourage interest, despite the unfortunate encroachment of housing which has occurred in recent years.

Visit the **museum** near the old market cross (east side), where there is a model of the battle and a full list of participants. Purchase a map of the excellent battle trail, which can be followed free of charge.

On the way to the abbey, pass through the old marketplace with **cross**. It was here that the Lancastrian captives, including **Edmund Beaufort, Duke of Somerset**, were beheaded two days after the battle.

Start and finish your battle trail walk at the abbey. Walking anticlockwise with the map of the battle trail, note the following:

- The **River Swilgate**, where many Lancastrians were slain or drowned as they fled back to the abbey after the battle.
- Lower Lode Road, the line of the old Gloucester–Tewkesbury road along which the Lancastrians marched.
- **Bloody Meadow**, again where many Lancastrians were slain. Information board at one end.
- **Tewkesbury Park**, where the plump of 200 Yorkist spearmen hid.
- **Lincoln Green Lane**, where the most intense fighting between Somerset and Richard, Duke of Gloucester may have occurred.
- (Taking the longer route) **Gupshill Manor**, now a pub and a good place for lunch, because they also have an information board. Queen Margaret stayed here before the battle. Note also Queen Margaret's Camp which is actually an older earthwork.

Bloody Meadow – scene of great slaughter during the Battle of Tewkesbury.

Gupshill Manor, Tewkesbury.

- On the return towards the abbey, note the monument in the **Vineyards** as you pass the playing fields.

While visiting Tewkesbury also visit these sites (see West Midlands) – all connected with the battle:

- **Didbrook church**.
- **Bushley place and church**.
- **Birtsmorton church**.
- **Little Malvern Priory**.

TORTWORTH, St Leonard's Church *
2 miles east of junction 14 on M5, north of B4509 to Wotton-under-Edge on minor road to Damery.

The tracery of the **south chapel** east window contains fragments of fine fifteenth-century Yorkist glass, including white roses and sunbursts (perhaps after the Battle of Tewkesbury?). Two heads and crowns are visible, one of which is said to be **Edward IV**; but bring your binoculars. While at Tortworth, why not visit nearby **Berkeley Castle**, which was the focus of an incredibly long-running inheritance dispute between the Berkeleys and the Talbots. This resulted in the Battle of Nibley Green (also nearby) in 1470, the last private battle in England. Stained glass in the great hall of the castle commemorates the feud.

WELLS, Cathedral *
Town centre.

In the **south-east transept**, a big unattributed tomb-chest to Dean Gunthorpe (d. 1498). Gunthorpe was dean of the Chapel Royal in Windsor under Edward IV, and King's Almoner. He was a distinguished academic, a Cambridge humanist, who had studied in Italy and became warden of King's Hall, Cambridge. In May 1483 Richard III appointed him Keeper of the Privy Seal in his government, at the same time as Bishop Russell, his predecessor, became Chancellor.

While you are in Wells, do have a meal or stay at **the George Hotel** in the High Street at nearby **Glastonbury**. Described by Pevsner as 'one of the most sumptuous of the small number of surviving inns of before the Reformation', its front archway is topped by the arms of **Edward IV** and of the abbey. Further east along the High Street, **St John the Baptist Church** contains fifteenth-century glass with sunbursts, and tombs of Richard Atwell (d. 1476) and his wife Joan (d. 1485), a wealthy cloth-merchant family who contributed to the church.

WIMBORNE, Minster ***
Town centre, west of River Stour.

In the **chancel** a fine tomb-chest for **John Beaufort, 1st Duke of Somerset** (1404–44) and his wife, Margaret Beauchamp of Bletsoe, Bedfordshire (d. 1482), widow of Sir Oliver St John. They were the parents of Lady Margaret Beaufort, in turn Henry Tudor's mother. Lady Margaret was the only surviving child of the marriage as the Duke died when Margaret was only 1 year old.

YEALMPTON, St Bartholomew's Church *
Village centre, south side of A379 Plymouth–Kingsbridge road.

In the north transept, a fine brass to Sir John Crokker (d. 1508). The Latin inscription tells us that Sir John was standard-bearer to Edward IV, presumably at the Battle of Tewkesbury (1471), where he was knighted. Hampton tells us that Sir John was one of those ordered by Edward to take St Michael's Mount from the Earl of Oxford in 1473. In October 1483 Sir John joined Buckingham's Revolt against Richard III in Exeter, but was not attainted when it collapsed. He may be the John Crokker who fought at Bosworth for Henry Tudor. He certainly assisted Henry's forces in the defence of Exeter against Perkin Warbeck in 1497.

EAST OF ENGLAND

ALDBURY, St John the Baptist Church ***
Western edge of village on road to Tring.

In the Pendley Chapel a fine tomb-chest and effigies of Sir Robert Whittingham (k. 1471) and wife, Katherine Gatewyne. He was Captain of Caen when it fell in 1450. Sir Robert became a household servant of Henry VI and an adherent of Edmund Beaufort, Duke of Somerset. From 1456 he was a founder member of the Prince of Wales' Council (receiver-general). He was a financier but very much a 'fighting accountant'. He fought at the First Battle of St Albans and at Wakefield. He was knighted after the Second Battle of St Albans (February 1461) and fought at Towton, after which he escaped with the King and Queen to Scotland. He took part in the abortive attack on Carlisle in June 1461. He was one of the Queen's inner circle and became keeper of her great wardrobe (his wife was one of her ladies-in-waiting) and joined her in exile in the 1460s at Koeur in the Duchy of Bar in France. He returned to England in April 1471 but was killed at the Battle of Tewkesbury (May). He was a true Lancastrian die-hard.

ASPENDEN, St Mary's Church **
Aspenden is at the southern end of Buntingford. From London, follow signs for Buntingford centre from A10, south exit. Turn first left (½ mile) to Aspenden. Right at T-junction to end of 'no through road'.

A **wall** tomb-chest and brasses to Sir Robert Clifford (d. 1508) and wife. Sir Robert was a member of the Clifford clan from Skipton, Yorkshire (they held lands in Hertfordshire, as well). The Cliffords were Lancastrians; Sir Robert's father and two brothers all died in the cause, while his nephew Henry was brought up in hiding in the Pennines (the 'Shepherd Lord'). However, be warned: Sir Robert may not have been nice to know.

He took part in Sir William Brandon's unsuccessful rising against Richard III at Colchester in October 1483 at the time of Buckingham's Revolt. He fought at the Battle of Stoke (1487) for Henry Tudor and was knighted after the battle. He became knight of the body and Master of Ordnance to Henry VII. In 1493 Sir Robert became involved with Sir William Stanley in the Perkin Warbeck conspiracy against Henry. Sir William was the brother of Henry VII's father-in-law, the Earl of Derby, and it was his intervention at the Battle of Bosworth that had saved Henry. Early in 1495 Sir Robert, bribed by Henry, turned King's evidence. Stanley was tried and executed in February 1495, and Warbeck's invasion in July ended in fiasco. The suspicion is that Sir Robert was in the King's service all along.

BACONSTHORPE, Castle **
3 miles east of Holt. From Holt, take minor road signposted Hempstead and Baconsthorpe. At east end of village, turn left on farm track to castle.

This is for you if you like your sites minimalist: there is no kiosk, no toilets, no audio-guide, no charge – just a farmyard, the castle remains and a lake, but a delightful picnic spot. Ignore the sixteenth-century hall, nearest the road. The original castle is further back. It was built between 1450 and 1486 by John Heydon (1405–79) and his son Sir Henry (1440–1504). Your enjoyment of this delightfully rural spot might be affected when you realise that we are celebrating one of Norfolk's most notorious characters. John Heydon was a lawyer, a member of William de la Pole, Duke of Suffolk's council and deputy steward of the Duchy of Lancaster. During the 1440s, under Suffolk's protection, he terrorised the local community through an extortion racket and by controlling the appointments of sheriffs. He featured on a Commons petition in 1451 listing twenty-nine people in the county who had been wronged by him. Unusually at this period, Heydon worked consistently with another 'gangster', Sir Thomas Tuddenham. They appear in the literature usually as a pair – Heydon and Tuddenham – just like Bonnie and Clyde. Tuddenham lived at Oxborough. Much time was spent feuding with John Mowbray, Duke of Norfolk and the Wingfields. Heydon has been described as 'even less scrupulous than Tuddenham!'

Baconthorpe Castle is the physical manifestation of these ill-gotten gains. Heydon typically ignored the usual permits required to build a castle. Both Heydon and Tuddenham had unhappy marriages – both their wives carried other men's babies (and Tuddenham's wife also entered a convent) – while Heydon's father-in-law married Tuddenham's mother-in-law. The Duke of Suffolk's murder in 1450 clipped their wings but they were not brought to justice until after Edward IV's accession in 1461. Tuddenham was executed but Heydon granted a pardon. However, his 'working' life was over – he received no more appointments. So ended one of the most notorious examples of the corruption and physical intimidation

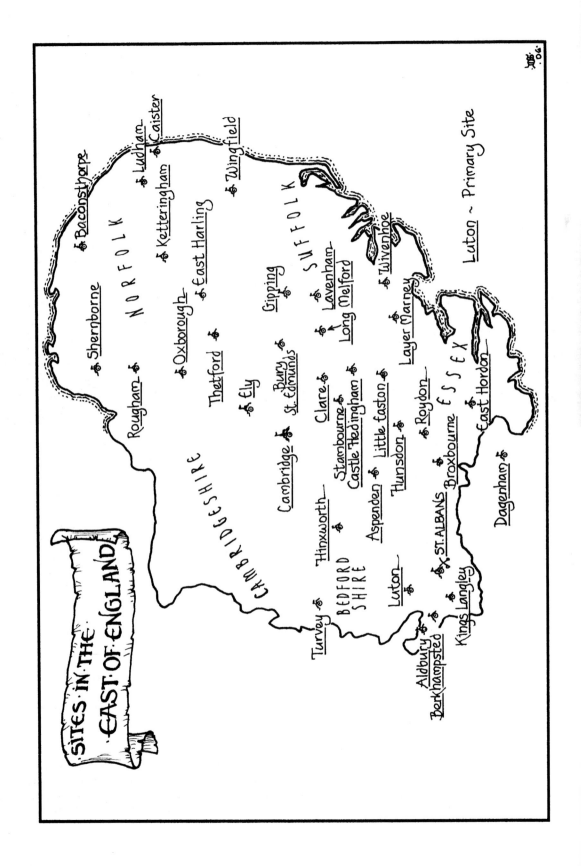

Sites in the East of England

Luton ~ Primary Site

NORFOLK

Baconsthorpe
Ludham
Caister
Wingfield
Ketteringham
Shernborne
East Harling
Rougham
Oxborough
Gipping
SUFFOLK
Thetford
Ely
Bury St. Edmunds
Lavenham
Long Melford
Wivenhoe
Layer Marney
Clare
Cambridge
Stambourne
Castle Hedingham
Little Easton
Roydon
ESSEX
East Horndon
CAMBRIDGESHIRE
Hinxworth
Aspenden
Hunsdon
Broxbourne
St. Albans
BEDFORD SHIRE
Luton
Dagenham
Turvey
Kings Langley
Aldbury
Berkhampsted

Baconsthorpe Castle, built by John Heydon.

that were so widespread at this period. His son Henry, also a lawyer, was knighted in 1485 and was also a builder. He built Salthouse church in Norfolk and the hall at West Wickham, Kent (now a school).

BERKHAMSTED, Castle (ruins) ** £

½ mile north-east of town centre, by railway station, on Ashridge road.

A large site, now mostly earthworks, unusual in originally having a double moat. The castle was owned by the Duchy of Lancaster in the fifteenth century. It was one of the Home Counties castles in which **Henry VI** spent his childhood and was a favourite of his. In 1448 it passed to **Queen Margaret of Anjou**. At the height of Jack Cade's Rebellion in June 1450, Henry fled here for one night en route to Kenilworth to join Queen Margaret, thus leaving London at the mercy of the rebels. To quote Griffiths, 'the abandonment of London by the frightened king was a fateful step', which came back to haunt the King and Queen in February 1461.

In 1469 Edward IV effectively banished his mother, **Cecily, née Neville**, from her London home, Baynard's Castle, to Berkhamsted Castle. (She dabbled too much in political matters during the Clarence–Warwick uprisings of that year.) It became her principal home until her death here in 1495. It was here that Richard, Duke of Gloucester came to stay in April 1483, prior to his bid for the throne.

There is a brass in **St Peter's Church** to Robert Incent (d. 1485), one of Duchess Cecily's servants. His son went on to found the local grammar school.

BROXBOURNE, St Augustine's Church **

2 miles south of Hoddesdon. From A1170 Hoddesdon–Cheshunt road take B194 Broxbourne–Waltham Abbey road. Church is on the edge of large green, just before railway station. Rectory next door.

In the **chance**l a delightful tomb-chest and enamelled brass to Sir John Say (d. 1474) and his wife, Elizabeth, née Cheyne, and canopied tomb to their son Sir William Say (died early sixteenth century)

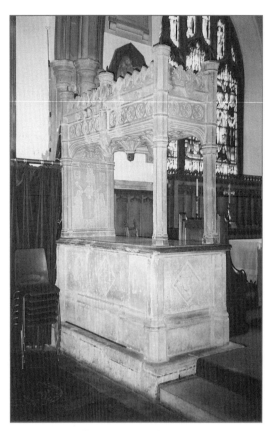

Tomb of Sir William Saye, Broxbourne church.

and wives. Here is a Lancastrian family who changed sides and became solid Yorkists (note Sir John's collar). Originally a client of the Duke of Suffolk in the 1440s Sir John became an esquire of the body to Henry VI and chancellor of the Duchy of Lancaster. He was elected Speaker in the troubled year of 1449 and then specifically named and formally indicted by Cade's rebels in 1450 as a traitor. Unlike others of the king's councillors, Say escaped with his life although he was threatened on Blackheath. He was a Council member from 1454–6 during York's First Protectorate, perhaps owing his position to links to Henry, Viscount Bourchier through his stepdaughter. This could also explain his conversion to the Yorkist cause in 1460, which led to his reappointment as chancellor of the Duchy of Lancaster in 1467. Sir John died in the mid-1470s.

Sir William, his son by Elizabeth Cheyne, was knighted at the coronation of Richard III and may have fought at the Battle of Bosworth (1485) for Richard.

BURY ST EDMUNDS, St Mary's Church *
Town centre, between cathedral and brewery.

Fine tomb-chest and effigies in **chancel** to Sir William Carew (d. 1501) and wife, Margaret. He was knighted on the field after the Battle of Stoke Field (1487) by Henry VII. He may have also fought for him at Bosworth. Note also the cadaver monument to John Baret (d. 1467) with the Lancastrian 'SS' painted on the aisle roof above. Mary Tudor, daughter of Henry Tudor and Elizabeth of York and sister to Henry VII, also has a monument in this church.

While you are in Bury, do stroll in the abbey gardens, just north of the cathedral. St Edmundsbury was one of the most important and wealthy monasteries in England, and the gardens give a good indication of the sheer size of these institutions. It is most likely that Humphrey, Duke of Gloucester, Henry V's last surviving brother, was murdered in his lodgings in Bury in 1447, not long after being summoned to see Henry VI, his nephew.

CAISTER, Castle (remains) * £
1 mile west of Caister-on-Sea. Signposted south to Motor Museum off A1064 Norwich road. Open mid-May–September (not Saturdays).

Somewhat bizarrely this castle coexists with a classic car museum. It was built from 1432 by Sir John Fastolf, one of the few heroes of the French wars, who fought at the battles of Verneuil, Patay and the Herrings. Sir John also made his fortune and used it to extend his lands in England. The castle was one of the first brick buildings in the country and was really more of a fortified manor house.

When Sir John died in 1459, he left only an oral will to his lawyer, John Paston, in which he gave all his East Anglian lands to Paston, who duly took over the castle. In August 1469, however, while Edward IV was imprisoned by the Kingmaker, **John Mowbray, 4th Duke of Norfolk** (who had first laid claim to the castle in 1452) laid down a full-scale siege of Caister with 3,000 men in an attempt to take it over. It was one of the few sieges to take place in England during the Wars. After five weeks, the Pastons surrendered because of lack of food and supplies. Much damage was done to the castle fabric when artillery fire was exchanged. For the next seven years, the Duke occupied the property, until his death in 1476. Within a few days, John Paston II occupied the castle and eventually regained title to the property from Edward IV upon payment of a fine. While not an event of any national significance, the feud over Caister is a very good example of the violence which regularly flared up between members of the aristocracy in East Anglia and elsewhere at this time.

CAMBRIDGE ****

City centre walk: King's Parade (head for King's College), St John's Street, Sidney Street and Silver Street.

Always a pleasure to visit, not least because of its compactness, Cambridge contains one of the finest medieval buildings in England, but is also full of surprises for the Wars of the Roses enthusiast.

Recommended walk: from King's Parade, turn left to visit **King's College Chapel** (£). The ultimate contradiction in the Wars of the Roses, this is the finest memorial in this guide but dedicated to the man whose incompetence and unfitness caused them. The chapel was founded in 1441 by **Henry VI** for a rector and twelve scholars, with links to Eton School (similar to those of Winchester School with New College, Oxford, which was founded in the 1370s by William of Wykeham). Work on the building went on until Henry's deposition in 1461. Not surprisingly, Edward IV provided no funds until 1477. Richard III

increased funding, but then, surprisingly, Henry Tudor stopped the work until 1508 (he was a renowned miser). Only after a visit to the city did Henry agree to finish the chapel. This was achieved by 1515, after Tudor's death. Hence, the first surprise is that King's is really as much a celebration of the Tudor triumph as of Henry VI himself. It is festooned inside and out with **Tudor emblems** – Tudor roses, red dragons, portcullises (the emblem of **Lady Margaret Beaufort**, Henry VII's mother), the crown in a thorn bush (from the Battle of Bosworth). Nevertheless, there is a statuette of Henry VI on the **lectern**, plus a likeness in the **west window glass**. It is altogether a monument matched only by St George's Chapel, Windsor, in turn designed to celebrate the Yorkist triumph of Edward IV.

Be careful not to miss the brass by the **altar** to Dr John Argentein (d. 1507), who was Edward IV's and Edward V's physician and the last man to see the latter alive in the Tower of London in the summer of 1483.

Return to King's Parade, and turn left up Trinity Street to **Trinity College**. Head for the **hall** in Great Court. At the north (far) end of the hall, behind the roped-off area and hidden away on the left-hand windows (west), is an absolutely delightful stained-glass portrait of **Richard, Duke of York**, he who

King's College, Cambridge, a celebration of Tudor triumph.

'gained battles in vain', and father of Edward IV and Richard III. Part of Richard's Mortimer estates were centred on nearby Clare, in Suffolk. The college hall is sixteenth century but very much in the Perpendicular style. Note the late hammer-beam roof.

Continue up St John's Street to **St John's College** and note the splendidly elaborate heraldic carving on the sixteenth-century **gatehouse**. The carving came from Queens' College. **Lady Margaret Beaufort** founded St John's posthumously in 1511.

Turn right down Bridge Street and Sidney Street. Proceed south to **Christ's College**. This was refounded by **Lady Margaret Beaufort** in 1505. Once again, the **gatehouse** is covered in an enormous coat of arms resplendent in Lady Margaret's Tudor devices.

Take Petty Cury to return to King's Parade. Turn left and proceed to Silver Street. Turn right and right again into Queens' Lane. **Queens' College** was refounded by **Queen Margaret of Anjou** in 1448 in order to emulate her husband Henry VI's foundation of King's 'to laud and honneurre of sexe feminine'. In 1465 **Queen Elizabeth Woodville** became 'foundress

Left: *Stained glass of Richard, Duke of York, Trinity College, Cambridge.*
Below: *Queens' College, Cambridge, founded by two fifteenth-century queens.*

by right of succession', necessitating the movement of the apostrophe. Front Court was built in 1448 and remains the best example in Cambridge of a complete medieval court. Old Hall and Cloister Court are also noteworthy. There is a portrait of Queen Elizabeth but it is rarely on view to the public. Note also the mathematical bridge at the rear of Cloister Court. Here is another surprise in Cambridge – that three senior female members of the royal families were very much involved in founding educational establishments exclusively for men at such an early date.

CASTLE HEDINGHAM

Castle, ** £
North-east edge of village. 01787 460261.

There was no military action here during the Wars but this castle formed the nucleus of the de Vere estates in East Anglia and was thus home to one of our heroes, **John de Vere, 13th Earl of Oxford** (d. 1513). The castle and grounds are a delight to visit and look exactly the part. The keep is Norman but the 13th Earl apparently added a good number of early Tudor outbuildings etc. once he had been restored to his lands after Bosworth in 1485. He built the **brick bridge** over the dry moat in 1496. John was visited in 1498 by Henry VII. Probably apocryphally, it is said that Henry was so upset by de Vere's apparent disregard for the new laws banning private liveries for armies that he fined him 15,000 marks (a small fortune at the time).

St Nicholas Church
Village centre.

The 13th Earl also carried out significant rebuilding in the church, e.g. the hammer-beam roof. However, we are looking for the frieze of shields above the **west window** *outside* the church. These refer to the **13th Earl** of Oxford and include a boar, his Lord Great Chamberlain's chain of state, and the notorious 'star on a shield badge' which was part of the dramatic confusion that took place at the Battle of Barnet (1471).

CLARE, Priory ***
South of village centre. Park in Castle country park and head over the river.

In the delightful ruins of the old priory we can ratchet back into the fourteenth century. Open to the elements near a tomb-chest is the grave of Lionel, 1st Duke of Clarence (1338–68), the second surviving son of Edward III and the man through whom **Richard, Duke of York** based his claim to the throne in October 1460. Lionel is buried with his first wife Elizabeth de Burgh (1332–63) through whom he acquired Clare Castle and estate. Lionel's second marriage was to Yolande Visconti, but he died shortly after the wedding, in Piedmont, Italy.

Also buried at Clare is Edmund Mortimer (1391–1425), son of Roger, who was Richard II's heir apparent and brother to Anne Mortimer, the mother of Richard, Duke of York. Edmund was technically the heir to the Mortimer claim to the throne, in whose name the Percys revolted unsuccessfully against Henry IV at the Battle of Shrewsbury in 1403, and Richard, Earl of Cambridge hatched the Southampton Plot in 1415. In fact, Edmund remained steadfastly loyal to both Henry IV and Henry V, personally alerting Henry V to the existence of the plot. Edmund died childless in 1425, when his vast estates and claim to the throne passed to his nephew Richard, Duke of York. The main centres of the Mortimer estates were in the Welsh Marches (Ludlow), in Ireland and at Clare. Do not forget to explore the **castle** nearby.

DAGENHAM, St Peter and St Paul's Church **
Surrounded by modern housing. Lies 200 yards north-west of B178 road (which links A1306 Dagenham–Grays road to A1112 Dagenham–Chigwell road), just before roundabout with A1112. Turn off B178 (Ballard's Road) and right into Church Lane.

An urban story for an urban site. The church contains a fine tomb-chest and brass of Sir Thomas Urswick (d. 1479) and wife. He was Recorder of London at the time of the 1471 conflict between Edward IV and Warwick the Kingmaker. In the run-up to the Battle of Barnet, it was Thomas who secretly let Edward IV and his followers into the city of London on 11 April 1471, through Bishop's Gate, at a time when it was not exactly clear which side the city was going to support in the ensuing conflict. Edward's swift action in sending King Henry VI back to the Tower (along with Archbishop George Neville of York, the Kingmaker's brother) ensured that the city's mind was made up.

A month later, having defeated the Kingmaker, Edward was busy on his Tewkesbury campaign. Kent meanwhile had been stirred to rebellion by Thomas Neville, the Bastard of Fauconberg (one of the natural sons of William Neville, Lord Fauconberg, uncle

Tomb-chest of Sir Thomas Urswick, Dagenham church.

of Warwick the Kingmaker). On 14 May his rebels launched a full-scale assault on the city, one of the rare occasions in the Wars when a town was attacked. Earl Rivers and the Earl of Essex were on hand with defending troops, but at the Aldgate it was Robert Basset and Thomas Urswick who raised the portcullis and sallied forth to defeat the rebels.

On Edward's triumphant return from Tewkesbury a week later, Thomas was knighted for his efforts, along with more than ten others – an unprecedented distribution of honours to civic dignitaries. A short time later, Sir Thomas was made Chief Baron of the Exchequer.

EAST HARLING, St Peter and St Paul's Church **
North-west of village centre on B1111 to Watton, near River Thet. Open summer afternoons.

This splendid church contains two items of interest. First is the wonderful stained glass in the **east window**, presented by Sir Robert Wingfield when the church was rebuilt in 1480. At the bottom of the window are two kneeling figures – Sir Robert and his wife Ann's first husband, Sir William Chamberlain. Sir William (d. 1462) was a war hero from France who opposed the Calais Earls in their drive from Sandwich in early 1460. He was made Knight of the Garter to replace Lord Welles. His son, Sir Robert Chamberlain, joined Edward IV in exile in 1470 and acted as one of his scouts when considering Norfolk as a possible landing place on Edward's return in 1471. (The decision was negative, so the fleet continued to Ravenspur, Yorkshire). Ann was the heiress to Sir Robert Harling. Her second husband, Sir Robert Wingfield (1430–81), was a member of one of the most unruly and violent families in East Anglia. Traditionally clients and neighbours of the Mowbray dukes of Norfolk, for some time they fell out and sided with the de la Pole dukes of Suffolk. Sir Robert was a second son, who was knighted in

Stained glass of Richard, Duke of York's head, Cirencester church.

Cecily Neville, Edward IV and Elizabeth Woodville kneeling before the Trinity, The Luton Guild Book.

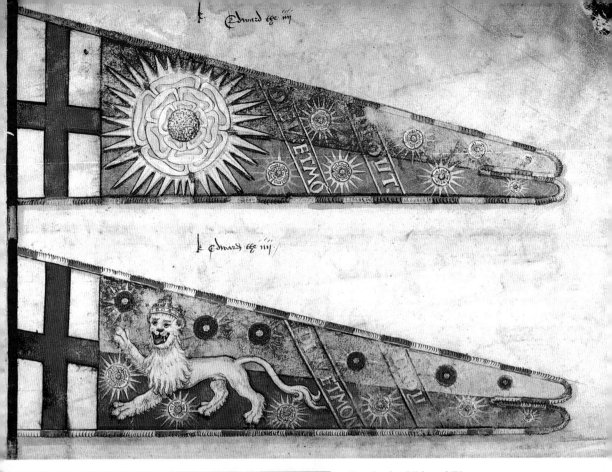

Standards of Edward IV.

The marriage of Edward IV and Elizabeth Woodville in 1464.

Stained glass portrait of Edward V, Coldridge church. The hovering crown indicates that Edward was never crowned.

Below, left: Garter stall plate of George, Duke of Clarence from St George's Chapel, Windsor.

Below, right: White boar emblem of Richard III on the pulpit of Fotheringhay church.

Weeper of Richard Neville, Earl of Warwick (the Kingmaker) on the tomb of his father-in-law Richard Beauchamp, Earl of Warwick, St Mary's Church, Warwick. It is the only surviving likeness of this overmighty subject.

Below, left: Garter stall plate of John Neville, Marquess Montagu, one of the Kingmaker's younger brothers, St George's Chapel, Windsor.

Below, right: Tomb of John de la Pole, Duke of Suffolk, Wingfield church, Suffolk.

Garter stall plate of William, Lord Hastings, Edward IV's loyal companion, St George's Chapel, Windsor.

Stained glass portraits of Elizabeth Talbot and Elizabeth Tilney, Duchess of Norfolk, Long Melford church, one of many windows that portray a large number of women.

The chapel of Wakefield Tower in the Tower of London where Henry VI is said to have been murdered by the Yorkists after the Battle of Tewkesbury in May 1471.

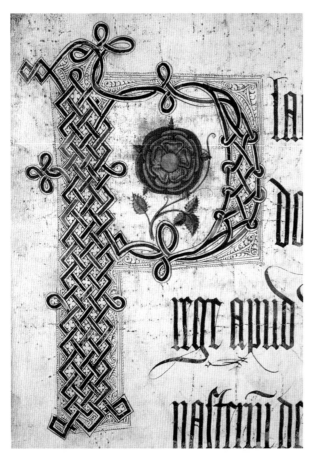

Lancastrian rose from a King's Bench Roll of Henry VII's reign.

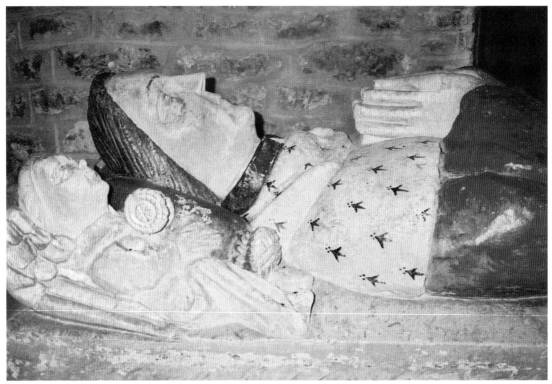

The tomb of Sir John Fortescue, Ebrington church. Sir John was tutor to Prince Edward (Henry VI's son) during exile in France in the 1460s.

The Tudor version of the royal line: Henry VII, Edward V (uncrowned) and Edward IV. From the painted screen of Bishop Oliver King's Chantry, Sir George's Chapel, Windsor.

Torrigiano's masterpiece, the effigy of Lady Margaret Beaufort, Westminster Abbey. Lady Margaret's scheming was crucial to the success of her son Henry Tudor.

The execution of Lancastrian Edmund Beaufort, Duke of Somerset after the Battle of Tewkesbury in May 1471.

Garter stall plate of Henry Stafford, Duke of Buckingham, executed by Richard III in late 1483 after his unsuccessful revolt.

Bodiam Castle. Sieges were rare in lowland England but one occurred here in 1483.

The delightful effigy of Sir Alexander Culpepper, Goudhurst church.

Herstmonceux Castle, an early brick building started by Sir Roger Fiennes in the early 1440s.

Sir Robert Harcourt's tomb, Stanton Harcourt church.

Stained glass portrait of Sir Robert Wingfield, East Harling church.

The roses ceiling in the tower of St Albans cathedral.

Stained glass portrait of Sir Thomas Montgomery, Long Melford church. Sir Thomas benefited from the death of his elder brother in 1462.

Oxborough Hall, built by Sir Edmund Bedingfield in the 1480s.

The Shernborne village sign commemorates Sir John Shernborne, who is buried nearby.

History lives on in strange ways – above, an Australian vineyard named after the Battle of Bosworth; below, a kneeler in Sutton Cheney church near the Bosworth battle site.

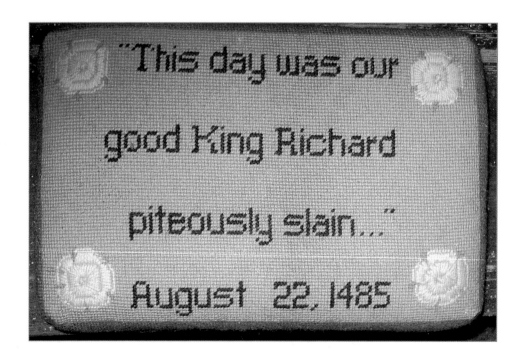

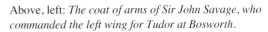

Above, left: *The coat of arms of Sir John Savage, who commanded the left wing for Tudor at Bosworth.*

Above, right: *Garter stall plate for Sir Thomas Burgh.*

The old hall at Gainsborough, rebuilt by Sir Thomas Burgh during the 1470s after being sacked by Lancastrians.

History lives on in strange ways – this filling station is next door to the battle site at Losecote Field.

A beer mat from the public house at Mortimer's Cross.

Yorkist suns commemorating the nearby battle on the roof of Tewkesbury abbey.

The fabulous tomb-chest and effigy of Richard Beauchamp, Earl of Warwick, father-in-law to the Kingmaker, St Mary's Church, Warwick.

Raglan Castle, built by William Herbert, Earl of Pembroke and his father.

The motte of Sandal Castle from where Richard, Duke of York was lured to his death in December 1460 at the Battle of Wakefield.

Roses placed at the battlefield cross on the 544th anniversary of the Battle of Towton. This takes place each year.

Dunstanburgh Castle. The Northumberland castles saw much action between 1461 and 1464.

1465 at Queen Elizabeth's coronation. He went into exile with Edward IV in 1470. Sir Robert gained notoriety as sheriff by failing to send a single prisoner into King's Bench (trial) for thirty-three years. He was on the Duke of Suffolk's council in the 1470s.

Sir William and Ann are commemorated by a tomb-chest and canopy in the **chancel**.

EAST HORDON, All Saints' Church **

This is a challenge to visit. The church is now all alone on a hilltop, cut off from the village by the A127 London–Southend road. It stands above the A127–A128 interchange, 4 miles south of Brentwood. From the interchange take the A128 north, and after ½ mile take the first turning left, signposted for the Halfway House Motel. The church is reached after ¼ mile, through a gate on the left. The church is managed by the Churches Conservation Trust (phone 01787 237132).

Once you are there, this site does not disappoint. The interior of this brick church is delightful in itself. Our interest is in the tomb-chest with brass commemorating Sir Thomas Tyrell (d. 1476) and wife. Sir Thomas was a significant player in 1450s politics as a member of Henry VI's Council and adherent of Edmund Beaufort, Duke of Somerset. He was sheriff and MP for Essex during his career and became a King's Knight. He was involved in the suppression of Cade's rebels in Essex in 1450 and was in fact specifically listed by the rebels as a target in their manifesto.

Sir Thomas was given a key task in October 1453, after King Henry's mental breakdown, to act as a link between the Council and Richard, Duke of York, which led to Richard coming back into the fold and his eventual appointment as Protector in March 1454. Tyrell was probably chosen for this delicate task because he had common ground with York, having fought in France under Bedford. He was one of the Lancastrians holed up in the Tower in July 1460 under the command of Lord Scales after the Yorkist invasion from Calais and the Battle of Northampton.

ELY, Cathedral ***

City centre.

This beautiful building is the setting for monuments to three important members of the governments during the Wars of the Roses. In the **south choir aisle** there is a tomb-chest with effigies commemorating the colourful John Tiptoft (c. 1417–70),

Earl of Worcester and two of his three wives. To modern eyes, the character and career of Tiptoft appear a total contradiction. On the one hand, he is remembered as an extremely cultured and learned man who studied classics in Italy and even impressed Pope Pius II with his erudition. His father, the first Lord Tiptoft, died in 1443 and John was promoted to earl at 22 years old. He was Lancastrian Lord Treasurer from 1452–4, and royal councillor, but was fortunate to be sent on a diplomatic mission to Italy in 1458. He delayed his return until late 1461, by which time it was clear the Yorkists would remain in power. Edward IV immediately placed him back in his old roles, adding Constable of England for good measure. He was a pillar of Edward's government in the 1460s. He spent two years in Ireland but was recalled after Warwick's coup in 1469. He again became Constable and, for a third time, Lord Treasurer.

Tiptoft is, however, also remembered as 'Butcher of England' because of the overzealous manner in which he carried out his duties as Constable. Traitors, however minor, were hanged, drawn and quartered, while Tiptoft introduced into England the Italian technique of impalement of offenders on wooden stakes after death. Unfortunately, in 1469 he chose some members of the Kingmaker's retinue for this treatment, for which he paid the ultimate price. On Henry VI's Readeption in 1470, Tiptoft was the only supporter of Edward IV's to be executed. Amid great public rejoicing, ice cool, he is said to have asked the axeman to use three blows rather than one in honour of the Trinity. In three blows, the learning in England was said to have been halved. Interestingly, Tiptoft's first wife, Cecily Neville (d. 1450), who is commemorated here, was the Kingmaker's sister, whose first husband was the infamous Henry Beauchamp, Duke of Warwick. Wife number two was Elizabeth Greyndour, widow of Reginald West, Lord de la Warr, and the third wife was Elizabeth Hopton. After a long gap, Elizabeth later married Sir William Stanley.

At the east end of the **north aisle**, the delightful Alcock Chantry celebrates the life of Bishop John Alcock (1430–1500), successively bishop of Rochester, Worcester and Ely, and president of the Council of Edward, Prince of Wales until 1483 (based at Ludlow). He then became a member of Richard III's Council and temporarily Lord Chancellor. He founded Jesus College, Cambridge and commissioned the superb stained glass of Edward IV's family in Little Malvern church.

A tomb-chest and effigy in the north-west bay of the presbytery celebrates <u>Bishop Richard Redmayne</u> (1458–1505), who came to Ely via Shap Abbey, St Asaph and Exeter. He was councillor to Richard III and was with the King when he received the Great Seal from Bishop Russell at the Angel in Grantham. He was pardoned by Henry VII in 1486 but implicated in the 1487 rebellion of the Earl of Lincoln, about which Henry complained to the pope. He did, however, recover favour with Henry and died a wealthy man.

GIPPING, St Nicholas's Church ****

3 miles north-east of Stowmarket, deep in the countryside. From A14 south take second Stowmarket exit on A1120 to Stowupland. After 2 miles, go straight on at corner on to minor road to Saxham Street and Gipping. Follow road round to left for 3 miles. Turn right to church on cul-de-sac.

This fabulous little church deep in the Suffolk countryside stands as a memorial to <u>Sir James Tyrell</u> (1445–1502), remembered by Sir Thomas More's history and by Shakespeare as one of the most notorious of murderers. On the eve of his execution by Henry VII for treason, Sir James is said to have confessed to having orchestrated the murder of the two Princes in the Tower in 1483 on the orders of Richard III.

Son and heir of William Tyrell, James was knighted after the Battle of Tewkesbury in 1471. He became a retainer of Richard, Duke of Gloucester. Tyrell became highly valued by Richard, often being given sensitive duties, e.g. escorting the Dowager Countess of Warwick to Richard's castle at Middleham, Yorkshire in 1476. During Richard's Second Coup in June 1483, Thomas Rotherham, Archbishop of York and a Woodville supporter, was committed to Tyrell's keeping for a time. Once Richard was installed on the throne, Tyrell was showered with rewards – knight of the body, Chamberlain of the Exchequer, Master of the Horse and Henchman. He received enough lands from attainders to boost his income to the level of a lord. He used this wealth to build this church, and which almost shouts 'James Tyrell' at you – his knot is everywhere, and even his name.

Pevsner, perhaps being uncharacteristically mischievous, puts the date of construction at '*c.*

Gipping church – heraldry of Sir James Tyrell. He is 'everywhere' in this building.

1483'. So the suggestion is raised that this church is built with money gained from the foulest of political murders, which shocked even contemporaries. The church guidebook takes a different approach, suggesting that most of the church was started from 1474.

No evidence has ever been put forward to implicate Tyrell in the murders. Henry VII never made Tyrell's confession public and no copy has survived, but contemporary chroniclers quickly latched on to Tyrell. He had certainly made an unusually smooth transition to Henry's rule in the mid-1480s for a former member of Richard III's inner circle. He continued to be knight of the body and Captain of Guisnes Castle, a position given to him in early 1485 by Richard (he thus missed Bosworth later that year). His background as Richard's 'odd job' man does make him a very credible suspect and most historians stick with Tyrell having done the deed. He could even have done the deed later for Henry himself. Certainly, this is a beautiful location and lovely church to ponder such hideous events. Gipping Hall was directly east of the church but only a moat survives. It was believed that the two Princes may have been hidden there.

HINXWORTH, St Nicholas Church **

South-east edge of village on Ashwell road. 2 miles north of Baldock, 2 miles north-east of A1. Turn off A1 1 mile north of Baldock services.

This delightful church houses brasses of <u>John Lambert</u> (d. 1487), his wife <u>Anne</u> (d. 1489) and their six children. John was a prosperous moneylender who dealt with both Henry VI and Edward IV. He was sheriff of the City of London. However, our main interest is in the eldest of his daughters, Elizabeth, who is known to history as <u>Jane Shore</u>, mistress of Edward IV, Lord Hastings and, probably, Edward's brother-in-law, the Marquis of Dorset. Elizabeth married William Shore. By 1476 she was petitioning the pope for annulment of her marriage on the grounds of non-consummation so that she could have children. Jane features in Shakespeare's *Richard III* and Sir Thomas More's works. She seems to have acted as a messenger in May and June 1483 between Hastings and Dowager Queen Elizabeth Woodville. At his second *coup d'état* in June of that year, Richard of Gloucester included Jane in his accusations of plotting to kill him (along with Hastings, Morton, the Dowager Queen, etc.). On Sunday 15 June, Jane was forced to do public penance at St Paul's, carrying a lighted taper and wearing only her kirtle. She was

Brass of Elizabeth née Lambert (known as Jane Shore, mistress of Edward IV), Hinxworth church.

then imprisoned. On her release, Jane attracted the attention of Richard's solicitor, Thomas Lynom, and remarried. Despite this, she died in 1527, widowed and destitute, her story re-emerging as a cautionary tale for later Tudor audiences.

HUNSDON, St Dunstan's Church **

1½ miles south of village on east side of minor road to Harlow (via A414) which forks off B180 Stanstead Abbots road.

The **east window** dates from the mid-fifteenth century. It commemorates <u>Sir William Oldhall</u> (d. 1460), whose badge can be seen. In north and south windows are visible the Yorkist badges of fetterlock and white rose. In the late 1440s Richard, Duke of York gave the manor of Hunsdon to Sir William, who had been his chamberlain since 1441. Oldhall built the house next door (much altered and extended by Henry VIII during conversion to a royal palace) and significantly rebuilt the church.

Oldhall had been a war captain with both Henry V and John, Duke of Bedford. By the mid-1440s he had become York's chief adviser in Rouen when York was Lieutenant-General. He continued this role back in England, becoming personally implicated in the anti-government events of the early 1450s – stirring up Cade's Rebellion, Suffolk's murder and York's Dartford fiasco. Oldhall became Speaker in 1450, even though he had never been an MP. He was seen by the Court party as York's strategist and 'Mr Fix-it'; he did at times keep some unsavoury 'friends' (e.g. Sir Thomas Tuddenham, Charles Nowell). After York's fiasco at Dartford he fled to sanctuary in St Martin-le-Grand, London. Initially, he was dragged out of the church by a group of Lancastrian nobles but, on Henry VI's orders, he was returned to sanctuary. Over the next months, however, he was stripped of his possessions, including the house in Hunsdon, which went to Edmund Beaufort, Duke of Somerset. He was attainted in May 1453 but this was reversed during York's Protectorate the next year.

He was present with the Duke of York at the rout of Ludford Bridge in the autumn of 1459, for which he was once again attainted. He was also captured and thus did not accompany the Duke of York in the flight to Ireland, where, interestingly, York found himself isolated from his closest allies and advisers (the Earl of Salisbury, Sir William Herbert, Sir Walter Devereux and Oldhall). He died at about the same time as his protector, York, in late 1460.

KETTERINGHAM, St Peter's Church *

4½ miles south-west of Norwich, close to A11. From Norwich turn left after the hall in Hethersett, down minor road to Ketteringham. Turn right at T-junction after 1 mile, and left after ½ mile into grounds of Ketteringham Hall. KAL.

In the **chancel** a mural brass to <u>Sir Henry Grey</u> (d. 1491/2) and his wife <u>Emma, née Appleyard</u>. Unfortunately, Sir Henry's figure is missing. He fought for Edward IV at the Battle of Tewkesbury alongside John Mowbray, 4th Duke of Norfolk and was knighted there. Sir Henry was buried in the chancel and his coat of arms can be seen on the bottom row of the **east window** – the red lion of Grey, rampant, joined with the three owls of Appleyard.

KING'S LANGLEY, All Saints' Church ***

1 mile north of M25, Junction 20. Church is at south end of village, just down from A4251 'old' Berkhamsted road.

In the **north-east chapel** a splendidly colourful tomb-chest commemorating <u>Edmund of Langley, 1st Duke of York</u> (1341–1402) and his first wife <u>Isabella of Castile</u> (c. 1355–92). Edmund was the fourth surviving son of Edward III and very much overshadowed by the third son, John of Gaunt. He was a political lightweight at this level. Richard II left him as regent while visiting Ireland in 1399. Edmund eventually sided with Henry Bolingbroke, Gaunt's son, after Gaunt usurped the throne during Richard's absence. Edmund had been created Duke of York in 1385 by Richard II thus founding the House of York. Edmund's two personal devices were a white rose and a fetterlock with a falcon in it. He completely rebuilt Fotheringhay Castle, given to him by his father. Isabella was the sister of Gaunt's second wife, Constance. She seems to have been a handful. Described by monastic chroniclers as a 'soft and lascivious woman', she was notorious for the number of her lovers.

Both Edmund and Isabella's corpses were exhumed in the nineteenth century. During the work, a third corpse was discovered in a coffin. Alison Weir tells us this is <u>Anne, née Mortimer</u> (1390–1411), daughter-in-law to Duke Edmund and wife to Richard, Earl of Cambridge, York's second son. She died soon after giving birth to her second child, Richard, later to become 3rd Duke of York. Anne therefore represented the crucial link between the Mortimer claim to the throne of England, held by her father Roger and then her brother Edmund, and the Yorkist dynasty. Edmund died childless in 1425, leaving Anne's son Richard as heir to the claim which was eventually to propel Richard's son to the throne as Edward IV in 1461.

LAVENHAM, St Peter and St Paul's Church ***

South-west side of town centre.

The excellent guidebook tells us that this magnificent church is in fact a celebration of the Tudor victory at the Battle of Bosworth (1485). **John de Vere, Earl of Oxford**, church patron, orchestrated a total rebuilding of the church from 1486, celebrating the battle's outcome, on which he personally had such an impact. The work was largely financed by the town's wealthy clothiers, the Springs and the Branches, and was finished by 1525. De Vere's personal contribution was the splendid **south porch**, which contains his heraldic devices of the **boar** and the **star**. In the south aisle interior is a parclose screen around a tomb-chest. This also includes some interesting heraldic carvings. De Vere was not buried here, but in Earls Colne Priory.

South porch, sponsored by John de Vere, Earl of Oxford after Bosworth, Lavenham church.

LAYER MARNEY, Tower and St Mary the Virgin Church ** £

1 mile south of B1022 Colchestrer–Tiptree road. From Colchester, turn left off B1022 after 6 miles, signposted to house. Church is round the back of the house. 01206 330784.

A great place to visit for the lover of Tudor brick. <u>Henry, Lord Marney</u> and his son <u>John</u> rebuilt the church and began building the **house** around 1510. Henry died in 1523 and John followed only two years later, so the house was unfinished, but what a monument to both men. Henry became Captain of the King's Bodyguard, councillor and Keeper of the Privy Seal under the Tudors and was ennobled. He had fought at the Battle of Stoke Field (1487) for Henry Tudor and was an executor of Lady Margaret Beaufort's will.

The **church** contains splendid tomb-chests and effigies to both men.

LITTLE EASTON, St Mary's Church ***

2 miles north-west of Great Dunmow. Take B184 Thaxted road out of Great Dunmow. After 2 miles, fork left and left again after ¼ mile. Church is on right after 1 mile.

Tucked away in this corner of rural Essex we suddenly come across a monument to two members of the fifteenth-century higher aristocracy who were close to royalty, both in terms of breeding and during their lives. A lovely canopied tomb-chest and enamelled brasses (still with some of their original colour) celebrates **Henry Bourchier, Earl of Essex** (1404–83) and his wife, **Isabel Plantagenet** (1409–84).

Isabel was the elder sister of Richard, Duke of York. On his side, Henry's mother, Anne, was the daughter of Thomas of Woodstock (Edward III's sixth son). Blood does not get much bluer than this. From the 1450s Henry was an early supporter of his brother-in-law, the Duke of York, and became

Engraving of the brass of Henry Bourchier, Earl of Essex and Isabel Plantaganet, Little Easton church.

a staunch supporter of Edward IV, being Lord High Treasurer of England from 1460–2 and 1471–83.

LONG MELFORD, Holy Trinity Church ****

In northern half of village, on the green, above the A1092 road to Haverhill.

At first sight this splendid Perpendicular church seems to offer just another commemoration of an East Anglian gentry family, in this case the Cloptons. There is a Clopton **chantry chapel** and a number of fifteenth-century memorials. The tomb-chest in the chancel of <u>Sir John Clopton</u> (d. 1491), Sheriff of Suffolk in 1452, is of particular interest. In early 1462 a Yorkist double agent unearthed

a Lancastrian plot to kill Edward IV led by John de Vere, 12th Earl of Oxford and his son Aubrey, in liaison with Queen Margaret of Anjou. On 12 February, Oxford, his son and four others, including John Clopton, were sent to the Tower. The other four were tried by John Tiptoft and savagely executed on Tower Hill; only Clopton was spared.

But Long Melford has much, much more – a unique collection of late fifteenth-century **stained glass** in the **north aisle**, containing portraits of East Anglian aristocrats, many of whom were either involved in the Wars of the Roses themselves or married to a participant. In fact the really unusual thing about the portraits is that they are mainly of women. Obtain a copy of the special guide to the stained glass. Here are the highlights:

- Elizabeth Talbot, wife of **John Mowbray 4th Duke of Norfolk** (d. 1476). She was mother of Anne Mowbray, who, aged 4, married Richard, Duke of York, Edward IV's second son, in 1478.
- Elizabeth Tilney, wife of **Thomas Howard, 2nd Duke of Norfolk** (d. 1524), who was prominent in Richard III's Second Coup in 1483 and was injured at Bosworth, where his father was killed.
- Elizabeth Howard, wife of **John de Vere, 12th Earl of Oxford**, who was executed by Edward IV in 1462. She was the sister of **John Howard**, later **1st Duke of Norfolk**.
- Anne Wenlock (née Danvers), wife of Lord John Wenlock, who was killed at the Battle of Tewkesbury (1471) (see Luton).
- Ann Darcy, wife of Sir John Montgomery of Faulkbourne, Essex, another of the 1462 conspirators executed by Edward IV. Sir John built Faulkbourne Hall from 1439; it is still in use as a private house.
- Sir Thomas Montgomery (1430–95), young brother of Sir John above. An early Yorkist who was one of Edward IV's personal companions, and knight of the body 1461–83. He fought at the battles of Towton, Tewkesbury and Bosworth, and was a Knight of the Garter. Edward used him as a diplomat and it was he who accompanied Dowager Queen Margaret of Anjou back to France in 1475 – no doubt a very satisfying task for a Yorkist. After Edward's death, Sir Thomas continued in Richard III's household but fell from grace after problems while deputising as Captain of the Calais garrison in 1484. He nevertheless fought for Richard at Bosworth.
- Sir Robert Clifford (d. 1508), who betrayed Sir William Stanley in 1495 (see Aspenden).
- Sir John Clopton (see chancel).
- Elinor Darcy, wife of Sir William Tyrell of Gipping, Suffolk, who was executed in February 1462 by the Yorkist regime for his part in the plot led by the Earl of Oxford. Sir William and Elinor were the parents of the infamous Sir James Tyrell, who may have murdered the Princes in the Tower (see Gipping).
- Elizabeth Fray, wife of Sir Thomas Waldegrave of Bures, who was knighted by Edward IV at the Battle of Towton (1461).

The original selection of portrait subject was not arbitrary. As Hampton points out, 'virtually every-one of these persons was in some way injured by one or both of the Yorkist Kings.' But is there something more? One window has Sir Thomas Montgomery flanked by his brother John and by Sir William Tyrell. Both John and Sir William were savagely executed with the Earl of Oxford for treason against the Yorkist regim in 1462. Sir Thomas, by contrast, became a pillar of the Yorkist regime, having been appointed sheriff of Norfolk by Edward IV from 1461. Does a theme of betrayal run through these portraits? Sir Robert Clifford, for example, is known to have turned King's evidence against Sir William Stanley in 1495.

LUDHAM, St Catherine's Church *
Village centre, on A1062 Hoveton – Potter Heigham road.

This church contains one of the best rood screens, showing **Henry VI** alongside ten saints. It was built in 1493 at the height of the campaign initiated by Lady Margaret Beaufort to have Henry made into a saint. The pope refused. Lady Margaret had particularly fond memories of her introduction to Court, when Henry showed her much kindness and is said to have personally championed Edmund Tudor as her husband – one of the rare examples when Henry's royal will comes through to us.

LUTON

St Mary's Church ***
South-east corner of town centre area, immediately next to university buildings. (tower) If church is closed, try PO (east end).

Modern Luton may win awards for being the worst town in England, but to the Wars of the Roses enthusiast it has two fine locations to visit. Here we encounter one of the rogues of our story – a rogue whose reputation was eventually his undoing. In the **Wenlock Chapel** is a plaque commemorating the founding of the chapel by Lord John Wenlock (1400–71) in 1461. Wenlock was killed at the Battle of Tewkesbury (1471) and initially buried in the abbey there, but later reinterred in this chapel. Wenlock was a self-made man and was everywhere. He was an experienced soldier (first fighting in France with Henry V when only 21), a diplomat, a household man for Henry VI and his queen and a politician (he was Speaker at least once). He was knighted in 1447/8. His war record is as long as any. He was badly wounded at the First Battle of

Memorial to John, Lord Wenlock, Luton.

St Albans (1455) fighting for Henry, but changed sides and supported the Yorkists at the rout of Ludford Bridge, escaping overseas afterwards with the three Calais earls. Consequently he was attainted in 1459. He assisted in the surrender of the Tower to the Yorkists in July 1460. He was made a Knight of the Garter and then fought with Warwick and Edward at Towton (having commanded the rear ward at Ferrybridge the previous day). He was ennobled later in 1461.

Then, in 1469, he chose to support Warwick and Clarence. In 1470, as Warwick was fleeing by ship from Edward IV in England, Wenlock famously refused to allow the fugitive entry into Calais, where he was Captain. He later claimed that he was actually protecting Warwick because Calais was a 'vipers' nest' full of treacherous people.

Through his old links with Queen Margaret, Wenlock found himself at the age of 71 commanding the Lancastrian centre division at Tewkesbury. Pre-battle planning with the overall Lancastrian commander, Beaufort, Duke of Somerset, proved difficult. The next day, Somerset led a charge at the climax of the battle, which was ultimately unsuccessful. He felt he had been disastrously let down by Wenlock and his division. Striding back to the Lancastrian centre position in a fury, Somerset is said to have gone straight up to the unsuspecting Wenlock and at a stroke felled him with his poleaxe. Somerset no doubt felt that Wenlock had in fact changed sides yet again and was acting treacherously (or rather not acting) to assist his old Yorkist friends.

In the Wenlock Chapel there is also stained glass to Lord John. Notice the tomb-chest and brass to Lady Alice Rotherham (d. 1490), whose brother-in-law Thomas was Archbishop of York under Edward IV.

Someries Castle (ruin) **

Approachable only from the south-east. Take the B653 Harpenden road out of Luton. After 2½ miles, turn left at crossroads to Chiltern Green and Kimpton. Go under railway and after 1 mile turn sharp to Dane Street and immediately left on narrow road. Proceed straight past Copt Hall, where road becomes unmetalled and is a dead end. Go as far as you can, and ruins are on left.

This is a site that must be approached walking backwards. By so doing, you can imagine that the castle is still located in the rural idyll it occupied 500 years ago. However, if you turn round you immediately realise that the site is now within 400 yards of the south side of the runway for Luton airport. Actually with the wind in the right direction it is still very pleasant, but a sense of humour helps here. Lord Wenlock used his accumulated riches to build this castle (really a brick fortified manor). The gatehouse, the chapel and some walling survive. The house is the earliest in Bedfordshire to use brick.

OXBOROUGH, Hall *** £
Signposted off A134 between Thetford and King's Lynn, 2 miles north-east of Stoke Ferry. NT. 01366 328258

The terracotta monuments in **St John's Church** and the moated house built in *c.* 1482 provide splendid memorials to Sir Edmund Bedingfield (1443–96) and his wife Margaret, née Scott (d. 1514). (The church is not part of the NT property, but next door.) Sir Edmund in fact played a modest part in the Wars of the Roses, being part of Henry VII's force at the Battle of Stoke Field (1487). His family came from Bedingfield, near Eye, in Suffolk. He inherited those estates but, in 1476, also inherited the estate at Oxborough from his grandmother, Margaret, née Tuddenham, sister of the infamous Sir Thomas Tuddenham who was executed for treason in 1462. Tuddenham had terrorised Norfolk during the 1440s and 50s. Sir Edmund moved his seat of power to Oxborough in order to build a grand new house. Meanwhile, in 1472, he had married Margaret Scott from Ashford, Kent daughter of a pillar of the Yorkist establishment, Sir John Scott (see Brabourne). Sir Edmund may have been Yorkist but he seems to have kept his head down until declaring for Henry VII ahead of Stoke Field.

The **hall** is a superb period survival. The huge gatehouse is fabulous (with echoes of Layer Marney – there were family connections) but unfortunately the great hall on the south side has gone. Internally, much use is made of the family device of falcon and fetterlock, very similar to that used by Richard, Duke of York. This device was not used by Edward IV; however, he developed the sunburst and roses device from the Battle of Mortimer's Cross.

ROUGHAM, St Mary's Church *
Village centre ½ mile north of B1145 Gayton–Litcham road.

This totally charming country church contains brasses to the Yelverton family. In the **chancel** north side

can be found a delightful brass, laid down in the early sixteenth century, of Sir William Yelverton (d. 1472) and wife. He was a judge of the King's Bench from 1443, became Lord Chief Justice and was knighted in 1460. He carried on a legal feud with the Pastons, which was ended when his grandson, William junior, married Ann Paston. William junior's step-brother, also William, is commemorated with a brass in the **nave**, north side of lectern. He died in 1510. He was an esquire of the body to Edward IV. Both brasses are under carpets.

Sir William senior was twice removed from the Bench, once for refusing to try Edmund, Earl of Somerset (who was accused of killing Sir Thomas Overbury), but was reinstated. Somerset had been Yelverton's mentor. Yelverton features in the Paston letters. He was on the Duke of Norfolk's council in 1450 and no lover of the fallen de la Pole, Duke of Suffolk. He was involved in trying to bring Thomas Tuddenham and John Heydon to justice. As executor of Sir John Fastolf, he was much opposed to the efforts of John Paston to take possession of Caister Castle.

ROYDON, St Peter's Church **
In village centre, on B181 Epping–Stanstead Abbotts road, just before river and railway.

The **Colt Chapel** (formerly the chancel) contains a floor brass to Thomas Colt (1425–67) and wife; he is in armour, with the indent of a Yorkist collar. Colt came from Yorkshire and was a lawyer and long-serving Neville household man. Initially he served the Earl of Salisbury and then transferred to his son when the latter became Earl of Warwick in 1449. He was MP for Cumberland and chief steward of the North Parks for the earldom. He became Warwick Chamberlain. Colt was present at Ludford Bridge in 1459 and then fled with Richard, Duke of York and John Wenlock to Ireland. He was attainted at the Parliament of Devils later that year.

Colt was in fact a 'fighting solicitor'. Perhaps surprisingly, he accompanied York and Salisbury to Wakefield in December 1460. During the battle, he was sought out and apparently wounded by Lancastrian Roger Thorpe, who was pursuing a family vendetta. Thorpe was the son of Thomas Thorpe, a former Speaker of the House of Commons. Thorpe senior clashed with Colt in 1454 and his son was seeking revenge. Colt later brought an action before Edward IV against Thorpe junior in 1462, although Thorpe had the last word, gaining

Terracotta tomb memorial of Sir Edmund Bedingfield, Oxborough church.

St Albans clock tower provides a great viewpoint for the old streets.

redress from Henry VII in the King's very first parliamentary bill.

After Towton, Colt became King's Attorney and Privy Councillor and was granted the tolls from the bridge at Ware, a Warwick manor. He moved to nearby **Nether Hall**. Wedgwood memorably described Colt as 'the great commoner of the Yorkist Revolution'. Another brass in the chapel commemorates his son John Colt (d. 1521) and wives. The remains of the early Tudor house built by John can still be seen 1½ miles south-west of Roydon on the minor road to **Lower Nazeing**. John's daughter Jane married Sir Thomas More, who will therefore have courted in this house.

ST ALBANS, Cathedral ***
Just south of city centre.

St Albans is a city dripping with action from the Wars of the Roses and proud of it. Two major battles were fought in or around the city, with much of the central

street pattern remaining. After the First Battle of St Albans, the Yorkist leaders accompanied Henry VI to the abbey (as it was then). The Lancastrian dead – the Duke of Somerset, Earl of Northumberland and Lord Clifford – were buried in the **Lady Chapel**, but there is no monument. The **tower ceilings** display red and white roses to make the connection. The **Wallingford Chantry** (1484) in front of the altar displays a rose in sunburst, the badge of Edward IV, but our main interest here is the **Chantry Chapel**, commemorating Humphrey, Duke of Gloucester (1380–1447), Protector to Henry VI in the 1420s. The youngest of Henry V's three brothers, he played an important part in the descent into the Wars of the Roses during the 1430s and 1440s, in that he represented the disaffected pro-war party against the Court party led by Cardinal Beaufort and, later, the 1st Duke of Suffolk, who had the ear of King Henry. He was probably murdered in his lodgings in Bury St Edmunds, upon which the mantle of the disaffected party moved to Richard, Duke of York.

In the chancel is a floor brass to Sir Antony Grey (d. 1480), who was the eldest son of that rogue Edmund, Lord Grey of Ruthin, who treacherously changed sides during the Battle of Northampton (1460), allowing the Yorkists an easy victory. Edmund was appointed Lord High Treasurer in Edward IV's reign and elevated to Earl of Kent in 1465. Treachery paid in those days. His son Anthony was knighted at Queen Elizabeth Woodville's coronation in 1465 and married Joan, one of the many Woodville sisters. He was part of Edward IV's French expedition in 1475.

THE FIRST BATTLE OF ST ALBANS (22 May 1455) ++++
Strategic Background and Campaign

Following the recovery of his wits, King Henry VI appeared unexpectedly in parliament in early February 1455 and dismissed the Duke of York from the office of Lord Protector. A Lancastrian backlash followed, in which the Duke of Somerset was freed from the Tower and restored to his positions of Constable of England and Captain of Calais, the Earl of Salisbury was dismissed as Lord Chancellor and his role given to Archbishop Bourchier, the Earl of Wiltshire became Treasurer and the Duke of Exeter was set free. By such partisan reaction, Henry ensured that from now on the nobility was split into two opposing camps.

By Easter 1455, both sides were plotting and York and the Nevilles (Salisbury and Warwick) were recruiting in the north and Warwickshire. The Court party announced a Great Council meeting at Leicester in late May. York, Salisbury and Warwick were not invited but instead were issued a summons to appear before it. Suspecting the worst, the Yorkists resolved to strike first by intercepting the King on his way to Leicester. York was looking both to gain control of the King and to eliminate his long-standing rival Somerset. Salisbury and Warwick had their eyes on the Earl of Northumberland and Lord Clifford, their antagonists in the north.

The Yorkist troops concentrated at Royston, in Hertfordshire. The leaders issued a manifesto which stated that they meant no harm to the King and that they had only marched south to ensure their own safety. The speed of the Yorkist concentration caught the Court party by surprise. Many nobles were still on their way to join the King after a late summons from Henry. The Yorkist force was probably slightly bigger than the royal one, 2,000/3,000 men compared with 2,000. In addition to the Nevilles, York had with him his 13-year-old son, Edward, Earl of March, plus Lord Clinton, Henry, Viscount Bourchier and his son Humphrey together with, perhaps, Lord Cobham. Henry VI had with him many more nobles, including Somerset, the Duke of Buckingham, Northumberland, Clifford, the Earl of Wiltshire and Jasper Tudor, Earl of Pembroke.

The King's force camped overnight at Watford. Unfortunately, Henry was offered contradictory advice on where to stand and fight by Somerset and by Buckingham. Buckingham advised a move to St Albans. Incredibly, at the last minute Henry put Buckingham in charge of the whole army and Somerset lost his office as Constable. Both sides then tried to negotiate but without success.

The Battle

On the morning of 22 May 1455 the Lancastrians established themselves in the marketplace and manned the east-facing gates at the ends of Sopwell Street, Shropshire Lane (now Victoria Street) and Cock Lane, together with the decayed thirteenth-century town ditch (or at least parts of it). The Yorkists camped in Key Field, to the east of the town, and positioned themselves to attack the gates.

Negotiations were attempted but quickly floundered, so at 1000 hours sharp York and Salisbury suddenly attacked the gates but soon began to suffer casualties in the narrow lanes. To relieve pressure, Warwick attacked the ditch between the gates, 'between the signs of the Key and the Chequer inns'

in Holywell Street (Chequer Street today), south of Shropshire Lane. Making his way largely unopposed, Warwick burst into the marketplace, completely surprising the Lancastrians, so that many were not yet in full armour, with helmets off. They had probably expected the negotiations to continue much longer. Note that some historians believe it was actually Sir Richard Ogle who achieved the crucial breakthrough, Warwick later claiming the credit.

As the alarm bell sounded in the marketplace, many of the Lancastrian defenders abandoned the gates for fear of being trapped, thus allowing the troops of York and Salisbury also to break through to the marketplace. As the Lancastrians attempted to rally around the King in the marketplace, mayhem ensued as Warwick's archers let fly at the massed ranks of nobles. In many ways, St Albans does not really do justice to the word 'battle': in modern parlance it was more of a one-sided gangster shoot-out. Aristocratic casualties were high. Dudley, Stafford (Buckingham's son, who subsequently died of his wounds), Dorset and Wenlock were injured; Clifford and Northumberland were killed. Somerset was cornered in the Castle Inn but was determined to die fighting; by tradition, he killed four men before being hacked to death. Do not miss the **plaque** on the corner of St Peter's Street and Victoria Street. Total casualties, though, were no more than 100, mainly Lancastrian, the commons having largely been spared.

Aftermath and Commentary

Wiltshire and Fauconberg escaped (the latter, as a Neville, may have been allowed to) but the other nobles were captured. The King himself was wounded in the neck by an arrow and, bleeding profusely, took refuge in a tanner's house. His standard had already been abandoned. Within the hour, fighting came to an end. The King was led to the abbey by the Yorkists. They went down on bended knee, declared themselves his 'humble servants' and asked for forgiveness. The Yorkist troops, who included many northerners, undertook much looting of the town and abbey. The next day, Henry was escorted back to London by York and the Nevilles and a crown-wearing ceremony at St Paul's organised on Whit Sunday. The Yorkists were back in charge of the government – a vicious way of conducting a parliamentary vote of no confidence on the government of the day.

St Albans is accurately referred to as 'a short, sharp affray in a street' but actually it does demonstrate well how a battle can be heavily influenced by the

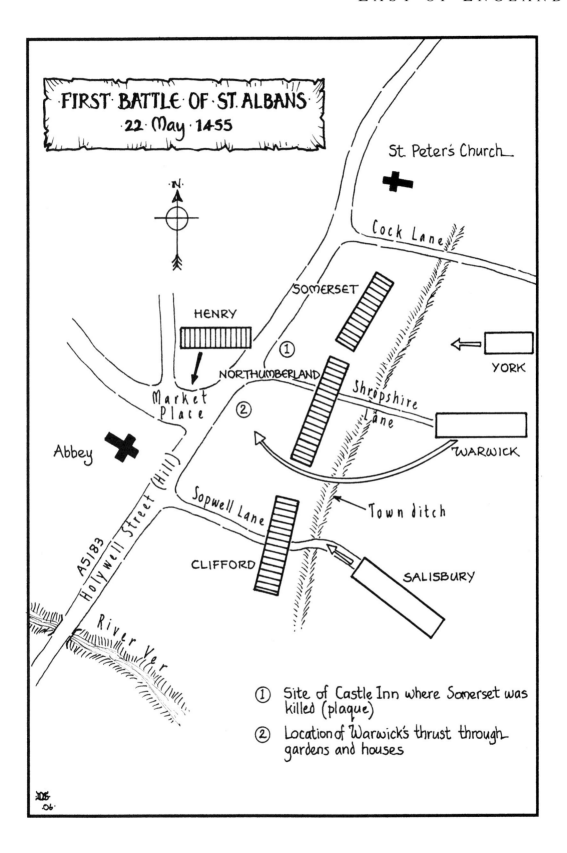

FIRST·BATTLE·OF·ST·ALBANS·
·22·May·1455

St. Peter's Church

N

Cock Lane

SOMERSET

HENRY

YORK

① NORTHUMBERLAND

Market Place

Shropshire Lane

② WARWICK

Abbey

Sopwell Lane

Town ditch

A5183 Holywell Street (Hill)

CLIFFORD

SALISBURY

River Ver

① Site of Castle Inn where Somerset was killed (plaque)

② Location of Warwick's thrust through gardens and houses

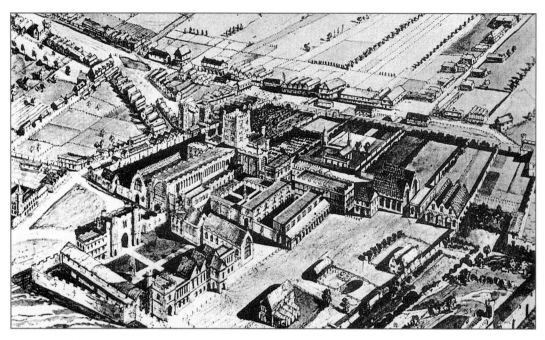

Reconstruction of St Albans from the south-west as it may have looked in medieval times. The Yorkists attacked from the fields to the east of the abbey and town centre.

Plaque marking the spot where Edmund Beaufort, Duke of Somerset was killed during the First Battle of St Albans.

strategic moves leading up to it. The Yorkists moved quickly throughout to engage the King on his journey to Leicester. Henry was thus struggling to recruit sufficient troops in time and may crucially have been short of archers. This would explain why Buckingham argued to occupy the centre of St Albans, where the Yorkist archers would be less effective. On the other hand, the cluttered townscape negated one of Henry's main advantages: the flying of the King's standard in the sight of both sides which was to prove so potent four years later at the rout of Ludford Bridge at deterring troops from engaging with an anointed king in the field. The townscape also, probably unexpectedly, gave Warwick the element of surprise.

Although the floodgates of the war did not open immediately after St Albans, scores would eventually have to be settled by the aggrieved Lancastrian families.

Location and What to See
The battle was fought in the town's **marketplace** and surrounding streets, the lines of which largely remain today. St Albans stands on the south-west edge of a low ridge sloping steeply down to the River Ver. The site is rewarding to visit, especially since a good aerial view can be gained from the **medieval clock tower** near the marketplace.

<table>
<tr><td colspan="2">Participants and Casualties</td></tr>
<tr><td>Lancastrian (~2,000 men)</td><td>Yorkist (2–3,000 men)</td></tr>
<tr><td>Henry VI</td><td>Richard, Duke of York</td></tr>
<tr><td>Edmund Beaufort, Duke of Somerset</td><td>Richard Neville, Earl of Salisbury</td></tr>
<tr><td>Humphrey Stratford, Duke of Buckingham</td><td>Richard Neville, Earl of Warwick</td></tr>
<tr><td>Henry Percy, Earl of Northumberland</td><td>Sir Thomas Neville</td></tr>
<tr><td>Thomas, Lord Clifford</td><td>Sir Richard Ogle</td></tr>
<tr><td>James Butler, Earl of Wiltshire</td><td>Sir David Hall</td></tr>
<tr><td>Ralph Butler, Lord Sudeley</td><td></td></tr>
<tr><td>William Neville, Lord Fauconberg</td><td>Casualties: Light</td></tr>
<tr><td>Jasper Tudor, Earl of Pembroke</td><td></td></tr>
<tr><td>Thomas Courtenay, Earl of Devon</td><td></td></tr>
<tr><td>Casualties: ~100 men</td><td></td></tr>
</table>

THE SECOND BATTLE OF ST ALBANS (17 February 1461) ++

Strategic Background and Campaign

With the death of his father, the Earl of Salisbury, and of Richard, Duke of York at the Battle of Wakefield in December 1460, Richard Neville, Earl of Warwick was left in sole command of the Yorkist government and of King Henry VI in London. Edward, now Duke of York himself, remained in the Welsh Marches. Warwick found time to elect himself, Sir John Wenlock, Lord Bonville and Sir Thomas Kyriell to the Order of the Garter. However, the large Lancastrian army which had triumphed at the Battle of Wakefield, led by Henry Beaufort, Duke of Somerset, was still in being and by the middle of January 1461 was massing in Yorkshire to strike for London in order to recover control of Henry VI. By 20 January the Lancastrian levies had combined with Queen Margaret's Scottish mercenaries (she had done a deal with King James), together with French and Welsh contingents, and began marching south. They created much propaganda material for the Yorkists by sacking many towns on the way south, being particularly severe on the Yorkist towns of Grantham, Stamford, Peterborough, Huntingdon and Royston, down the Great North Road. Such behaviour only reinforced southerners' prejudices against 'wild' northerners, creating panic in London, but, at the same time provided for Warwick a rallying call to Yorkists in the south. Large numbers of armed men began arriving in London every day ready to save the south.

Both armies were therefore large, although by now the discipline of the northern 'veterans' of the Battle of Wakefield was suspect. The Lancastrians reached Royston, near Cambridge, around 10 February and abruptly turned westwards. Warwick led out his army from London on 12 February, comprising men from Kent, East Anglia and the rest of the south, accompanied by King Henry. This was very much a north vs south battle. On the 13th, Warwick arrived in St Albans, the scene of his military triumph in 1455. This time, he was unclear of the exact movements and destination of the Lancastrian forces. He therefore drew up his army spread out over a 2-mile front from the centre of St Albans to Nomansland, just south of Wheathampstead, in order to cover the possible routes of attack by the Lancastrians from the north. Adopting a very defensive posture, Warwick dug in over the next three days, utilising a whole range of military paraphernalia to deter his enemy, which on the day seemed to have negligible effect, like caltrops, handgunners, nets, etc.

The Battle

On the evening of 16 February Warwick received reports that the Lancastrians had overrun a Yorkist outpost at Dunstable, north-west of St Albans on Watling Street. However, he was not sure of the veracity of this information, so chose to ignore it. In fact it had been correct. After halting a while, Queen Margaret's army set out on a night march down Watling Street, arriving at St Albans (St Michael's Church) from the west at around 6.00 a.m. A force led by Andrew Trollope moved up George Street towards the marketplace. Its arrival took the Yorkists completely by surprise – even the gates of the town ditch in George Street stood open and unmanned. Trollope penetrated to the market square but then encountered Montagu's (John Neville, Warwick's brother) archers, who inflicted such severe casualties on the Lancastrians that they were forced to retreat

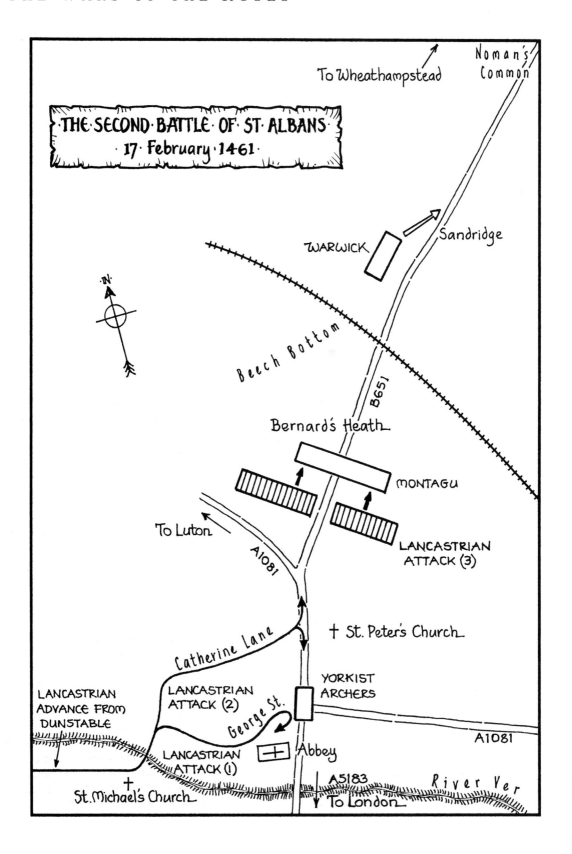

back to St Michael's Church. However, the scouts reported that, unbelievably, another route into the town centre was unguarded, through Catherine Lane. A combined attack here and up George Street was successful this time, with the Yorkist archers eventually being overrun and the town centre occupied by the Lancastrians.

There was now a pause in the fighting while the Lancastrians refreshed themselves after the rigours of the morning and the night march. This enabled Montagu to redeploy his main force (the left wing of Warwick's army) from Beech Bottom to Bernard's Heath, so that it faced south-west towards the Lancastrian army now occupying the town centre. He also sent a message to Warwick (who was deployed at Sandridge) calling for reinforcements from the Yorkist main battle as quickly as possible because Somerset was about to attack with the entire Lancastrian force. However, communication between the Yorkist battles proved very difficult over the 2-mile front, perhaps caused by the terrain of tall hedgerows and narrow lanes. Warwick did not react until it was too late for Montagu. Shortly after midday, the Lancastrians attacked Montagu's force, who put up a spirited defence. In the end, sheer weight of numbers told and Montagu was slowly pushed down the gentle slop of Bernard's Heath.

Eventually, relief was forthcoming in the form of Warwick, personally leading a cavalry force towards Bernard Heath. However, it was too late – one of the Kent captains, called Lovelace, and his retinue are alleged to have deserted from Montagu's force and joined the Lancastrians. The Yorkist line broke and scattered and Montagu was captured (but surprisingly not executed). Once Warwick realised what was happening, he ordered his cavalry to turn back and set about rallying his infantry in Nomansland and leading them back to St Albans. However, it was now almost dark and Yorkist morale was low. Under cover of night, many troops simply disappeared. Warwick himself left the field of battle at the head of his remaining infantry (probably about 4,000 men). It was a shambles.

Aftermath and Commentary

As darkness descended, King Henry was found by the Lancastrians, laughing and singing under a tree, guarded only by Lord Bonville and Sir Thomas Kyriell. He was reunited with his wife and 8-year-old son, Prince Edward. Queen Margaret promptly insisted on the executions of Bonville and Kyriell, despite the fact that Henry had promised their safety.

They had already been pardoned once as Yorkist rebels. Prince Edward was allowed to announce the orders of execution. Henry was unable to stop widespread looting in St Albans town and in the abbey by the Scottish mercenaries, despite pleas from the abbot.

The Lancastrians had gained both their strategic objectives at the Second Battle of St Albans:

• The recovery of King Henry from Warwick's clutches. (At each major battle, Henry was brought along with whichever army because he provided legitimacy to their particular cause. He played no part whatsoever in command.)
• With the heavy defeat of the Yorkists, and Warwick's 'retreat' westwards, London was at the mercy of the Lancastrians. An opportunity existed for the King and Queen to reoccupy the natural centre of English government after four years of governing from Coventry and Kenilworth.

The converse, of course, was that Warwick had failed totally with his two strategic objectives, i.e. to avoid both the above. Any conventional assessment would say that his military performance at St Albans was feeble. The Yorkists lost because a number of serious mistakes were made. Intelligence on Lancastrian troop movements before the battle was poor and then ignored. Complete surprise at the Lancastrian attack from Dunstable meant that the defences of the town centre were unmanned. Finally, Warwick's inability to reinforce Montagu at the vital moment was crucial to the result. Communication between the different elements of the army was disastrously slow. Perhaps Warwick was struggling to exert full control over his large army and over his fellow magnates. The question, though, is, was the Second Battle of St Albans a conventional battle?

What happened next constitutes one of the most extraordinary episodes in the Wars of the Roses. After the battle, the Lancastrian army pushed on to Barnet and entered negotiations for access to the city. Here, however, the Yorkist propaganda about the destruction wrought by Queen Margaret's northerners came into its own. Londoners had never been strong supporters of King Henry; his flight from the city during Jack Cade's Rebellion in 1450 was not forgotten. They were therefore very reluctant to allow the Queen's hordes into their city. A delegation of Lancastrian noble ladies – the Dowager Duchess of Bedford, the Duchess of Buckingham and Lady

Scales – was sent to Queen Margaret by the Council to explain their views and negotiate. Margaret seemed more interested in acquiring victuals for her army than in gaining access to the capital. Events dragged on until rumours began to circulate that a large Yorkist force led by Edward, Duke of York and Warwick was approaching London from the west. Margaret withdrew most of her army back to Dunstable, leaving a detachment at Barnet. Her northerners began to desert as they saw no further prospects of booty and were getting hungry. The city refused access to the 400 of her best troops who had marched from Barnet to Aldgate.

By 24/25 February, Margaret abandoned her attempt to enter London, rather than risk large civilian casualties, and pulled back fully to Dunstable. Earl Rivers afterwards admitted to the Milanese ambassador, 'and so the Lancastrian cause was lost irredeemably.' With the benefit of hindsight, her decision seems incredible but she may have been influenced by her French upbringing, where the King of France had managed to govern that country quite adequately for years without controlling Paris.

What made her decision so wrong was what came next. On 27 February, Edward of York and Warwick, backed by their armies, reached London and were immediately admitted to the city. They had combined their forces after the Battle of St Albans at Burford (a Warwick town) or Chipping Norton in the Cotswolds as Edward hurried to London on 22 February and then marched straight to the capital. Edward was cheered enthusiastically by the populace; he was of course returning a victor after his success at the Battle of Mortimer's Cross. Edward and Warwick then broke the political 'paradigm'. Arguing that King Henry's behaviour since the Act of Accord of October 1460 – in 'allowing' Richard, Duke of York to be assassinated at Wakefield and in knighting thirty Lancastrians after the Battle of St Albans – made the Act itself invalid, they put forward Edward as the valid heir to the Mortimer claim to the throne of England, rather than just Henry's heir as stated in the Act. This argument might have carried weight with Yorkist supporters but the Lancastrians had never even accepted the Act of Accord. The two of them went a step further: in the first few days of March a number of carefully managed ceremonies were held, proclaiming Edward, Duke of York as King Edward IV of England. There were now two rival kings in the land. Warwick's brother, George Neville, Bishop of Exeter played a prominent part in these well-researched ceremonies.

So Warwick may have only been going through the motions at the Second Battle of St Albans, his priority being to survive so that he could assist in putting Edward on the throne?

Participants and Casualties

Lancastrian (more than 25,000)
Henry Beaufort, Duke of Somerset
Henry Percy, Earl of Northumberland
Henry Holland, Duke of Exeter
John Talbot, Earl of Shrewsbury
Lords Roos, Grey of Cobnor, Clifford, Welles,
    Willoughby
Andrew Trollope (knighted)

Yorkist (~25,000 men)
Richard Neville, Earl of Warwick
William Fitzalan, Earl of Arundel
John Mowbray, Duke of Norfolk
John de la Pole, Duke of Suffolk
Lords Fauconberg (William Neville), Bonville,
    Berners
Sir John Wenlock
Sir Thomas Kyriell
Henry VI being held by Warwick

Casualties: Yorkist deaths are estimated at 4,000. Perhaps 2,000 Lancastrians died, the figure reflecting the stout resistance put up by Montagu's outnumbered Yorkists

---

Location and What to See
The action of this battle covers an unusually large area from **St Michael's Church** on the western outskirts of St Albans to **Nomansland** in the north (1 mile south of Wheathampstead on the B651 to St Albans). There are two centres of interest for this battle:

- The **market square** in the town, where the archery duels were fought along George Street and Catherine Street. This can be visited at the same time as the sites associated with the First Battle of St Albans, which are very close by.
- The second centre is on **Bernard's Heath**, where the main mêlée between Montagu and the

Lancastrians occurred. It is on the B651, 1 mile out of St Albans. There is only a street called Archers Fields to be seen on the heath. At the north end of Bernard's Heath, fork left before the railway cutting on the road which leads back to the A1081 to Harpenden. **Beech Bottom** is the ancient linear earthwork, ¼–½ mile on the right, which formed part of Warwick's original defensive line and from which Montagu had to redeploy to Bernard's Heath when it at last became clear the Lancastrian forces were attacking from the west, not the north.

- **Nomansland Common** (where the undergrowth so hampered communication between the Yorkist forces) is on the B651 to Wheathampstead (1 mile south of that town). The undergrowth is still there but there is also a good pub!

SHERNBORNE, St Peter and St Paul's Church **

2 miles north-east of Dersingham, at hamlet crossroads.

This delightfully situated little church stands across from the green and the **hamlet signpost**, which sports a representation of the knight <u>Sir Thomas Shernborne</u> (d. 1458). Sir Thomas and wife <u>Jomana de Chevneys</u> also have a memorial brass on the wall of the church chancel. Jamona was French and was one of Queen Margaret of Anjou's ladies-in-waiting. Sir Thomas became Queen Margaret's Chamberlain of the Household, a position which demanded total loyalty and discretion. If it were possible, an interview with Sir Thomas would no doubt tell us much about the Wars in the badly documented 1450s. He was also

sheriff of Norfolk and Suffolk in 1452. The site of his old manor house with moat can be seen ½ mile west of the church on the road to Ingoldisthorpe.

STAMBOURNE, St Peter and St Thomas's Church*

In lovely countryside, north-west of Castle Hedingham. From A1017 Braintree–Haverhill road turn left at Man's Cross, just beyond Great Yeldham. Turn right after 2½ miles in Stambourne village and church is on right after ⅓ of a mile.

A delightful rood screen from the sixteenth century, painted with four figures of saints. <u>**Henry VI**</u> is represented standing on an antelope and holding an orb. Henry VII did petition Rome to have his predecessor beatified but was unsuccessful. Clearly, however, Henry VI was accepted here (and elsewhere in the country) as an unofficial saint.

THETFORD PRIORY OF OUR LADY (ruins) ****

½ mile west of town centre, north of Little Ouse river. Turn sharp left off old A11 going north just after bridge.

Church monuments of fifteenth-century nobles and magnates are surprisingly rare. The reason is that before the Reformation a large proportion of these wealthy people were buried in monasteries, often as patrons. Their tombs were invariably lost at the Dissolution of the monasteries in the sixteenth century or afterwards. Thetford Priory was the burial place of the Mowbrays and Howards, Dukes of Norfolk, powerful participants on the side of York

Thetford is very proud of its medieval connections.

Detail from a portrait of Thomas Howard, Earl of Surrey, later 2nd Duke of Norfolk, at Arundel.

throughout the Wars. Fortunately the remains of the tomb-chest of **John Mowbray, 4th Duke** survive at the east end of the south aisle. He died in 1476. The local council have kindly indicated with small **plaques** where **John Howard, 1st Duke**, but a new creation (k. 1485), and his son **Thomas, 2nd Duke** (1443–1524) were also buried. At the Dissolution, the Howard 3rd Duke removed their tombs for safekeeping.

This is a great place for a quiet picnic. It is a far cry from Canterbury Cathedral or Warwick Castle but entry is free and the priory has a great gatehouse.

TURVEY, All Saints' Church *

In village centre, on sharp bend just off A428 Bedford–Northampton road.

In the **south side aisle**, fine tomb-chest and effigies of <u>Sir John Mordaunt</u> (d. 1506) and his wife, <u>Edith Latimer</u>. Sir John fought at Bosworth and at

Stoke Field for Henry Tudor. He was subsequently appointed King's Sergeant and Speaker of the Commons. Just before his death, he became Chancellor of the Duchy of Lancaster.

WINGFIELD, St Andrew's Church ****

Wingfield is a small village 2 miles west of Fressingfield. Take road out of Fressingfield to Hoxne. After 2+ miles turn right across stream to Wingfield. Church is up hill on right.

This is about as good as it gets. This large but charmingly unrestored church houses the monument to a duke who fought in the Wars of the Roses and to his wife, sister of kings. What's more, because the church was collegiate before the Reformation, this is the original resting place of the monuments; they have not been brought from a nearby monastery. All this is set in delightful countryside.

The only disappointment is that **John de la Pole, 2nd Duke of Suffolk** did not really pull his weight

Tomb of John de la Pole, Duke of Suffolk and Princess Elizabeth, Wingfield church.

in the Wars. He did fight at the Second Battle of St Albans and Ferrybridge/Towton and he did support Edward IV in 1471, but he was never a major player in the way his position almost demanded. The fascinating tomb-chest lies in the **chancel north side**. His armour is a very good representation of the period; note also the tilting helmet and the Yorkist and Tudor badges on the canopy. Princess Elizabeth (1444–1503) was the fourth surviving child of Richard, Duke of York and Cecily Neville and therefore sister to Edward IV and Richard III. Married in mid-1461, she had eleven surviving children by Duke John. Because of the royal blood, their eldest son, John de la Pole, Earl of Lincoln, was groomed by Richard III as his heir (Richard's own son had died in 1484). Lincoln was killed at the Battle of Stoke Field (1487). The rest of the brood continued to trouble the Tudors well into the reign of Henry VIII.

The **east window** was sponsored by Duke John's father, **William de la Pole, 1st Duke** who was Henry VI's chief minister in the 1440s. Some original glass remains. A mile north-west lies **Wingfield Castle**, built in the fourteenth century by the de la Pole forebears. The grounds are private but a glimpse can be obtained from the common on the west side.

WIVENHOE, St Mary the Virgin's Church ***

Leave Colchester on A133 to Clacton. After approximately 2 miles, take right B1028 to Wivenhoe. Follow signs to quay/ station. Church is on left before the descent to the quay. Summer weekend afternoons.

This memorial is a gem. Not only do we have a lovely **floor brass** still with colour but it also involves a significant Lancastrian die-hard from the 1460s and 70s. Added to this is an interesting personal story. William, Viscount Beaumont and Lord Bardolf (1438–1507) was the son of John, given the first viscountcy in England in 1440. John

a staunch Lancastrian supporter was killed at the Battle of Northampton (1460). The family estates were in the east Midlands and Lincolnshire.

William fought at Towton (1461) and was taken prisoner. He was subsequently attainted, then pardoned but still disinherited. His lands were given to William, Lord Hastings. In 1471 Beaumont joined Warwick for the Barnet campaign. After preliminary brushes with Edward IV's troops at Newark and at Leicester, Beaumont formed part of the high command at Barnet, probably on the right wing alongside John de Vere, Earl of Oxford. After the defeat, both men escaped to Scotland. In 1473 the two men occupied St Michael's Mount in Cornwall, where they were besieged by Yorkist troops. Eventually they submitted and Beaumont was imprisoned for the next twelve years in the castle at Calais.

William married well, to Joan Stafford, daughter of the Duke of Buckingham in 1452; but before 1477 the marriage 'had been put aside' with no offspring. On reinstatement of his lands, he remarried in 1486, to Elizabeth Scope (d. 1537), daughter of Sir Henry, perhaps 'trading down' to a younger but less upmarket Yorkist model. Intriguingly, within a year William had lost his senses – more likely caused by his time imprisoned in Calais. In 1487 he and Elizabeth went to live with his long-standing friend the Earl of Oxford, at first at Castle Hedingham and then at Wivenhoe. Oxford was first given control of Beaumont's lands, followed in 1495 by his person. Oxford's wife, Margaret Neville (the Kingmaker's sister), died in 1506, followed by William's death in 1507. Oxford proceeded to marry Beaumont's widow in 1508, who became Countess of Oxford, enjoying regular visits to the Tudor Court. Oxford died in 1513, leaving Elizabeth a second-time widow for twenty-four years. Elizabeth is also commemorated here in brass. Again, there were no children. We must surely admire Oxford's compassionate approach to his friend's mental illness.

EAST MIDLANDS

ASHBOURNE, St Oswald's Church **

½ mile south-west of town centre on Leek road (spire).

The **Boothby Chapel** in the north transept is a treasure trove for the medievalist. It contains fine tombs to the powerful Cockayne and Bradborne families – in particular to two Sir John Cockaynes (d. 1447 and d. 1504). Ashbourne belonged to the Duchy of Lancaster and the Cockaynes were distinguished officials for the north of England. They had assumed the status of local squire in Ashbourne. Sir John I wears an 'SS' collar. But we are really interested in the appropriately defaced alabaster **floor slab** which commemorates his son, Sir John II, the 'black sheep' of the family. Storey sees him as a 'lawless and dissolute ruffian' who, in his own time, was described as 'one of the two dozen men who were "notoriously and universally throughout all this your realm famed and noised, known and reputed severally, for open robbers, ravishers, extortioners and oppressors".'

Sir John II's career provides good examples of the vicious internecine warfare of the Deryby-shire gentry during the fifteenth century. Cut off geographically from the centres of power and lacking effective lordship from the local magnates (the dukes of Buckingham, Lord Grey of Cobnor) the gentry here were a law unto themselves who engaged in an orgy of property disputes based on the principle of hit first, go to law second. On the other hand, few of these people actually turned out to fight formal battles during the Wars because of this same lack of magnate control. Cockayne was not an exception, just an extreme.

His father died when he was 16 years old and he was excluded from his inheritance outside Ashbourne until his mother died some time after 1466. He joined the service of the earls of Stafford (later dukes of Buckingham) in 1439 and married Agnes Vernon from Haddon Hall. By 1443 Cockayne had fallen out with his stepfather, Thomas Bate, and attacked his home at Polesworth in Warwickshire. In 1449 Cockayne attacked separately two of his near neighbours, Philip Okeover from Okeover and Ralph Basset from Blore, both across the River Dove in Staffordshire, killing deer and smashing fences and houses. He was supported by Thomas Meverell and Thurstan Vernon. By the end of the year, his exploits were known to parliament. In 1452 he assisted Nicholas Longford and Nicholas

Mongomery on a raid on their Shirley/Brailsford neighbours. In May 1455 he also took part in the notorious Elvaston raid (near Derby), when a force of 1,000 led by Nicholas Longford attacked the house of Walter Blount, the prominent Yorkist in Derbyshire. A year later, he escaped retaliatory ambush by Thomas Blount. In December 1461 Edward IV appointed a commission to arrest Sir John, who was said to be 'leading a band of marauders'.

By 1485 Sir John was looking to atone for his past behaviour and founded a chantry chapel in this church with Richard Vernon, Nicholas Montgomery and the Okeover brothers. In 1494 he was forced to sell off virtually all his lands to the father-in-law of his grandson (his son, Thomas, not surprisingly, had been killed in a duel in 1488) to pay off his debts. He was given a weekly allowance and lived to be 82 years old.

South-west Derbyshire is blessed with a remarkable number of survivals of these feuding gentry. While in Ashbourne, why not visit **Norbury**, St Mary's Church. The Fitzherbert tomb-chests are wonderful, with rare Yorkist collars. Take the B5032 Uttoxeter road, turn left over the Dove bridge at Ellastone (B5033) and left again in Norbury on the Snelston road. The church is set back in trees on the left. A great spot.

Cubley church is east of the A515 Uttoxeter–Ashbourne road, just south of Great Cubley. Tomb-chests remain to two Sir Nicholas Montgomerys (d. 1435 and 1494). The elder was Constable of Tutbury Castle, part of the Duchy of Lancaster, the younger an associate of Sampson Meverell in his feud with the Bassets of Blore.

ASHBY ST LEGER, St Leodegarius's Church ***

3½ miles north of Daventry. Turn off A361 on minor road to Watford Gap. Church is at end of village as road bends left.

This small village is positively dripping with history. As you approach the church, note the timbered gatehouse. Tradition has it that in the upstairs room the Gunpowder Plot was hatched in 1605. Robert Catesby, whose mother owned the house, was one of the conspirators. The Catesbys acquired Ashby in the thirteenth century and became one of the leading gentry families in Northamptonshire. The church is their memorial. On

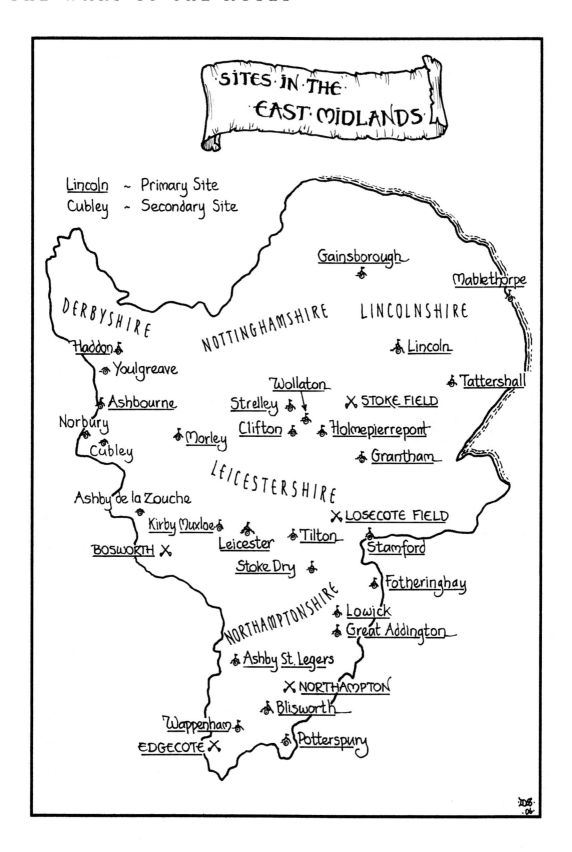

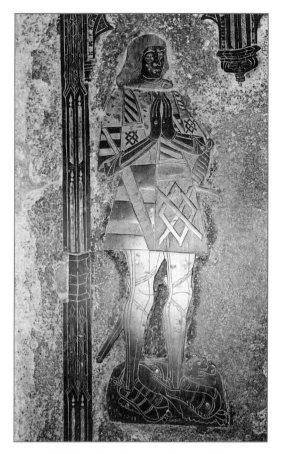

Brass of William Catesby, one of Richard III's henchmen, Ashby St Leger church.

introduced Catesby to Richard, Duke of Gloucester in April 1483, who seems to have taken to him immediately. Catesby played a major role in Richard's Second Coup in June 1483, during which he acted as Richard's double agent and entrapped Hastings for planning treason against the Protector. Catesby relayed all to Richard, resulting in Hasting's almost immediate and illegal execution on 13 June 1483.

Catesby was amply rewarded with lands that doubled his income. He became knight of the body, councillor, King's Secretary, Chancellor of the Exchequer and finally Speaker, in January 1484. Such a rise to fame won him no friends among his contemporaries. He was seen as a man with a total lack of scruple and became notorious as a member of Richard III's 'kitchen cabinet', immortalised in William Collingbourne's doggerel, 'The Cat, the Rat and Lovell our Dog, Ruleth all England under Hog [Richard III's emblem]'. Collingbourne paid the full price for this and other treasons.

William was the only man executed after the Battle of Bosworth. Captured after the battle, he was beheaded three days later at Northampton. He had at least, in 1484, opposed point-blank Richard III's suggestion that he, Richard, should marry his niece, Elizabeth of York. He claimed that Richard's northern following would not go along with it.

BLISWORTH, St John the Baptist Church *
West side of village, near canal.

A splendid tomb-chest with good brasses to Roger Wake (d. 1504) and wife Elizabeth Catesby, sister of the ill-fated William junior. Roger fought at Bosworth (1485) for Richard III. He held significant lands in this county and in Somerset and Lincolnshire and had been granted lands forfeited by his near neighbours the Woodvilles of Grafton Regis by Richard in 1483. After the battle, Roger was attainted but this was reversed in 1487.

Roger's father, Thomas, was a supporter of Warwick the Kingmaker. In 1469 when Warwick's conflict with Edward IV came to a head, Thomas gained notoriety by accusing his neighbour, Jacquetta, Dowager Duchess of Bedford and mother of Queen Elizabeth Woodville, of using witchcraft to ensnare Edward IV into marriage with her daughter. Jacquetta was taken to court in London but on the day Thomas's witnesses let him down and refused to testify.

the chancel floor is a brass to Sir William Catesby (d. 1479) and wife. He was a prominent Lancastrian who was knighted by Henry VI in 1453. He fought at the battles of Northampton (1460) and Towton (1461). He may also have fought at the Battle of Wakefield (1460) and acquired a share of the Duke of York's lands after his death at this battle, and he became steward and Constable of Wigmore Castle, Herefordshire. Later he became a retainer of Warwick and Clarence.

Tucked away at the eastern end of the church, to the right of the **altar**, under a carpet, is a fabulous brass to Sir William's son, another William Catesby (c. 1440–85), and his wife Margaret, daughter of Lord Zouche (d. 1494). William became a lawyer at Inner Temple and built up a successful practice with members of the aristocracy, especially in the Midlands. He became a retainer and indeed the protégé of William, Lord Hastings. Hastings

Brass of Roger Wake, Blisworth church.

THE BATTLE OF BOSWORTH (22 August 1485) +++++

Strategic Background and the Campaign

In June 1483 Richard III, backed by his faithful northerners, usurped the throne of England and incarcerated his nephews, the former Edward V and his brother Richard, Duke of York, in the Tower. By the end of the summer, the boys had disappeared from view, never to be seen again. In October, the south of England rose in rebellion against Richard III, under the leadership of Henry, 2nd Duke of Buckingham. Buckingham himself was captured and executed by Richard in early November. Henry Tudor attempted to land a force from France to join the rebellion but was beaten by bad weather. Nevertheless, Henry, despite a weak claim to the throne, emerged from the revolt as the leading Lancastrian claimant because of an agreement between his mother, Lady Margaret Beaufort, and Dowager Queen Elizabeth Woodville that Henry would marry Elizabeth of York, the Dowager Queen's daughter by Edward IV. This commitment

was made public at Rennes Cathedral at Christmas 1483, and was crucial to attracting newcomers to Henry's cause from former supporters of Edward IV in the south of England. After the rapid collapse of Buckingham's Revolt and the attainting of many rebels by Richard III, a stream of exiles from England made their way to join Henry in France.

After much negotiating, Henry obtained direct military assistance and funding from Louis XI, King of France. By July 1485 Henry's invasion fleet, commanded by the French Admiral de Gasenove, was ready to sail from Harfleur in Normandy. On August 7, after good weather, it reached Milford Haven in west Wales, where Henry's uncle, Jasper Tudor, had many contacts. Landing at Mill Bay, Henry chose the more lengthy northerly route into England because it afforded less chance of a hostile reception than the direct route via south Wales. Initial recruitment of new supporters was slow, but at Newton, near Welshpool, the powerful Welsh leader Rhys ap Thomas, who had been shadowing Henry's force, finally 'came on board'. Henry proceeded via Shrewsbury, Lichfield and Tamworth to Merevale Abbey near Atherstone, which was reached on 21 August. Henry had had an inconclusive meeting with Thomas, Lord Stanley (Henry's mother's fourth husband) and his brother Sir William in an attempt to agree how these powerful affinities should join him.

Meanwhile, King Richard had based himself in the heart of England at Nottingham Castle. Richard would probably have known of Henry's landing within three days, and immediately set about arraying forces to repel the invader. On 17 August Richard moved to Leicester, ready to cut off any attempt by Henry to turn south for London. Richard's considerable force arrived in the Atherstone–Market Bosworth area on 21 August and camped for the night.

The Battle

The Battle of Bosworth is one of *the* decisive battles of English history because it ushered in the awesome Tudor era. Yet it has always been controversial. Like so many of the battles of the Wars of the Roses, we know frustratingly little about the details of how the battle unfolded. In Bosworth's case, there is general consensus on the overall pattern of the battle. The problem is the exact location and the detail of the tactical deployments.

However, we are indeed fortunate that, in 1974, Leicestershire County Council boldly opened a Battlefield Centre on the site traditionally held to

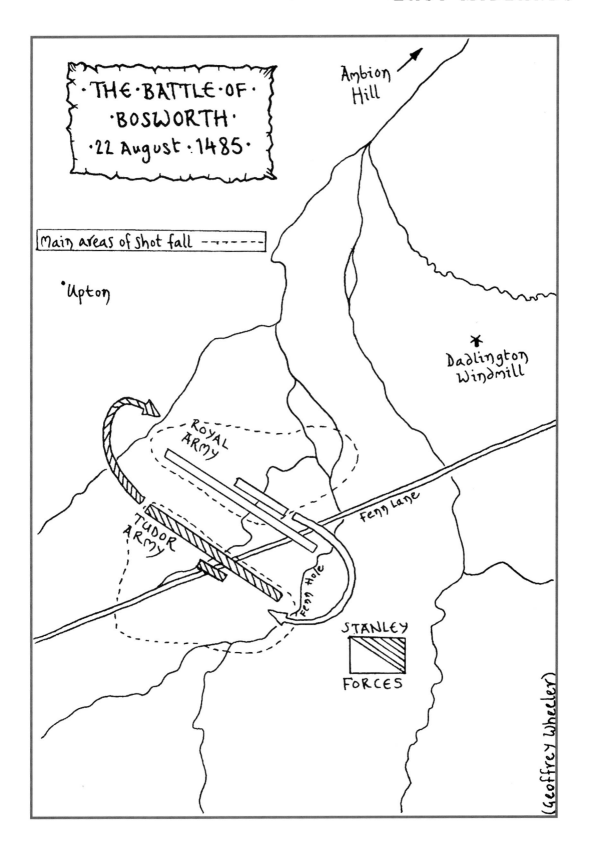

THE·BATTLE·OF·
·BOSWORTH·
·22 August·1485·

Ambion Hill

Main areas of shot fall ------

·Upton

Dadlington
Windmill

ROYAL
ARMY

TUDOR
ARMY

Fenn Lane

Fenn Hole

STANLEY

FORCES

(Geoffrey Wheeler)

be the location of the battle, at Ambion Hill, between Shenton and Sutton Cheney. The 1985 anniversary led to new research into the battle, which has resulted in much speculation about the true battle location. Finally, after more than twenty years' effort, it looks as if the true battlefield has now been located 2 miles southwest of Ambion Hill at a place called Fenn Hole. Soil sampling and metal detector work suggest the battle took place on very flat terrain straddling Fenn Lane, a Roman road running from Fenny Drayton to Sutton Cheney. More than 25 pieces of lead munition have been recovered from the site and the existence of a marsh during medieval times has been proven at Fenn Hole. It is now certain that the County Council has invested at the wrong site! Peter Hammond's recent book provides an excellent account of the latest thinking. Ambion Hill now becomes Richard's overnight camp, whilst Henry Tudor's army spent the night near Merevale Abbey. On the morning of the battle, both armies made their way to the Fenn Hole area.

The main episodes of the battle are seen as:

- The usual exchange of archery and cannon fire, in this case probably of short duration.
- The vanguards engage. The Yorkists, led by John Howard, Duke of Norfolk, the Lancastrians by John de Vere, Earl of Oxford. The mêlée lasted about an hour and led to the death of the Duke of Norfolk. Oxford's force employed superior technique, using a wedge involving French pikemen. Norfolk's forces may well have been routed. His son, Thomas Howard, took over command of the Yorkist van but may have ordered his men to lay down their arms. (This action may therefore have saved Thomas from subsequent execution.)
- King Richard spotted Henry Tudor with his household detaching themselves from the centre force and riding in the direction of the Stanleys, perhaps in order to obtain a final confirmation of the allegiance of these notorious 'trimmers'. Richard had assembled an elite force of cavalry before the battle with just this opportunity in mind. Cavalry had made little impact in the earlier battles in the Wars of the Roses because of their ineffectivness against archers. However, Richard may have been influenced by contemporary reports of the Battle of Toro in Spain (1476), where a charge of heavily armoured knights secured victory for King Ferdinand of Castile.
- Richard ordered his elite troop to ride straight at Henry. What an awesome sight that must have

been, with Richard wearing his crown. His tactical innovation almost worked. The two forces clashed. Richard personally killed Henry's standard-bearer, Sir William Brandon, and knocked the giant Sir John Cheyne from his horse with a battle hammer. He may have got within a few feet of Henry. However, Sir William Stanley had finally committed to Henry and, as his large force engaged with Richard's troop, the King was surrounded and overwhelmed, finally being cut down by pikemen. In fact, Tudor may have employed a defensive wall of French pikemen, who used new tactics to prevent Richard's force breaking through. The King had been out-thought on the battlefield. The rest of Richard's army appear to have remained inactive.

Aftermath and Commentary

Tradition has it that Richard's crown was found under a hawthorn bush on a small hill by Thomas, Lord Stanley at nearby Stoke Golding. Here, Stanley placed the crown on Henry Tudor's head, so instigating a new dynasty after more than 300 years of Plantagenet rule in England – and what a dynasty it was to be. The hill is still known as Crown Hill.

Richard's body was stripped and carried on a horse's back to Leicester, where it was displayed for two days. He was buried in Greyfriars in that city.

William Catesby was captured on the battlefield and executed two days later in Leicester marketplace. He was a hated member of Richard's inner circle and his was the only execution to take place after the battle.

Some of Richard's followers escaped to fight again another day, including his boyhood friend Francis, Viscount Lovell (see also Battle of Stoke Field). Henry had to establish his new regime and rebellions rumbled on into the 1490s, but none really threatened.

In truth, the battle had been won by treachery on a grand scale. The combined force of the Stanleys numbered 5,000 men and tipped the balance. The Stanleys both prospered after Bosworth. Thomas was made Earl of Derby by a grateful Henry VII, and William received grants of land and offices making him the wealthiest commoner in England. Treachery really did pay in the Wars of the Roses. Throughout their duration, Lord Stanley had shown himself the master 'trimmer'. The family has prospered to this day, counting among their ancestors a nineteenth-century prime minister and the founder of the horse race.

The inactivity of the rest of Richard's army after Norfolk's death was also critical. Its surviving commanders, Henry Percy, Earl of Northumberland and Thomas Howard, Earl of Surrey were imprisoned by Henry VII but released quite soon; Surrey became a Tudor stalwart. Percy was never forgiven in Yorkshire for his seeming lack of support for Richard and indeed was murdered by tax rebels at Topcliffe in 1489, tradition telling us that his household troops just stood about and watched. Tudor doggerel catches the flavour of Bosworth: 'Jock of Norfolk be not too bold, for Dicken they master is bought and sold!'

Exam syllabuses often insist that, in 1485, out went the Middle Ages, and in came modern history. Actually the start of the Tudor era did not produce a seismic shift in society. Life continued much as before but without the dislocation of war and with an improving rural economy. The truly seismic shift occurred from 1530, which ushered in the Tudor Revolution and the Reformation.

In hindsight, the Bosworth campaign superficially looks like one almighty gamble. Henry Tudor landed in a far-flung part of the country, with no credible claim to the throne, with a small army and no military experience. Nevertheless, Richard III with a larger army and with proven military success managed 'to snatch defeat from the jaws of victory'. At the vital moment, Richard could not command the allegiance of a large part of his force, including his northerners, led by Henry Percy, Earl of Northumberland. He found himself isolated, with only his household troops around him, and overwhelmed by a suddenly hostile force led by Sir William Stanley.

Participants and Casualties

Yorkist > c. 12,000	*Lancastrian (Tudor and Stanleys), approx. 5,000*
Richard III	Henry Tudor
Lord Dacre of Gilsland	John de Vere, Earl of Oxford
Walter Devereux, Lord Ferrers	Jasper Tudor, Earl of Pembroke
Thomas, Lord Dacre of the South	Thomas, Lord Stanley
Thomas, Lord Maltravers	Sir William Stanley
John Howard, Duke of Norfolk	Sir William Berkeley
Thomas Howard, Earl of Surrey	Sir Reginald Bray
Henry Percy, Earl of Northumberland	Sir John Cheyne
Sir Ralph Assheton	Humphrey Cotes
Sir Henry Bodrugan	Piers Courtenay
William Catesby	Sir Giles Daubeny
Sir Gervase Clifton	Sir Simon Digby
Sir Marmaduke Constable	Sir Richard Edgcumbe
Sir John Huddleston	Sir John ap Ellis Eyton
Sir Thomas Mackenfield	Sir Richard Guildford
Sir Thomas Montgomery	Sir Robert Harcourt
Sir Henry Pierrepont	Sir Piers Legh
Henry Vernon	Thomas Lovell
	Richard Nanfan
Casualties: ~1,000	Sir David Owen
	Sir John Savage
	Sir Rhys ap Thomas
	Sir Roger Tocotes
	Casualties: Light

Location and What to See

The **Battlefield Visitor Centre** is located between Sutton Cheney and Shenfield in open country off the A447, south of Market Bosworth. Access is free. It is signposted and offers diorama facilities, a fine range of Wars of the Roses books and a café. The traditional story of the battle is represented *in situ* on Ambion Hill, with rival standards flying. Obtain a copy of the excellent battle guide and take the **battle trail**. You will pass **King**

King Dick's Well, Bosworth.

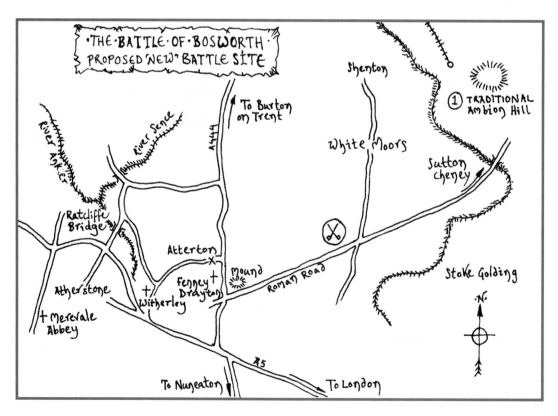

Dick's Well. Near Shenton station look for the modern **field memorial** to Richard III where he was killed.

Visit **Sutton Cheney** church, where the Richard III Society have placed a memorial to the king.

To find the new battlefield site, turn left out of the visitor centre on to the minor road to Market Bosworth. Under the railway go left at the T-junction. After 1 mile, turn right onto Fenn Lane westwards towards Fenny Drayton. The battlesite straddles Fenn Lane after 1 mile after the joining minor roads and a small stream (Fenn Hole). The site runs along Fenn Lane to a farm (which has a barn already named Tudor Barn!) There is nothing yet marking the site but there is a public footpath across it. Note this is a working farm, though.

Return to the crossroads 1½ miles to the east. Turn right through Dadlington, turn second right and right again at T-junction into **Stoke Golding**. Follow the road west straight for ⅓ mile to the brow of the downslope. This is **Crown Hill**. There is a classic **blue plaque** on the gate of a bungalow commemorating the 'crowning' of Henry Tudor after the battle here (not actually mentioned in the sources until 1605). Note also the decorated village sign. This is a village that has recently got the message.

A mile west of Atherstone lies the **Church of Our Lady, Merevale**, on the B4116 Sheepy Magna to

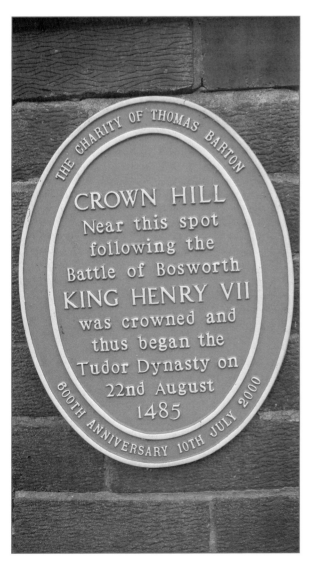

Above: *The arms of John de Vere, Earl of Oxford displayed at Bosworth battlefield.*

Over Whitacre road. It is half a mile south-west of the B4116–A5 roundabout on a hill. **Henry Tudor** is said to have stayed at Merevale Abbey (of which this church was part) the night before the battle and his army camped nearby. In the **south aisle** is an original stained-glass figure of St Armel, an obscure Breton saint adopted by Henry Tudor during his exile in France before 1485 and seen also on his tomb in Westminster.

CLIFTON, St Mary's Church **

On southern outskirts of Nottingham. Cross Trent on A52. Immediately take A453 right to M1 south. Pass Trent University on right and in Clifton village turn right up dead-end to old village. Church and hall are at the end. Thursday mid-morning service.

In the **north transept**, there are two brasses to Sir Robert Clifton (d. 1478) and to his son, Sir Gervase Clifton (d. 1491), members of an old-established, upper-gentry family. Sir Robert was an early supporter of Edward IV, being present at the Battle of Towton (1461). He was knighted at Edward's coronation that year. However, a Sir Gervase Clifton also fought for Lancaster at Towton, indicating intra-familial rivalries. Hampton tells us that this was Sir Robert's brother, who also fought for Lancaster at Tewkesbury (1471). This Gervase was a long-serving supporter of the dukes of Somerset. He was executed after that battle. Sir Robert founded a chantry college in this church in 1476.

Sir Robert's son, another Gervase (d. 1491), followed his father's Yorkist leanings. He was an esquire of the body to Edward IV and a member of the Hastings affinity. He was summoned to receive his knighthood at the coronation of Edward V but this never happened. Instead, he was made Knight of the Bath at the coronation of Richard III in 1483. He gave good service to Richard during Buckingham's Revolt in the autumn of 1483 and was rewarded with extra lands in Derbyshire, Leicestershire and Huntington. He became a knight of the body during 1484 and a member of Richard's 'northern mafia'. At Bosworth, he stuck with Richard (he had no option really since Richard based himself in the summer of 1485 at Nottingham).

There is some confusion as to whether he was killed at Bosworth; it is more likely that he was badly wounded but survived. He married Agnes, née Constable, daughter of Marmaduke of Flamboro'.

A Gervase Clifton fought for Tudor at the Battle of Stoke (1487).

THE BATTLE OF EDGCOTE, (26 July 1469) ++
Strategic Background and the Campaign

From the announcement of Edward IV's engagement to Elizabeth Woodville in September 1464, his relationship with Warwick the Kingmaker steadily deteriorated. By late 1467, it had reached breaking point; Warwick found himself unable to influence Edward any longer and withdrew to his estates. There was a temporary reconciliation of sorts in early 1468 but it lacked sincerity. Warwick had begun to flatter Edward's brother George, Duke of Clarence with promises of glory.

In the spring of 1469 there were local rebellions in Yorkshire, led by Robin of Holderness and Robin of Redesdale. The former agitated for the restoration of Henry Percy as earl of Northumberland. It was suppressed by John Neville, the current Earl of Northumberland, and its 'Robin' executed. Robin of Redesdale, however, eluded Neville. Concerned about these revolts, Edward headed to East Anglia and began mustering an army. He commanded the Earls of Pembroke and Devon to muster troops and meet him in the east Midlands. He seemed in no hurry initially, finding time to have a week's holiday with his queen. However, on 10 July at Newark, his actions suddenly became more urgent. He had learned that Robin of Redesdale was heading south with a large army. 'Robin' was most probably Sir William Conyers of Marske, brother of Sir John, who was steward of Warwick's lordship of Middleham, the centre of Neville power in Yorkshire. Sir William was accompanied by other members of the tight-knit Richmondshire gentry – a formidable force. The rebels issued a manifesto that accused the King of excluding from his Council the lords of his blood (Warwick, Warwick's youngest brother, George Archbishop of York and, until recently, Lord Chancellor of England, and the King's brother, George, Duke of Clarence) and listening only to his favourites, e.g. William Herbert, Earl of Pembroke, Humphrey Stafford, Earl of Devon, Lord Audley and the Woodvilles. Very threateningly, the manifesto compared the favourites to those of the deposed kings, Edward II and Richard II.

Meanwhile, under cover of these risings, Warwick and Clarence had sailed over to Calais with Warwick's daughter Isabel. On 11 July she and Clarence were married by George Neville. King

Edward had specifically forbidden this union but Warwick had secretly obtained papal dispensation. After only two days of festivities, the party returned to England. They received a warm welcome in Kent. Warwick continued his theme of needing to purge Edward of his favourites rather than removing him entirely. He was allowed into London and given a loan of £1,000. Very quickly he moved onwards, heading for the Midlands to link up with Redesdale.

Edward remained stationary in Nottingham, waiting for Pembroke and Devon to join him. In fact, Redesdale bypassed Nottingham in the drive to join up with Warwick and Clarence, also hoping to cut Edward off from London. Unbeknown to them, the opposing armies of Redesdale and Pembroke and Devon were on a collision course somewhere between Banbury and Northampton. Pembroke's force was made up almost entirely of Welshmen from Monmouthshire and Glamorgan, Devon's of men from the West Country. Their forces had combined in the Cotswolds.

The Battle
On 23 July a royalist cavalry force led by Devon and Pembroke's brother Richard Herbert was reconnoitring and clashed with the Redesdale army. On the 24th the royalists were arranging billets in Banbury when Devon and Pembroke had a furious row over lodgings and a comely wench. Devon had arrived first but Pembroke pulled rank. Devon responded by removing his troops to Deddington Castle, ten miles to the south. This was a complete disaster for the royalists, because King Edward had dictated that Devon's force should comprise only archers, Pembroke's only men-at-arms and cavalry. The next day, the 25th, Pembroke clashed with Redesdale. The Welshmen, despite the lack of archers, got the better of the struggle and occupied the hill at Edgcote/Upper Wardington. The 'rebel' Sir Henry Neville, son of Lord Latimer, was captured and executed.

The main battle took place on the 26th, on the plain called Danes Moor, surrounded by the Edgcote, Culworth and Thorpe hills. The royalists' lack of

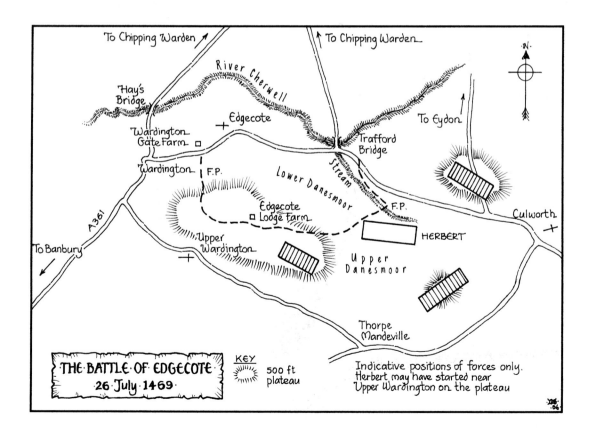

archers probably led to their army being manoeuvred down from Edgcote Hill on to Danes Moor, where a mêlée ensued. Despite the heroic efforts of Sir Richard Herbert with his poleaxe, the Welshmen had no answer when John Clapham and William Parr arrived with the first contingent of Warwick's army marching from London. With cries of 'A Warwick! A Warwick!', the Welshmen were put to the sword. They were probably encircled and the Herbert brothers were taken prisoner.

Aftermath and Commentary

This battle was particularly hard fought. The Welsh acquitted themselves well but were overwhelmed. The high number killed has led to Edgcote being dubbed the 'Welsh Flodden'. At least in the short term, the effects of this defeat were cataclysmic for the royalists. The Herbert brothers were executed by Warwick in Northampton the next day. This was completely illegal, since they were purely serving their king. The Earl of Pembroke touchingly requested that his younger brother be spared, but this was to no avail of course, as far as Warwick was concerned. The Earl of Devon's force retired from the area. Earl Rivers and his brother Sir John Woodville were captured at Chepstow and beheaded in Coventry in August. The Earl of Devon was murdered by the mob in Bridgwater on his return. Edward meanwhile eventually left Nottingham and was heading south when the news of the disaster at Edgcote reached him. Very quickly, his own army melted away and he was left with just his brother Richard, Duke of Gloucester, William, Lord Hastings and a few loyal retainers.

Perhaps trying to return to London, Edward allowed himself to be taken prisoner on the road outside Olney, Buckinghamshire, perhaps at a manor belonging to the Kingmaker's wife, Anne Beauchamp. Warwick sent his brother, George, Archbishop of York to do the job. Edward was taken to Warwick Castle and then imprisoned at Middleham Castle in Yorkshire. The others were dismissed. At this moment the Kingmaker was just that, he had two crowned kings of England under lock and key (the other, Henry VI, was in the Tower). For a brief period he held the reins of power, but it was not to last. Edward was too smart for that.

At first sight, Edward's performance in this campaign looks sluggish in the extreme. His 'eyes and ears' were clearly at fault; were they infiltrated? Normally such a vigorous and decisive general, Edward was just the opposite in 1469.

Participants and Casualties

Royalists (~10,000 men)
William Herbert, Earl of Pembroke
Humphrey Southwick, Earl of Devon
Sir Richard Herbert
Sir Richard Herbert of Ewyas, bastard son of
    William

Rebels
Sir William Conyers
Sir John Conyers
Sir William Parr
Sir Geoffrey Gate

Casualties: Royalists ~2,000 men

Location and What to See

Details of the exact location and of the manoeuvres in the battle are even more scarce than usual for Edgcote and there are no monuments or tombs to see. Despite this, a visit here is one of the most enjoyable and rewarding on offer from the Wars because Danes Moor is set in beautiful, unspoiled countryside. A two-stage approach is recommended on a visit:

• First, drive around the Danes Moor area. Turn off the A361 Banbury–Daventry road at Wardington. Take the second right to Edgcote and continue via Trafford Bridge to Culworth. Before the church, turn right downhill to Thorpe Mandeville. Turn right at the end of that village to Upper Wardington and return to Wardington. This will give you a great idea of the unusual high/low plateau country around Edgcote.

• Take the Edgcote road again. After 1 mile, park at Wardington Gate Farm. Take the public footpath up the west side of Edgcote Hill via Hill Barn, Douglas's Barn, Edgcote Lodge Farm yard to Danes Moor. Cross the stream (a tributary of the upper reaches of the River Cherwell) and ascend towards Culworth. Turn left on the

The track leading down to Upper Danes Moor.

Trafford Bridge, and it looks like the Battle of Edgecote might have occurred just a few months earlier!

footpath towards Trafford Bridge. Rejoin the Edgcote road and turn left. Walk past Trafford Bridge Farm, Edgcote House and return to Wardington Gate. The first part of the walk takes you along the higher ground on which the royalist army encamped. After Edgcote Farm the path crosses Danes Moor itself, and the last leg leads past Edgcote House. Altogether a two-hour walk during which you will be unlucky if you meet anybody.

FOTHERINGHAY *****
Village centre, 3 miles north-east of Oundle

Castle
As a place to visit for the fifteenth-century historian, Fotheringhay has just about everything you could want – tombs of key members of the Yorkist family, a beautiful church, the scant remains of one of the Yorks' seats of power, a delightful riverside setting on the Nene and a good pub.

At the east end of the village, the castle was the original seat of power of the dukes of York,

renovated by Edmund, 1st Duke after 1385. Unfortunately only a grassy mound remains. Fotheringhay is, of course, most famous as the place where Mary Queen of Scots was executed in 1587 by Queen Elizabeth. When he inherited the throne of England, James I ordered the castle to be completely destroyed. It was. The castle was also the birth place of **Richard III** (b. 1452) and other Yorkist siblings. A **plaque** by the river records this fact. The Yorks were often at Fotheringhay. Edward IV famously visited here in 1469 before the action commenced against his brother Clarence and the Kingmaker. Bring a picnic to the lovely riverside setting.

St Mary and All Saints' Church
Village centre.

For maximum visual effect, approach Fotheringhay from the south-west, turning off the A605 Thrapston–Peterborough road 1 mile beyond Oundle, via Tansor village. As you approach Fotheringhay, the church with its fabulous octagonal tower rising above

Fotheringhay church.

the Nene and surrounding fields surely represents one of the sights of rural England. The church was rebuilt by the 2nd and 3rd Dukes of York as a college, which was disbanded at the Reformation and the church size much reduced. The tower and the crossing **fan-vaulting** are adorned with the falcon and fetterlock device of the dukes, and the **pulpit** with further emblems including **Richard III**'s **white boar**.

On either side of the **altar** are tombs commemorating the following members of the House of York:

Edward, 2nd Duke of York (k. 1415 at the Battle of Agincourt)
Richard, 3rd Duke of York (k. 1460 at the Battle of Wakefield)
Cecily, née Neville, wife to Richard (d. 1495)
Edmund, Earl of Rutland, son of Richard (k. 1460 at the Battle of Wakefield)

Richard, the 3rd Duke of course led the Yorkist cause in the 1450s and memorably claimed the throne in 1460 without success. Note that the remains of Richard and his son Edmund were initially buried in Pontefract in early 1461, after they had been killed at the Battle of Wakefield. Their reburial in the family vault at Fotheringhay somewhat intriguingly did not take place until 1476, when the chief mourner was **Richard, Duke of Gloucester**, although Edward IV was also present. Precedence problems between Cecily, the widow and mother, and Queen Elizabeth Woodville could have been the reason for the delay; in the event, Cecily did not attend. The similar reburial of the Neville family members at Bisham Abbey (Richard, Earl of Salisbury and his son Thomas) took place in 1463. The current tombs were erected late in the sixteenth century on the orders of Elizabeth I, after their originals were despoiled during the Reformation – the fate of the tombs of so many aristocrats. Edmund, 1st Duke of York is buried in King's Langley parish church.

Note the **plaque** on the main street just east of the church.

GAINSBOROUGH, Old Hall **** £

Gladstone Street, north side of town centre, near
All Saints' Church. EH. 01427 612669.

This is a remarkable survival of fifteenth-century architecture. Over the centuries, the hall has been used for a wide range of activities – linen factory,

Masonic lodge, theatre and ballroom, as well as a private residence – but it has survived largely intact. The hall was built around 1450/60 by Sir Thomas Burgh (c. 1430–96), one of Edward IV's favoured courtiers in the 1460s. It serves as a memorial both to Sir Thomas and to an important episode in the Wars of the Roses. In February 1470 Lord Welles (step-brother to Lady Margaret Beaufort), his son Sir Richard and two brothers-in-law, Sir Thomas Lande and Sir Thomas Dymmock, sacked this manor, driving Burgh from the shire and carrying off his goods – just another example of aristocratic violence in this period. The difference here is that Edward IV determined to intervene personally in this case. Burgh, as one of Edward's favoured team, had been showered with lands and honours in Lincolnshire – steward of Bolingbroke Castle, constable of Lincoln Castle and grants of attainted lands. He had been one of those joining Edward on his departure from Middleham Castle in 1469 after imprisonment by the Kingmaker. Edward stood by his man and advanced north to Stamford. The result was the Battle of Losecote Field and the execution of Lord Welles, Sir Richard Welles and Sir Thomas Dymmock. Burgh was present at Losecote Field and also fought at Towton (1461), Hexham (1464), Barnet and Tewkesbury (1471).

He rebuilt the house in the 1470s and 80s and **Richard III** stayed here in 1483. Richard made him Knight of the Garter. Sir Thomas attended the coronations of both Richard III and Henry VII. He was ennobled as Lord Burgh in 1487 by Henry. Burgh married Margaret Roos, and their son Edward was knighted after the Battle of Stoke Field by Henry Tudor.

GRANTHAM, Angel and Royal Hotel **

North end of town centre.

Here is an entry with a difference. One of the oldest inns in Britain, it is still based upon the contemporary façade and structure. In October 1483 **Richard III** was staying here when he heard news of Buckingham's Revolt. The letter he wrote to Chancellor Russell demanding the Great Seal is displayed outside the upper room in which Richard stayed. Richard used the Great Seal to confirm the **Duke of Buckingham**'s death warrant. Buckingham was executed in Salisbury marketplace in front of Richard in November 1483.

Do enjoy a meal in this delightful period hotel here or treat yourself to an overnight stay.

The Angel and Royal Hotel, Grantham, where Richard III was staying when Buckingham's Revolt began in 1483.

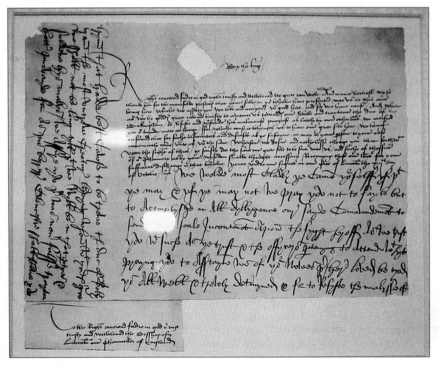

*Facsimile of a
letter written
by Richard III
at the Angel and
Royal Hotel.*

GREAT ADDINGTON, All Saints' Church *
In village centre 3 miles north of Irthlingborough, on minor road to Woodford and Islip.

An alabaster effigy with 'SS' collar of <u>Henry Vere</u> (d. 1493), who joined Henry Tudor just a few days before Bosworth and fought in the battle (1485). He was JP and Sheriff of Northamptonshire later in Henry's reign. His eldest daughter married into the Mordaunt family of Turvey, Bedfordshire.

HADDON, Hall (near Bakewell) ** £
2 miles south-east of Bakewell, on A6. 01629 812855.

Haddon was the principal seat of the powerful <u>Vernons</u>, 'Lords of the Peak', who were buried at Tong. From 1370 the Vernons were great builders at Haddon, updating and extending the original twelfth-century castle. We are interested in <u>Sir William</u> (d. 1472) and <u>Sir Henry</u> (d. 1515) (see Tong). The house retains much of this medieval flavour (especially the lower courtyard, the chapel, the banqueting hall and the dining room) and should not be missed.

While at Haddon, why not visit the delightful village of **Youlgreave**, 3 miles west. Take the A6 south from Haddon, turn first right on the B5056 and right again on the minor road to Youlgreave. The church is in the village centre and contains a tomb-chest to <u>Thomas Cockayne</u> (k. 1488). Thomas was a member of the unruly Cockayne family from Ashbourne, son of John II, and was killed in a duel. He died before his father; as a consequence his tomb-chest was made smaller than normal.

HOLME PIERREPONT, St Edmund's Church *
3 miles east of Nottingham city centre, 1 mile west of Radcliffe on Trent. Take A52 (Grantham) to Radcliffe. Turn left into village. After ½ mile, turn hard left before village centre. Proceed west for 1 mile along unmade road. Church on right.

A fine alabaster effigy and tomb-chest to <u>Sir Henry Pierrepont</u> (d. 1499), with Yorkist collar. Sir Henry fought as an early Yorkist at Towton (1461), was knighted at Tewkesbury (1471) but switched to Henry Tudor at Bosworth. Henry was both sheriff

Haddon Hall, home of the Vernons, known as 'Kings of the Peak'.

Truncated tomb-chest of Sir Thomas Cockayne, Youlgreave church.

and JP during his career. A William Pierrepont fought for Henry at the Battle of Stoke Field (1487). In fact, Henry is said to have lodged at Holme Pierrepont the night before Stoke and prayed in this church.

Also note the **red-brick house** adjacent to the church. This is the entrance range of the great early sixteenth-century courtyard house, no doubt built to reflect the enhanced fortunes of the Pierrepont family after Bosworth. By the seventeenth century, the family had become earls of Kingston.

KIRBY MUXLOE, Castle *

2 miles north-west of Leicester Forest East services, just west of M1–A46 junction. Signposted in village. N.B. From M1, can only be reached directly from south, via junction 21A.

In the 1470s **William, Lord Hastings** was a great builder. Much favoured by a grateful Edward IV after 1471, Hastings conceived Kirby as the very latest design of castle/fortified manor in red brick. After Hastings' death in 1483, it remained unfinished, work having ceased immediately the news of his execution reached Leicester. This is an ideal picnic spot to break your journey on the M1 – so much more pleasant than the nearby motorway services. Hastings also built the Hastings Tower at **Ashby de la Zouch castle**.

LEICESTER ****
City centre, west side.

Given its strategic position in the middle of England, Leicester was always going to get involved in the Wars. It was here that Lord Hastings joined Edward IV with 3,000 men on his march south to recover his throne in spring 1471. It was a key moment. But it is with Richard III that Leicester is most closely connected. It was from Leicester that Richard crossed the Soar and marched out to meet Henry Tudor at Bosworth in 1485. It was back to Leicester that Richard's body was brought, slung over a horse, and buried in the Greyfriars. Until recently, Leicester

Kirby Muxloe Castle, started by William, Lord Hastings but never finished.

hid this association with Richard very successfully. However, in recent years the Richard III Society and the city council have done a super job in ensuring that the link is recognised. You are in plaque country now; around the west side of the city centre can be seen

- A **plaque** to Richard in **Greyfriars Street**, where his tomb may have been. The Greyfriars was dissolved during the Reformation and has now completely disappeared. Henry VII eventually paid for a modest tomb for Richard but this was lost and Richard's remains, by tradition, thrown into the Soar – the coffin for many years being used as a horse trough.

- A fine floor slab to Richard in the **chancel** of Leicester **Cathedral**.
- A modern **statue** of Richard at the north end of **Castle Gardens** off St Augustine Road, by the canal. Nearby, in Castle Street, is a **plaque** which commemorates the fact that Leicester greeted two different kings within two days in August 1485.
- An older **plaque** on the river/canal bridge over the Soar in **St Augustine Road** (A47).
- In Highcross Street is a **plaque** to mark the spot where the Blue Boar Inn stood. Richard III stayed here before Bosworth, when the inn was called the White Boar, Richard's emblem. The innkeeper rapidly changed its name on hearing the result at Bosworth!

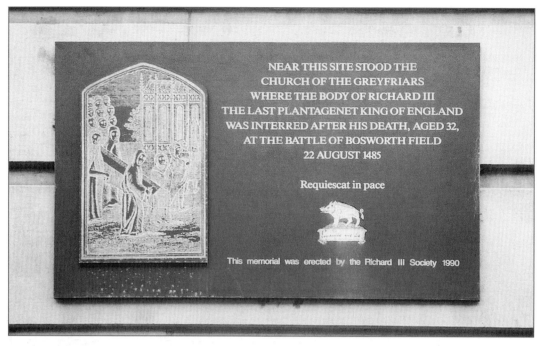

Plaque near Richard III's burial place, Greyfriars, Leicester.

LINCOLN, Cathedral ***
City centre on hill.

Women took a surprisingly high profile in the politics of the Wars of the Roses – Queen Margaret of Anjou, Lady Margaret Beaufort, Queen Elizabeth Woodville – but here in Lincoln are the tombs of a mother and daughter who played more conventional roles in our story. In this cathedral in 1396, John of Gaunt (Duke of Lancaster, Earl of Lincoln) married his third wife, Katherine Swynford, who had been his mistress on and off since 1371. There were already four Beaufort children and all were legitimated by Richard II in 1397. Katherine was the common great-grandmother to both Edward IV and Lady Margaret Beaufort, and great-great-grandmother to both Henry VII and his queen, Elizabeth of York.

Katherine's tomb (d. 1403) lies on the **south side** of the **chancel**, next to that of her youngest child, Joan Beaufort (d. 1440), who was second wife to Ralph Neville, Earl of Westmorland and who bore an illustrious brood of twelve surviving children, including Richard, Earl of Salisbury (the King-

Bow Bridge, Leicester. Leicester Council have put a lot of effort into commemorating Richard III, but it is obviously not always appreciated locally.

Detail from a miniature of the Neville family at prayer, showing Joan Beaufort, Countess of Westmorland, and her daughters, Bibliothèque Nationale, Paris MS Lat 1158.

maker's father) and Cecily, who married Richard, Duke of York and was mother to Edward IV and Richard III.

Joan has another importance to our story. On Ralph's death in 1425, his estates in northern England were divided unequally between the twelve children of his first marriage, to Margaret Stafford, and those born by Joan. Joan's children, with their royal blood, received more than their fair share. The two branches of the family split. A legal reconciliation was achieved in 1443 after Joan's death, but this did not prevent the two branches taking opposite sides in the Wars, the senior Westmorland line staying with Lancaster, the junior branch joining Richard, Duke of York from the mid-1450s.

On the south side of the **retrochoir** is a chantry chapel to <u>Bishop John Russell</u> (d. 1494), Bishop of Lincoln from 1480. Russell was educated at Winchester and New College, Oxford and was a respected man of learning. He had diplomatic experience and in 1474 succeeded Thomas Rotherham as Keeper of the Privy Seal. He was executor of Edward IV's will and took part in his funeral ceremony at Windsor. In May 1483 Richard, Duke of Gloucester appointed Russell to be Chancellor in place of Archbishop Thomas Rotherham. He supported Richard throughout his reign but was troubled when Richard seized the throne. Richard did, on two occasions, reclaim the Great Seal from Russell – once famously during Buckingham's Revolt in October 1483 (see Grantham) and once just before the Battle of Bosworth in July 1485. From 1483 Russell was also Chancellor of Oxford University. He was a friend of the young Thomas More.

While you are in Lincoln, why not walk down to the High Street south of the cathedral. The street passes under the **Stonebow**, in which is housed Lincoln's Guildhall and council chamber. They have a fine collection of civic insignia, including a **sword** given to the city by Henry VII after the nearby Battle of Stoke Field, at which the Yorkist leader John de la Pole, Earl of Lincoln was killed (the sword may have been his). There is an organised tour of the chamber (tel.: 01522 873256).

THE BATTLE OF LOSECOTE FIELD
(Empingham) (12 March 1470) ++
Strategic Background and the Campaign
In September 1469 King Edward IV released himself from captivity by Warwick the Kingmaker at Middleham Castle, Yorkshire and made his way back to London, accompanied by his supporters (his brother, Richard, Duke of Gloucester, the earls of Arundel, Essex and Northumberland, and William, Lord Hastings). An uneasy truce prevailed at Westminster between Edward and Warwick and George, Duke of Clarence, Edward's other brother. In August, Warwick had called a parliament for October, at which, so it was rumoured, Warwick and Clarence intended to denounce Edward as a bastard and replace him with Clarence, a true son of Richard, Duke of York. Nothing came of this because Warwick received little support from his fellow nobles and was struggling to run the country without Edward.

Edward was able to reassert his authority and rebuild support to fill the gap left by Warwick's destruction of his 'evil' councillors, William Herbert, Earl of Pembroke and the Woodvilles. Edward obtained Council support for a clear statement that his heir to the throne was Elizabeth, his eldest daughter, not his brother the Duke of Clarence. Elizabeth was then betrothed to George, the son of John Neville, Earl of Northumberland (Warwick's brother). George was made Duke of Bedford. The couple were still only minors but nevertheless this move represented a clear snub to Clarence.

Warwick and Clarence were unlikely to accept the status quo. A spark to further rebellion occurred when, in February 1470, the house of Sir Thomas

Burgh of Gainsborough was raided and destroyed, and belongings stolen. Sir Thomas was Edward IV's principal supporter in Lincolnshire, a Knight of the Chamber and Master of the Horse. The raid was led by Sir Robert Welles, son of Richard, Lord Welles and Willoughby, a Lancastrian family prominent in Lincolnshire (see Methley), accompanied by Sir Thomas Dymmock and Sir Thomas de la Laude. Clarence is very much seen as the instigator of this rebellion, taking the lead ahead of Warwick because he was the more powerful in Lincolnshire. For this campaign, however, Edward was back to his usual decisive and dynamic best. He summoned Lord Welles and Sir Thomas Dymmock to London to explain events. They were detained at his pleasure.

Clarence secretly called for Sir Robert Welles to muster his 'rebel' forces, while Edward arranged for a royalist army to concentrate at Grantham on 12 March. Sir Robert went public, posting notices in every church with a call to arms asking for men to meet at Ranby Hawe, near Lincoln. On 7 March, Edward reached Royston, Cambridgeshire, where he heard the rebels were heading for Stamford to meet up with Yorkshire rebels led by Sir John Conyers and Lord Scrope of Bolton. To confuse matters, Warwick and Clarence sent a letter to Edward saying they would join him to help suppress the rebels. Lord Welles and Sir Thomas Dymmock were meanwhile brought before Edward again at Huntingdon. Under interrogation, they both confessed to their parts in the revolt but did not reveal Warwick's or Clarence's part.

Lord Welles was forced to write a letter to his son, Sir Robert, saying that if he did not submit to the King, both Welles and Sir Thomas would be put to death. The rebels, by now heading for Leicester to meet up with Warwick and Clarence, doubled back to Stamford as Sir Robert Welles attempted to save his father's life. The two armies arrived at about the same time in the Stamford area, the rebels 5 miles to the north-west of the town in the parish of Empingham in Rutland, Edward over the county border in Stamford itself. Edward's scouts confirmed that the rebels were arrayed and ready for battle, so he moved up the Great North Road to confront them.

The Battle
The engagement was more a slaughter than a battle. Events started with the execution of the hapless Lord Welles and Sir Thomas Dymmock in front of both armies. Edward knew how to be ruthless when he needed to. As the rebels, led by Richard

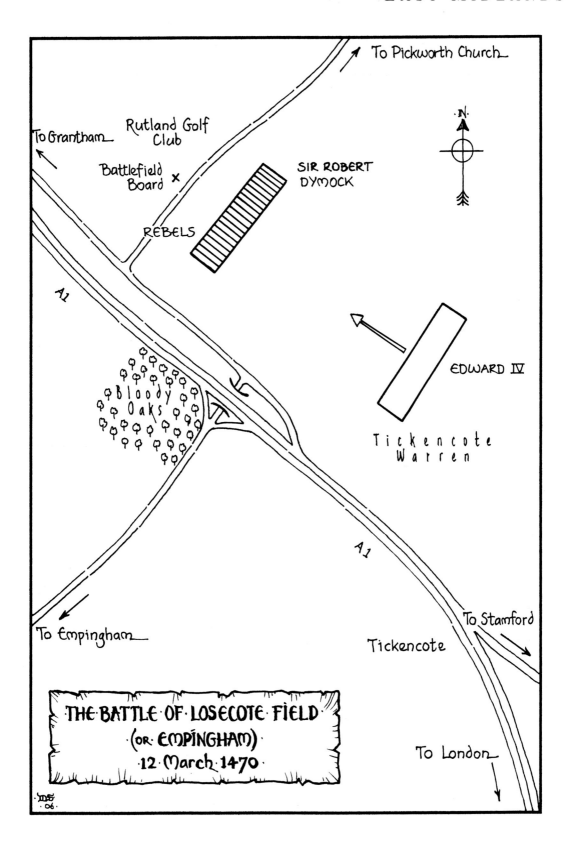

To Pickworth Church

Rutland Golf Club

To Grantham

Battlefield Board ✕

SIR ROBERT DYMOCK

REBELS

A1

Bloody Oaks

EDWARD IV

Tickencote Warren

A1

To Stamford

To Empingham

Tickencote

THE BATTLE OF LOSECOTE FIELD (OR EMPINGHAM) 12 March 1470

To London

Warren, moved forward with cries of 'A Warwick! A Clarence!' Edward ordered his cannon to open fire, causing heavy casualties among the rebel levies. When the royalists charged, the rebel line began to break even before the armies clashed. As the rebels fled the field, they discarded their livery jackets, provided by Warwick or Clarence, thus giving the battle its name. Edward captured the Duke of Clarence's envoy and had clear proof that his brother and Warwick had masterminded the revolt. Sir Robert Welles, Sir Thomas de la Laude and Richard Warren were captured as the rebels were routed.

Aftermath and Commentary

After the battle, Edward tried to insist that the principal conspirators disband their army and come to him. Warwick and Clarence of course refused but, importantly, had not been able to recruit enough troops to confront Edward on their own. The two armies proceeded northwards on parallel courses, the rebels via Rotherham, Edward via Doncaster. At Doncaster, Sir Robert Welles and Richard Warren were executed in front of the entire army. They had confessed not only to the involvement of Warwick and Clarence in the revolt, but also that its principal aim was to put Clarence on the throne.

Meanwhile, John Talbot, Earl of Shrewsbury had defected from Clarence to the King, taking with him many supporters from the north Midlands; likewise Sir William Parr, one of Warwick's captains from Cumberland. Warwick and Clarence found few new supporters at Rotherham. Having tried their luck with Lord Stanley in Lancashire, they were eventually forced to flee the kingdom from Dartmouth, seeking exile in France.

Edward had now recovered control of his kingdom after the humiliations of 1469. His military talents had returned. His vigorous campaign and ruthless pursuit of the rebels in the end ensured an easy victory. But if the Lincolnshire rebels had indeed joined together with the more 'professional' troops of Warwick and Clarence, there could have been a very different result. John Neville, Earl of Northumberland dealt with the risings in Yorkshire. These northern rebels never did meet up with those from Stamford. Edward pardoned their leaders (Sir John Conyers, Lord Scrope of Bolton and Robert Hildyard) in York later, in March. For Clarence, the rebellion was nothing short of disastrous. Not only had he personally taken the lead in organising it (rather than Warwick) but one of the main reasons for its failure was the lack of success the two conspirators had in recruiting supporters. The message was clear to Clarence (and to Warwick himself) – the country did not want him as King in place of his brother (and anyway was he up to the job?).

In true Wars of the Roses fashion, however, on the cusp of his triumph, Edward managed to 'snatch defeat from the jaws of victory'. At the end of March, he announced he was reinstating Henry Percy to the traditional family title and estates of Earl of Northumberland at the expense of his military bulwark in the north, John Neville (Warwick's brother). Neville was compensated with lands in the south-west and with promotion to Marquis Montagu. This was a miscalculation – it pushed Montagu into Warwick's camp and led directly to the debacle of Edward's flight from Doncaster via King's Lynn to the Netherlands in November 1470, and the Readeption of King Henry VI.

Participants and Casualties

Royalists
Kind Edward IV
John Mowbray, Duke of Norfolk
John de la Pole, Duke of Suffolk
John Stafford, Earl of Wiltshire
John Tiptoft, Earl of Worcester
William, Lord Hastings
John, Lord Howard
John Donne

Rebels
Sir Robert Welles
Sir Thomas de la Laude
Sir Thomas Dymmock
Richard Warren

Location and What to See

The battle was fought astride another Roman road, the Great North Road or A1, 5 miles north-west of Stamford between Tickencote Warren and the present-day Rutland Golf Club. It is therefore easy to find but unfortunately there is not too much to see. You will not want to stop on this fast section of the A1 dual carriageway. Take the Bloody Oaks turn-off and underpass to Empingham and Pickworth.

What to see:

- **Bloody Oaks** is the stand of trees on the north-west side of the A1. It is named after the slaughter of the rebels in 1469 and can be viewed from the south from the minor road to Empingham. On your way north on the A1, call in at the Texaco service station at Tickencote (1 mile south-east). It is called Star Bloody Oaks – well done, Texaco!
- The battle site. Go under the A1, take the minor road north-east towards Pickworth. After 200 yards is a local authority **information board**, very much where the battle action was.
- **Pickworth**. Take the minor road north-east from battlefield for 3 miles to Pickworth. The village is entered on a right-hand bend with church ahead. Park here. To the left of the church can be seen an old standing arch in the property adjacent. This is all that remains of the medieval church that was attacked and burned after the battle by Yorkist troops hunting rebel fugitives. A number took sanctuary in the old church but the Yorkists ignored this tradition.

LOWICK, St Peter's Church **
2 miles north of Islip on A6116 Corby road. Turn off left from new bypass. KAL.

You should visit Lowick for the church alone. Simon Jenkins describes it as a 'hidden masterpiece of English Perpendicular' financed largely by the wealthy Greene family of nearby Drayton House. The octagonal tower, completed after 1470, is stunning.

However, Lowick has more for the student of the Wars of the Roses. Sir Henry Greene (d. 1468) and his wife are buried here, commemorated by a fine tomb-chest and brasses. Henry was pardoned by Edward IV in 1462, although he does not seem to have fought at Towton the previous year. The couple had no sons but provide a good example of how the upwardly mobile and wealthy gentry could better their family through marriage. Their daughter, Constance, married John Stafford, the youngest of three sons of Humphrey Stafford, 1st Duke of Buckingham. During the period that Edward IV was bolstering his support in the struggle against the Kingmaker in 1469, John, a natural Lancastrian, was

Looking across the A1 at Bloody Oaks from the Losecote Field battlefield. Even Edward IV's household troops would have been no match for this lot.

made Earl of Wiltshire (although he received little extra land endowment to support this position).

John and Constance's son Edward Stafford, Earl of Wiltshire (d. 1498) was born in 1470 and was present at the coronations of both Richard III and Queen Elizabeth of York in 1487. He fought for Henry VII at the battles of Stoke (1487) and Blackheath (1497). He is commemorated by the handsome tomb-chest and effigy near his maternal grandparents.

MABLETHORPE, St Mary's Church *
¾ mile south-west of resort centre. Turn right off A1104 from Maltby, 1 mile from sea. Church ½ mile on left side.

Tomb-chest with brasses on the **north wall** to Sir Thomas Fitzwilliam (d. 1494) and wife Margaret Harrington, a Yorkist family. He was elected

*Brass to Sir Henry Greene, Lowick church.
Sir Henry's substantial wealth proved useful to the junior branch of the Staffords, ennobled by Edward IV as Earls of Wiltshire.*

Below: *Edward Stafford, 2nd Earl of Wiltshire, Lowick church.*

Recorder of London on 19 June 1483 and then took an important part in the meeting at the Guildhall five days later, at which the Duke of Buckingham entreated the citizens of London to offer the crown to Richard, Duke of Gloucester – a key step in Richard's second *coup d'état*. Fitzwilliam's role was to repeat Buckingham's words. It was still possible for him to speak as Recorder in Henry VII's first parliament in 1485 and he was knighted in 1486. He was later Speaker of the Commons.

MORLEY, St Matthew's Church **

Turn right off A608 Derby–Heanor road, approx. 3 miles
north-east of Derby. Church is in trees on left.
Saturday p.m. in summer.

This church is a treasure trove for the medieval historian. There is an interesting brass with inscription to John Sacheverell, who was killed at the Battle of Bosworth (1485) fighting for Richard III. John had married the Stathum heiress, whose family is also commemorated in brass in this church. John Stathum (d. 1452) was a retainer of Ralph, Lord Cromwell in the 1440s.

THE BATTLE OF NORTHAMPTON (10 July 1460) +

Strategic Background and the Campaign
The debacle of the Ludford Bridge campaign in the autumn of 1459 left the Yorkist leaders not only exiled but also attainted, with Queen Margaret in command of mainland England. On paper at least, she appointed James Butler, Earl of Wiltshire and Henry Beaufort, Duke of Somerset as Lieutenant of Ireland and Captain of Calais respectively, to replace the Duke of York and the Earl of Warwick. However, in practice it proved impossible to dislodge either 'rebel'; York was popular with the Irish, while the Kingmaker threw his immense energy and expertise into conducting a naval and land defence of Calais. Somerset led an expeditionary force to Calais but with no success, while Warwick raided Sandwich in Kent and destroyed a Lancastrian fleet under construction.

At the end of June 1460 Warwick was ready with 2,000 men accompanied by the Earl of Salisbury (his father), Edward, Earl of March and John, Lord Audley (son of the Lancastrian commander killed at the Battle of Blore Heath who had defected to the Yorkists). They landed at Sandwich, which Salisbury's brother Lord Fauconberg had been holding, and made quickly for London, reaching it

in early July. Amazingly, they found only a small Lancastrian force here, led by Lord Scales, who retreated into the Tower once he realised that the city leaders did not intend to resist the 'Calais Earls'. The main Lancastrian army was in fact at Coventry with the King and Queen, covering possible attack from both Calais and Ireland. After only a three-day stay, the Yorkist force moved up from London in two columns – one northwards towards Ely, the other north-west via St Albans. Salisbury and Sir John Wenlock were left behind to besiege the Tower.

The Lancastrians, meanwhile, were slowly moving southwards, allowing time for their many supporters to join them. However, the northern retinues under the Earl of Northumberland and Lord Clifford never made the battle. It is clear that the speed of the Yorkist earls' advance from Calais took the Lancastrians by surprise and proved decisive for the final result because the Lancastrian army was significantly below strength.

The Battle
The Lancastrians reached Northampton and dug into a traditional defensive position backing on to the River Neve with stakes, entrenchments and a ditch at the front, together with field guns. They numbered 10,000–15,000 men, led by Humphrey, Duke of Buckingham, John Talbot, Earl of Shrewsbury, Thomas Percy, Lord Egremont, John, Viscount Beaumont and Edmund, Lord Grey of Ruthin, who commanded the right wing.

After pausing for two days at Dunstable to allow extra contingents to join, the Yorkists advanced towards Northampton. It is probable that they spent the night of 9 July on Hunsbury Hill, south-west of Northampton, which overlooks the Nene. Heavy rain disrupted proceedings but the Yorkists arrayed west of Delapré Abbey in three divisions led by Lord Fauconberg, the Kingmaker and the 18-year-old Earl of March with John Mowbray, Duke of Norfolk.

In contrast with the low turn-out at Ludford Bridge the previous autumn, the Yorkists had for the first time a respectable company of nobility – Viscount Bourchier, Lords Abergavenny (Neville), Audley, Say and Sele, Scrope of Bolton and possibly Clinton and Stanley. The Duke of York himself remained in Ireland. Warwick had also brought with him Thomas Bourchier, Archbishop of Canterbury and the Papal Legate, perhaps with a view to obtaining a favourable deal and truce. As usual, therefore, efforts were made to mediate, but these were summarily dismissed by Buckingham for

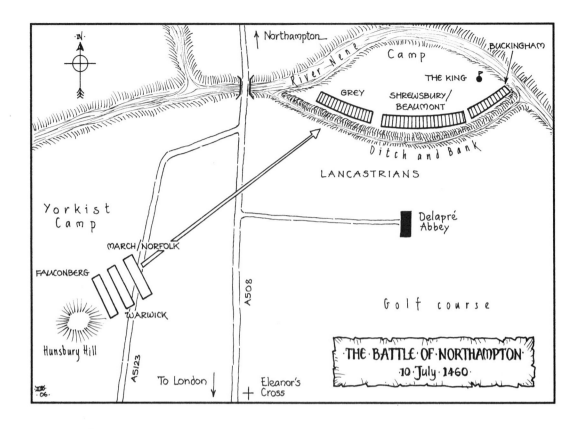

THE·BATTLE·OF·NORTHAMPTON·
10·July·1460·

the Lancastrians. The clerics retreated to the nearby Eleanor cross to view the battle.

In the early afternoon, the Yorkist trumpets announced the simultaneous advance in three battles. Initially the troops found the going hard in slippery conditions. The rain, however, also seems to have completely nullified the Lancastrian artillery. But the battle was effectively decided by the sudden treachery of Lord Grey of Ruthin, who ordered his troops on the Lancastrian right to assist the opposing Yorkists in ascending the entrenchments. The Lancastrian army was thrown into confusion, and within thirty minutes the fighting was over. Royal soldiers fled towards Northampton, a number drowning in the river. Buckingham, Shrewsbury, Beaumont and Egremont were caught in or in front of their tents and slain as they stood by the Yorkists. The King was captured by a Yorkist archer and the Yorkist leaders found him in his tent, where they paid due homage. He was escorted to Delapré Abbey and then via Northampton to London. The Tower soon capitulated to the Yorkists.

Aftermath and Commentary

The failure of the Lancastrian forces to concentrate at Northampton was calamitous. In fact, the relatively few peers who were present were kinsmen of the Duke of Buckingham. Even without Grey of Ruthin's treachery, the Yorkists would probably have won through weight of numbers, although casualties on both sides would have been much higher. As at the First Battle of St Albans, speed of concentration was key. Treachery in the Wars of the Roses usually paid off; Edward IV made Grey of Ruthin Earl of Kent in 1465, and he was briefly Treasurer of England in 1463.

The Battle of Northampton represents another 'change of government' during Henry's reign brought about by force of arms. Henry was well treated by the Yorkists but he now resided in London. In came Warwick as 'Chief Minister'; for the moment, Richard, Duke of York was supine in Ireland. 'Out' went Queen Margaret, who fled to Wales with Prince Edward. Warwick could never himself be king but he had now achieved his first goal – to govern the country himself, with Henry as a 'constitutional' monarch.

> *Participants and Casualties*
> Yorkists outnumbered Lancastrians, whose troops from the north had not yet arrived.
>
> **Yorkist**
> Richard Neville, Earl of Warwick
> Edward, Earl of March
> John Mowbray, Duke of Norfolk
> William Neville, Lord Fauconberg
> Viscount Bourchier
> Edward Neville, Lord Abergavenny
> Lord Say and Sele
> Lord Scrope of Bolton
> Thomas, Lord Stanley (possibly)
>
> **Lancastrian**
> King Henry VI
> Humphrey Buckingham, Duke of Buckingham
> John Talbot, Earl of Shrewsbury
> John, Viscount Beaumont
> Thomas Percy, Lord Egremont
> Edmund Grey, Lord Grey of Ruthin
> Sir John Beaumont
>
> Casualties: Yorkist light, Lancastrian 300 dead

Location and What to See

The battlefield lies south of the River Nene, east of the A508 Northampton–Roade road. Most accounts of the battle place the Lancastrian position as backing on to the river in an area now occupied by an industrial estate and a cosmetics factory. A walk along the **north** bank of the Nene in the park adjoining the A428 road is instructive. Otherwise a visit to **Delapré Abbey**, further south down the A508, is useful, though nothing remains from the period. Some commentators put the battle lines immediately south of Delapré Abbey, now a golf course. The **Eleanor cross** where the clerics waited during the battle is well worth a visit. It actually marks where the funeral cortège carrying Eleanor of Castile's body halted for the night on its way to London in 1290. It lies ¾ mile south of the abbey on the east side of the A508.

Finally, **Hunsbury Hill** Country Park can be visited on the south-west side of the A45 ring road, west of the A508 roundabout. This is the likely site of the Yorkist camp and contains Iron Age earthworks. Perhaps Northampton is not proud of its association with a Wars of the Roses battle, although the museum does display a medieval inscription. But then there is nothing really to be proud of about this shameful affair.

POTTERSPURY, Queen's Oak **

1½ miles north-west of village. 400 yds north of Potterspury Lodge School. Access on foot only. See map. Park on minor road off A5 to Yardley Gobion in tiny hamlet (called Moor End) after 1 mile. Take Grafton Way footpath through gate (signposted to the Gullet).

This has to be a favourite because it is so different. There is no blood and thunder, no tomb, no treachery, but what this site has is romance (although a good imagination helps). Behind the Steiner School at Potterspury Lodge, about ½ mile off the A5 (Watling Street), can be found the Queen's Oak, said to be planted at the spot where in 1464 **King Edward IV** first met Dame **Elizabeth** Grey (née **Woodville**), flanked by her two young sons, while he was hunting in Whittlebury Forest nearby.

Elizabeth is said to have thrown herself at Edward's feet in an attempt to lobby for her rightful inheritance from her husband, Sir John Grey (killed at the Second Battle of St Albans, fighting for Lancaster), which was being withheld by her mother-in-law. She had struck a deal with William, Lord Hastings, who no doubt set up the meeting. Tradition has it that Edward and Elizabeth were married within the month, the deal now irrelevant. The rest is history. Cynics may say that tradition is probably invention in this case, but a visit to the site reveals it to be in a very credible location. It is on the old road from Watling Street (i.e. London) to Alderton and Grafton Regis (the Woodville home). Now only a track, it does cross the nearby stream over a well-engineered bridge. The location is also well hidden from prying eyes on Watling Street, so a busy king could divert off the Roman road for a discussion in some sort of privacy.

The interesting thing here is that the oak tree in question is only two or three years old and in a plastic tube (actually there are two of them at present). The remains of the previous one lie nearby, having been set on fire some years ago. Perhaps the new one is the third since 1465, but it certainly needs visiting to ensure that the sapling gets established. Take a picnic; you are unlikely to be disturbed. An hour's round walk.

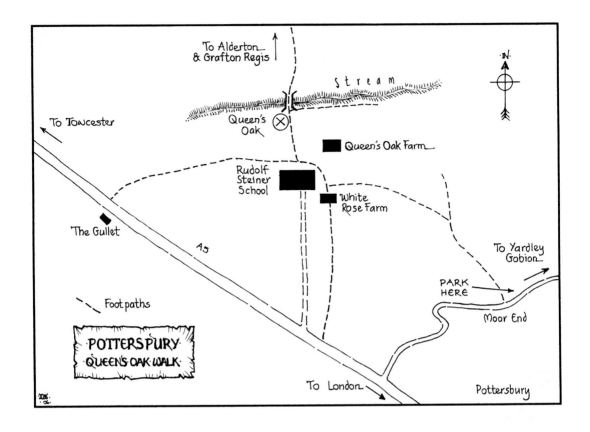

Map: POTTERSPURY QUEEN'S OAK WALK

STAMFORD, St Mary's Church *

Town centre.

Stamford is a fine town to visit. Its four splendid medieval churches are all centrally situated. In January 1461 the Lancastrian troops of Margaret of Anjou sacked Stamford en route to the Second Battle of St Albans (the dukes of York held the manor of Stamford). St Mary's nave and aisles had to be rebuilt after suffering fire damage. In the **chancel** there is a tomb-chest with effigies to Sir David Phillip (d. 1506) and his wife, Anne Semark. Sir David was a Welshman who was in exile with Henry Tudor in France and fought at the Battle of Bosworth (1485). He became an esquire of the body to Henry and steward to Lady Margaret Beaufort, who lived at nearby Collyweston. You might like to visit the fifteenth-century **Browne's Hospital**, founded by a wealthy wool merchant in 1475. It is located in Broad Street.

STOKE DRY, St Andrew's Church **

High up in the centre of the hamlet on the Stockerston–Lyddington minor road. 2 miles south-west of A6002 crossroads.

This is a little gem high above a reservoir. Stoke Dry was the home of the Digbys. For a change we are interested primarily in the tomb and **incised slab** of a woman, Jacquetta, née Ellis of Devon, who married Sir Everard Digby. Sir Everard was killed fighting for Lancaster at Towton (1461) and attainted, leaving Jacquetta to bring up their fourteen children on little or no income. They are also shown on this slab. Family tradition has it that all six sons fought for Henry Tudor at Bosworth (1485). The church monuments to Everard (see Tilton) and Simon (see Coleshill), the two eldest, survive. Jacquetta survived her husband by thirty-five years, dying in 1496, and unusually is buried alone. Another Everard (d. 1540) is buried here.

THE BATTLE OF STOKE FIELD (16 June 1487) ++

Strategic Background and the Campaign

In the chaos that followed Richard III's death at the Battle of Bosworth in 1485, a number of senior Yorkists were able to escape, one of whom was Francis, Viscount Lovell (Richard's friend from boyhood). Lovell took sanctuary in

Tomb of the indefatigable Lady Jacquetta Digby, Stoke Dry church.

Colchester Abbey with Sir Humphrey and Sir Thomas Stafford. In April 1486 they broke out and raised rebellion at Middleham, the former Neville stronghold in Yorkshire, and in Worcestershire. Neither revolt attracted much support. Henry offered pardons to the rebels in Middleham and Lovell was forced to flee. The Staffords were forcibly removed from sanctuary in Oxfordshire and Sir Humphrey executed. Lovell was eventually forced into exile in Burgundy at the court of Margaret, Dowager Duchess of Burgundy and sister to Richard III, where John de la Pole, Earl of Lincoln, who had been Richard III's heir, later joined him. Nevertheless, there was still considerable residual support for the Yorkist kings in the country.

During 1486 an Oxford priest named Richard Simons had been training one of his scholars, Lambert Simnel, to impersonate Edward Plantagenet, Earl of Warwick, who was the Duke of Clarence's son. Barred from his inheritance through attainder, Edward had been placed in the Tower by Henry VII as soon as he gained the throne. Simnel provided a plausible figurehead whose name gave an aura to the enterprise around which Yorkists could rally. Margaret of Burgundy supplied finance for German mercenaries led by a Captain Martin Schwartz. Simnel was taken to Ireland, which had long been pro-Yorkist and where the support of Gerald Fitzgerald, Earl of Kildare was obtained, perhaps through promises of home rule. In late May 1487 Lambert Simnel was 'crowned' King Edward VI at Christ Church, Dublin. A number of die-hard Yorkists joined Simnel in Ireland – Richard Harleston, Sir Henry Bodrugan, Sir John Beaumont. Henry VII meanwhile had moved his military base up to Coventry/Kenilworth.

On 4 June the rebel Yorkists landed on the Lancashire coast near Piel Island, close to Barrow in Furness, in an area where a Yorkist sympathiser, Sir Thomas Broughton, held lands and influence. Travelling via Carnforth and Sedburgh, the army headed for Yorkshire, where old Neville and Ricardian sympathies were at their strongest. Moving quickly, but recruiting as they went, in four days the Yorkists had reached Masham, near Ripon. Lords Thomas Scrope of Masham and John Scrope of Bolton offered support and assistance in Yorkshire but may not actually have journeyed south. The Yorkists found the City of York barred to them so they bypassed it and proceeded down the Great North Road. They camped for the night at Bramham Moor, where Sir Henry Clifford, the 'Shepherd Lord', attempted to engage the rebels but was routed by them.

As soon as King Henry heard about the landing, he assembled his forces and headed northwards. He was accompanied by an impressive array of peers and not just mainstream Lancastrians – the Earl of Shrewsbury, who had fought for Richard III at Bosworth, was there, together with Sir Edward Woodville. By 11 June the royal army had reached Loughborough. The rebels meanwhile marched south via Castleford, Doncaster and Southwell, which was reached on 14 June. The rebels decided not to confront the defenders of Newark Castle in order to cross the River Trent, but instead crossed at Fiskerton, where the river was wide and shallow (they had good local knowledge). Camping overnight in water meadows just over the river, they remained hidden from view from the nearby Fosse Way.

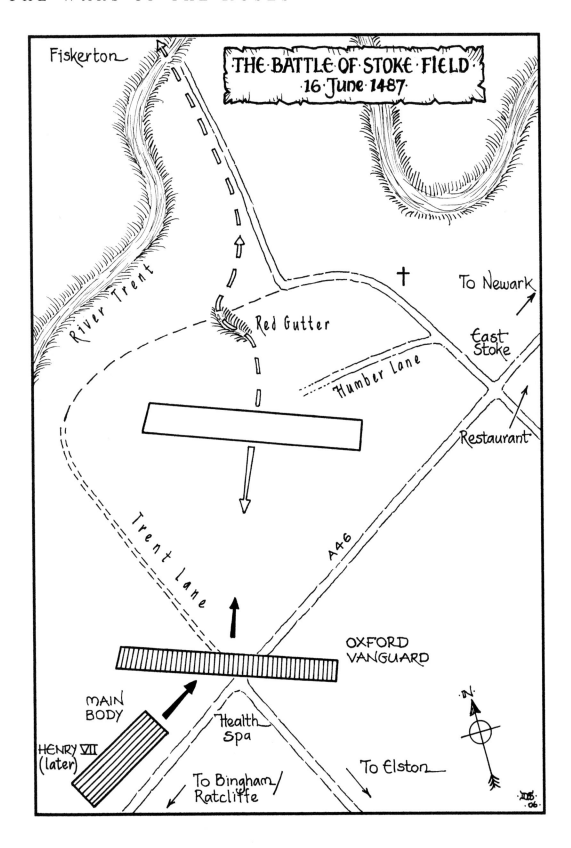

Fiskerton

THE·BATTLE·OF·STOKE·FIELD
16·June·1487·

River Trent

To Newark

East Stoke

Red Gutter

Humber Lane

Restaurant

Trent Lane

A46

OXFORD VANGUARD

MAIN BODY

Health Spa

HENRY VII (later)

To Elston

To Bingham/ Ratcliffe

·N·

The Battle

Early in the morning of 16 June the Yorkists had time to choose their ground before arraying for battle. Although they had recruited perhaps 9,000 or 10,000 men, they were short of solid support from the nobility. They did have the impressive German mercenaries, but then again, the Irish troops led by Thomas Geraldine were poorly equipped.

Henry's forces were unaware of the exact location of the rebels. In fact they did not realise that the rebels had crossed the Trent, because their camp was so well hidden. Accordingly they set out from Radcliffe in the direction of Newark in 'column' marching formation, not in 'line across' battle formation. The vanguard, under John de Vere, Earl of Oxford, came across the rebels quite suddenly near East Stoke. Oxford was therefore forced to advance to the attack rather than risk being exposed to the enemy while he waited for Henry's reinforcements to move up. Goaded by Oxford's superior archery fire, the rebels charged down the slope and for over an hour held their own against his more regular troops. Oxford's line steadily gave way until he was reinforced by the main body of the army led by Jasper Tudor, Duke of Bedford, arriving 'hot foot' from Radcliffe. The rebels were now badly outnumbered; their line soon began to waver and, after three hours of conflict, it broke. In the rout, the slaughter was particularly heavy in 'Red Gutter' as men tried desperately to clamber back down towards the Trent.

Aftermath and Commentary

Lambert Simnel was captured in the rout and put to work in the royal kitchens. He never troubled Henry again. Lincoln was killed in the battle, much to Henry VII's anger; he had hoped to interrogate him. Lovell was never seen again. Tradition has it that he either drowned in the Trent while trying to ride to safety or he starved to death in a secret hide-out in his family home at Minster Lovell, Oxford-shire, where a walled-up skeleton was found in the eighteenth century. The conspiracy was crushed. Edward, Earl of Warwick remained incarcerated in the Tower of London until 1499 when Henry VII had him executed in an attempt to mollify the Spanish ambassador ahead of his son's wedding to Catherine of Aragon (but that is another story).

The military turnout for Henry Tudor at this battle was very impressive. He was now able to establish fully the Tudor dynasty. But something had gone badly wrong with Henry's scouting on the morning of the battle. It had been unexpectedly hard fought and, against a more formidable opponent, the effect could have been disastrous.

Participants and Casualties

Yorkists (~5,000)	Tudor (~6,000)
John de la Pole, Earl of Lincoln	King Henry VII
Francis, Viscount Lovell	Jasper Tudor, Duke of Bedford
Lambert Simnel	John de Vere, Earl of Oxford
Sir Thomas Broughton	Edward Grey, Viscount Lisle
Sir James Harrington	Sir Gilbert Talbot
Sir Henry Bodrugan	George Talbot, Earl of Shrewsbury
Sir Jonn Beaumont	Lord Strange
Thomas Fitzgerald (Irish)	Sir John Cheney
Captain Martin Schwartz (German)	Sir John Savage
	Sir Rhys ap Thomas
	Sir Antony Browne
	Charles Somerset
	Sir Richard Pole
	Sir Edmund Bedingfield
	Sir William Carew
	Sir Amyas Paulet
	Sir Simon Digby
	Sir David Philip
	Sir John Mordaunt
Casualties: Yorkist ~5,000 dead	Tudor ~3,000 dead

Recently constructed monument to the dead from the Battle of Stoke Field.

Location and What to See

The battle was fought astride the Fosse Way (now A46) between Newark and Nottingham, just west of East Stoke village. The A46 is a very busy and fast trunk road. The battle site itself is on private land but can be viewed as follows:

- Turn north off the A46 in **East Stoke** to the church. Here there is a recent memorial to the dead from the battle.
- Continue northwards on a very minor dead-end to the River Trent opposite **Fiskerton** village (where Viscount Lovell may have drowned with many others and where the rebels camped overnight).
- Return to the woods at Stoke Park and walk 50 yards westwards. **Red Gutter** leads up the escarpment in the woods.
- Walk further westwards by the river until a left turn is reached (**Trent Lane**) and take this track south-east. The fields on your left are where the

battle was fought. The Yorkist right wing was on the high ground by Burham Furlong, where Henry raised his standard to signify victory.
- Return to your car and drive back towards East Stoke. Two hundred yards before the A46 crossroads, turn sharp right along **Humber Lane**. Drive and walk to the end to get a different view of the Yorkist position.

STRELLEY, All Saints' Church *

On the north-west outskirts of Nottingham, squeezed between A6002 and M1 (no direct access). Leave M1 at junction 26. Take A6002 south to Stapleford. After 2 miles, turn right at traffic lights up dead-end to Strelley Hall and church. KAL.

A fine collection of medieval church monuments and brasses to the Strelley family, including a **double brass** to Sir Robert Strelley (1420–87) and his wife. Sir Robert was introduced into the household of Henry VI in 1451/2 by his uncle, Archbishop Kemp of Canterbury (his mother, Isabella, was Kemp's sister). A sheriff of Nottingham and Derby, he raised troops for King Henry in February 1452, when Richard, Duke of York threatened London as he campaigned against Edmund Beaufort, Duke of Somerset. He accompanied the troops to London and was present at the Dartford fiasco when York was tricked by Henry and the Duke of Somerset into surrender. Robert remained a firm Lancastrian supporter and was knighted during 1459/60, perhaps before the Battle of Northampton. He took part in the Barnet–Tewkesbury campaign in 1471. His gentry neighbours described him as overly 'acquisitive' – a common fault in that era.

TATTERSHALL ***

½ mile south-west of village centre on A153 Horncastle–Sleaford road. NT. 01526 342543.

The grouping of the large **Holy Trinity Church** and **castle** provide a splendid memorial to Ralph, 3rd Lord Cromwell (1393–1456 – no relation!). The church was originally collegiate and was built after his death under the supervision of Bishop Waynflete. It took fifty years to complete. Cromwell is commemorated in a brass in the **north transept**, although his head is missing ('posthumously', like his namesake's). The adjacent brass of his wife, Margaret Deyncourt, has been lost. She was a substantial heiress in her own right but the marriage was childless.

Tattershall Castle, built by Ralph, Lord Cromwell.

Cromwell's money bag emblem, from a fireplace in Tattershall Castle.

Cromwell was knighted at Agincourt. From 1422 he was a member of the King's Council as a supporter of Cardinal Beaufort. For a record ten years, from 1433–43, he was Lord High Treasurer of England, at that time probably the most difficult job in the country, given the position of Crown finances. It was, however, also the most lucrative job, with ample scope for further financial 'enhancements' before he retired from office in 1443. In short, Cromwell was a wealthy man. He was also a great builder; in addition to Tattershall, he built a large fortified mansion at South Wingfield in Derbyshire (which can be visited), and he built extensively at Collyweston near Stamford. Cromwell showed great skill in exploiting every loophole in the property law in order to increase his estates. This led him into many disputes with other landholders (Ampthill, in Bedfordshire, and South Wingfield, as well as the Percy manors in Yorkshire). He was briefly imprisoned in Wallingford Castle in 1454 after clashing violently with the Duke of Exeter.

He was a member of Richard, Duke of York's Council but did not support him militarily. As Cromwell was childless, his nieces Joan and Maud, née Stanhope (his sister Margaret's daughters) were his heiresses. They also have brasses in the north transept. Maud was first married in 1448 to Lord Willoughby de Eresby, who had been part of the escort for Queen Margaret of Anjou to England in 1445. Her second marriage, in 1453, was to **Sir Thomas Neville**, second son of Richard Neville, Earl of Salisbury. After the wedding at Tattershall, Maud quickly got a taste of what she had let herself in for. The bridal party, including Maud, Salisbury, Thomas and his brother John were returning to the family estates in Yorkshire when they were confronted by their Percy rivals fully armed, led by Lord Egremont, at Heworth Moor, just north of York. Much abuse was hurled but fortunately there were no casualties. The bridal party continued on safely. The particular reason that the Percys were so incensed about the wedding was that Cromwell's estate included manors which they regarded as traditional Percy property (Wressle and others in Yorkshire and some in Lincolnshire). To see it pass to their arch-rivals, the Nevilles, was too much.

Some time later, the Kingmaker forcefully accused Cromwell of being 'the beginner of that journey [battle] at St Albans' (First Battle, 1455) in front of the King. Cromwell's new-found alliance with the Nevilles was abruptly broken. Sir Thomas Neville being among the Yorkist casualties at the disastrous Battle of Wakefield (1460), Maud then married Sir Gervase Clifton, a Lancastrian who was subsequently executed after the Battle of Tewkesbury (1471). Then followed twenty-six years of widowhood; Maud was, of course, wealthy in her own right. It is interesting that in the brass she chose to be known as Lady Willoughby.

Joan's first marriage was to **Sir Humphrey Bourchier**, eldest son of the Yorkist Earl of Essex. He was granted the title of Lord Cromwell but was killed at the Battle of Barnet (1471). She then married Sir Robert Radcliffe, another Yorkist supporter.

As a result of the falling-out with Warwick, in his will Cromwell had caused a sensation on his death in 1456 by only leaving a portion of his estates to his nieces. The families-in-law were furious, and straight after the funeral Neville and Bourchier led the way in stripping the estate of furnishings etc. The elder sister, Joan, and husband inherited Tattershall and South Wingfield. In 1471 Tattershall was confiscated by the Crown and subsequently given by Henry VII to his mother, Lady Margaret Beaufort. The castle was restored in 1912 by Viscount Curzon and has a particularly interesting interior, including stained glass installed by him.

TILTON-ON-THE-HILL, St Peter's Church *
Village centre on B6047 Market Harborough–Melton Mowbray road.

In the **south aisle** a tomb-chest and effigy of Sir Everard Digby (1440–1509), son and heir of the Sir Everard killed at the Battle of Towton (1461) and attainted. Sir Everard II was sheriff and MP for Rutland and fought at the Battle of Bosworth (1485). The family tradition is that all six Digby brothers

were present on that day on the side of Henry Tudor (see Stoke Dry and Coleshill). The family were certainly well rewarded after the battle by Henry Tudor, which enabled Everard to fund the rebuilding of this church in 1490, including the delightful clerestory windows.

WAPPENHAM, St Mary's Church *
Small village 3 miles north of A43 at Syresham. From A43 follow signs to Syresham and Wappenham, church at western end.

Floor brass to Sir Thomas Billing (d. 1481), Chief Justice of the King's Bench from 1469, and his first wife, Katherine Gifford. Billing was of lower-class origins, and his patron was Edmund, Lord Grey de Ruthlin – not a great start in life (see the Battle of Northampton). He conducted two particularly controversial trials in 1477, that of Thomas Burdet, the supporter of Edward IV's brother George, Duke of Clarence who was subsequently executed, and, in 1478, the extraordinary trial of George himself, when Edward IV was chief witness. Clarence was privately executed in February 1478, allegedly in a butt of Malmsey wine. Hampton tells us that Billing 'is regarded as one of the least worthy holders of his high office, sycophantic, corrupt and unjust'. He is not, then one of our heroes.

WOLLATON, St Leonard's Church *
West side of city, ¼ mile south of A609 Nottingham–Ilkeston road, just north of north-west corner of Wollaton Park.

There are two memorials of interest in this church. On the north wall of the chancel a tomb-chest, brasses and cadaver to Sir Richard Willoughby (d. 1471). On the south side of the chancel a tomb-chest, effigies and cadaver to Sir Henry Willoughby (d. 1528) and his four wives. Sir Henry fought for Henry Tudor at the nearby Battle of Stoke Field (1487). Henry was knighted after that battle. Sir Henry's will referred to five coal pits which even in the late fifteenth century were earning good profits. A century later they had increased sufficiently to permit the building of the magnificent Elizabethan mansion in the adjacent park.

WEST MIDLANDS

ASTLEY, St Mary's Church and Castle **
North side of village. Turn off B4102 Nuneaton–Hampton in Arden road towards Ansley. Church on right. KAL.

This fascinating building was originally a much larger collegiate church formed by Sir Thomas Astley in the fourteenth century. Under the **tower** are the only three monuments remaining from the college, placed together but, in fact, originally separate.

The man represents Sir Edward Grey, Lord Ferrers of Groby (d. 1457). Sir Edward was the eldest son of Reginald Grey (Lord Grey of Ruthin) by his second wife, Joan Astley, the heiress to the Astley estates. Sir Edward married Elizabeth Ferrers, heiress to the Ferrers title, based at Groby, Leicestershire. Sir Edward and Elizabeth's eldest son, Sir John Grey, became in 1452 the first husband of Elizabeth Woodville, later Edward IV's queen. After their marriage, the couple probably resided at the adjacent castle. The sting in the tail here is that on Sir Edward's death in 1457, Elizabeth his wife, as the Ferrers heiress, chose to keep the title herself and not to pass it on to her son, Sir John. Elizabeth Ferrers then married Sir John Bourchier, an early Yorkist, so perhaps dynastic politics were getting in the way here. Sir John Grey was a staunch Lancastrian and cavalryman. He was killed fighting for Lancaster in February 1461 at the Second Battle of St Albans. The title finally passed to Thomas Grey, Marquis of Dorset, Elizabeth's grandson, in 1483 on her death.

The delightful middle lady is Elizabeth Talbot, co-heiress of the Lisle titles and estates, the junior title of the powerful Talbot earls of Shrewsbury. Elizabeth's father was killed at the Battle of Castillon, France in July 1453, fighting alongside his own father John Talbot, 1st Earl (see Whitchurch). Elizabeth married Sir Edward Grey (1442–93), second son of Sir Edward above, who is also buried in this church (no monument). Sir Edward became a councillor to Warwick and to Clarence in the 1460s. He supported Richard III's coup in 1483 and was quickly rewarded with both his title and lands. He seems to have disengaged himself from Richard before Bosworth, since he was also in favour with Henry VII.

The third effigy is that of Cecily Bonville (1460–1529), daughter and heiress of William Bonville, Lord Harrington, killed at the Battle of Wakefield (1460), and Katherine Neville, the Kingmaker's sister. She held lands in Devon and was the second wife of **Thomas Grey, Marquis of Dorset**, the eldest son of Sir John Grey and Elizabeth Woodville above. The Marquis is also buried in this church. Cecily either had a heart of gold or was long-suffering. Grey was a notorious womaniser, competing with Hastings and even Edward IV for the hands of mistresses, including Jane Shore. Yet the couple had fifteen children before Thomas died in 1501. It is from this eldest direct line that Lady Jane Grey, the nine-day queen in 1553, was descended. She spent time in this church and castle.

The **castle** is derelict and closed and looks dangerous. Its origins are thirteenth century but most of the features are Elizabethan.

AYMESTREY, St John Baptist and St Allmund's Church *
Village centre on A4110 Hereford–Wigmore road.

In the chancel an incised slab to Sir John Lingen (d. 1506) and his wife, Elizabeth Burgh (d. 1522). His figure is obscured. Sir John was involved in the 1456 south Wales raid with other early Yorkists (e.g. William Herbert and Thomas Vaughan). In February 1461 he fought for his neighbouring landowner, Edward, 4th Duke of York, at the nearby Battle of Mortimer's Cross, thus helping Edward in his drive for the throne of England.

BADDESLEY CLINTON, House and St Michael's Church **
Signposted west off A4141 Warwick–Solihull road, in Baddesley Clinton village. NT. 01564 783294.

Described by Pevsner as 'the perfect late medieval manor house', Baddesley Clinton was built in the mid- to late fifteenth century by John Brome and his son Nicholas, with later additions by Sir Edward Ferrers, Nicholas's son-in-law. A visit here is thus worthwhile just for the house but, in fact, offers yet another example of the violence endemic in the fifteenth century among the middle and upper classes. John Brome (k. 1468) was a wealthy lawyer from Warwick who became Under-Treasurer of the Exchequer in the mid-1440s. He was appointed by Henry Beauchamp, Duke of Warwick to be Warwick Chamberlain in 1445. However, on the Duke's death, Brome was immediately dismissed by the new Earl of Warwick, Richard Neville, who instead appointed Thomas Colt. Brome then lent his support to Margaret Talbot, Countess of Shrewsbury in her Beauchamp inheritance dispute

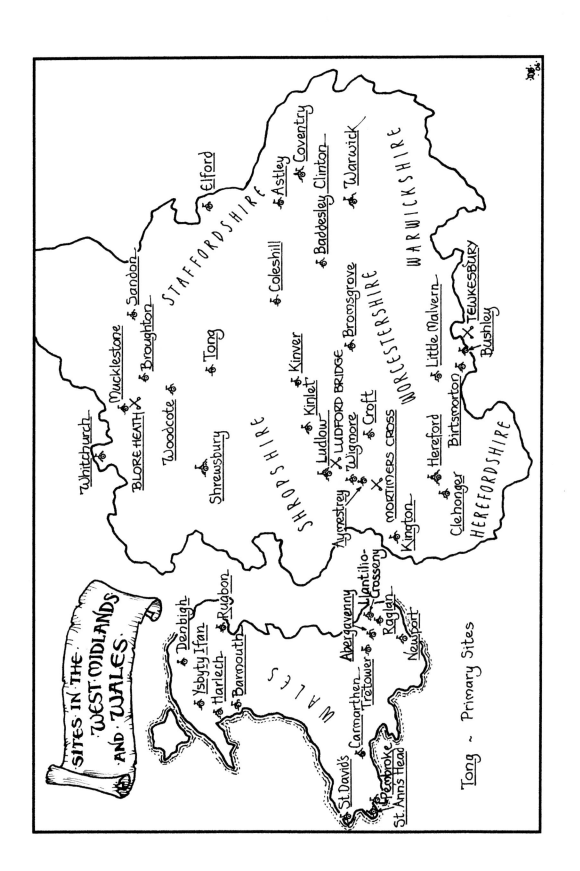

SITES IN THE WEST MIDLANDS AND WALES.

Whitchurch

Muckleston

Sandon

Broughton

BLORE HEATH

Woodcote

Elford

STAFFORDSHIRE

Tong

Astley

Coventry

Baddesley Clinton

Warwick

WARWICKSHIRE

Coleshill

Shrewsbury

Kinver

Kinlet

LUDFORD BRIDGE

Bromsgrove

WORCESTERSHIRE

Little Malvern

Tewkesbury

Bushley

SHROPSHIRE

Ludlow

Wigmore

Croft

Birtsmorton

Aymestrey

MORTIMERS CROSS

Hereford

Kington

Clehonger

HEREFORDSHIRE

Denbigh

Ruabon

Abergavenny

Llantilio-Crossenny

Raglan

Newport

Ysbyty Ifan

Harlech

Barmouth

WALES

Carmarthen

Tretower

St. David's

Pembroke

St. Ann's Head

Tong ~ Primary Sites

Baddesley Clinton, built by John Brome.

with Warwick. This was not necessarily an astute move, given the Kingmaker's ruthlessness. True to form, four times in 1450 and 1451, Brome's properties (no doubt including this house) were attacked by members of Warwick's affinity. At one stage, in 1450, the Kingmaker's inherited title was suspended and Brome reinstated as Warwick Chamberlain. However, the Kingmaker got his man in the end.

John Brome was murdered by one John Herthill, steward to the Kingmaker, in November 1468 in the porch of the Whitefriars Church in London. In accordance with the culture of the time, the matter did not rest there. John's second son, Nicholas (d. 1517), avenged his death in 1471 by murdering Herthill at Longbridge, 3 miles south-west of Warwick. Nicholas was obviously something of a hothead. In the mid-1480s he returned home to Baddesley Clinton unexpectedly to find the local priest 'chokinge his wife under ye chinne' and so slew him. No doubt in big trouble, Nicholas obtained pardons from both the pope and the King. His penance was to erect the tower on the Baddesley Clinton church and a steeple at nearby Packwood. The house guidebook tells us

that 'Nicholas died in 1517 extremely humble and penitent and is said to have been buried under the **church porch** so that he will be trodden on by all who enter.' A nineteenth-century stone just inside the south door of the church marks the spot.

The church also contains a tomb-chest to Sir Edward Ferrers (1465–1535) and his wife Constance (Nicholas's daughter). The **east window** contains glass of Nicholas Brome and Sir Edward and Lady Constance. The interior of the house is largely sixteenth and seventeenth century, but very pleasant. There is some good armorial glass, including some of Sir Edward Ferrers.

BIRTSMORTON, St Peter and St Paul's Church **

*House and church ½ mile north of A438 Tewkesbury–
Ledbury road. 1 mile after Sledge Green, turn north up
minor road. Church on left.*

A lovely house and church pairing. The church contains a tomb-chest to Jane, née Coleshill in memory of her three husbands, Sir John Nanfan (1400–59) being the second On the tomb south side is a kneeling figure

Weeper of Sir Richard Nanfan in Birtsmorton church.

of Sir John in armour, plus Sir Richard and Sir John junior, his sons. Sir John was an esquire of the body to Henry VI from 1447 and Governor of Jersey 1451–7. He was a retainer of the Beauchamp earls of Warwick who managed their lands during the difficult period 1436–50. His son, <u>Sir Richard</u> (1445–1507), was attainted after being involved in Buckingham's Revolt in 1483. He fled to France but returned with Tudor to fight at the Battle of Bosworth. He became a knight of the body to Henry VII.

The family hailed from Cornwall and, after a successful spell in the French wars, Sir John bought **Birtsmorton Court**, next door. Here, in May 1471, the fugitive **Queen Margaret of Anjou** sought shelter after the Battle of Tewkesbury with her old friend Jane Nanfan. The Court is still there, delightfully positioned behind trees; much of the fourteenth- and fifteenth-century house remains, surrounded by a moat. It is a private house but you can catch a glimpse from the church (better in winter). The Queen did not stay long, probably moving on to Little Malvern Priory. The Nanfans were upper gentry, holding further lands in Wales, Buckinghamshire and Warwickshire.

THE BATTLE OF BLORE HEATH
(23 September 1459) ++

Strategic Background and the Campaign

This battle was part of the September/October campaign in 1459 which culminated in the rout of Ludford Bridge near Ludlow, when the Yorkist leaders were forced to flee into exile. Richard Neville, Earl of Salisbury had raised an army of Yorkshire and north-country retainers in response to Richard, Duke of York's appeal to meet at Ludlow, Shropshire along with Salisbury's son Richard Neville, Earl of Warwick. York desired to confront King Henry VI as they had done at St Albans in 1455. Coming from the north, Salisbury had reached Blore Heath, between Newcastle-under-Lyme and Market Drayton, when he was confronted by a Lancastrian force led by James Touchet, Lord Audley. This force had been raised in Cheshire in the name of Queen Margaret's son, Edward Prince of Wales, and was separate from King Henry's main Lancastrian army which lay 10 miles away. Henry had, in fact, summoned Thomas, Lord Stanley and his brother Sir William with 2,000 troops to join the Prince's army from Lancashire. Thomas began his war as he meant to continue – he volunteered to

command the Lancastrian vanguard but, when turned down, he held his troops off and sulked only 6 miles away. Sir William, for his part, sent troops to join the Yorkist army.

The Battle

Audley was a surprise choice for Lancastrian commander. He was a local landowner but had only limited military experience in France. His army contained a large proportion of cavalry. Audley's orders from Queen Margaret, unusually, were to take the Earl of Salisbury prisoner. Second in command was John, Lord Dudley. Most of the knights were from Cheshire and Lancashire. The Lancastrians occupied a very strong defensive position but not such a good position from which to launch offensive manoeuvres uphill to the ridge.

The Yorkists were outnumbered by at least 2:1. However, their troops were experienced and comprised trusty northerners (including Salisbury's youngest sons, Sir Thomas and Sir John Neville, Sir Thomas Harrington, Sir Thomas Parr and Sir John Conyers). Their position was also strong defensively; offensively, they had the advantage of the westward slope. They also had the major advantage in Salisbury

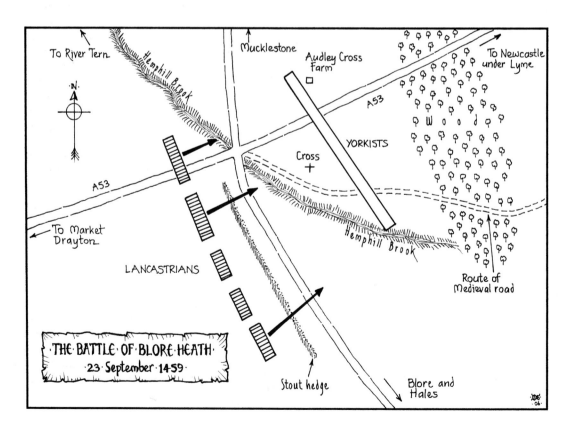

of a commander with vast experience of warfare in France and in the northern Marches.

The decisive moment of the battle probably came right at the beginning at around midday. In order to break the defensive deadlock, Salisbury somehow feigned a retreat with a wagon laager on his right wing. The wings may also have been hidden over the ridge. The less experienced Audley fell for the ruse and ordered an assault by his cavalry (perhaps believing Salisbury to be retreating?) across Hemphill Brook and up the slope. In the time-honoured fashion in late medieval battle the Yorkist archers shot the horses from under the Lancastrian knights, who were finished off by the Yorkist infantrymen. A second cavalry assault failed, so the knights dismounted and a Lancastrian infantry force of some 4,000 men engaged in ferocious hand-to-hand fighting lasting well into the afternoon. In either the second or third attack Lord Audley was killed. A splendid **stone cross** and inscription marks the spot (on private land) near the aptly named Audley Cross Farm. Lord Dudley took over command.

The remaining Lancastrian cavalry was held behind lines to the west. At some stage they decided that the hand-to-hand mêlée was not going well so they left the field. It is also possible that as many as 500 of the Lancastrian infantry defected to the Yorkists. The Lancastrian line broke and perhaps 2,000 were killed many in the ensuing rout. The Lancastrians became trapped at the River Tern, 2 miles west at a place since called 'Deadman's Den'. Lord Dudley was captured.

Aftermath and Commentary
Salisbury's strategic objective had been to fight through and continue his march to Ludlow. This was achieved. His forces spent the night south of Market Drayton – there is a prominent hill 1 mile south, close to the minor road to Sutton, called **Salisbury Hill** presumably because his army camped there – and then marched to Ludlow, evading King Henry's waiting army, and joined up with York and the Kingmaker. So this was superficially a clear-cut Yorkist victory, in fact the one and only time in the Wars when the two sides approximated to Lancashire (plus Cheshire) versus Yorkshire (plus the far north). Actually with the non-engagement of Lord Stanley, it was a Lancashire second team versus a crack Yorkshire outfit. Stanley helpfully sent Salisbury a letter of congratulation and promised future support.

However, Salisbury managed to turn victory into defeat by allowing a substantial part of his army, including his two sons, to return home to the north. The engagement at Blore Heath had been very hard fought and the Yorkists had themselves been badly mauled. Salisbury's strategic objective was to get as many troops to Ludlow as possible to support the Duke of York. In the event, neither the Duke of York nor Warwick the Kingmaker had mobilised as many men as expected either. Consequently the Yorkist army at Ludlow was desperately short of men (perhaps outnumbered 3:1 by the King's force). 'The St Albans Three' had no option but to flee in the middle of the night. Blore Heath had been a pyrrhic victory and a strategic defeat for the Yorkists.

Salisbury's sons were in fact captured in an ambush at Acton Bridge, along with Sir James Harrington, and incarcerated in Chester Castle. Queen Margaret, by tradition watching the battle from the tower of nearby Mucklestone church, took a very dim view of Salisbury's aggressive intent, especially since most of Audley's troops had been raised in Prince Edward's 'home' county of Cheshire. In the Act of Attainder of late 1459, Salisbury and his wife were singled out for particularly harsh treatment. His behaviour at Blore Heath may have led directly to his own execution in December 1460, the day after he was captured by the Lancastrians at the Battle of Wakefield.

Participants	
Yorkist ~5,000 men	*Lancastrian ~ 10,000 men*
Richard Neville, Earl of Salisbury	James Touchet, Lord Audley
Sir Thomas Neville	John Sutton, Lord Dudley
Sir John Neville	Sir John Stanley
Sir Thomas Harrington	Sir William Catesby
Sir John Conyers	Sir Richard Booth
Sir James Metcalfe	Sir John Skidmore
Sir Thomas Mountford	Sir John Egerton
Sir Thomas Parr	Sir Thomas Dutton
Sir John Wenlock	Sir Thomas Hesketh
	Sir John Legh
Casualties: 2,000 dead	Casualties: 500 dead

Monument to James Touchet, Lord Audley, Lancastrian commander killed in the Battle of Blore Heath.

Location and What to See

This battlefield can be accurately located. The armies arrayed east–south-west across the Newcastle-under-Lyme–Market Drayton road (now A53), 2 miles east of Market Drayton, near a minor road crossroads leading north to Mucklestone and south to Blore village. *The A53 is single-carriageway, busy and fast with no pavement: take great care on foot and do not park on it.* Park on the Blore road just after the crossroads. The Lancastrian position commenced behind the stout hedge on the west side of this road. The Yorkists lay across Audley Cross Farm on the crest of the ridge, 1 mile east.

- The battlefield can best be viewed from the minor road to Blore, where parking is also possible.
- A fine **battlefield cross** lies on private land opposite Audley Cross Farm. It marks the spot where Lord Audley was killed.
- Visit nearby **Mucklestone church**, 2 miles north, from whose tower Queen Margaret is reputed to have watched the battle. (See separate guide entry.)

BROMSGROVE, St John the Baptist's Church **

Town centre area, west of A38 on hill top (spire).
PO: 01527 878801.

Fine alabaster effigies and tomb-chest of Sir Humphrey Stafford (d. 1450) of Grafton and his wife, Alienora. A member of the powerful Stafford family headed by the Duke of Buckingham, Sir Humphrey has the unenviable reputation of being part of 'the spark which lit the flames' of the Wars of the Roses in June 1450. After the confrontation and climb-down at Blackheath, Kent, Jack Cade's rebels were dispersing when Humphrey and his kinsman, William, decided to pursue some of the rebels more closely. Their force of some 400 men were led into an ambush near Sevenoaks, probably at the Stafford manor at Tonbridge, and both men killed along with a number of their supporters. Cade stripped the corpses and took over Humphrey's expensive armour and accessories. Encouraged by this success, Cade's rebels entered London and the crisis escalated (see Cade Street).

Effigy of Sir Humphrey Stafford, the other half of the Stanton Harcourt feud, in Bromsgrove church.

Sir Humphrey had also been involved in the Stafford–Harcourt feud, a classic example of the aristocratic violence endemic under Henry VI. This culminated in the 'Siege of Stanton Harcourt church' by Sir Humphrey in May 1450 (see Stanton Harcourt).

BROUGHTON (Staffs), St Peter's Church *
Stands on south side of B5026 Eccleshall–Loggerheads road, 1 mile north of Wetwood. KAL.

This seventeenth-century church contains original fifteenth-century stained glass on the south side of the chancel, which commemorates Sir John and Ellen Delves. Delves was a finance man, being Treasurer to the Duke of Clarence's household and later holding the same post in Henry VI's household during the 1470/1 Readeption. He fought for Henry and was killed at the Battle of Tewkesbury (1471), a family tragedy since his son was executed after the battle. The glass was removed from nearby Doddington Castle in Cheshire (the Delves seat) when the Broughtons acquired Doddington by marriage in the eighteenth century.

BUSHLEY, St Peter's Church *
½ mile north of A438 Tewkesbury–Ledbury road. Village centre.

In the **nave** a charming brass to Thomas Payne (d. 1500) and his wife, Ursula. He was a wool merchant who gained fame because he gave shelter to **Queen Margaret of Anjou** as she fled westwards after the Battle of Tewkesbury (1471). The timber-framed house where she stayed is still known as **Paynes Place** and is the big farm midway along the back lane to the A438. Head south from the church and turn right at the crossroads. The house is ¼ mile on the left.

CLEHONGER, All Saints' Church **
¼ mile north of B4349 Hereford–Vowchurch road, 3 miles south-west of Hereford. Turn sharp right to church and village centre.

Absolutely delightful wall brasses to Sir John Barre (1415–83) and his second wife, Jane Greyndour, née Rugge. Pevsner calls them 'very swagger',

Wall brass of Jane née Rugge, second wife to Sir John Barre, in Clehonger church.

highlighting the rare intrusion of humour into church memorials. A very early supporter and assistant of Richard, Duke of York, by 1459 Barre had become a Lancastrian (he was a brother-in-law of William Catesby the elder). He was elected to the Coventry parliament that year as MP for Herefordshire and in 1460 received manors previously belonging to the Earl of Salisbury as reward for good service against the Yorkist earls. As a consequence he was arrested in August 1460 after the Battle of Northampton on the orders of the Kingmaker. He received a pardon in 1468. Barre held lands in Hereford, Gloucester and Hertfordshire.

COLESHILL, St Peter's and St Paul's Church **
Town centre just south of B4114 Castle Bromwich–Nuneaton road. Lunchtimes on Wednesday and Saturday in summer.

The chancel contains a number of Digby tombs, of which the oldest commemorates Sir Simon Digby (d. 1519) and his wife, Alice. Sir Simon joined Henry Tudor's force at Tamworth the day before the Battle of Bosworth with a 'choice band' of men, having deserted from Richard III's army at the last minute. He is alleged to have brought with him information on Richard's intended battle plan which could have been decisive for Henry. But it was a gamble: Sir Simon would have suffered an unenviable fate if Henry had lost and he had been captured alive. Family tradition also has it that all six Digby brothers fought at Bosworth for Henry. Simon again fought for Henry at the Battle of Stoke Field (1487) with his brother John. In 1495 he was granted the manor of Coleshill forfeited by Sir Simon Mountford, who was found guilty of treason after supporting Perkin Warbeck's rebellion. Digby, as Deputy Constable of the Tower, had conducted Mountford to his trial. Digbys still hold land in Coleshill today.

COVENTRY ****
By the fifteenth century, Coventry was among the four biggest cities in England, based on prosperity from first wool and then cloth. Its strategic position in the kingdom ensured that it had a castle, a priory and the best-defended city walls in the country. Despite the damage Coventry suffered in the twentieth century, much survives of interest from the old centre.

St Mary's Hall £
City centre, south side of old cathedral.

This medieval hall built in the fourteenth century superbly celebrates Coventry's role as capital and Court of England during the reign of Henry VI and Queen Margaret of Anjou in the years 1456–60. The now-demolished castle was the formal seat of government. St Mary's housed the attendant Court. In mid-1456 Queen Margaret left London, perhaps fearful that the young Prince Edward (then aged 3) might be at risk from the lawlessness now endemic in London. London had never warmed to Henry VI's French queen, nor forgiven Henry for deserting the townspeople at the height of Jack Cade's Rebellion in July 1450. Margaret did not return until late 1457. By September 1456 Henry VI joined his wife and child in Coventry and the process of national government moved with him. At a Great Council there in October, Henry announced the changes to the key government positions (Chancellor and Treasurer) that spelled the end of the Duke of York's Second Protectorate. In total, Henry spent more than 50 per cent of his time in Coventry during these four years. Communication with the government departments back in London was, of course, fraught with difficulties and further weakened an already ineffective administration. The infamous Parliament of Devils was held here in November 1459, at which the Duke of York and the three Calais Earls were finally attainted. The Lancastrian defeat at the Battle of Northampton in July 1460 brought to an end Coventry's and St Mary's moment of glory. Apparently fervently Lancastrian in this period, Coventry is held to have changed sides in early 1461 and sent 100 men to fight for Edward, now Duke of York, at the Battle of Towton.

St Mary's, very much in period, contains splendid **stained glass** and early Tudor tapestry, which both feature key participants in the Wars. There is a statue of **Henry VI** in the kitchens (somehow appropriate). The stained glass portraits constitute a veritable Lancastrian shrine:

Edward III
Richard II
Henry IV
Henry V
Henry VI
John, Duke of Bedford } Henry V's
Humphrey, Duke of Gloucester } brothers
Richard Beauchamp, Earl of Warwick and Isabella Despenser his wife
Humphrey Stafford, 1st Duke of Buckingham.

The tapestry was made in the 1490s for the visit of **Henry VII** and **Queen Elizabeth of York**. They are depicted as two kneeling figures (or they may be Henry VI and Queen Margaret of Anjou).

St Mary's Priory (remains)
'Old' city centre, north side.

The scant remains of Coventry's first religious house, where **Henry VI** often used to lodge while in Coventry (Queen Margaret stayed in the house of a rich merchant).

City Walls (remains)
Continue north to the Look Street Gate and walls in Lady Herbert's Garden. Also visit Swanswell St. Gate. This is all that remains of the substantial medieval city walls, containing twelve towers, and the longest in England. It was here in March 1471 that **Warwick the Kingmaker** and his army took shelter when pursued by Edward IV as he sought to reclaim his throne. On at least two occasions, Edward and his brothers, backed by their army, thundered around these very walls challenging Warwick to battle. Warwick, in true cautious style, declined the challenge and had to be winkled out by Edward IV's rapid march on London. Warwick's defeat at the Battle of Barnet was the result.

CROFT CASTLE, St Michael Chapel ** £
Castle is on the north side of B4362 Mortimer's Cross–Orleton road, 3 miles east of Mortimer's Cross. National Trust signposts. NT. 01981 590509.

Superb tomb-chest and effigies to <u>Sir Richard Croft</u> (1438–1509) and his wife <u>Eleanor</u>, née Cornwall, widow of Sir Hugh Mortimer. Croft and his younger brother Richard are immortalised through the survival of a letter written by the young Edward, Earl of March and Edmund, Earl of Rutland, Duke of York in 1454 complaining about the behaviour of the two Croft brothers, who were probably lodged at Ludlow with the Yorks. No matter, the brothers turned into loyal supporters of King Edward, since Richard fought for Edward at the battle of Mortimer's Cross (1461), Towton (1461) and Tewkesbury (1471), after which he was knighted. He had accompanied Edward into exile in 1470. The battlefield of Mortimer's Cross lay on Richard's land. Richard is reputed to have been the man who captured Edward, Prince of Wales at Tewkesbury before handing him over to Edward, who had him murdered. The alternative version is that the Prince was killed in open battle.

Richard became governor of Ludlow Castle and, as a result, by 1478 was seen as a Woodville man (the Woodvilles dominated the Council of Wales from Ludlow). However, Richard became a member of Richard III's household after Edward IV's death. Nevertheless, by 1487 Richard was prepared to fight for Henry Tudor at the Battle of Stoke Field, after which he was created knight banneret – evidence, perhaps, that he was a skilled trimmer.

ELFORD, St Peter's Church **

Elford is 4 miles north of Tamworth on A513 Burton-on-Trent road. Church is on west side of village and off A513.

The brochure in the church tells us that in the **Stanley Chapel** is a tomb-chest and effigy of <u>Sir John Stanley</u> (d. 1476), who fought in true Stanley style for Lancaster at the Battle of Blore Heath (1459) and for York at the Battle of Tewkesbury (1471). However, the armour of the effigy looks a lot earlier in style (perhaps an old effigy was reused?). Actually this chapel was restored in the nineteenth century, so that might be the problem. Sir John rests alone but was actually married three times. Note also the effigy of a child on the floor who was killed by a real tennis ball around 1460; he was the grandson of Sir John. The tomb of <u>Sir William Smythe</u> (d. 1525) and wives is of interest because his first wife was <u>Isabel Neville</u>,

youngest daughter of John Neville, **<u>Marquis Montagu</u>** (the brother of Warwick the Kingmaker).

HEREFORD, Cathedral **

City centre.

In the **south-east transept** are brasses to <u>Sir Richard de la Bere</u> (d. 1514) and his two wives. Sir Richard was sheriff of Herefordshire eight times under Henry VII. He was made knight banneret at the Battle of Stoke Field (1487) after fighting for Henry. He lived at Kinnersley Castle, west of Hereford. In addition, off the **north chancel aisle** is <u>Bishop John Stanbury</u>'s delightful chapel, built in 1480, with fan vaulting throughout. Stanbury died in 1473, having been chaplain and confessor to Henry VI. His alabaster monument resides outside in the aisle. Off the Lady Chapel, south side, is <u>Bishop Edmund Audley</u>'s chapel, built in 1502. Audley was younger

Effigy of Sir John Stanley, Elford church.

brother of John, Lord Audley and actually moved to the see of Salisbury before he died. (See Shere and Blore Heath.)

KINGTON, St Mary's Church **

½ mile north-west of town centre on old A44 to New Radnor.

In the **Lady Chapel** a superb tomb-chest and effigies of Thomas Vaughan of Hergest (k. 1469) and his wife, Ellen, née Gethin (she was known as 'Ellen the Terrible'!). Thomas fought for William Herbert, Earl of Pembroke at the Battle of Edgcote in 1469 and was killed along with a large number of other Welshmen.

KINLET, St John the Baptist's Church *

Kinlet lies at the junction of the B4194 Bewdley–Bridgnorth road with the B4363 Cleobury Mortimer–Bridgnorth road. The church is reached 1 mile north-west on a minor road direct from the junction (to school).

The park of Kinlet Hall was extended in the eighteenth century, the village moved and the road diverted; the church remains in the grounds of the hall. There are two splendid medieval tomb-chests with effigies in the **chancel**, commemorating members of the Blount family and their wives. Sir Humphrey Blount (d. 1471) was knighted by Edward IV immediately after the Battle of Tewkesbury in 1471. He wears a Yorkist sun-and-roses collar. His grandson, Sir John (d. 1531), displays a Lancastrian 'SS' collar by contrast.

KINVER, St Peter's Church *

The church stands high above the village on the southern edge.

In the **Hampton Chapel** a badly damaged effigy of John Hampton (1390–1472), esquire of the body of Henry VI, 1437–61. John was said to be a constant companion of Henry VI and assisted in his Eton College project. In 1445 he accompanied Margaret of Anjou to England and became her Master of Horse. In 1450 his head was demanded by Jack Cade's rebels but he escaped. He stood by the royal family in the late 50s and was pardoned by Edward IV in 1462. From 1447–61 he held the office of Constable of Colchester Castle. He died at the extreme age of 82, in the same year as intruders had broken into his home, nearby Stourton

Castle. Note the splendid brass of Sir Edward Grey (d. 1528) and his two wives.

LITTLE MALVERN, St Giles' Priory Church ***

Just off A449–A4104 T-junction, as A4104 descends to Upton.

By tradition this wonderfully situated priory is the place where **Queen Margaret of Anjou** was apprehended by Edward IV's troops in May 1471, four days after the Battle of Tewkesbury. Immediately following the battle, Margaret and her party (which included Anne Neville, the Kingmaker's daughter, who was married to Prince Edward) appear to have moved between safe houses at Paynes Place, Bushley and Birtsmorton Court. Sir William Stanley's force probably caught up with her at Little Malvern, 'a poor religious place', which the priory certainly was, supporting only a prior and four monks by that date. Sir William took the opportunity to tell Queen Margaret that her son was dead. She seems to have fallen apart at this news (I am sure Anne Neville was not too thrilled either) and launched into a diatribe against the Yorkists. She had to be dragged almost senseless from the priory. She continued in this vein when brought before Edward at Coventry, who is said to have considered executing her, so dreadful were her insults.

The importance of Margaret's capture should not be underestimated. It marks the end of the middle part of the Wars of the Roses. With her son, her husband and the Duke of Somerset dead and Margaret herself in captivity, there was no one to continue the Lancastrian resistance. Edward IV was finally sole and complete master in his realm.

However, the priory itself contains a treasure. In the **east window** are the remains of a superb six-panel set of stained glass depicting **Edward IV** and his family, including **Edward V**, plus Bishop Alcock of Worcester. Three are now missing (including Edward IV and Richard of York). Bishop Alcock, who was a Chancellor under Edward IV and a tutor to the princes, restored the run-down priory in 1480–2 (see Ely).

THE 'ROUT' OF LUDFORD BRIDGE (12/13 October 1459) +

Strategic Background and the Campaign

In August of 1456 Queen Margaret moved Henry VI from Westminster to Coventry/Kenilworth, from where she ruled as de facto regent. An uneasy peace

Little Malvern Priory, set in delightful countryside.

held for the next three years, with York in Ludlow, the Earl of Salisbury at Middleham and Warwick the Kingmaker, his son, hanging on to Calais. By 1459 Margaret felt strong enough to act against the three St Albans 'traitors'. She called a Council meeting at Coventry in June, to which all the magnates and other councillors were called, except the 'St Albans Three'. Charges of treason were laid against them. To counter this, the Duke of York called a meeting at his Marcher Castle at Ludlow, with the two earls each expected to arrive in force with armed troops. His aim seems to have been to engage the Lancastrian army and seize the king, just as he had done at St Albans four years earlier.

The Kingmaker's Calais contingent (led by Andrew Trollope) had to struggle across the breadth of England from Sandwich narrowly avoiding interception near Coleshill, Warwickshire by Henry Beaufort, 3rd Duke of Somerset and his Lancastrian forces. Salisbury, for his part, had to traverse the north of England. On the road westwards from Newcastle-under-Lyme to Market Drayton, Salisbury's army encountered Lancastrian forces digging in at Blore Heath. In the ensuing battle, Salisbury emerged the clear victor but, in the fierce fighting, sustained heavy casualties; quite a number of his troops had to return home to Yorkshire. His two sons, Sir Thomas and Sir John Neville, were taken prisoner

in Cheshire. Nevertheless, by late September the three elements of the Yorkist forces had concentrated at Ludlow.

However, numbers were very disappointing. In addition to the casualties sustained by Salisbury's retinue, Warwick's Midland retainers were thin on the ground, while even the Duke of York had had trouble in mobilising troops from his Marcher heartlands. Neither Sir William Herbert nor Roger Vaughan were there, having been skilfully manoeuvred away from York by Queen Margaret over the last two years. As in 1452 at Dartford, only two other minor peers joined the Yorkists – Lords Clinton and Grey of Powis. On the other hand, as many as twenty peers may have been present in Henry VI's army now menacing the Marches. It is likely that the Yorkists were outnumbered by as many as 3:1.

Nothwithstanding, the Yorkists took the initiative and marched to Worcester. Between Worcester and Kidderminster, they confronted the Lancastrian army, which was displaying the royal banner, but then declined to fight. They retreated to Worcester, where they swore an indenture in the cathedral, recognising royal pre-eminence, and then moved to Tewkesbury. Here they crossed the Severn and headed north-west to Ludlow. This decision meant that Richard, Duke of York was abandoning any attempt to link up with his support in the rest of England and was concentrating on defending his Marcher lordships. While at Worcester, King Henry made offers of pardons for the Yorkists, except those involved in the Battle of Blore Heath. This offer was publicly rejected by the Kingmaker.

The 'Rout'

By 12 October, the Yorkists were drawn up in the fields south-east of Ludford Bridge. Morale seems to have been low because of the disparity in numbers. King Henry offered a pardon to all who deserted the Yorkists, while the Yorkist leaders spread rumours that the King was already dead. The Yorkist guns fired randomly at Lancastrian lines in the gathering dusk. The Lancastrian leaders were Henry Beaufort, Duke of Somerset, Humphrey Stafford, Duke of Buckingham and Henry Percy, Earl of Northumberland. King Henry and Queen Margaret may have been in the rear. Then, some time in the evening, Andrew Trollope took up the King's offer and led his crack Calais contingent over to the Lancastrian lines. The Yorkist position was now hopeless. Around midnight, the Yorkist leaders excused themselves that they were going back to Ludlow Castle to refresh and rode off into the night, leaving their army with banners flying to fend for itself. In medieval times this was seen as particularly dishonourable. Although casualties were virtually non-existent, the 'rout' was a catastrophe for the Yorkist leaders, especially Richard, Duke of York.

Aftermath and Commentary

Immediately after escaping from the battlefield, the Yorkist leaders split up. The Duke of York, his second son the Earl of Rutland and Lord Clinton headed to Ireland, where York was Lieutenant. The Nevilles and, perhaps surprisingly, York's eldest son, Edward, Earl of March slipped through England and sailed to Calais. For certain, York lost a lot of prestige over this debacle, which was so reminiscent of the fiasco of Dartford in 1452. In the chaos of the abandonment, York also became separated from many of his close councillors, like Sir William Oldhall, who were captured and not able to join him in Ireland. His woe was complete when the Yorkist army surrendered the next morning, the leaders taken prisoner and Ludlow, York's home town, sacked, looted and worse. York's wife, Cecily, bravely took his two younger sons, George and Richard (the future Richard III), into Ludlow marketplace and awaited their fate. Actually, they were well looked after, being sent to live with Cecily's sister Anne, Duchess of Buckingham.

The Yorkists looked down and out; indeed the Duke of York himself was never the same force again. At the November 1459 parliament – the Parliament of Devils – they were attainted and their lands parcelled out to deserving Lancastrians. Even Salisbury's wife, Alice, was singled out for attainder. Queen Margaret now seemed very much in control – but see the Battle of Northampton.

Participants

Yorkist
Richard, Duke of York
Edward, Earl of March
Richard Neville, Earl of Salisbury
Richard Neville, Earl of Warwick
John, Lord Clinton
Richard, Lord Grey of Powis
Sir Walter Devereux

Lancastrian
Henry VI
Henry Beaufort, Duke of Somerset
Humphrey Stafford, Duke of Buckingham
John, Viscount Beaumont
William Fitzalan, Earl of Arundel
John, Lord Clifford
Richard West, Lord de la Warr
Thomas Courtenay, Earl of Devon
Thomas Percy, Lord Egremont
Henry Holland, Duke of Exeter
Henry, Lord Fitzhugh
John, Lord Lovell
Henry Percy, Earl of Northumberland
Thomas, Lord Roos
Thomas, Lord Scope of Masham
John Talbot, Earl of Shrewsbury
Lionel, Lord Welles
James Butler, Earl of Wiltshire

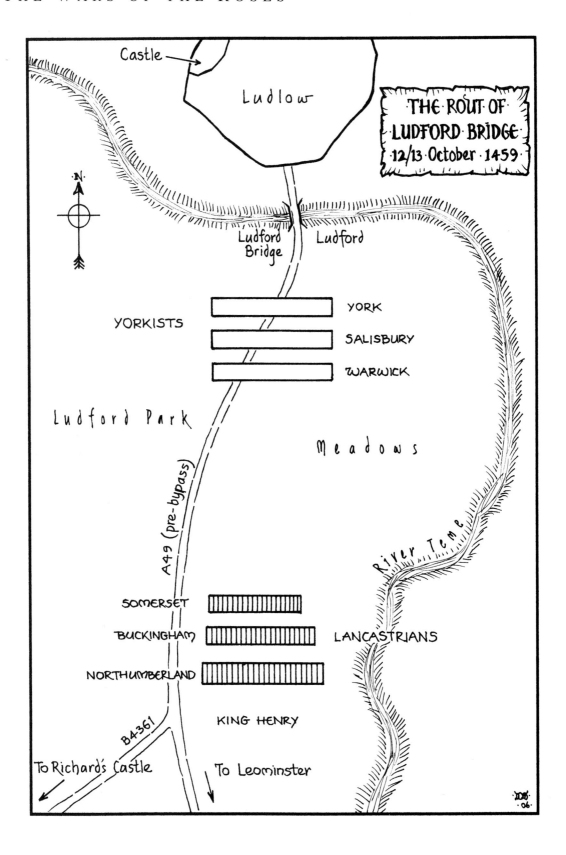

Castle

Ludlow

·N·

THE·ROUT·OF
LUDFORD·BRIDGE
·12/13·October·1459·

Ludford
Bridge

Ludford

YORKISTS

YORK

SALISBURY

WARWICK

Ludford Park

Meadows

A49 (pre-bypass)

River Teme

SOMERSET

BUCKINGHAM

NORTHUMBERLAND

LANCASTRIANS

B4361

KING HENRY

To Richard's Castle

To Leominster

Ludford Bridge with the River Teme in full spate.

Location and What to See

The opposing armies were drawn up straddling the medieval road south to Hereford, south-east of Ludford Bridge in the bend of the River Teme. The current road (B4361, 'old' A49) follows a somewhat different course. The position was well fortified in defensive array with guns, carts and stakes. The pursuing Lancastrian army aligned to the south of the Yorkist position. The fields where the armies formed up can still be seen from the B4361. Otherwise, there is nothing to see except **Ludford Bridge** itself, a splendid fifteenth-century structure on the south side of Ludlow. The Yorkist leaders may have crossed it as they shamefully slipped away from the battlefield.

LUDLOW ****

Ludlow has everything for the historian of the Wars of the Roses – castle, church and battle nearby.

Castle £

Town centre. 01584 873355.

Ludlow was the principal seat of the Mortimer Marcher lordship, which was inherited through his deceased mother, Anne Mortimer, by Richard, Duke of York in 1425. Edward, Earl of March and his brother Edmund, Earl of Rutland spent much time at this castle as boys. A letter survives indicating that the boys played with their neighbours, the Croft brothers. Edward as king developed the castle into the seat of the Prince of Wales's Council (the future Edward V), under the control of the Woodvilles. The two princes mainly lived here from 1473. Indeed they were in residence in April 1483 when Edward IV died. Prince Edward was en route from Ludlow to London with Anthony Woodville, Earl Rivers when they were waylaid by Richard, Duke of Gloucester and Henry Stafford, Duke of Buckinghamshire on 30 April at Stony Stratford. (See guide entry.)

In front of the castle is the marketplace. Nothing remains but it was here in 1459, after the rout of Ludford Bridge, that Cecily, Duchess of York stood her ground against the victorious Lancastrians with the younger members of her family – George and Richard, later dukes of Clarence and Gloucester.

St Lawrence's Church

Just east of the marketplace.

This splendid Perpendicular church provides something of a celebration of the Yorkist cause, although the Tudors get a look in. It contains superb fifteenth-century **misericords** with Wars of the Roses emblems and Victorian stained glass of the York family in the **west window**.

The bonus to Ludlow is the famous **Feathers Hotel** in the Bull Ring, with Tudor origins but boasting an Edward IV room. A great place to stay.

THE BATTLE OF MORTIMER'S CROSS
(2 February 1461) +++

Strategic Background and the Campaign

In early December 1460, at the same time as the Earl of Salisbury and Richard, Duke of York had headed north for Sandal Castle, Edward, Earl of March, York's eldest son, had left London for the Welsh Marches. His intention was to suppress the Lancastrian uprisings in Wales against York's Third Protectorate inspired by Jasper Tudor, Henry VI's stepbrother from his base at Pembroke. He also sought to recruit forces for the Yorkist cause. Edward was probably at York's town of Shrewsbury when he heard of this father's death in early January 1461. Quite soon, he moved on to Wigmore Castle, near Ludlow. Edward was planning to return to London with his recruits, who included Sir Walter Devereux (York's steward in his Welsh lordship) and Sir William and Richard Herbert of Raglan. He moved down to Hereford when he received intelligence that a large Lancastrian force led by Jasper Tudor, his father Owen Tudor and James Butler, Earl of Wiltshire was moving north east-wards towards Ludlow, perhaps with the intention of moving into England and reinforcing Queen Margaret's northern army. Wiltshire had sailed from the Continent with a force of mercenaries, Bretons and French to Pembroke where he was joined by his Irish retinue (he held lands in Ireland and had been appointed Lieutenant by Margaret). By late January they had joined up with the Tudors. Edward turned his army round from Hereford and marched 17 miles to intercept the Lancastrians at Mortimer's Cross just two miles from his own castle at Wigmore.

The Battle

There ware no field guns on either side. The Lancastrians made the first move at about midday. Wiltshire's mercenaries on the Lancastrian left pushed back Devereux's Yorkists, who broke and scattered across the river taking the Lancastrians with them. (Interestingly, exactly the same thing happened to Edward's forces at Barnet in 1471, when Hastings' left wing scattered downhill pursued by the Earl of Oxford's strong force.) Owen Tudor, on the Lancastrian right, tried to outflank the Yorkist left under Herbert by marching in a wide arc towards Kingsland. In the centre, Edward (still only 18 years old and in his first major command) led his men with confidence and succeeded in pushing back Pembroke's division, whose line suddenly broke and the force scattered westwards.

Owen Tudor's manoeuvre was unsuccessful and led to his left flank being dangerously exposed to Herbert's men, who took full advantage of the opportunity. Tudor's force broke and fled towards Hereford. Meanwhile, by the time Wiltshire had regrouped his mercenaries and led them back across the river, Edward in the centre and Herbert on the left had all but finished off the Lancastrians. It is said that, on realising this, the mercenaries simply sat down and waited for events to unfold. Owen Tudor's men may have made a last stand near the present battlefield monument at Kingsland. Tudor, Sir John Throckmorton and others were captured. Pembroke and Wiltshire both escaped to fight another day.

Aftermath and Commentary

Owen Tudor, Sir John Throckmorton and eight other gentry were executed in Hereford marketplace as rebels. Edward, still smarting from his father's assassination at Wakefield, perhaps saw the execution of Henry VI's stepfather (Owen Tudor had 'married' Catherine of Valois, Henry's mother) as some sort of revenge. Tudor was perhaps 60 years old by then and was of course the grandfather of the future Henry VII.

Edward had for now purged Wales of Lancastrian 'rebels'. He was free to restart his march to London to join up with Warwick. Perhaps surprisingly, Edward was not in a hurry (given that Queen Margaret's army was advancing on London from the north). He did not leave Hereford until after 19 February when he heard the news of Warwick's defeat at the Second Battle of St Albans. But it was a fine performance for a first military command by Edward.

On the morning of the Battle of Mortimer's Cross, Edward claimed that his army saw three rising suns in the sky – a phenomenon known as a parhelion. Edward saw this as a sign from God that a new age was dawning. He adopted the sunburst as his favourite badge and so launched his bid for the crown of England.

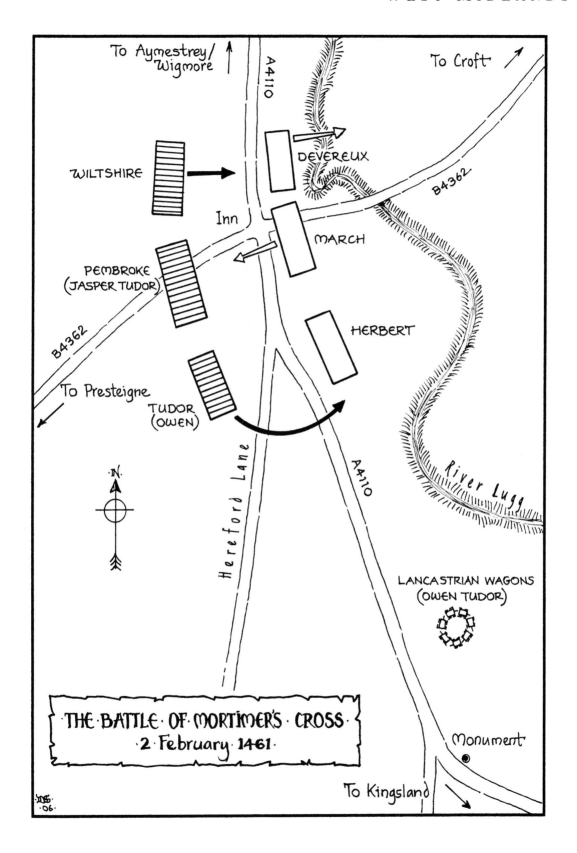

To Aymestrey/Wigmore ↑

A4110

To Croft ↗

WILTSHIRE

DEVEREUX

B4362

Inn

MARCH

PEMBROKE
(JASPER TUDOR)

B4362

HERBERT

To Presteigne

TUDOR
(OWEN)

River Lugg

N.

Hereford Lane

A4110

LANCASTRIAN WAGONS
(OWEN TUDOR)

THE·BATTLE·OF·MORTIMER'S·CROSS·
·2·February·1461·

Monument

To Kingsland

The Battle of Mortimer's Cross from John Speed's map of Herefordshire. It shows the parhelion observed on the day of the battle.

Participants and Casualties

Yorkist (~11,000 men)
Edmund, Duke of York
Sir William and Sir Richard Herbert
Sir Walter Devereux
Sir John Lingen
Sir Richard Croft
Sir Roger Vaughan of Tretower
Lord Grey of Wilton
Lord Audley

Lancastrian (~ 8,000 men)
Jasper Tudor, Earl of Pembroke
James Butler, Earl of Wiltshire
Owen Tudor
Sir Thomas Percy
Sir John and Sir William Scudamore
Sir John Throckmorton

Casualties: Heavy as the contest was hard fought; more than 3,000 Lancastrians were killed

Location and What to See
The battle took place across what is now the crossroads of the A4110 Hereford–Craven Arms road and the B4362 Presteigne–Orleton road in the surrounding meadows near the River Lugg. Most commentators assume a north–south alignment of the opposing forces on the basis that the Lancastrians were arriving from the west and the Yorkists deployed with the Lugg to their backs. An alternative theory is an east–west alignment with the Yorkists to the north, caused by a Lancastrian advance from the south. This location is proud of its battle.

- The **Mortimer's Cross Inn**. A must for a pint and/or food. Do not miss the pub sign and beer mats.
- The battle monument is located at **Kingsland**, probably the scene of Owen Tudor's last stand.
- Both **Aymestrey church** and **Croft Castle** chapel should be visited to see the monuments to Sir John Lingen and Sir Richard Croft, who both fought here. (See separate guide entries.)
- The ruins of **Wigmore Castle**, 3 miles north, should also be visited. (See separate guide entry.)
- **Hereford Museum** contains the remains of a helmet found in the River Lugg below Mortimer's Cross, which is believed to have found its way into the river after the battle.

MUCKLESTONE, St Mary's Church *
2 miles north of A53 Market Drayton–Newcastle-under-Lyme road on B5026 from Loggerheads to Woore.

By tradition, **Queen Margaret of Anjou** watched the unfolding drama of the battle of nearby Blore Heath (no doubt to her horror) in 1459 from the tower of this church. In the church **west window** is a stained-glass memorial to Queen Margaret, **Henry VI** and the Battle of Blore Heath.

At the east end of the churchyard is an **anvil**, and on the wall of the house opposite a **plaque**. These commemorate the tradition that the Queen departed from the church in something of a hurry as the Lancastrian line at Blore Heath collapsed. In order to outwit any pursuing Yorkist, her horse was shod by the village blacksmith the wrong way round! The rout of her Cheshire knights would have upset her but within a few weeks, in their turn, the Yorkists had fled the country.

SANDON, All Saints' Church *
1 mile north of A51 Rugeley–Stone road, just as Sandon village is reached from Rugeley. Turn right up long dead-end directly opposite B5066 Stafford turning.

In a lovely setting adjacent to Sandon Park, the church contains four fine incised slabs on tomb-chests commemorating members of the Erdeswick family, who held Sandon from the fourteenth century to the seventeenth century. The Erdeswicks were a powerful gentry family in Staffordshire who were aligned with the Stafford dukes of Buckingham. On the **south side** of the chancel lies Hugh Erdeswick (d. 1500) and his wife, Elizabeth. Hugh fought at the Battle of Bosworth (1485) for Henry Tudor. Note also another Hugh, his father, who died in 1473.

SHREWSBURY **
Town centre.

A Yorkist town which contains a statue of **Richard, Duke of York** in the **Market Square**. On **Wyle Cop** on the climb to the town centre from English Bridge, there is a **plaque** commemorating **Henry Tudor**'s

This pedeftal is erected to perpetuate the Memory of an obstinate, bloody, and decifive battle fought near this Spot in the civil Wars between the ambitious Houfes of York and Lancaster, on the 2nd Day of February 1461 between the Forces of *Edward Mortimer*, Earl of March, (afterwards *Edward the Fourth*) on the Side of York and thofe of *Henry the Sixth*, on the Side of Lancafter.

The King's Troops were commanded by *Jafper Earl of Pembroke*, *Edward* commanded his own in Person and was victorious. The Slaughter was great on both Sides Four Thousand being left dead on the Field and many Welfh Perfons of the firft diftinction were taken Prisoners among whom was *Owen Tudor* (Great-Grandfather to *Henry the Eighth*, and a Defcendent of the illuftrious *Cadwallader*) who was afterwards beheaded at Hereford

This was the decifive Battle which fixed *Edward* the Fourth on the Throne of England who was proclaimed King in London on the Fifth of March following.

Erected by Subfcription in Year 1799.

Monument at Kingsland to the Battle of Mortimer's Cross.

stay here in August 1485, en route for Bosworth. It is unlikely he stayed the night but may have been served a meal here.

TONG, St Bartholomew's Church ***
Tong is immediately north of junction 3 of M54 on A41 to Newport. Turn right off A41 to village.

This former college contains a treasure trove of medieval monuments. Two are of particular interest. In the **nave** there is a tomb-chest with lovely brasses

of <u>Sir William Vernon</u> (d. 1467) and his wife, <u>Margaret Swynfen</u>. In the **Golden Chapel** (south transept) are a tomb-chest and effigies of <u>Sir Henry Vernon</u> (d. 1515), Sir William's son, and wife <u>Anne Talbot</u>, daughter of the 2nd Earl of Shrewsbury.

The Vernons' principal residence was Haddon Hall in Derbyshire but they also owned Tong Castle. The college here was founded in the early 1400s and became the mausoleum of the Vernons following their acquisition of it in 1446. The Vernons were powerful members of the upper gentry with lands

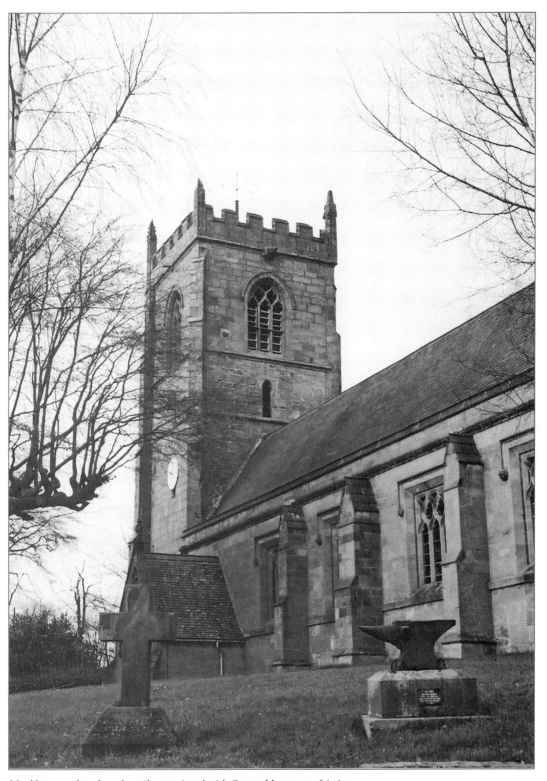

Mucklestone church and anvil, associated with Queen Margaret of Anjou.

Tomb-chest of Hugh Erdeswick, Sandon church.

Left: *The Golden Chapel, Tong church.*

around Bakewell. They were known as 'Kings of the Peak'. They were involved in a number of notorious disputes among members of the unruly Derbyshire gentry in the 1450s (Longford–Blount, Meverell–Basset and Gresley–Vernon). They were followers of Humphrey Stafford, 1st Duke of Buckingham, an ineffective lord. Sir William inherited the Treasurer-ship of Calais from his father Sir Richard (whose monument is also here) in 1450 and was involved in suppressing Cade's Revolt in the southern counties in that year.

In general the Vernons were unlucky or ineffective in their choice of overlord. Sir Henry was successively a retainer of Warwick, Clarence, Hastings and Richard III. For this reason, perhaps, the Vernons did not 'punch their weight' on the national stage. In fact Clarence used Sir Henry to raise troops for him in the north Midlands in 1471 but Vernon did not put in an appearance for the Barnet/Tewkesbury campaign. He was present, though, for Richard III at Bosworth (see Haddon Hall).

WARWICK ****

Collegiate Church of St Mary's
North-east side of town centre.

Head for the **Beauchamp Chapel** on the south side of the church. Here is probably the finest medieval, non-royal church monument in England – the tomb, effigy and hearse of <u>Richard Beauchamp, 13th Earl of Warwick</u> (1382–1439). This is just as well, as the church literature describes Richard as 'Medieval England's Greatest Knight'. Let us be clear this is not our Earl of Warwick, Richard Neville the Kingmaker – it is his father-in-law, whose youngest daughter, Anne, became the Kingmaker's wife in 1436. However, Richard Beauchamp himself is important to our story. Beauchamp was very much involved in the French wars and was councillor to both Henry V and Henry VI.

On his deathbed, Henry V entrusted Beauchamp to be tutor to his baby son, Henry VI surely a thankless task. At the time of Richard's own death, he was Governor of Normandy. Marrying into the Despenser fortune after the death of his first wife in 1422, Beauchamp had become one of the two richest men in England, alongside Richard, Duke of York. It was the inheriting of this Beauchamp wealth and titles in 1447 through his wife Anne that transformed Sir Richard Neville at the age of 19 into one of the foremost magnates of the fifteenth century.

This came about in a way which was far from straightforward. Richard Beauchamp, above in fact, had a son, Henry, by his second wife who was aged 15 in 1439 when he inherited the earldom. Henry Beauchamp is one of the forgotten men of medieval England. Since his father was Henry VI's tutor, the two Henrys were childhood companions and friends. Henry Beauchamp was made up to duke by King Henry in 1445 (the only man to hold the title Duke of Warwick). However, Beauchamp seems to have been a thoroughly nasty piece of work and there were concerns that he was a bad influence on the impressionable King. By 1447 Henry Beauchamp was dead, aged only 22, and his only child, Anne, aged 2, had become the ward of the Duke of Suffolk, then the most powerful man in England below the King. Note that in 1436 Henry Beauchamp had married the Kingmaker's sister Cecily in a 'sister swap', when the Kingmaker also married Henry's sister Anne. However, within three years the infant Anne above was also dead. The elder Anne Beauchamp, the Kingmaker's wife and Henry's

sister of the full blood, was now the heir to her brother's fortune.

This was very nice for Sir Richard Neville, but it gets better. Anne Beauchamp had three sisters of the half-blood – Richard Beauchamp's daughters by his first wife, Elizabeth Berkeley (d. 1422). The wonderful golden **weepers** on Richard Beauchamp's tomb show us they were all married (as you would expect) to powerful members of the aristocracy:

- Margaret, married to <u>John Talbot, Earl of Shrewsbury</u> (killed at the Battle of Castillon in 1453 – see Whitchurch).
- <u>Eleanor</u>, married to **Edmund Beaufort, Duke of Somerset** (killed at the First Battle of St Albans, 1455).
- <u>Elizabeth</u>, married to <u>George Neville, Lord Latimer</u> (d. 1469) brother of the Earl of Salisbury.

Obtain a copy of the **guide-card** in the church, which elaborates on these marriages. It includes some of the most powerful participants in the Wars of the Roses. Five of the seven male weepers died violent deaths in the next thirty years, two at the hands of the Neville members on this tomb.

These sisters of the half-blood had expected to get a share of the Beauchamp inheritance. The dispute went to law in Hereford, with the result that Richard Neville junior triumphed. Michael Hicks indicates that the jury was 'overawed'. At this crucial moment, the Kingmaker's half-brothers-in-law were conveniently absent in France. Thus Richard Neville came about his enormous fortune, so crucial to the Yorkist cause between 1455 and 1464 (further enhanced when he inherited the earldom of Salisbury after his father was executed in 1460). Note the **weeper** at the right end on the south side of Richard Beauchamp's tomb. This represents **Richard Neville, Earl of Warwick** and is the only monument we have to this supremely powerful magnate.

Castle ££
South side of town centre, on north bank of River Avon. Signposted. 0870 442 2000.

This was the principal seat of the medieval earls of Warwick. Surprisingly little remains of Richard Neville, the Kingmaker, here. He was not much of a builder and often 'had bigger fish to fry' in London.

Externally the castle looks very much as it would have done during the Wars of the Roses, since its greatest building period was the fourteenth century.

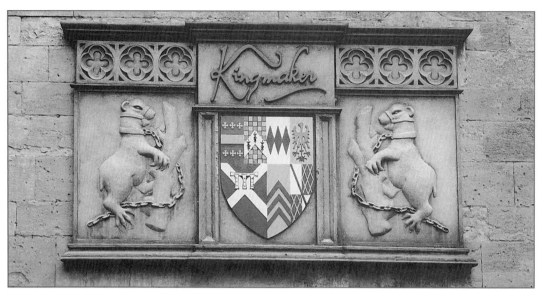

Kingmaker Exhibition, Warwick Castle.

Note the **Clarence Tower**, built in the late fifteenth century but not named after him until the nineteenth century. **George, Duke of Clarence** held the castle from 1471 to his death in 1478, having inherited it through his wife, Isabel Neville, the Kingmaker's elder daughter. It then passed to his brother **Richard, Duke of Gloucester**, who had married the Kingmaker's younger daughter, **Anne Neville**.

The castle is most famous as the place where the Kingmaker imprisoned **Edward IV** after his capture at Olney near Northampton in the summer of 1469. As a result, he had two Kings of England in prison at the same time. Henry VI had been in the Tower since 1465. Edward had his revenge when, in the run-up to the Battle of Barnet (1471), he occupied this castle and the town and had himself proclaimed king (for a second time, of course) from these very walls.

Entrance to the castle is pricey but it is great fun for children and there is a special **Kingmaker exhibition**.

WHITCHURCH (SHROPSHIRE), St Allmund Church **

Town centre, north side.

In the **Lady Chapel**, a tomb-chest with effigies of John Talbot, 1st Earl of Shrewsbury (d. 1453) and his wife, Margaret Beauchamp. John was one of the few heroes of the French wars, who, in 1441, combined with Richard, Duke of York at Pontoise in Ile-de-France and famously captured the still-warm bed of the recently departed Dauphin. John was involved in France from the 1420s, making his name as a brilliant and daring tactician. In 1453 the English were urged by the Gascons to return to Bordeaux, lost to the French the year before. The French were expelled from the town but, in mid-July, Talbot, now aged over 70, was lured into battle at Castillon, 15 miles to the east. The English defeat was total, and Talbot and his son John perished. So ended the Hundred Years War. Even the French called him 'the English Achilles' and erected a monument at the spot where he was killed. Within the month, Henry VI suffered a major mental breakdown and the clock began ticking towards the Wars of the Roses speeded up. It is believed that the defeat and the loss of his French lands were the major cause of Henry's breakdown. Domestically Talbot was conventionally Lancastrian, supporting the King against Richard, Duke of York at the fiasco of Dartford in 1452.

Outside the **south porch** is an inscription to John Talbot. Both John and Margaret appear as weepers on the tomb of Richard Beauchamp, Earl of Warwick in Warwick church.

WIGMORE, Castle *

Take path north-west from village centre, past church.

The home of the Mortimer earls of March and the dukes of York in turn. **Edward, 4th Duke of York**

Incised slab memorial to Humphrey Cotes and wife, Woodcote Chapel.

knew the castle well from his boyhood based in Ludlow. He stayed here the night before the Battle of Mortimer's Cross, where he launched his drive for the throne of England in February 1461. A splendid historical site without frills. This is how castles should be – with an air of mystery.

WOODCOTE, Chapel **

2 miles south of Newport (Shropshire) on west side of A41 Newport–Wolverhampton road. At the rear of old people's home now occupying Woodcote Hall. KAL.

Like so many other aristocratic houses, Woodcote Hall is no longer a private home. The chapel survives but is under threat of closure, so do make a visit to this little gem. It is kept locked but a key

is available locally. This unpromising location is lit up by a superb **incised slab** to Humphrey Cotes (d. 1485) and his wife. Humphrey joined Henry Tudor's army as it passed by from Shrewsbury en route to Bosworth Field. He mustered his men 1 mile north-west of the hall on **Muster Hill**, which can be reached by taking the first left off the A41 north to Chetwynd Aston, and immediately left again on a narrow lane. Muster Hill is on your left at the first bend. There is a poignancy to the scene there. Although backing the winning side, Humphrey did not return to Muster Hill. He was killed in the battle. As usual, we have little idea what happened to his household and tenants who had mustered here, but most likely a fair number did not return home either.

WALES

For map of Wales see p. 191.

ABERGAVENNY, St Mary's Priory Church **
Town centre, on east leg of central one-way system.

The **Herbert Chapel** provides a superb mausoleum of medieval tomb-chests and effigies, three of which are of interest.

Sir Richard Herbert of Coldbrook (k. 1469) and his wife. A younger brother to William Herbert, Earl of Pembroke (see Raglan), Richard fought at the Battle of Mortimer's Cross and helped William drive Jasper Tudor out of Wales in 1461/2, for which he was granted new lands in Herefordshire. Richard seems to have acted always in tune with his elder brother. Unfortunately this meant taking the

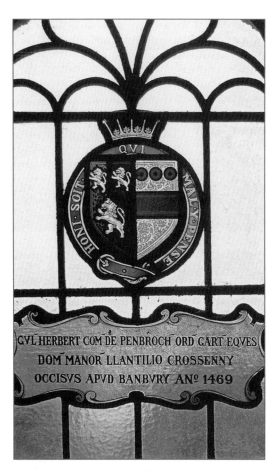

Stained glass of William Herbert in Llantilio Crossenny church.

downs with the ups. He was captured at the Battle of Edgcote (1469) with his brother and executed the next day by Warwick the Kingmaker in Northampton. Richard (who was very tall) is said to have achieved prodigious feats with his poleaxe in the battle but to no avail.

Sir Richard Herbert of Ewyas (d. 1510), a natural son of William Herbert, Earl of Pembroke, who also fought at Edgcote.

Sir William ap Thomas (d. 1460) and his wife, Gwladys (d. 1454), daughter of the Welsh hero Sir David Gam, killed at Agincourt in 1415. They were the parents of the Herbert brothers. Sir William began life as the fifth son of minor Welsh gentry. He also fought at Agincourt and was knighted by Henry VI in 1426. He first married Elizabeth Berkeley (d. 1421), and then Gwladys (the 'Star of Abergavenny'), who was the widow of Sir Roger Vaughan of Brewardine. Sir William became known as the 'Blue Knight of Gwent'.

While you are in Abergavenny, why not visit the delightful and surprisingly large **Llantilio Crossenny parish church**. In the nave north aisle, there is splendid Tudor glass celebrating William Herbert, Earl of Pembroke (k. 1469) and Sir David Gam, above. The village lies between Abergavenny and Monmouth on the B4233. The church lies east of the B4233 on the southern edge of village. For William Herbert, see Raglan.

BARMOUTH, House by Harbour *
On harbour front, Davy Jones' Locker restaurant.

This is the perfect place to combine the Wars of the Roses with a family holiday. Enjoy a meal across from the harbour and soak in the atmosphere of the 1460s. This fifteenth-century building, called **Ty Gwyn**, served as **Jasper Tudor**'s base as he sought vainly to maintain the Lancastrian presence in Wales after the defeats at the battles of Mortimer's Cross and Towton in 1461. It was owned by Griffith Vaughan, Jasper's chief agent in north Wales. Jasper used this port to sail in and out of Wales, ensuring that he eluded capture and kept the Lancastrian/ Tudor cause alive. Its proximity to Harlech Castle, the last Lancastrian stronghold, just up the coast, was of course crucial. In June 1468, for example, he disembarked from exile in Normandy with just three ships and fifty men before departing on his celebrated *chevauchée* across north Wales, gathering supporters as he went (and back again).

CARMARTHEN

St Peter's Church **
Town centre, east side. Summer. 01267 237117.

<u>Sir Rhys ap Thomas</u> (d. 1525) – tomb-chest and effigies. A grandson of Griffith ap Nicholas, who dominated west Wales in the mid-fifteenth century, Rhys entered his inheritance without licence in 1473. By 1485 Rhys had, himself, become the predominant force around Milford Haven. After Henry Tudor's landing at Dale Bay, Rhys at first sat on the fence and shadowed Henry's force. This was for two reasons – firstly, Richard III had taken his young son, Gruffydd, as hostage, and secondly, he was busy negotiating favours from Henry before committing.

Eventually, Rhys did join Henry at the Long Mountain, near Welshpool, when he brought 1,800–2,000 men to the Tudor cause. Richard III was said to be furious when he heard the news. Rhys's contingent went all the way to Bosworth, where they formed part of the Earl of Oxford's vanguard and helped break the Duke of Norfolk's line, which resulted in the Yorkist commander's death. After Bosworth, Rhys received his rewards from Henry and became the most powerful man in Wales in the early Tudor period.

Castle
Town centre above river, next to council offices.

While in the town down do visit the castle, situated on the north bank of the river near the bridge. Castle ruins in south Wales are often put to good use – Brecon is next to an hotel, Hay is a bookshop and Carmarthen abuts the council offices next door. This castle was fought over during the 1450s by the Tudor brothers and William Herbert. In 1456 it was besieged by Herbert and Walter Devereux during the Yorkist raid into south Wales. The castle fell and its commander **Edmund Tudor**, father of Henry VII, was captured and incarcerated in the castle. In November 1456 Edmund died here, allegedly of plague.

DENBIGH, Castle * £
South end of town on hill. Signposted.
Cadw: 01745 813385.

The command of castles as military strongholds was not an important feature of the Wars of the Roses, except in Wales and in Northumberland. Quite a number of castles saw some action in these areas; Denbigh suffered more than most.

Denbigh was a Mortimer stronghold, inherited by **Richard, Duke of York** in 1425. In 1457 Henry VI appointed his half-brother, **Jasper Tudor**, to be Constable of Denbigh but it was not until after the rout of Ludford Bridge in September 1459 that Jasper felt strong enough to move against the fortress. It surrendered to him in early 1460, while York was still in Ireland. After the Battle of Northampton (July 1460), the Kingmaker demanded the castle's surrender back to the Yorkists and it was besieged. One Robert Bold was appointed as Yorkist constable in readiness but, in fact, the Lancastrians, under Roger Puleston (Jasper's deputy), held out until January 1462, during which time the castle suffered much damage. Because his castle was still in Lancastrian hands in October 1460 when he returned from exile in Ireland, Richard, Duke of York was forced to land on the Wirral prior to marching to London, rather than risk a landing in hostile north Wales.

In July 1468 Jasper launched his *chevauchée* from Barmouth across north Wales. He besieged Denbigh without success but burned the town within the **walls north** of the **castle**. Much of these walls survives today. It is said that, as a result, the townspeople abandoned the ancient site within the walls and rebuilt their houses on the present site of the town, further north.

HARLECH, Castle *** £
Town centre, difficult to miss. CADW: 01766 780552.

Harlech gave shelter to **Queen Margaret of Anjou** in July 1460 as she fled to Scotland after the Yorkist victory at Northampton. After Towton, Sir William Herbert and Lord Ferrers (Walter Devereux) were charged with securing Wales for York. They successfully besieged a number of key strongholds so that, by spring 1462, Harlech stood alone for the Lancastrians on the fall of the Carreg Cennen castle. A visit to this fabulous location will immediately tell you why – it was virtually impregnable and so held out for a further six years.

In 1468 <u>William Herbert</u> (now ennobled) and his brother Sir Richard (see Raglan and Abergavenny) launched a determined effort to take the castle with forces numbering about 10,000. Approaching the castle in two wings from north and south, they laid waste the countryside and put down a siege. In fact

Harlech Castle, scene of a rare siege in 1468.

the Lancastrian defenders, led by David ap Eynon and Sir Richard Tunstall, held out for less than one month before surrendering on 14 August 1468. Fifty prisoners were taken, including Eynon. All of Wales was now Yorkist and Herbert had reached the peak of his career; he was made Earl of Pembroke (Jasper's title) by Edward IV.

The 'Men of Harlech' folk song is said to have been composed in memory of this siege.

NEWPORT, Cathedral *

High up, north-west of city centre (tower).

The remains of a tomb-chest monument with **plaque** to Sir John Morgan of Tredegar (1493). Sir John, along with Richard Griffith, was one of the very first to join Henry Tudor's army after it had landed at Dale. Three days into the march, they joined at Cardigan, which was known to Sir John from his days as an officer in Edward IV's army in west Wales in the 1470s. At this uncertain time, they were most welcome, especially as they were friends of the powerful Rhys ap Thomas, who had not yet committed his retinue to Henry. Sir John

fought at the Battle of Bosworth and was rewarded with his knighthood. He was also made constable/steward of Newport Castle by Henry VII. Henry well recognised his debt to those who accompanied him to Bosworth.

PEMBROKE, Castle ** £

Close to town centre. Signposted. 01646 681510.

This magnificent ruin looks every inch a castle. Here in the **Henry VII Tower** (in the outer ward), the recently widowed **Lady Margaret Beaufort** gave birth to **Henry Tudor** on 28 January 1457, the future King of England. Margaret was only 13 years old and had lost her husband, Edmund Tudor, two months before. The birth was difficult and Margaret had no more children, despite two further marriages.

The castle and earldom of Pembroke were granted to Edmund's brother, **Jasper Tudor**, by their stepbrother, Henry VI, in 1454 as Henry sought to bolster the small Lancastrian royal family. Jasper was the first earl for a long time actually to live at the castle. He instigated many renovations and

THESE
FRACMENTS OF ALABASTER
ARE THE ONLY REMAINS OF A MONUMENT
WHICH ONCE STOOD IN THE BODY OF THE CHURCH
ERECTED AS THE ARMS DENOTE, TO THE MEMORY OF
SIR IOHN MORGAN OF TREDEGAR
✠ KNIGHT OF THE HOLY SEPVLCHRE, WHO
DIED 1493, AND HIS WIFE IANET DAUGHTER AND HEIRESS
OF DAVID MATHEW, OF LANDAFF, ESQUIRE

Plaque to Sir John Morgan of Tredegar, Newport cathedral.

improvements to the structure. When his elder brother, Edmund, died in 1456, he took his heavily pregnant sister-in-law, Lady Margaret Beaufort, under his wing to live in this castle.

After the Yorkist successes at Mortimer's Cross and Towton in 1461, Pembroke was besieged by Sir William Herbert by land and sea. Led by Sir John Skydmore, the Lancastrian forces surrendered at the end of September 1461 after a short siege. Herbert captured the 4-year-old Henry Tudor and

Lady Margaret Beaufort. He went on to purchase the wardship of Henry Tudor and brought him up at his seat of Raglan Castle. After the Lancastrian Readeption in 1471, once again Yorkist forces moved on Pembroke Castle, where Jasper and his nephew Henry were besieged. They fled to France via Tenby. In 1485 it was held for Richard III by the loyal Richard Williams. It was he who informed the king of Henry Tudor's arrival in Wales on 11 August.

Henry VII Tower, Pembroke Castle, birthplace of Henry Tudor.

RAGLAN, Castle **** £

1 mile north-east of Raglan. Accessible only from eastbound dual carriageway of A40 beyond Raglan roundabout. CADW: 01291 690228.

This splendidly imposing ruin looks every inch the medieval castle. Building was started in the 1430s by William ap Thomas, a retainer of Richard, Duke of York, who had purchased the property from his stepson, James, Lord Berkeley. It replaced the old-established manor house. William probably built the Great Tower and the Southgate. On William's death in 1445, the castle passed to his son, another William, who took the surname Herbert. This second William was responsible for the fabulous gatehouse and the Closet Tower. Raglan thus serves as a fitting monument to father and son, who between them in the space of fifty years rose from being the fifth son of minor Welsh gentry to being among the wealthiest peers in the realm, and Earl of Pembroke. Sir William Herbert's career is, however, very much a roller-coaster affair.

Sir William returned from France an experienced soldier, having been captured at the Battle of Formigny in 1450, when Normandy was lost. He became the Duke of York's constable, and steward of the lordships of Usk and Caerleon. With his father-in-law, Walter Devereux (Herbert married his daughter Anne), he participated in the general lawlessness of the 1450s in the Welsh Marches. They occupied Hereford in 1456 and overawed a jury into convicting some of their enemies, who were then executed. They seized Carmarthen and Aberystwyth castles and imprisoned Edmund Tudor, Earl of Richmond in the former.

In the subsequent government inquiry, which finally reached a verdict in 1459, Herbert was pardoned but Devereux convicted. This clever strategy by Queen Margaret ensured that, very surprisingly, Herbert was not present with the Duke of York at the rout of Ludford Bridge in September 1459, thus contributing to the farce that ensued. Nevertheless, by early 1461 William reverted to the Yorkists and did play a major role at the Battle of Mortimer's Cross in February as second in command to Edward, who was by now the Duke of York. Herbert was present at Towton and was knighted after the battle.

Edward IV as king now used his close relationship with Herbert to develop him very rapidly into a virtual 'viceroy' of Wales. He was showered with a bewildering array of lands, titles and offices, culminating in the earldom of Pembroke in 1468, and Knight of the Garter. He was the first Welshman since the conquest of Edward I to achieve a high position in English politics and penetrate the upper ranks of the aristocracy. Militarily, Herbert did a good job – Jasper Tudor was driven out of Wales and Harlech Castle was finally taken in 1468. Herbert even had time to engage in commerce and shipping, thus enhancing his burgeoning wealth.

Unfortunately, Herbert was seen by his peers in England as grasping, ruthless and vengeful, particularly by Warwick the Kingmaker; the two men were in fact far too alike and had land disputes in south Wales. For Warwick, Herbert had become the symbol of Edward IV's tendency to ignore the old-established magnate councillors and to promote into high office talented men, but from the wrong background. Sure enough, when Warwick and Clarence rebelled in 1469, Herbert was one of the 'evil counsellors' of Edward referred to in their manifesto. Herbert and his younger brother, Sir Richard, met their nemesis at the Battle of Edgcote in July 1469 and were executed in Northampton the next day by Warwick (completely illegally). Herbert's Welshmen fought heroically but were overwhelmed. His force had no archers, he had a major falling-out the day before the battle with the Earl of Devon, who did have archers, and the royal army itself was nowhere to be seen on the day. Had Herbert been thrown to the wolves?

In 1468 Edward carved out specially from his Marcher lordship of Usk a lordship of Raglan for Herbert, of which the castle was the centre. Herbert also acquired the wardship of young Henry Tudor, who resided here. On William's death, his wife, Anne, looked after Henry.

RUABON, Parish Church (Wrexham) *

Southern edge of town, west of A483 bypass.

In the **north chapel** a fine tomb-chest and effigies commemorating John ap Elis Eyton (d. 1526) and Elizabeth Calveley (d. 1524). He fought for Henry Tudor at the Battle of Bosworth (1485) and was rewarded with large estates in Ruabon and an annuity of 10 marks. He sports the Lancastrian 'SS' collar.

ST ANN'S HEAD (Dale/Mill Bay) ***

St Ann's Head is best approached on the B4327 from Haverfordwest via Dale. Drive to coastguard station.

Henry Tudor's invasion force left Honfleur at the mouth of the Seine in Normandy on 1 August 1485. With fair southerly winds they reached Milford Sound unopposed just before sunset on 7 August. They anchored in Mill Bay, which is immediately east of the cottages at the old coastguard station. Join the Pembrokeshire Coastal Path eastwards to get a better view of this bay. It is difficult to see Mill Bay as the main disembarkation point for an army of 4,000–5,000 men; the cliffs are surely too precipitous? Perhaps Mill Bay was the place where a landing party scrambled up the cliffs and then moved to secure Dale Castle, two miles away. By August 1485 Richard III's soldiers providing coastal protection had been conveniently withdrawn. That achieved, the main fleet could sail into nearby Dale Bay and disembark using the gently shelving beach there – a much more practical solution. The road to the Battle of Bosworth had started.

An excellent road walk can be undertaken by continuing north-eastwards round Dale Point to Dale Village. Head westwards past the church to the castle remains. Rejoin the coastal path on the west side of St Ann's Head and head south to return to your car.

ST DAVID'S, Cathedral **

City centre, signposted.

In the sanctuary is the splendid tomb-chest and brass of **Edmund Tudor, Earl of Richmond** (1430–57), father of Henry VII. Edmund was initially buried in Carmarthen Priory, the town where he died. At the Dissolution, his tomb was brought to St David's. The brass is a nineteenth-century replacement.

TRETOWER, Court *** £

3 miles north-west of Crickhowell, on left of A479 Talgarth road. CADW: 01874 730279.

Sir William ap Thomas bought Tretower Castle in 1420. His son by Gwladys Gam, William Herbert, gave the property to his maternal stepbrother, Sir Roger Vaughan the younger, in 1457. Sir Roger began the transformation of an existing but relatively new house to the east of the thirteenth-century round keep. He rebuilt the north and west ranges – his son, Sir Thomas, the gatehouse. Tretower Court therefore not only represents a rare example in Wales of a splendid late medieval country residence, it also provides a fitting tribute to this branch of the powerful Vaughan family of Bredwardine, Herefordshire.

Roger Vaughan the elder of Bredwardine and his second wife Gwladys Gam (who subsequently married Sir William ap Thomas) produced three sons, the eldest of whom was another Roger. Roger the younger was an early Yorkist who joined his stepbrother, William Herbert, and Walter Devereux in the 1456 south-west Wales raid against Edmund

Tudor. Once Warwick the Kingmaker had control of the government in July 1460, he appointed Roger and others to prevent all assemblies in Wales. Roger fought for Edward, Duke of York at the Battle of Mortimer's Cross in February 1461 and was subsequently blamed for leading Owen Tudor, Henry Tudor's grandfather, to his execution in Hereford marketplace after the battle. This act led to a ten-year feud with Jasper Tudor, Owen's son, which only ended with Sir Roger's execution by Jasper at Chepstow Castle in 1471, after the Battle of Tewkesbury.

His son is recorded as Thomas but there is some doubt over parentage. Thomas was attainted as a Yorkist rebel at the Parliament of Devils in 1459 and, through his efforts in Wales, he helped to prevent Jasper Tudor's force from joining up with the Lancastrian army in the 1471 Tewkesbury campaign before the battle. Vaughan became a retainer of the Duke of Buckingham, but in 1483 he sided with Richard III after the failure of Buckingham's Revolt. From his Tretower base, Thomas set out for Brecon, where he stormed and plundered the principal castle in Wales of his own lord, apparently having no scruples about hitting a man when he was down.

Buckingham was executed and Vaughan was granted the lordship of Brecon by a grateful Richard III. (Brecon Castle still stands on the west side of the town, adjoining an hotel.) In 1485 Vaughan was deployed by Richard as part of this defence in south Wales against possible invasion by Henry Tudor. Henry, however, chose the northern route into England.

YSBYTY IFAN, St Ioan's Church *

Northern edge of village, 1 mile south of A5, east of B4407 (not the prominent non-conformist chapel).

On entering this church, you are confronted in the **nave** with a sight of great pathos. On the floor lie the battered effigies of Rhys Fawr ap Meredydd and his family. Rhys fought for Henry Tudor at the Battle of Bosworth, where his deeds made him a genuine hero. Richard III's last, desperate cavalry charge at the climax of the battle hit Henry Tudor's bodyguard hard. Sir William Brandon, his standard-bearer, was killed by Richard's own lance. In the mêlée, Rhys Fawr, a large man, grabbed hold of the fallen red dragon standard and kept it aloft (so important in medieval battles). How inappropriate, therefore, that in death Rhys Fawr's effigy has lost its head and both legs.

His son Robert is also commemorated in monastic dress, but without his head. His wife Lowry's effigy is intact.

YORKSHIRE

ALLERTON MAULEVERER, St Martin's Church *

East of A1. From A1 take A59 Knaresborough–York road and then, after ¾ mile, minor road (no through road) left to church. Redundant Churches Trust. 01423 330467

In this delightful church are battered effigies of Sir John Mauleverer (d. 1475) and his wife, Alyson née Banks. A Percy retainer, he fought at the Battle of Wakefield (1460), where he was knighted by Henry Percy, 3rd Earl of Northumberland, and the Battle of Towton (1461). Hampton tells us that by 1465 he was in the service of John Neville, who had been given the Northumberland earldom by Edward IV.

The Mauleverers also took part in the later phases of the Wars through Sir Thomas and Halnath, who were well thought of by Richard III. Sir Thomas fought at the Battle of Bosworth (1485) and at the Battle of Stoke Field (1487).

BARDEN, Tower *

On B6160 Bolton Abbey–Burnsall road, just south of Barden village.

This splendid tower house celebrates one of the most unusual 'participants' in the Wars of the Roses, Henry, 10th Lord Clifford (1454–1523). After the slaughter of his father at the First Battle of St Albans, John 'Butcher' Clifford, 9th Lord swore to avenge his death by hunting down the members of the York family. He formed an elite force called the Flower of Craven to do so. A good start was made at the Battle of Wakefield, where Richard, Duke of York and Edmund, his son, were killed. However, York's eldest son, Edward IV, was then declared king, and at the Battle of Ferrybridge (1461) 'Butcher' Clifford and most of his men were cut off from their allies and destroyed. Clifford's wife was so concerned for the safety of her son in these vengeful times that she sent him away to be brought up in a shepherd's family (he was 7 years

Barden Tower, home of the 'Shepherd Lord'.

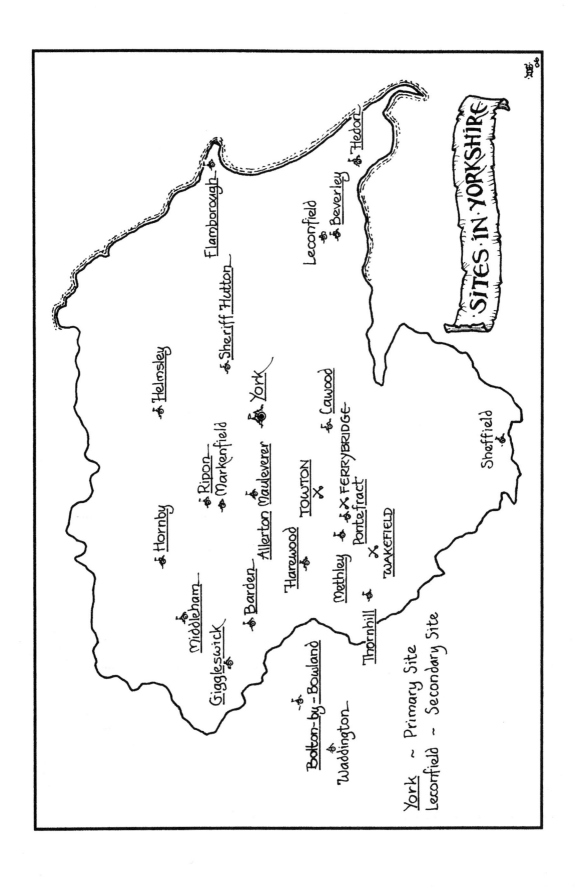

SITES IN YORKSHIRE

Hedon
Beverley
Leconfield
Flamborough
Sheriff Hutton
Helmsley
York
Cawood
Ripon
Markenfield
Allerton Mauleverer
FERRYBRIDGE
Pontefract
TOWTON
Harewood
Hornby
Methley
WAKEFIELD
Barden
Thornhill
Middleham
Sheffield
Giggleswick
Bolton-by-Bowland
Waddington

York ~ Primary Site
Leconfield ~ Secondary Site

old at the time). Wordsworth celebrated the story as the 'Shepherd Lord'. After the Battle of Bosworth, Henry returned to his former life, now Lord of Skipton. In 1487 he attempted to halt the southwards march of Lambert Simnel's Yorkists. At Tadcaster his force and camp were overrun and the rebels continued southwards 'with their tails up'.

Henry was a man of modest ways. He preferred to live here in what was a Clifford hunting lodge rather than in Skipton Castle, the family seat. He built the adjoining chapel and cottage, now a restaurant.

BEVERLEY, The Minster ****
South-east side of town, near railway.

The pre-Reformation Minster was a collegiate church and became by the late medieval period the mausoleum of the Percys. One of their principal houses was Leconfield, just north of the town.

At the end of the north aisle in the **Percy Chapel**, a large, plain tomb-chest commemorates **Henry Percy, 4th Earl of Northumberland** (k. 1489) and his wife, <u>Maud Herbert</u>, daughter of William,

Earl of Pembroke, a Yorkist favourite in the 1460s. This man is famous for doing nothing – twice! One occasion was when he failed (or was unable) to support Richard III on the battlefield of Bosworth in 1485; the other was when he obligingly laid low after Edward IV's landing at Ravenspur in 1471, when Edward reclaimed his throne. Beverley seems somewhat ashamed of this monument; it rarely features in the Minster brochures and there is no signage. This is understandable – the 4th Earl was a harsh and cruel man who was murdered by his own peasants at Topcliffe. Note the stained glass in the chapel.

Also visit **St Mary's Church**, just north of the town centre. On the chancel roof is a set of wooden roof panels depicting the Kings of England, erected in 1445. **Henry VI** is thus the last panel. Note the nearby **North Bar**, built in *c.* 1410.

Just 2 miles north of Beverley on the A164 Driffield road lie the remains of the moat and enclosure of Leconfield fortified **manor house**, one of the main houses of the Percys in the fifteenth century. **Henry VI** stayed here in 1448 during his

Tomb of Henry Percy, 4th Earl of Northumberland, Beverley Minster.

one and only visit to the north in a forty-year reign. It did not seem to affect his following up here though. The site lies ½ mile west of the A164, accessible on a public footpath just south of the village.

BOLTON BY BOWLAND, St Peter and St Paul's Church **
East side of village.

This church was rebuilt in the fifteenth century by Sir Ralph Pudsay (*c.* 1390–1468). His large tomb and splendid brasses survive in the **Pudsay Chapel**. He is depicted with all of his three wives – Matilda Tempest, Margaret Tunstall and Edwina – and twenty-five children (seventeen of whom were borne by Edwina). Margaret is buried here. Sir Ralph was knighted in 1448. He is recorded as having given shelter and hospitality to Henry VI in nearby Bolton Hall during his wanderings in the north-west among Lancastrian sympathisers after the Battle of Hexham in 1464.

His son Sir John gained notoriety through being named as one of the murderers of Richard Neville, Earl of Salisbury at Pontefract Castle in 1460 by Salisbury's widow, Alice. Sir John predeceased his father. A nice brass remembers Sir John's son Henry Pudsay (d. 1520) and wife, Margaret.

While at Bolton, do look in at nearby **Waddington Hall**. **Henry VI** is said to have dined at the Hall in July 1465 before his capture in nearby Clitheroe. The Hall survives as a private house on the east side of the main street. Sir Richard Tempest (see Giggleswick), his host, appears to have set a trap for him from which Henry, with the help of Sir Richard Tunstall, escaped. However, soon afterwards, Henry was apprehended just across the Ribble at Brungerley Bridge in a wood called Clitherwood or Pigshill, accompanied only by Dr Thomas Manning, former Dean of Windsor, Dr Bredon and a squire called Ellerton. Henry was taken to London, his feet tied to the stirrups, and imprisoned in the Tower. Sir Richard Tempest and the members of his family who assisted him were well rewarded with lands in the north-west confiscated from Tunstall. Treachery won yet again.

CAWOOD, Castle **
On B1223 Selby–Tadcaster road, just south-east of village centre crossroads.

All that remains of this 'castle' is the **gatehouse** dating from the time of John Kemp, Archbishop of York from 1426–51 (see Canterbury). The 'castle' was in fact the medieval palace of the Archbishops and, together with the grounds, acts as an unusual monument to the youngest of the **Neville** brothers **George** who was made Archbishop by Edward IV in 1464 – no doubt with some encouragement from his brother, Warwick the Kingmaker. His inauguration banquet was held in this palace and a detailed account of its incredible splendour and extravagance has survived. Historically it is an important moment. It defines the high-water mark of the Nevilles; within a decade, all three brothers had been destroyed by Edward. Not for the first time or last, the Yorkists had 'pressed the self-destruct button'.

The magnificent banquet was attended by more than 2,000 people and involved the consumption of 104 oxen, 1,000 muttons, 400 swans, 2,000 geese, 104 peacocks, 608 pikes/breams, 204 bitterns, 400 herons, 1,000 egrets, 500 stags/bucks, 12 porpoises/seals, 2,000 hot custards, 4,000 cold tarts, 300 tons of ale, and 100 tons of wine. Invited were a goodly proportion of the nobility of England. In addition to the three Neville brothers were the dukes of Gloucester (later Richard III) and Suffolk, the earls of Oxford, Westmoreland and Worcester, lords Hastings, Stanley, Cromwell and Dacre among others, all with wives plus members of the gentry.

Behind the gatehouse the castle grounds survive as a public open space – a pleasant place for a picnic. Try 6 September, the anniversary of the banquet held in 1465.

FLAMBOROUGH, St Oswald's Church **
On B1255 Bridlington–Flamborough road at south-west end of village. Thursday mid-morning service.

An **altar tomb** with a twenty-five-verse inscription to 'Little' Sir Marmaduke Constable (d. 1520). The Constables had lived at Flamborough since the thirteenth century. Originally a Percy retainer, Sir Marmaduke transferred to Richard, Duke of Gloucester. He was a distinguished soldier who accompanied Edward IV to France in 1475 and took part in the Scottish campaigns in 1481/2. He was knighted in 1481. He was made knight of the body by Richard III and helped suppress Buckingham's Revolt in the autumn of 1483. He was one of the northern gentry sent down by Richard III to the southern counties to keep them quiet. He was given the former Buckingham lands at Penshurst and Tonbridge in Kent with orders to suppress private armies. Richard's move caused much resentment among the Kentishmen but Constable was probably successful, because, five months later, he was given the Stewardship of the Honour of Tutbury and the Shrievalty of Staffordshire. Sir Marmaduke was rewarded with grants of land, including the manor of Market Bosworth in Leicestershire. He fought for Richard III at the Battle of Bosworth but made his peace with Henry VII and was retained as knight of the body. He did not support Perkin Warbeck at the Battle of Stoke Field (1487), although a Philip Constable of Flamborough did.

Marmaduke survived to lead the left wing at the Battle of Flodden (1513), when the Scots were routed and their King James IV killed. Interestingly, his tomb inscription makes no mention of his involvement with Richard III. Legend has it that he died from swallowing a toad while drinking water. Round the bend towards the village centre lie the remains of the tower of the Constable **fortified manor house**.

GIGGLESWICK, St Alkeda's Church **
Village centre.

Recumbent effigy with 'SS' collar to <u>Sir Richard Tempest of Bracewell</u> (d. 1488). He started the Wars as a Lancastrian, fighting at the Battle of Wakefield, where he was knighted by 'Butcher' Lord Clifford (he was a Clifford retainer), and at the Battle of Towton, where Clifford was killed. He was attained by Edward IV but later pardoned.

Sir Richard in fact has a special place in the events of the Wars of the Roses. It was he who in July 1464 betrayed his position as host to the fugitive **Henry VI** after the Battle of Hexham at his Waddington home and soon afterwards organised an ambush across the River Ribble at Clitheroe with members of his family (see Bolton). Henry was captured and despatched to the Tower. Sir Richard was granted valuable extra lands in the north-west. He fought at the Battle of Bosworth and, like many northerners, by then he was supporting the Yorkist Richard III. He is said to have been buried with the head of his favourite horse.

Flamborough 'Castle', home of the Constables.

HAREWOOD, All Saints' Church ***

*In grounds of Harewood House ¾ mile west of T-junction
between A659 and A61. Park in Church Lane, just north
of T-junction. Walk ½ mile along lane westwards and turn
left into churchyard. Churches Conservation Trust. Open
with house.*

This church contains a splendid collection of six
medieval tomb-chests and effigies, three of which are
of particular interest for the Wars of the Roses.

Sir William Gascoigne (1404–62) and his wife,
Margaret Clarell of Aldwark, with Yorkist collar and
rare Lion of March pendant. In 1425 Sir William and
Margaret were married clandestinely. He was the
grandson of Judge Gascoigne, also displayed in this
church. Exact identification of these monuments at
Harewood has been particularly difficult, not least
because there were four (if not more) Sir William
Gascoignes successively through the fifteenth century.
This Sir William's son also died at roughly the same
time as his father, in the early 1460s, to complicate
matters further. The excellent literature in the church
gives the latest thinking, followed here. The family
was originally Lancastrian. Sir William, the son,
above, was knighted at the Battle of Wakefield (1460)
and fought at the Battle of Towton (1461). As a result,
Sir William senior was pardoned by Edward IV in
1462 but not attainted. There must have followed
a quick and apparently wholehearted conversion to
the Yorkist cause in time for Sir William's death
before 1465.

Sir William Gascoigne IV (1450–87) and his wife,
Margaret Percy, sister of the 4th Earl of Northumberland. This marriage reflects the reduced status of
the Percys after Towton and superficially seems to
suggest a marriage between two newly Yorkist, but
traditionally Lancastrian, families. At the marriage
of Edward IV's second son, Richard, Duke of
York, to the Mowbray heiress in 1478, Sir William
IV was made Knight of Bath. Like so many former
Lancastrians, he had become a retainer of Richard,
Duke of Gloucester and was made knight banneret
by him in 1482. He fought for Richard at the Battle
of Bosworth but appears to have been quickly
reconciled to Henry VII. The family lived at nearby
Gawthorpe, later demolished as the Harewood estate
was expanded.

Edward Redman and his wife, Elizabeth Huddleston
(1455–1510). Edward was a great-grandson of the
Sir Richard also commemorated in the church. He
succeeded in 1482 to the family estates in Yorkshire
and Cumberland on the death of his brother Sir

William, although he himself was never knighted.
His father, Sir Richard, had been a Neville retainer.
He himself supported Richard III and was somewhat
favoured by him. He helped to suppress Buckingham's
Revolt in the south in late 1483 and was among the
'implants' of northern gentry put there by Richard as
king. He was made sheriff of Somerset and Dorset
and granted lands. He does not appear to have fought
at the Battle of Bosworth but took some while to be
reconciled to Henry Tudor. He sensibly avoided being
drawn into the Battle of Stoke Field (1487) and was
finally recognised by Henry when appointed Sheriff of
Cumberland and Westmorland in 1495.

HEDON *

*South side of town centre in Baxtergate in the back garden
of Holyrood House.*

This entry is rather different. In the back garden
of this retirement home is the Hedon Cross, which
was washed up on the beach at Kilnsea (near Spurn
Point) in 1818 and re-erected here by a developer
who had pretensions to construct an elegant Georgian
square – sadly never achieved. Tradition has it
that the cross was originally located at Ravenspur
(a long-vanished port on the west side of Spurn
Point) and commemorates the landing of either
Henry IV (in 1399) or **Edward IV** (in 1471), or
both, and their subsequent attainment of the throne
of England.

Edward's landing at Ravenspur in March 1471
with his brother, Richard, Duke of Gloucester,
Lord Hastings and others was not auspicious. They
had tried to land near Cromer in Norfolk but were
warned off that the Lancastrians had the area well
defended. Storms then intervened and the ships
achieved landfall in the Humber at different points.
Having collected his scattered army together, Edward
was then menaced by a Lancastrian force led by Sir
Martin del See from Barmston on the east coast.
Edward's force was refused entry into Hull but
allowed access by Beverley (Percy territory). At York,
Edward had to repeat Henry IV's 'trick' of saying
that he was only returning to England to claim his
dukedom of York before he was admitted to the city.
Initially, support rallying to his cause was meagre
and did not really pick up until Hastings joined him
at Leicester and the 'ball was rolling'. After emphatic
victories at the Battles of Barnet and Tewkesbury,
Edward was able to end the Readeption of Henry
VI and regain control of his kingdom before the end
of May.

Hedon Cross by tradition commemorates Edward IV's landings at Ravenspur.

HELMSLEY, All Saints' Church **
Village centre.

In the north-west corner of the **baptistry** is the tombstone and brass of Thomas, Lord Roos of Hamlake and his wife, Philippa Tiptoft. Originally buried at Rievaulx Abbey, at the Dissolution the bodies were brought to this church and buried under the chancel. Roos was a Lancastrian die-hard who was a close ally of Henry Beaufort, Duke of Somerset. Through his mother, Eleanor Beauchamp,

whose second husband was Edmund Beaufort, Duke of Somerset, he was involved in the opposition to Richard Neville junior's Warwick inheritance in the late 1440s. He was associated with his Percy neighbours in the 1450s and was something of a naval man, who owned ships. He was involved with Somerset in 1457 in an unsuccessful attempt to seize (or murder) Warwick the kingmaker in the City of London with 400 men. In 1459 he and Somerset attempted to regain Calais from Warwick.

In the early phases of the Wars, he was very active in the fighting on the side of the Lancastrians; he fought at the First Battle of St Albans (1455), the Battle of Wakefield (1460) and the Second Battle of St Albans (1461). He did not actually fight at the Battle of Towton, as he stayed behind in York with the King and Queen while the battle was being fought. After the disastrous defeat, he accompanied them in flight to Scotland. In 1461 he was attainted and proved an irreconcilable Lancastrian who, by June 1461, was raising Henry's standard in Durham. He was very much involved in the subsequent struggle to control the military strongholds in Northumberland against Warwick the Kingmaker and his younger brother, John Neville, Lord Montagu. He fought at the Battle of Hedgeley Moor (where he and Somerset deserted Sir Ralph Percy) and was captured at the Battle of Hexham (1464). Two days later he was executed at Newcastle with Lord Hungerford.

His title and lands were later restored to his son, Edmund, who unfortunately was mentally incapacitated. On Edmund's death, the title fell to Sir George Manners of Etal in Northumberland through his mother, Eleanor (Edmund's sister). From George are descended the dukes of Rutland (see Windsor). The Rooses had principal seats at Belvoir Castle in Leicestershire and **Helmsley Castle** which can be visited nearby.

Much mutilated memorial brass to Thomas Mountford, Hornby church.

HORNBY, St Mary's Church **

West of A1, 3 miles south of Catterick, turn left off A1 on minor road for 3 miles, through Hackworth to Hornby.

Richmondshire played a disproportionately important part in the Wars of the Roses through the powerful Conyers family, retainers of first the Nevilles and then Richard III. Hornby was the seat of one branch of the family; there were Conyers of Hornby at the battles of Blore Heath, Towton, Edgcote and Bosworth.

In the **south chapel** is a brass of Christopher Conyers (died c. 1464) and his wife, Ellen Ryleston. They had a large family, including the soldiers Sir John, Knight of the Garter, Sir Richard (of South Cowton) and Sir William, who was killed at the Battle of Edgcote (1469) fighting for Warwick the Kingmaker as 'Robin of Redesdale'. His elder brother, Sir John, took over command during the battle, with success. Christopher's grandson through Sir William was ennobled by Henry VII in 1494.

Note also the fine brass of Thomas (d. 1489) and Agnes Mountford and fifteen children. The Mount-

fords of nearby Hackworth and the Strangeways were also retainers of the Nevilles. A Sir Thomas Mountford fought for the Nevilles at Blore Heath. Do get a view of nearby **Hornby Castle**, (private) home of the Conyers, which was built in the fourteenth century.

METHLEY, St Oswald's Church ***

On A639 Castleford–Leeds road at south end of village, near cricket ground.

This church contains an extensive collection of monuments. In the **Waterton Chapel**, the tomb-chest and effigies commemorate Lionel, Lord Welles (1406–61) and his first wife, Jane Waterton. Lord Welles was killed at the nearby Battle of Towton, fighting for Lancaster. He was close to the dukes of Somerset, being their joint Lieutenant with Earl Rivers in Calais in the 1450s. He accompanied Somerset on the ignominious attempt to reclaim Calais in 1457 from Warwick. He was extremely active in the early phase of the Wars, fighting at the Battle of Blore Heath (1459), the Battle of Wakefield (1460) and the 2nd Battle of St Albans (1461).

In 1447 Welles married Margaret Beauchamp, the mother of Lady Margaret Beaufort. The Welles were powerful landowners in Lincolnshire. Welles was posthumously attainted by Edward IV after Towton. He was buried in Methley because it had been the home of his first wife's family, the Watertons. Sir Robert Waterton (d. 1425) is commemorated with tomb-chest and effigy. He was an esquire to Henry IV, Master of the King's Horse and Constable of Pontefract Castle at the time that Richard II was starved to death in its dungeons in 1400. Sir Roger was also tutor to Richard, Duke of York, who lived with the family at nearby Methley Hall (demolished 1963).

MIDDLEHAM, Castle **** £
Village centre. EH. 01969 623899.

In the centre of this delightful village stands Middleham Castle, a principal seat of the Nevilles since 1270. The castle passed to the junior branch of the Nevilles, **Richard, Earl of Salisbury**, on the death of his mother, Joan Beaufort, in 1440. It became his principal seat and Salisbury carried out many alterations during the twenty years before his execution in 1460. In 1454 Lord Egremont, the Percy heir, was imprisoned here after an armed skirmish with the Nevilles at Stamford Bridge, near York.

The castle was next inherited by Salisbury's son, **Warwick the Kingmaker**, who used it as his main base in the north. **Edward IV** stayed here shortly after the Battle of Towton in 1461 but made an unwelcome return in August 1469 as Warwick's prisoner after the Battle of Edgcote. King Edward was taken into 'custody' by Warwick's brother George Neville (Archbishop of York) at Olney in Northamptonshire after Edward's forces melted away on the news of William Herbert's catastrophic defeat near Banbury. Initially, Edward was sent to Warwick Castle and then was moved up to Yorkshire. Amazingly, therefore, the Kingmaker had two Kings of England imprisoned at the same time – Edward in Middleham and Henry VI still languishing in the Tower after four years. No wonder he has been given the title 'Kingmaker'.

On the Kingmaker's death at the Battle of Barnet in 1471, the castle was granted to **Richard, Duke of**

Middleham Castle, stronghold of the Nevilles and of Richard, Duke of Gloucester.

Gloucester, Edward's youngest brother. Richard had already spent three years here in the mid-1460s as a member of the Kingmaker's family in the manner of aristocratic sons at that time. In 1472 Richard married Anne Neville, the Kingmaker's younger daughter. Middleham became the centre of Richard's northern power base, which he used to such devastating effect to seize the throne in June 1483.

Richard's only son, **Edward of Middleham**, was born in this castle in 1474, possibly in the **Prince's Tower**. He became Prince of Wales in 1483 but died here in 1484 (see Sheriff Hutton).

Either Warwick or Richard added the upper chamber of the Great Hall. Do also visit **St Mary's Church**, which houses a modern memorial to **Richard III**.

PONTEFRACT, Castle ** £
North of A645 Pontefract–Ferrybridge road at north-east end of town.

The remains of this once imposing castle are limited but do represent the site of two key events in the evolution of the Wars of the Roses. Firstly, it was in a dungeon here that Richard II was reputedly starved to death in 1400, leaving Henry IV as the undisputed Lancastrian ruler of England. Sir Roger Waterton (see Methley) was governor of the castle at the time. Pontefract was a principal seat of the Duchy of Lancaster. John of Gaunt, Henry IV's father, had carried out many modifications to the castle in the late fourteenth century.

Secondly, it was to this castle that **Richard Neville, Earl of Salisbury** was brought as a prisoner for ransom by the victorious Lancastrians after the Battle of Wakefield at the end of 1460. He was, however, executed the next morning, allegedly by commoners disaffected with his lordship in Yorkshire. This execution made the Battle of Wakefield a total disaster for the Yorkists. Salisbury, together with his own son Sir Thomas, **Richard, Duke of York** and his son Edmund, Earl of Rutland (all three killed at the Battle of Wakefield) were buried in Pontefract. Their remains were subsequently reinterred in lavish ceremonies in their family mausoleums at Bisham Abbey and Fotheringhay.

Pontefract was regularly used as a royal prison. Here, Sir Thomas Vaughan (see Westminster Abbey) and possibly Sir Richard Haute were sent by Richard, Duke of Gloucester after their arrest at Stony Stratford in Buckinghamshire with Edward V in April 1483. On 25 June Vaughan, **Antony**

Woodville, Earl Rivers, **Sir Richard Grey** and Sir Richard Haute were beheaded in this castle in the presence of Thomas Percy, Earl of Northumberland.

Edward IV is said to have stayed at the castle on the eve of the Battle of Towton in late March 1461.

RIPON, Cathedral **
City centre.

In the north transept are somewhat battered tomb-chest and effigies to Sir Thomas Markenfield (d. 1497) and his wife, Eleanor Conyers (daughter of Sir John, Knight of the Garter), who lived at nearby Markenfield Hall. Sir Thomas appears from relative obscurity on Richard III's usurpation in 1483. He helped to defeat Buckingham's Revolt in October 1483 and then was one of the three dozen or so northerners to be sent down to the south of England by Richard in an attempt to subdue the region. Not surprisingly, this policy proved to be a grave error by Richard and was much resented by the southern gentry. Sir Thomas was granted eight manors in Somerset from lands confiscated from Lancastrian 'rebels' such as Sir Robert Willoughby, Sir Roger Tocotes and Sir Thomas St Leger.

By December 1484 Sir Thomas was a knight of the body to Richard III and Sheriff of Yorkshire. He fought for Richard at Bosworth but was not attainted. In fact, perhaps surprisingly, he served out the last two months of his shrievalty under Henry VII.

Markenfield Hall is 2 miles south of Ripon, east of the A61 Harrogate road. It is a remarkable survival of a fortified and moated manor built in the early fourteenth century and largely unchanged externally. It is open for two weeks every year in May and July (01765 603411). Note that the turning off the A61 is sharp.

SHEFFIELD, St Peter and St Paul's Cathedral **
City centre, north side of Fargate.

In the **Shrewsbury Chapel**, a fine tomb and effigies celebrate the 4th Earl of Shrewsbury, George Talbot (1468–1538) and his two wives, Anne Hastings and Elizabeth Walden. He was the great-grandson of the great John Talbot, scourge of the French, who was killed at the Battle of Castillon in 1453. The family pedigree was strongly Lancastrian. George inherited at 5 years old and was married to Anne Hastings, daughter of William, Lord Hastings. Not surprisingly, therefore, aged 17 George fought for Richard III at the Battle of Bosworth (his uncle Sir Gilbert

Markenfield Hall, near Ripon.

Tomb of George Talbot, Earl of Shrewsbury and his two wives, Sheffield cathedral.

233

Talbot upheld family tradition and sided with Henry Tudor). Henry sensibly pardoned him and restored the Talbot lands in 1486, George having carried the sword at his coronation. He also attended Henry's wedding to Elizabeth of York in that year. George joined Henry at the Battle of Stoke Field (1487) and was made Knight of the Garter in 1487.

Note that the Talbots were traditionally buried at Worksop Priory but because George lived until 1538, the priory had already been dissolved, so this tomb is original to the cathedral. Only a few participants in the Wars survived beyond 1530.

SHERIFF HUTTON

St Helen's Church ***

At the end of straight dead-end, running east from village centre (near castle).

In the **south-east corner** of the church, the Gower/Sutherland chapel contains a worn brass inscription to Sir Thomas Gower (k. 1485), a retainer of Richard III with lands in Sheriff Hutton and nearby Stittenham. Gower was Constable of Sheriff Hutton Castle in 1483/4. He fought for Richard at the Battle of Bosworth and was killed there.

In the north side in the **St Nicholas Chapel** is a floor brass to Thomas Wytham (d. 1481) and his wife, Agnes, née Thweng (d. 1495). Thomas was a long-term servant of both Salisbury and his son, Warwick the Kingmaker. From 1454–64 he was Chancellor of the Exchequer to Henry VI and Edward IV (a household position). The Thwengs lived at nearby Cornborough Manor.

The main interest in this church is the free-standing alabaster effigy, in the **north aisle**, of a young man, said to be **Edward, Prince of Wales** (d. 1484), only son of Richard III. Born in 1473 to Anne, née Neville, Richard's wife, he was a sickly child. He was invested as prince and knighted by Richard in September 1483 at York Minster in the presence of Archbishop Rotherham and other dignitaries. In 1478 he was made Earl of Salisbury. He died at Middleham Castle on 9 April 1484, just one year to the day after the death of Edward IV, while his parents were staying at Nottingham Castle. They were devastated. Richard's regime now began to look very shaky. His queen, Anne Neville, died later that year. Note also the Yorkist sunbursts in the stained glass in this aisle.

Also buried in this church was George Neville, one-time Duke of Bedford (*c.* 1457–83) and the only son of the Kingmaker's youngest brother, John Neville, Marquis Montagu. George was thus the only male offspring of the four sons of Richard Neville, Earl of Salisbury, who inherited Middleham and Sheriff Hutton by virtue of tail male at a time when Edward IV's troubles with the Kingmaker were particularly difficult. Hence, in 1469 Edward created George Duke of Bedford with the idea of marrying him to his eldest daughter, Elizabeth of York, in an attempt to shore up Montagu's support for Edward against the Kingmaker. This move in fact failed spectacularly a year later, when Montagu suddenly declared for his brother at Doncaster. Montagu and the Kingmaker were eventually killed in April 1471 at the Battle of Barnet. George became 'redundant' and an embarrassment to Edward IV. In 1478 he was degraded from the dukedom because he lacked the means to support it. Edward then gave the title to his third son, who unfortunately died young (and is buried in St George's Chapel, Windsor).

George was also blocked from inheriting his mother's Inglisthorpe lands after her death, surely a man very badly treated by Edward IV (like his father before him).

Castle ***
Southern edge of village. 01347 878341.

The scant but imposing remains of this important fortress can be visited by appointment. Alternatively you can walk round the outside. With Middleham Castle, this forms the core of the junior Neville inheritance passed down from Joan Beaufort to her eldest son the **Earl of Salisbury**, and then successively to the Kingmaker and to **Richard, Duke of Gloucester**. The castle was often used to house political prisoners. Earl Rivers was imprisoned by Protector Richard, Duke of Gloucester before his execution at Pontefract after Richard's Second Coup in June 1483; and then in 1484 a whole group of royal prisoners formed something of a house party under John de la Pole, Earl of Lincoln (maternal nephew to Richard and probably his heir presumptive after the death of Richard's son). They included **Princess Elizabeth**, Edward IV's eldest daughter (whom Richard had wanted to marry), and one or two of her sisters, as well as **Edward Plantagenet, Earl of Warwick** (Clarence's young son) and his elder sister Margaret. It was from Sheriff Hutton that Elizabeth and the Earl of Warwick were escorted by Sir Robert Willoughby under orders from the victorious Henry Tudor after the Battle of

Sheriff Hutton Castle, one of the power bases of the Nevilles.

Bosworth in 1485. The one was destined for marriage to Henry as his queen, honouring the pledge he made in France at Christmas 1483. The other was secretly taken to the Tower, never to emerge alive.

THORNHILL, St Michael's Church **

Village centre on B6117 Horbury–Dewsbury road.
Wednesday mid-morning service.

The **Savile Chapel** contains a wonderful collection of monuments and stained glass. The Saviles were associated with the dukes of York before 1399, being constables of Sandal Castle. There are two tomb-chests and effigies of interest: firstly an alabaster one of <u>Sir John Savile I</u> (d. 1481) and his wife, <u>Alice Gascoigne of Gawthorpe</u>, with York collars. John I was also a retainer of Richard Neville, Earl of Salisbury. He was Sheriff of Yorkshire 1454/5 during all the troubles between Percy and Neville. He fought with Salisbury at the Battle of Blore Heath in September 1459 and may have been present at the rout of Ludford later that year.

Sir John's son, John II, and his wife, Jane Harrington, are featured in the splendid fifteenth-century stained glass in the east window of this chapel, along with William Savile, donor of the window, and son of Sir John II (who died in 1481), and William's brother Sir John III and first wife, Alice Vernon. A most unusual wooden tomb-chest and effigies also commemorate <u>Sir John Savile III</u> (d. 1504) and his two wives, <u>Alice</u>, above, and <u>Elizabeth Paston</u>. Sir John III was very much part of Richard III's northern 'mafia' who were sent south after Buckingham's Revolt in 1484 to keep the peace. He was made Constable of the Isle of Wight and granted lands in Wiltshire/Hampshire and Devon. Sir John III wisely did not show at the Battle of Bosworth for Richard III.

THE BATTLE OF TOWTON
(29 March 1461) +++++
Strategic Background and the Campaign
Edward IV had been proclaimed king by the citizens of London in early March, carefully coordinated by the Neville family under the Earl of Warwick

(the Kingmaker). After the defeat of Warwick at the Second Battle of St Albans in February, the Yorkist regime had lost custody of the Lancastrian King, Henry VI, which had been regained by Queen Margaret of Anjou. Their regime in London therefore had no legitimacy and in desperation they were forced to acclaim their own king. Since the 'assassination' of his father, Richard, Duke of York, in late 1460 at the Battle of Wakefield, Edward was heir to the rival Mortimer claim to the throne of England. The Yorkists were, however, only a minority faction among the nobility; only eight or nine peers accompanied Edward to Towton. Full legitimacy in the eyes of the whole country could only be gained on the field of battle against the Lancastrians.

By 11 March, Edward and Warwick began leaving London for Yorkshire, where the vast but unruly Lancastrian army was now encamped around the city of York itself. The Yorkist army was recruited largely in Kent, East Anglia, the Welsh Marches (Edward's veterans from the Battle of Mortimer's Cross) and the Midlands (where Warwick held sway). Progress northwards was deliberately slow to allow new recruits to join. By 27 March, the army had reached Pontefract Castle, although the Duke of Norfolk's retinue was delayed because the Duke was very ill (he died later that year).

Meanwhile the Lancastrians, led by the Duke of Somerset and fresh from their stunning victories at the battles of Wakefield and Second St Albans, had taken up a defensive position 15 miles south-west of York, across the River Wharf on a plateau near the village of Towton. With Somerset were eighteen or nineteen other peers and more than sixty knights and gentlemen. A very large proportion of the aristocracy was therefore engaged at this crucial encounter, but decisively in favour of the incumbent Lancastrians. Interestingly a large proportion of Lancastrian forces at Towton came from Yorkshire in the retinues of Percy, Clifford and Roos.

Precursor to the Battle at Ferrybridge

Between Edward's army at Pontefract and the plateau at Towton lay the formidable obstacle of the River Aire in winter flood. The Great North Road crossed the Aire by bridge at Ferrybridge (as it still does today). Edward's first tactical objective was to force a crossing of the bridge and then move his large army up through Sherburn in Elmet to Towton. This proved no easy matter and had it not been for the full-scale battle fought a day later at Towton, this encounter itself would have qualified for a separate battle entry.

Immediately on arrival at Pontefract, Edward sent a force under the Duke of Suffolk to command the crossing of the Aire. It was found that the Lancastrians had destroyed the wooden bridge as they moved up to their Towton 'fortress', so the Yorkist advance party set about rebuilding the structure later that day. They guarded the bridge overnight but were surprised early on the 28th by a Lancastrian cavalry force led by Lord Clifford, which killed many men, including Lord Fitzwalter, their commander, and took control of the bridge.

Edward ordered his main army forward to Ferrybridge, where they engaged Clifford's troops on the bridge. Frustrated by high casualties, Edward then ordered Lord Fauconberg (Warwick's uncle), Sir Walter Blount and Robert Horne, a Kentish captain, to lead a flanking attack via Castleford and a crossing of the Aire, 3 miles upstream. Clifford seems to have got wind of this manoeuvre, because he ordered his troops to pull back to Towton before they were intercepted by Fauconberg. It was too late: Fauconberg's mounted archers caught Clifford at Dintingdale as dusk fell. Both Clifford and Lord John Neville (both major figures at the Battle of Wakefield) were killed almost within sight of the Lancastrian position at Towton. They were not reinforced by Somerset, perhaps suggesting that visibility was very poor by this time.

The Battle

After the hard-fought crossing of the Aire, Edward moved up his army in late evening to Sherburn in Elmet, with the vanguard reaching Saxton village, just south of Towton, in atrocious winter conditions of extreme cold, snow and ice. His men were probably short of food as the baggage train had not yet arrived.

The numbers of men engaged on both sides were very large. Despite the medieval habit of badly exaggerating numbers, this battle is usually reckoned to have been the biggest in English history, with unfortunately the greatest number of casualties. The battle site itself, being a wide plateau, tends to support this view. There is no mention on either side of artillery.

Ferrybridge – and they say the camera never lies! Visit this idyllic spot on the Aire, scene of the battle in 1461.

The Yorkist front line viewed across Towton Vale from the Lancastrian line.

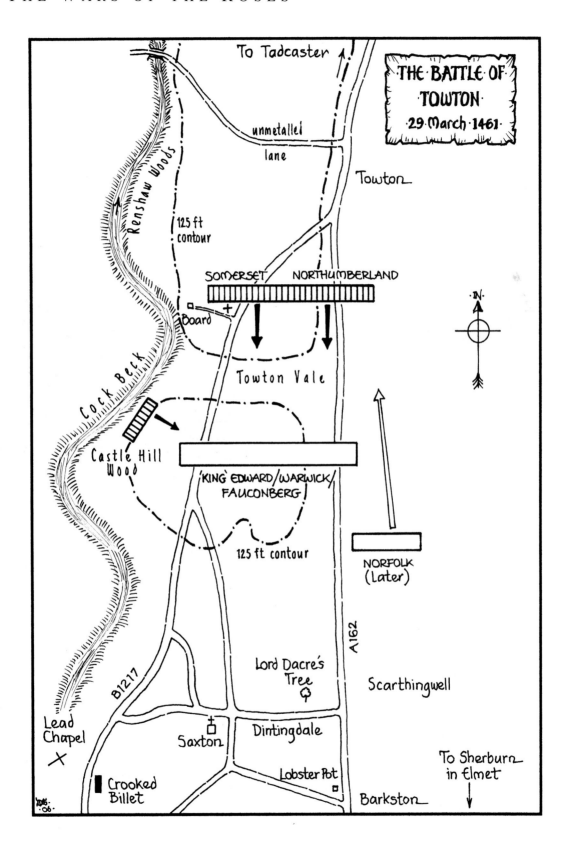

To Tadcaster

unmetalled lane

THE BATTLE OF TOWTON
29 March 1461

Renshaw Woods

125 ft contour

Towton

SOMERSET   NORTHUMBERLAND

Board

Cock Beck

Towton Vale

N

Castle Hill Wood

KING EDWARD/WARWICK/
FAUCONBERG

125 ft contour

NORFOLK
(Later)

A162

B1217

Lord Dacre's Tree

Scarthingwell

Lead Chapel

Saxton

Dintingdale

To Sherburn in Elmet

Crooked Billet

Lobster Pot

Barkston

Dintingdale, near Towton – the hawthorn tree marks the east end of the Yorkist rear lines.

The two armies took some time to get into formation the next morning, but by 9.00 a.m. they were ready, lined up across the shallow Towton vale. Exact details of what happened on Towton battlefield are, as usual, lacking but one thing we do know is that neither King Henry nor Queen Margaret was present with the Lancastrian army. Henry claimed that he could not possibly be on a battlefield on a day such as Palm Sunday. More likely, Queen Margaret feared that if he were now found by Yorkists on a battlefield he would be killed. The couple remained at York. It was snowing and the wind was blowing into the faces of the Lancastrians. Lord Fauconberg, leading the Yorkist van, ordered more than 10,000 archers into the shallow valley to unleash their volleys. The Lancastrians replied, but many arrows fell short because of the strong wind and were picked up and reused by the Yorkist archers. The casualties caused to the Lancastrians

were beginning to sap morale, so the Duke of Somerset gave the order to advance.

Sheer weight of Lancastrian numbers, a successful cavalry charge and a flanking attack by mounted spears from Castle Wood enabled the Lancastrian right, led by Somerset and Andrew Trollope, to pressure the Yorkists, move forward and threaten to break their line down the western slope of the plateau. Some Yorkists may have fled down to Lead but the line held. On the left wing of the Lancastrian army, the Earl of Northumberland was slow to engage and so lost the opportunity to convert the success of the right wing into victory. On this flank, the two sides initially fought to a standstill but then the Lancastrians began to give ground. The fighting at Towton was so intense and lasted for so long that it had to be halted from time to time to clear away the large number of bodies. The battle lasted all day.

Signet ring said to have belonged to Henry Percy, 3rd Earl of Northumberland.

The Earl of Northumberland was killed in the mêlée and then, crucially, the Duke of Norfolk's retinue arrived on the field in mid-afternoon to reinforce the Yorkist right. They outflanked the pivoting Lancastrian line, causing the struggling Lancastrian left to break and flee the field. The rout and chase at Towton were particularly bloody as men became trapped crossing the River Cock and the River Wharfe at Tadcaster, where the bridge had already been destroyed by the Lancastrians.

Aftermath and Commentary

In the end, Towton was an emphatic Yorkist victory but it had been 'a damned close thing'. Casualties on both sides were heavy, although those of the Lancastrian aristocracy were much higher, perhaps reflecting the slaughter in the rout. Forty-one captured Lancastrian knights were executed although many were spared. Both Edward and Warwick must take credit for the logistical and organisational triumph that underpinned the battle. The Yorkists mobilised and moved north quickly in the middle of winter. Their concentration of all their forces may have been a last-minute affair but it worked. Quite who deserves the tactical credit is unclear; perhaps Lord Fauconberg was the unsung hero of Towton. Politically the battle was not totally decisive, at least in the short term, because Henry and Margaret were able to flee to Scotland along with the Dukes of Somerset and Exeter, Lord Roos and Sir John Fortescue. From here, they were able to organise resistance to King Edward IV centred on Northumberland and Wales. Although dragging on until 1464, at no time did this activity threaten the English heartlands. In practice, therefore, Towton was decisive in that no Lancastrian uprising or invasion threatened English heartlands until Edward so unexpectedly quit his own kingdom in 1470. Edward IV was crowned in Westminster Abbey on Sunday 28 June 1461.

Immediately after the battle, Edward proceeded to York, where he ordered the heads of his father and brother to be taken down from Micklegate Bar. The Earl of Devon was found hiding in the city and executed.

Location and What to See

The eighteenth-century **bridge** over the River Aire at Ferrybridge still stands, on the line of the old Great North Road, just to the north of the village. It would have been here or hereabouts that the preliminary fighting would have taken place.

The battle of Towton itself was fought on the 100ft plateau on the line of the A162 Ferrybridge–Tadcaster road and the B1217 Towton–Hook Moor road. It is easily the most satisfying battlefield from the Wars of the Roses, being an impressively large area and virtually unspoiled. The western edge of the plateau down to the Cock Beck looks the part and makes particularly chilling viewing when you realise that probably thousands of Lancastrians died trying to flee down its slopes in conditions of snow and ice in the dark, wearing their suits of armour. If they survived the descent, they probably drowned in Cock Beck. The battlefield is best explored using both a car and on foot.

The Dacre Cross is a good place to start. Situated next to the B1217 about 1½ miles south of Towton, it defines the western end of the initial Lancastrian

Participants and Casualties

Yorkist (~25,000 men)	*Lancastrian (~30,000+)*
King Edward IV	Henry Beaufort, Duke of Somerset
Richard Neville, Earl of Warwick	Henry Percy, Earl of Northumberland
William Neville, Lord Fauconberg	James Butler, Earl of Wiltshire
John, Lord Clinton	Henry Holland, Duke of Exeter
Thomas, Lord Stanley	Thomas Courtenay, Earl of Devon
Sir John Fogge	Sir Andrew Trollope
Sir John Wenlock	Richard Woodville, Earl of Rivers
Sir William Stanley	Sir William Catesby
William, Viscount Bourchier	Randolph, Lord Dacre
Edward Brooke, Lord Cobham	Sir John Delves
William Fiennes, Lord Saye and Sale	Sir Everard Digby
Thomas Fitzalan, Lord Maltravers	Sir William Gascoigne
Edmund, Lord Grey of Ruthin	Robert, Lord Hungerford
Sir Robert Harcourt	Sir James Luttrell
Sir William Hastings	Sir John Mauleverer
Sir William Herbert	John, Lord Neville
Sir John Howard	Thomas, Lord Roos
Sir Thomas Montgomery	Sir Richard Tempest
Sir John Scott	Lionel, Lord Welles
Sir John Saye	Sir Robert Whittingham
John, Lord Stourton	
John Sutton, Lord Dudley	
Sir Roger Tocotes	
John Touchet, Lord Audley	
Sir John Dinham	

Casualties: Towton is generally believed to be not only the largest battle ever fought in Britain, but also the most bloody. Total casualties were high, especially in the rout. King Edward estimated 28,000, of which 8,000 were Yorkist – an overestimate but indicative of the intensity of the struggle

position in front of the Towton vale dip and looks across to the Yorkist line above the other side of the vale. It is an awesome sight, for here the two armies did most of their fighting. Each year, wreaths of red and white roses are placed on the cross on or near 29 March. An **information board** is located 300 yards off the road, westwards along a farm track. From here, **Bloody Meadow** can be viewed down off the plateau to the south.

As you proceed southwards by car for 1 mile on the B1217 down Towton vale, **Castle Hill Woods** (which housed the Lancastrian spear party) can be seen by turning right on the unmetalled road just before Lead Mill Farm. A short walk on this road gives access to **Cock Beck**. There are burial mounds to the right of the road.

Half a mile further south-west along the B1217 brings you to Lead. The **Crooked Billet** is a convenient place for a pint and meal. (The Earl of Warwick may have lodged here before the battle but

Stained glass memorial in the Lead Chapel, near Towton.

it is unlikely to have been a pub at the time.) Do not miss **Lead Chapel** in the field opposite the pub. It was standing in 1461 and is a little gem. The Richard III Society have placed a **stained-glass** memorial in the east window.

Briefly retrace your footsteps up the B1217 and take the first right to **Saxton** churchyard. By the south-east corner of the church is a large **tomb-chest** surrounded by an iron railing above the burial site of <u>Lord Dacre of Gilsland</u> (k. 1461), who was killed during the battle by an arrow in the neck while his helmet was off. Dacre is said to be buried alongside his horse. Next to it is a modern **stone memorial** which marks the 1996 reburial of the dead excavated in recent times by the University of Bradford.

Take the southerly minor road east out of Saxton for 1 mile towards Barkston Ash (Headwell Lane). At the crossroads with the A162 is a stone **'lobster pot'**, said to be the original base for Dacre's Cross. Some 600 yards north of here is **Dintingdale**, where Lords Clifford and Neville came to grief.

Proceed northwards for 2 miles to Towton (try the Rockingham Arms). At the northern end of the village, park and walk along the 'Old London Road' footpath, which descends off the plateau and leads to the bridge over **Cock Beck** where so many Lancastrians were slain or drowned as a bridge of bodies formed. After 200 yards, note the undulations in **Chapel Hill** on the left, where Richard III is said to have built a chapel.

THE BATTLE OF WAKEFIELD (30 December 1460) ++++

Strategic Background and the Campaign

After the Battle of Northampton in July 1460, Warwick the Kingmaker had possession of Henry VI and governed the country from Westminster. He concluded a treaty with Henry, Duke of Somerset, allowing Henry to take up sanctuary in France in exchange for abandoning his campaign against Calais. Edward, Earl of March and the Earl of Salisbury were with Warwick. Queen Margaret had fled to Wales, while Richard, Duke of York bizarrely remained in Ireland.

Finally, at the beginning of September, York landed near Chester and, accompanied by Cecily Neville, his wife, made his way to London, entering the city with his sword held uppermost and trumpets playing. What followed is one of the most extraordinary non-events in English history. In Westminster Hall, York claimed the throne of England by right of being descended from Edward III's second son, Lionel. He laid his hand on the empty throne, but instead of thunderous applause from the assembled lords, there was deathly silence. Bear in mind that the assembly consisted largely of Yorkist lords. There followed a furious row between the Yorkist leaders. The Kingmaker claimed variously that the Archbishop of Canterbury and his own father, Salisbury, were against the move, not wishing to break their vows of allegiance to Henry VI. What is incredible is that Warwick and York had spent two months together in Ireland in the spring of 1460 when these matters would have been endlessly discussed. Furthermore, Warwick had visited York in Shrewsbury while on the latter's journey south to London. The final outcome after long discussions involving both Houses of Parliament was the Act of Accord passed by parliament on 24 October 1460 – Henry would remain king, and on his death, York and his heirs would take the crown (however, York was ten years older than Henry). This of course was unacceptable to Queen Margaret, because Prince Edward was disinherited.

York now headed a Third Protectorate. Meanwhile, Somerset returned suddenly from France and then proceeded north to York. The Lancastrian forces quickly concentrated at Hull – retinues of the Earls of Devon and Northumberland, Duke of Exeter, Lords Clifford, Roos and Neville (senior branch) – a major achievement in winter. They began harassing the Yorkshire estates of York and Salisbury. The Yorkist government in London was taken by surprise, so early in December, York and Salisbury, with two of their sons, set out with a small force to deal with the 'uprising', recruiting on the way. Meanwhile, York had sent his eldest son, Edward, to suppress another Lancastrian 'uprising', by Jasper Tudor (Henry VI's stepbrother) in Wales. The War of Succession had begun.

Recruitment on the way north was slow and the weather very wet. At Worksop, York's army was ambushed by a Lancastrian contingent led by Andrew Trollope. This was beaten off and the force reached York's castle of Sandal near Wakefield on 21 December 1460. Unfortunately provisions at the castle were low because the Lancastrian army had already taken up positions around Sandal, thus hindering foraging parties leaving the castle. The Lancastrians were operating from nearby Pontefract Castle, belonging to the Duchy of Lancaster. A Christmas truce may have been arranged with Somerset, to last

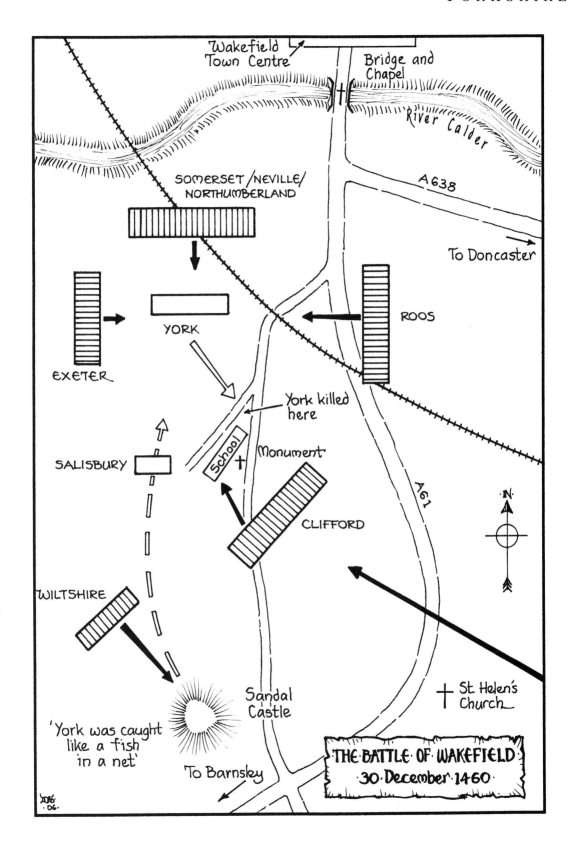

Wakefield Town Centre

Bridge and Chapel

River Calder

SOMERSET /NEVILLE/ NORTHUMBERLAND

A 638

To Doncaster

ROOS

YORK

EXETER

York killed here

School

Monument

SALISBURY

CLIFFORD

A 61

N

WILTSHIRE

St. Helen's Church

'York was caught like a fish in a net'

Sandal Castle

To Barnsley

THE BATTLE OF WAKEFIELD
30 December 1460

until Epiphany. York meanwile had sent to his son Edward for reinforcements.

The Battle

York had to send out regular foraging parties to keep his army fed, which left his forces stretched. On 30 December a returning party was attacked north of Wakefield Green by Somerset and Devon's forces. Against the advice of his councillors, the Duke of York decided to sally forth to relieve the party. Salisbury stayed put in the castle. York's decision may have been influenced by the arrival over Wakefield Bridge, to the north, of Lord John Neville, the younger brother of the mentally infirm 2nd Earl of Westmorland, and stepbrother to Salisbury. The two branches of the Neville family had been set against one another by the will of Ralph Neville, 1st Earl (d. 1425), which left the bulk of his property to the junior branch headed by Salisbury. The senior branch had remained staunchly Lancastrian. Lord John Neville had fought against Salisbury at the Battle of Blore Heath in September 1459. Neville had allegedly visited the Duke of York at Sandal and received a commission of array to raise troops for him (up to 8,000 men). (This John Neville should not be confused with Salisbury's son and the Kingmaker's younger brother of the same name, who also fought at the Battle of Blore Heath, but for his father.) Believing Neville to be leading a relieving force, as commissioned, York possibly saw the opportunity to envelope the Lancastrian force. Another theory is that the ruse involved men under Andrew Trollope's command dressing in the livery of Warwick the Kingmaker – the bear and ragged staff. These men may even have gained access to Sandal Castle. It is difficult to believe that any of these ruses would have worked if Salisbury had been aware of them.

Once York had engaged with Somerset and Devon, it became quickly clear that Neville was not leading a relieving force for the Yorkists but was in fact on the Lancastrian's side. On to the field then appeared further Lancastrian contingents led by Roos, Northumberland and finally Clifford. All had been waiting at some distance from Sandal behind tree and hill cover. The trap was sprung and York's smaller force was surrounded and overwhelmed 'like a fish in a net'. Salisbury and his son, Thomas, led out the Yorkists remaining in the castle to reinforce the beleaguered York, but it was to no avail. Still outnumbered, they were forced to retreat southwards towards the castle. York, Sir Thomas Neville and many of the Yorkists were killed. York was probably killed by Sir James Luttrell of Dunster, who had a personal grievance. The battle had lasted barely an hour. Salisbury escaped but was captured by Andrew Trollope's men during the night and taken to Pontefract Castle. He was publicly beheaded the next day. As his position weakened, York had sent away his second son, Edmund, Earl of Rutland, with Sir Robert Aspall. Lord Clifford, entering the fray late from the south, spotted their flight and pursued them on to Wakefield Bridge, where he famously slew Rutland 'as your father slew mine'. (It might have been in Kirkgate, north of the bridge.) After the battle, the severed heads of York, Salisbury, Rutland and Thomas Neville were placed on Micklegate Bar in York, 'so that York may look on York'.

Aftermath and Commentary

Wakefield was a total and utter disaster for the Yorkists. They were beaten on all fronts – by superior mobilisation and concentration, by skilful deception and by treachery. In effect they entered a lions' den and did not return. The top two Yorkist leaders had been killed at a stroke. It was now over to the younger generation. On the positive side, they still held King Henry, and Edward, Earl of March had now become 4th Duke of York and Henry's heir under the Act of Accord.

Wakefield remains the hardest of the Wars of the Roses battles to comprehend fully. How could two commanders as experienced as York and Salisbury get it so wrong so many times? York was no soldier – he was too important for that – but his military adviser, Sir David Hall, was with him. Why 'put your head in the lion's mouth' in the middle of winter when his own following in Yorkshire was not large? Where were Salisbury's much-vaunted northern retainers from Richmondshire? Why sit tight in hostile territory for so long? Deception and treachery are the answers, but to what depth does the treachery go? Interestingly a well-substantiated tradition states that the Wakefield Tower in the Tower of London is so named because it was used to house prisoners after the battle (although the chroniclers do not mention many prisoners who were not put to death). However, London and the Tower were in the hands of Warwick's Yorkists at the time, so surely they would not hold Yorkist prisoners from the battle?

Participants and Casualties	
Yorkist (~5,000 men)	**Lancastrian (~ 25,000 men)**
Richard, Duke of York	Henry Beaufort, Duke of Somerset
Edmund, Earl of Rutland	Percy, Earl of Northumberland
Richard Neville, Earl of Salisbury	Lord Clifford
Sir Thomas Neville	John, Lord Neville
Sir David Hall	Thomas Courtenay, Earl of Devon
Sir Thomas Parr	Henry Holland, Duke of Exeter
Sir Thomas Harrington	Andrew Trollope
Thomas Colt	Thomas, Lord Roos
	Humphrey, Lord Dacre of Gilsland
	Sir James Luttrell
	Sir Robert Whittingham
	Sir William Gascoigne
	Sir John Mauleverer
	Sir Richard Tempest
Casualties: ~ 2,000 died	Casualties: light

Location and What to See

Sandal Castle lies ½ mile west of the A61 Wakefield–Barnsley road, 2 miles south of Wakefield. The turning off the A61 is opposite Sandal Magna church. The castle stands in a magnificent setting above the River Calder but was badly slighted in the Civil War (a **visitor centre** has recently opened). The battle was fought to the north of the castle, between the Calder and the A61. Inevitably there are different theories as to the exact alignment of the opposing forces. Most of this area is now covered by housing.

However, we know the location of the death of **Richard, Duke of York**, because a splendid **monument** was re-erected in 1898 in Manygates Lane on Wakefield Green. (Edward IV had erected a wooden cross here after his father's death, which was destroyed in the Civil War.) It stands alongside an old school about ½ mile south of the railway bridge. (There is a view that the actual location of York's death occurred at the junction of Manygates Lane and Milnthorpe Lane, just yards to the north.) The main mêlée probably occurred even further to the north, on the line of the railway. As York retreated towards the safety of Sandal Castle, he was surrounded and killed.

The **chapel** on Wakefield Bridge (over the River Calder) near which York's second son **Edmund, Earl of Rutland** was traditionally killed, is still used. Built in the fourteenth century, it has a restored Victorian front. The bridge is very busy today, but you can park next to the chapel.

Victorian monument to Richard, Duke of York close to where he is thought to have been killed.

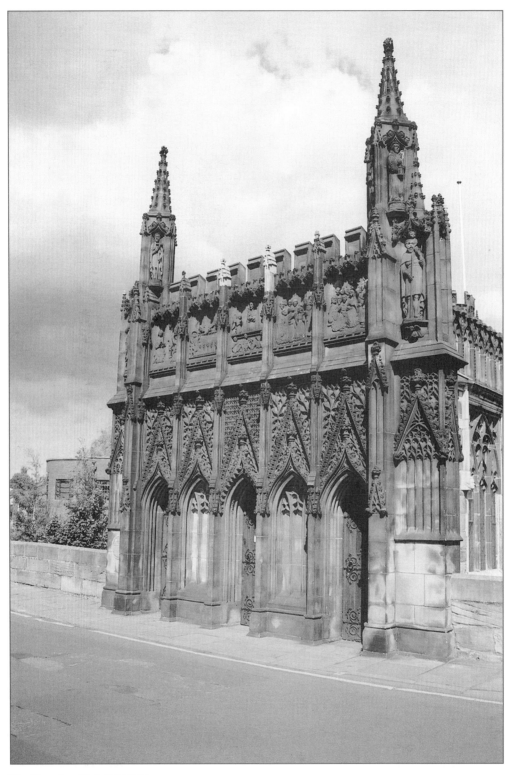

The Chapel on Wakefield Bridge.

Death of Edmund, Earl of Rutland on Wakefield Bridge, December 1460. Painting by E.F. Skimmer.

YORK ***

Micklegate Bar

South-west corner of city wall, near railway station.

It was here, at New Year 1461, that the severed heads of **Richard, Duke of York**, his second son Edmund, Earl of Rutland, **Richard Neville, Earl of Salisbury** and his second son Sir Thomas Neville were displayed after their deaths at the Battle of Wakefield, overwhelmed by a large Lancastrian force. Queen Margaret of Anjou, the Lancastrian war leader, is said to have ordered their display, so that 'York may look upon York'. This event provides one of the abiding images of the Wars of the Roses. Within three months, though, a victorious King Edward IV entered York 'hot foot' from the Battle of Towton and ordered the heads to be taken down and buried. King Henry VI and Margaret had remained in York during the battle but then had fled to Scotland.

The Minster

North edge of city walls.

The altar in the **St Nicholas Chapel** (north transept) sits upon a tomb-chest of Archbishop Thomas Rotherham of York (d. 1500). Previously Bishop of Rochester, then Lincoln, Rotherham was promoted to York in 1480. He was Lord Chancellor when Edward IV died in April 1483. He was a Woodville/Edward V supporter and in fact delivered the Great Seal to Queen Elizabeth. He was present at the Council meeting in the Tower on Friday 13 June 1483 at which Richard, Duke of Gloucester staged his second coup, and was imprisoned. He did not hold high office again. He died of plague at Cawood Castle, the palace of the medieval archbishops.

He is thought to have been the son of Sir John Scott of Brabourne, Kent, and to have taken the name of his birthplace. He was a great benefactor to York and to Rotherham.

Micklegate Bar, York, on which the severed heads of the defeated Yorkist leaders were displayed after the Battle of Wakefield.

Richard III Museum at Monk Bar, York.

In passing the **north choir aisle**, note the tomb of Archbishop Thomas Savage (d. 1507), who was a younger son of Sir John Savage and Katherine Stanley (see Macclesfield). His main interest as Archbishop is said to have been hunting, and he lived like a nobleman, not a cleric.

The choir screen in the nave contains statues of kings. The one on the extreme right represents **Henry VI** and was made in 1810. Over the years, it has received at times 'improper reverence' and has had to be removed on several occasions. The 'improper reverence' may be a reference to Henry's unofficial sainthood.

Note the Tudor roses on the **south transept** rose window, and the stained glass of Henry VI and Cardinal John Kemp (d. 1454) (see Canterbury) in the **Zouche Chapel** off the south-west choir aisle.

Monk Bar
North-east corner of city walls, near Minster. Open year round.

Here is something completely different. The privately run **Richard III Museum** has an interactive style that is ideal for children and school parties but also informative for adults, plus a good range of books. The upper storey was added by Richard III in 1484.

THE NORTH

ASHTON-UNDER-LYNE, St Michael's and All Angels Church **
South side of town centre, alongside A635 to Stalybridge.
Close to roundabout at east end (tower). 0161 308 2795.

This church contains fabulous **stained glass** in the **south aisle** of this church. Donated over four generations by the powerful Assheton family, this original glass (1460–1517) commemorates

- Sir John Assheton (d. 1428) and his four sons and three daughters. He was one of Henry V's top commanders and fought at Agincourt. He is a contender for the original 'Black Knight' of local legend. His son Sir Ralph, by his second wife, is the other (see Middleton).
- Sir Thomas de Assheton (d. 1457) and Elizabeth de Byron, his wife. He was an alchemist, licensed by Henry VI to search for the Philosopher's Stone, which would transmute base elements into gold. Unfortunately, he did not succeed.
- Sir John Assheton (1425–84) with his three wives, Dulcie, Margaret and Isabella. He was an ardent Lancastrian who was knighted at the Battle of Northampton (1460) and probably fought at the Battle of Towton (1461). Sir John contributed to the building of the present church.
- Sir Thomas Assheton (1447–1516) with his three wives, Elizabeth, Anne and Agnes. He married a fourth in 1512 but left no male heirs. He fought for Lancaster.

In the north aisle, the Kings' Window displays medieval glass of three saintly kings, including **Henry VI**.

DUNSTANBURGH, BAMBURGH, ALNWICK, Castles *** £
For directions, see later in entry.
Dunstanburgh: 01665 576231. Bamburgh: 01668 214515.
Alnwick: 01665 510777.

After Edward IV's great victory at the Battle of Towton in March 1461, he quickly achieved effective control of the English heartlands. However, Lancastrian resistance continued in two areas – Wales and Northumberland. In the latter, Percy retainers had quickly garrisoned these mighty fortresses, built to resist the Scots in the north of the county. For the next three years, control of the castles was hotly disputed between the Lancastrians led by the Duke of Somerset, Lords Roos and Hungerford/Moleyns and Sir Ralph Percy, with interventions by Queen Margaret with France and Scottish troops, and the Yorkists led by the Kingmaker and his younger brother John Neville, Lord Montagu, with distant support from Edward IV. These campaigns constituted a mini-war in the far north. Castles changed hands repeatedly, as did control of the region. Lancastrian efforts ultimately proved futile as no major towns were secured (both Carlisle and Newcastle were besieged but successfully defended for the Yorkists) and no threat to the south developed.

The campaigns came in waves. By the autumn of 1461, Warwick the Kingmaker had secured Alnwick and Dunstanburgh. In November, Sir William Tailboys took them back for Lancaster with a raiding party from Scotland and with the help of some treachery from Sir Ralph Percy.

In July 1462 Yorkist forces came north under Lord Hastings and Sir John Howard and obtained Tailboys' surrender at Alnwick, where Sir Ralph Grey was made captain. Bamburgh was also taken for the Yorkists by Sir William Tunstall. In October Queen Margaret led an invasion force which landed near Bamburgh with Pierre de Brézé and a sizeable contingent of French troops. The Lancastrians quickly regained Bamburgh and Alnwick without long sieges. Henry VI's standard was raised at Bamburgh but little local support was forthcoming.

The Yorkists reacted quickly by raising a huge force led by the Kingmaker and thirty-nine other nobles (the largest number to serve in the late medieval period), which came north in November 1462. All three castles were subject to full-scale sieges. Alnwick was defended by Hungerford, Sir Robert Whittingham and 300 men (mostly French); Bamburgh by Somerset, Lord Roos, Jasper Tudor, Earl of Pembroke and Sir Ralph Percy; Dunstanburgh by Sir Richard Tunstall and Sir Thomas Finderne – a fairly motley collection of Lancastrian die-hards.

The Kingmaker, Montagu, the Earl of Kent (William Neville, uncle to the Kingmaker), Lords Scales (brother to Queen Elizabeth Woodville) and Ogle commanded for the Yorkists. Warwick based himself at Warkworth Castle near Alnwick and coordinated the sieges through a daily visit to each, a round trip of 60 miles each day. Bamburgh and Dunstanburgh capitulated by Christmas Eve 1462, Alnwick by early January 1463. However, by May

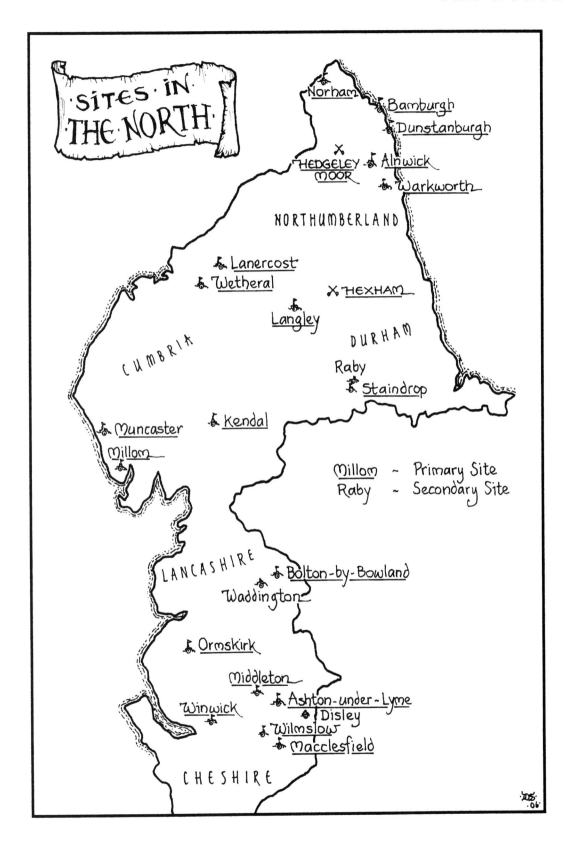

SITES IN THE NORTH

Norham
Bamburgh
Dunstanburgh
✗ HEDGELEY MOOR
Alnwick
Warkworth

NORTHUMBERLAND

Lanercost
Wetheral
✗ HEXHAM
Langley

DURHAM

CUMBRIA

Raby
Staindrop

Muncaster
Millom
Kendal

Millom — Primary Site
Raby — Secondary Site

LANCASHIRE

Bolton-by-Bowland
Waddington

Ormskirk
Middleton
Ashton-under-Lyme
Winwick
Disley
Wilmslow
Macclesfield

CHESHIRE

1463, all three castles were back in Lancastrian hands, betrayed by Sir Ralph Grey and Sir Ralph Percy, who returned to their Lancastrian roots.

Early in 1464 there was widespread civil unrest in more than fifteen counties in England. Encouraged by this, the Lancastrians in Northumberland went on full offensive led by the Duke of Somerset, recently returned to the Lancastrian fold from his flirtation with the Yorkists. From February to late March they extended their hold to castles in the Tyne Valley (e.g. Bywell, Hexham and Langley), plus Skipton in Yorkshire. However, disaster struck in April and May when they were defeated at the battles of Hedgeley Moor and Hexham by Lord Montagu. Most of the leaders were executed.

The Yorkists were then able to move on the three castles for the last time. Alnwick and Dunstanburgh surrendered without a fight but Sir Ralph Grey at Bamburgh refused. Edward IV's new siege artillery, utilising modern technology, was therefore fired in anger for the first time. The great gun 'Dijon' badly damaged the castle, and Sir Ralph was knocked unconscious. Sir Humphrey Neville took command of the garrison and quickly agreed terms. Sir Ralph, badly injured, suffered the full penalty for treason at Doncaster in July 1463. King Edward was now master of all England and Wales, with the exception of Harlech Castle, which did not surrender until 1468.

All three castles can be visited today. **Alnwick Castle** is still the home of the Percys and lies in the north-west corner of this small town on the B6341 to the Charltons. There is little fifteenth-century atmosphere internally though. **Bamburgh Castle** cannot be missed in daylight; it dominates the village whichever way you approach. Again, there is little to see inside that is of interest, so my recommendation is to spend your time walking on the beach by this castle in order to appreciate fully its superb location. **Henry VI** held a small Court here in 1464.

The best castle to visit is **Dunstanburgh**. Turn off the B1339 Alnmouth–Embleton road to Dunstan and Craster on the coast. From Craster, a splendid thirty-minute walk along the shore northwards brings you to the castle, which stands majestically ahead of you throughout the walk. The magnificent ruins were built on a rocky outcrop above the sea. A bonus here is **Queen Margaret's Cove** at the south-east edge of the outer bailey, near the Egyncleugh Tower (sometimes called Queen Margaret's Tower). Tradition has it that during the Wars of the Roses, **Queen Margaret of Anjou** was lowered from the tower to a waiting ship in the cove in heavy seas, so that she could escape a siege.

THE BATTLE OF HEDGELEY MOOR (25 April 1464) ++

Strategic Background and the Campaign

Early in 1464 there was widespread civil protest from Cornwall to Leicestershire against Edward IV's government. While Edward was distracted, Henry Beaufort, Duke of Somerset reneged on his pardon, rejoined his Lancastrian comrades in Northumberland and went on the offensive. Having failed to take Newcastle, he embarked on a major military campaign for two months. Accompanied by Sir Humphrey Neville, Lord Roos, Lord Hungerford and others he managed to overrun Norham Castle and Hexham, thus making deep inroads into the Tyne Valley. This offensive had already threatened the crucial talks that Edward had arranged with the Scots, now scheduled for late April in York. Lord Montagu, the Kingmaker's brother, was ordered to meet the Scottish envoys at Norham and to escort them to York.

This proved a perilous undertaking. Near Newcastle, Montagu just managed to avoid an ambush laid by Sir Humphrey Neville's Lancastrian force. After leaving Newcastle, Montagu continued northward with a large force. Some 9 miles north of Alnwick, his army encountered the Lancastrians drawn up across the old Roman road to Wooler.

The Battle

The Lancastrians were led by Somerset, with Lord Roos on the left and Sir Ralph Percy on the right. Even before the Yorkists could fully engage, the Lancastrians' left wing, led by Roos and Lord Hungerford, broke and fled, leaving Somerset and Sir Ralph Percy to cope on their own. They continued to advance and the mêlée developed. However, very soon the rest of the Lancastrian force fled, leaving only Sir Ralph Percy and his household retainers. Tradition has it that as Percy received his death blow he made one last leap for freedom. He is said to have covered 12 yards, now immortalised in the small battle-site park by two rocks placed this distance apart.

Aftermath and Commentary

This was an overwhelming victory for the Yorkists. Montagu was able to regroup and push on to Norham. The Scottish envoys were then escorted successfully down to York.

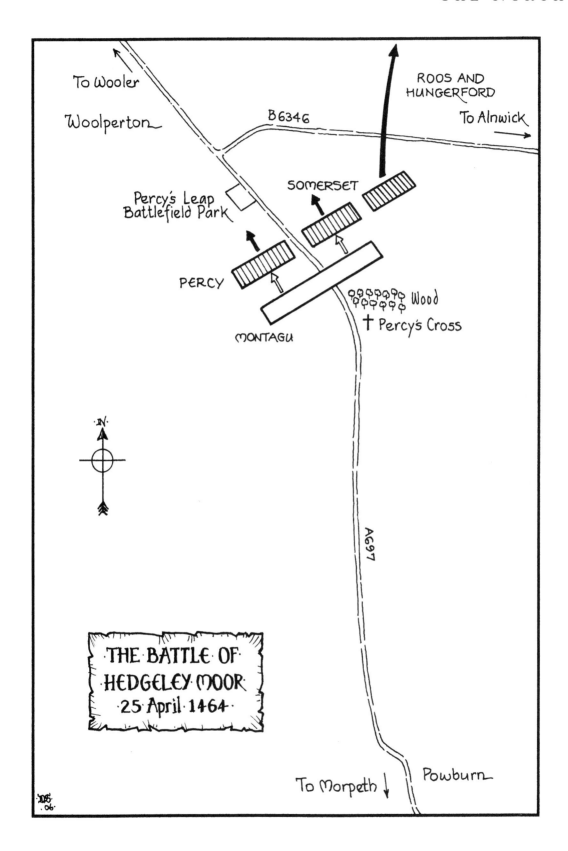

To Wooler

Woolperton

B6346

ROOS AND
HUNGERFORD

To Alnwick

SOMERSET

Percy's Leap
Battlefield Park

PERCY

MONTAGU

Wood

✝ Percy's Cross

·N·

A697

THE·BATTLE·OF·
HEDGELEY·MOOR·
·25·April·1464·

To Morpeth ↓

Powburn

Participants and Casualties

Yorkist (~5,000 men)
John Neville, Lord Montagu

Lancastrian (~5,000 men)
Henry Beaufort, Duke of Somerset
Lord Roos
Robert, Lord Hungerford (and Moleyns)
Sir Ralph Percy
Sir Ralph Grey
Sir Henry Bellingham

Location and What to See

The small **battlefield park** stands on the west side of the A697 Morpeth–Wooler road, 2 miles north of Powburn village, just before the right fork on the B6346 to Alnwick.

Percy's Cross is ½ mile south of the park, on the east side of the A697 on a fast bend. The splendid cross is behind a cottage and can be accessed from the stand of conifers.

THE BATTLE OF HEXHAM (15 May 1464) ++

Strategic Background and the Campaign

King Edward IV, alarmed at the success of the Lancastrians in penetrating the Tyne Valley in early 1464, had vowed in late March to mobilise a large army and march north to deal with them once and for all. Edward was now making preparations for that event. Notwithstanding their poor showing at the Battle of Hedgeley Moor, the Lancastrians

The Percy Cross on Hedgeley Moor.

254

had regrouped at Alnwick and re-entered the Tyne Valley with King Henry at their head and reinforced by Henry, Duke of Somerset, and were looking for a swift victory in the north before Edward arrived. Meanwhile, Montagu, after his successful escorting of the Scottish envoys, made his way back to Newcastle. Here he received intelligence that the Lancastrian army had reached Hexham and was encamped 2 miles south of the town alongside a river called Devil's Water.

The Battle
Montagu appears to have achieved almost total surprise soon after dawn. The Lancastrians led by Somerset had just enough time to flee their camp and redeploy a little upstream. They were, however, hopelessly trapped between the river and the western slope of the hill on which Montagu had been able to deploy. Montagu led the bulk of his forces in the centre flanked by Lords Willoughby and Greystoke (both former Lancastrians). His centre moved first in a rapid downhill charge which soon pushed back Somerset's men towards the river bank. Panic may have set in as men had to choose between drowning or being crushed. The whole length of the Yorkist line now engaged, but very soon Lords Roos and Hungerford were repeating their tricks from Hedgeley Moor and fleeing with their retinues across

a ford upstream from the battle. The Lancastrian line then broke and men fled for their lives. Somerset and his retainers were captured.

Aftermath and Commentary
This battle in effect represents the destruction of Lancastrian resistance in the north. The leaders were rounded up after the battle and executed at a number of locations in the north – Somerset at Hexham the next day, Roos and Hungerford at Newcastle. Sir William Tailboys was also found hiding in a coal-pit and executed at Newcastle.

While his army slept in the open, King Henry had lodged at Bywell Castle, just down the Tyne. Montagu quickly dispatched a party to capture him but he had already fled when they arrived. They did, however, find his coronated helmet, which Montagu subsequently presented to Edward IV. The other Tyne Valley fortresses, like Langley Castle, also fell quickly to the Yorkists. All that remained was for them to besiege Alnwick, Dunstanburgh and Bamburgh castles, still held by the Lancastrians. The first two fell easily; the last required a full-scale siege and bombardment, a rare event in the Wars of the Roses, and submitted in early July 1464.

A grateful King Edward meanwhile invested Montagu with the lands and titles of the Percy earls of Northumberland.

Participants and Casualties

Yorkist (~4,000 men)
John Neville, Lord Montagu
Lord Willoughby
Lord Greystoke

Lancastrian (~500 men)
Henry Beaufort, Duke of Somerset
Thomas, Lord Roos
Robert, Lord Hungerford (and Moleyns)
Sir Ralph Grey
Sir Humphrey Neville

Casualties: They were heavier on the Lancastrian side but low by contemporary standards. The main impact of the battle was to scatter the Lancastrian commanders, who were then hunted down, captured and executed

---

Location and What to See
The battlefield lies 2 miles south of Hexham on the B6306 Slaley/Blanchland road just over the narrow bridge over **Linnels Bridge** which crosses the river known as Devil's Water. The steep-sided valley is today heavily wooded and so visibility is limited. Try a visit in winter. This location is highly instructive; it shows that the numbers of combatants must have been limited and that the Lancastrians were caught in a hopeless position between the

river and the steep slope. It is almost as if Somerset thought he had found an excellent hide-out tucked away off the main Tyne Valley. Unfortunately it was also a death trap if an enemy did know that you were there. Was it an insider who passed on the intelligence to Montagu? Travel uphill towards Slaley. Just before the junction with the B6307 Corbridge road, stop and look north-west; a longer view of the slope down to the river and Linnels Farm can be obtained.

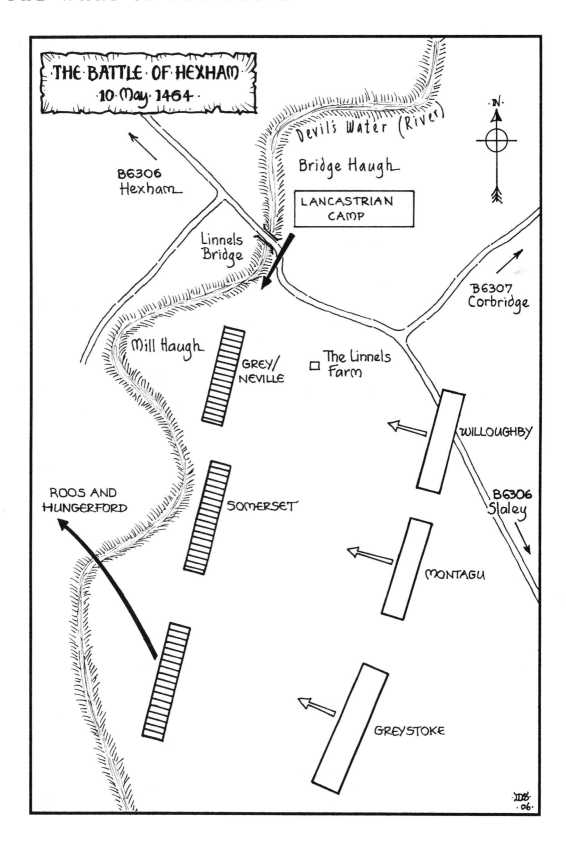

THE BATTLE OF HEXHAM
10 May 1464

B6306 Hexham

Devil's Water (River)

Bridge Haugh

LANCASTRIAN CAMP

N

Linnels Bridge

B6307 Corbridge

Mill Haugh

GREY/NEVILLE

The Linnels Farm

WILLOUGHBY

ROOS AND HUNGERFORD

SOMERSET

B6306 Slaley

MONTAGU

GREYSTOKE

The view down to Linnels Farm and Devil's Water as seen by John Neville before the Battle of Hexham.

KENDAL, Holy Trinity Church **
On southern approach to town on A6, ½ mile south, right-hand side.

In the **Parr Chapel** is the large tomb of Sir William Parr (d. 1484), a member of the powerful family based at the nearby castle. Sir William was a retainer of the Nevilles and fought at the Battle of Edgcote (1469) for Warwick the Kingmaker. William, Sir Geoffrey Gate and John Clapham led the mounted troop which decisively reinforced the northern army on the second day of the battle. The Earl of Pembroke's Welsh forces mistakenly thought the whole of Warwick's army had arrived and succumbed. At Doncaster in 1470 Sir William took up Edward IV's offer of a pardon and deserted Warwick and Clarence.

Early on in Edward's march south from Ravenspur the next year, Parr joined him at Nottingham with Sir James Harrington and 600 men. He fought at both the battles of Barnet and Tewkesbury. He was rewarded by Edward, becoming Controller of the Household. With his brother Sir John, he was one of Edward's chief supporters in the north-west and was appointed deputy to Richard, Duke of Gloucester in the West March. He was elected Knight of the Garter. He was a participant at Edward's funeral in 1483 and Richard III's coronation later the same year. He was a member of Richard's Council. Sir William was the grandfather of Queen Catherine Parr, Henry VIII's sixth wife.

Note the brasses to the Bellinghams, who lived at Burneside and were arch-rivals of the Parrs.

LANERCOST, Priory *** £
2 miles north-east of Brampton, signposted off A6071 (old A69), 1½ miles east of Brampton centre on minor road. EH. 01697 73030.

Two fine tomb-chests survive in the remains of the priory. They celebrate the first and second Lords Dacre of the North, Humphrey and Thomas. Humphrey (d. 1485) fought at the Battle of Towton for the Lancastrians alongside his brother Ranulph, Lord Dacre of Gilsland. Ranulph was killed in the battle and is buried in Saxton churchyard near the battlefield (see Towton). Sir Humphrey avoided capture but was attainted. He took part in Queen Margaret's attack on Carlisle in June 1461. The town was besieged but then relieved by Yorkist forces led by Lord Montagu, the Kingmaker's brother. Humphrey also raided deep into Durham, raising the standard of Henry VI at Brancepeth. Meanwhile he had reoccupied his own castle at nearby Naworth, thus proving to be a real thorn in the side of the Yorkists.

Humphrey was involved in a prolonged dispute over the Dacre succession with Sir Richard Fiennes, who had married his sister Joan Dacre. In 1463 Edward IV split the barony and Humphrey became Lord Dacre of the North. Later he became a supporter of Richard, Duke of Gloucester, being a councillor and Lieutenant of the West March in September 1484, much to the annoyance of the Percys. This wardenship was renewed under the Tudors and laid the basis of the Dacres fortunes later in that dynasty. Interestingly, Humphrey had the reversion of the Tower of London during the summer of 1483 when the Princes disappeared. There is no evidence to link him with events there though. Humphrey died two months before the Battle of Bosworth.

His son and heir, Lord Thomas (d. 1525), fought at Bosworth for Richard III but sensibly was not tempted by the Lambert Simnel rising in 1487. Reconciled to Tudor, he commanded the right wing at the Battle of Flodden in 1513.

LANGLEY, Castle *
West side of A686 Haydon Bridge–Alston road, about 1 mile south of Haydon Bridge. Hotel.

This tower house is now a luxury hotel, so go on, treat yourself and stay here, because it played a part, albeit small, in the mini-war in the north. Acquired by the Percys through marriage in the fourteenth century, it was lost to the Crown in 1461 when the 3rd Earl of Northumberland was posthumously attainted by Edward IV after the Battle of Towton. In early 1464 the castle was recaptured by the Lancastrians during their push down into the Tyne Valley. However, it was quickly recovered by the Yorkists after the Battle of Hexham in May that year. Later that month, the castle was granted to John Neville, the Kingmaker's brother, when Edward elevated him to the earldom of

Langley Castle, a Percy stronghold which was fought over in 1464.

Northumberland. In true Wars of the Roses fashion Neville was deprived of the earldom and Langley in 1470, as Edward strove to outwit the Kingmaker and his family, and the earldom returned to Henry Percy as 4th Earl. This perverse manoeuvre led directly to Edward IV's flight to Burgundy and the Readeption of Henry VI.

MACCLESFIELD, St Michael's Church ***
South side of town centre, above railway station.

In medieval times, among the aristocracy at least, it was a common custom for eldest sons to be given the same Christian names as their fathers. In some cases, furthermore, the same name would also be given to the eldest son of a second wife. From a distance of more than 500 years this can make accurate genealogy a real challenge. In this church we have exactly this situation and more. There are effigies here of at least four John Savages with dates of death between 1492 and 1528. Not only does uncertainty exist over the identification of each effigy, but also there is some confusion in the history books over who did what.

This is a pity, because this is a splendid collection of tomb-chests and effigies. We can at least be certain that one of these commemorates the Sir John Savage who commanded Henry VII's left wing at both the Battle of Bosworth (1485) and of Stoke Field (1487). The consensus is that he was the Sir John II who died in 1492 at the siege of Boulogne (he was the 'professional' soldier) and whose effigy lies between the **Savage Chapel** and the **chancel**. This Sir John joined Henry Tudor just days before Bosworth (he had previously been arrested by Richard III), along with Sir Simon Digby – see Coleshill) and Sir Brian Sandford and a considerable number of men. He was a cavalry expert and a nephew of Thomas, Lord Stanley through his mother. So this man was an important part of the Tudor fighting machine. He became a Knight of the Garter in 1488.

Sir John II was the son of the Sir John I (d. 1495), whose tomb-chest and effigies lie on the south side of the **chancel** alongside his wife, Katherine Stanley. He was also present at the Battle of Bosworth as a member of Stanley's retinue, but dispatched to assist

Effigies of Sir John Savage I and his wife Katherine Stanley, Macclesfield church.

Henry Tudor with three other knights. Intriguingly he sports a Yorkist collar (unlikely in 1495), but this may indicate that he was the Sir John who fought at the Battle of Tewkesbury for Edward IV. Sir John I became a knight of the body to Henry VII.

Sir John III and IV lie in the **Savage Chapel**, having died in 1527 and 1528. One of them may also have fought at Bosworth. Finally in the north chancel is an unidentified effigy (d. 1475). The lack of clarity does not really matter here. We can be sure that we are in the presence of major supporters for Henry Tudor in this church.

The Savages lived at Clifton, on the south bank of the Mersey near Runcorn. The site is now part of a chemical works named Rock Savage.

MIDDLETON, St Leonard's Church **
½ mile north of town centre on A664 to Rochdale (use junction 19 off M62 and come south).

Although long ago swallowed up by Greater Manchester, this splendid church perhaps surprisingly houses a brass to one of the more colourful characters of our tale. Sir Ralph Assheton (1420–89), his wife Margery Barton and thirteen children are commemorated in the **chancel**. Sir Ralph was born into the Assheton family of Ashton-under-Lyne, the youngest son of the second wife of Sir John Assheton. His wife came from Middleton. They moved away to Yorkshire (Fritton-in-Redesdale). Sir Ralph worked his way up to be a Knight of the Body of Edward IV and was made a knight banneret by Richard, Duke of Gloucester during the Scottish campaign of 1482. He continued as a knight of the body under Richard III, being brought down south in May 1483 as part of the first wave of Richard's northern implants. He attended Richard's coronation and was granted lands in Kent.

He helped suppress Buckingham's Revolt in October 1483, gaining much notoriety for brutal suppression. His habit of wearing black armour gained him the title 'the Black Knight'. On 24 October 1483 he was appointed Vice-Constable by Richard, with the power to try treason cases without appeal, i.e. Ralph was chief enforcer. Tradition has it that he ordered prisoners to be rolled downhill in barrels containing spikes. A ditty of the time ran:

Sweet Jesu for they mercy's sake,
And for thy bitter Passion,
Save us from the axe of the Tower,
And from Sir Ralph of Assheton.

He fought for Richard at the Battle of Bosworth but was not attainted and appears to have made his peace with Henry VII. Sir Ralph is said to have been murdered by his peasants in 1489. A harsh and uncharismatic man, Sir Ralph is a candidate for the origins of the old tradition of parading and destroying an effigy each Easter Monday in Ashton-under-Lyne, known as 'Riding the Black Lad'.

MILLOM, Holy Trinity Church **
On A5093 to Duddon Bridge, 1 mile north of town centre/railway station. This is not the church near the town centre.

The Huddlestons were Neville retainers who, like so many northerners, switched to Richard, Duke of Gloucester after Warwick's death in 1471. In this church are two tomb-chests which commemorate late fifteenth-century Huddlestons. There is a problem of identification because three generations of male heirs died between 1485 and 1503 – Sir John (d. 1494), his son Sir Richard (d. 1484/5) and the latter's son Richard (d. 1503). My preference is for Sir John and his wife to be associated with the fine tomb-chest with effigies, and for Richard junior and wife Elizabeth Dacre be celebrated by the coarser, plain tomb-chest (the guidebook says the opposite).

Sir John was an esquire of the body to Henry VI but became an early Yorkist, involved with both Newcastle and Cockermouth castles in 1460/1. He stayed with the Nevilles in 1469/70 and was arrested by Edward IV after Warwick's escape to France in 1470. Sir John prospered under Richard III, becoming sheriff of Cambridgeshire. He was a kinsman of Sir James Harrington of Hornby, Lancashire, another prominent Richard III supporter in the north. Sir John fought for Richard III at the Battle of Bosworth, escaped and took refuge with another son, Henry, in the Lakeland Fells. He was involved in an attempted rising led by Francis, Lord Lovell in 1486 but was pardoned. However, by late 1486 he was in Fleet Prison with Sir James Harrington. Sir John had the sense to avoid the 1487 Lambert Simnel revolt, even though the invasion force landed at nearby Barrow.

His son, Sir Richard, married Margaret, the natural daughter of Warwick the Kingmaker (how did he find the time?), receiving a £200 p.a. grant of lands in Norfolk and Richmondshire for his sins. Sir Richard was much favoured by Richard

III, becoming keeper of the lands of Thomas Grey, Marquis of Dorset when they were forfeit after Buckingham's Revolt in 1483, and Constable of Beaumaris Castle and Captain of Anglesey. Sir Richard died in late 1484.

Richard junior died before gaining his majority. The church lies next to the ruins of **Millom Castle**, inhabited by the Huddlestons and now partly incorporated into a private farmhouse.

MUNCASTER, Castle and grounds **

Muncaster Castle lies on the A595 Barrow–Whitehaven road. (More detail below.) 01229 717614.

The castle lies in delightful country with the sea on one side and the Wasdale hills behind. It is also a place which over the centuries has been proud of its involvement with the Wars. Here, in 1464, the then owner, Sir John Pennington, as a Lancastrian sympathiser, gave hospitality to the wandering **Henry VI** and his small band after the Lancastrian defeat at the Battle of Hexham. Although the castle

has medieval elements, the internal atmosphere is not fifteenth century. However, the family does have in the castle a number of items which by tradition are said to have belonged to Henry, including a **lock of his hair**, a **commode** in the King's bedroom, the **'Luck of Muncaster'**, a **drinking horn** (only a replica is on view), and a later **painting** (even the brochure describes it as awful).

Of most interest is an **octagonal high tower** built in the late eighteenth century by the then Lord Muncaster as a folly to mark the spot where, by tradition, King Henry was found by a local shepherd on Muncaster Fell and brought to meet Sir John Pennington at the castle. The tower is nearly a mile up the hillside from the castle and can be seen from the A595 south of Muncaster. It is not currently open to the public but can be more closely observed by following the public bridleway north-east from the A595 on the sharp bend north of the castle car park. Climb towards Chapel Hill and then turn right on a circuitous path steeply down through conifer forest to the tower. In total it is a 45-minute walk.

Eighteenth-century monument to Henry VI, Muncaster Castle.

NORHAM, Castle ** £

½ mile east of village on minor road to Horncliffe.
EH. 01289 382329.

Norham commanded a ford of the Tweed and thus stands on the English–Scottish border, our most northerly site and close to Berwick. It was owned by the Bishop of Durham and, because of its location, had a long and continuous history of warfare. In early 1463, while both Edward IV and Warwick the Kingmaker were in the south, the Lancastrians regained control of the key Northumbrian fortresses of Alnwick, Bamburgh and Dunstanburgh, largely through defections by the 'Yorkist' commanders Sir Ralph Percy and Sir Ralph Grey. Meanwhile Queen Margaret of Anjou had been busy securing French and Scottish support and military assistance for the Lancastrian cause. During July, a full-scale invasion force of the young Scottish king James III, his queen Mary of Gueldes, Pierre de Brézé, **Queen Margaret** and Grey and their forces crossed the Tweed and laid siege to Norham. The castle held out for eighteen days until a force led by **the Kingmaker** and **Lord Montagu** (his brother John Neville had just been made Warden of the East March), arrived from the south and raised the siege. The Lancastrian multinational force panicked and fled back into Scotland. Montagu in turn raided some 63 miles into Scotland. This rout was important because it effectively ended Franco-Scottish cooperation with the Lancastrians. During her own flight, Queen Margaret and Prince Edward are said to have been robbed of their jewellery by a gang of thieves who then proceeded to argue among themselves, allowing the royal pair to escape, but without the jewellery.

Geographically isolated, Norham fell to the Lancastrians again in early 1464, when their fortunes reached a new high in Northumberland (probably through treachery). In April, Montagu was on his way to Norham to escort Scottish envoys to meet Edward IV at York for peace negotiations when he encountered Lancastrian forces at the Battle of Hedgeley Moor (Woolperton) led by Somerset. After his victory, Montagu continued on his way to Norham, met up with the envoys, and thence escorted them to York.

ORMSKIRK, St Peter & St Paul's Church ****

Town centre on west side on A570 Skelmersdale–Southport road on a bend. 01695 572143.

In the **Derby Chapel** are two sets of battered effigies brought here after the Dissolution from nearby Burscough Priory. These modest monuments com-memorate one of the most significant and successful participants in the entire wars – **Thomas Stanley, Earl of Derby** (1435–1504). It was the Stanleys' defection from Richard III to Henry Tudor on the battlefield at Bosworth that ensured victory for Tudor.

The effigies on the left represent Thomas and his first wife, Eleanor Neville (*c*. 1440–70), sister to Warwick the Kingmaker. They married in 1454, a marriage of great political statement given that the Stanleys had hitherto been solid Lancastrians. The right-hand effigies have never been a pair in life or death. The man is the third Earl of Derby (d. 1572) while the woman is none other than **Lady Margaret Beaufort** (1443–1509), Henry Tudor's mother and Thomas, 1st Earl's second wife. They were married in 1472 in what was to prove the greatest politico-military partnership of the age, culminating in Henry Tudor's capturing the throne of England. But this is not Lady Margaret's spiritual home. After Henry became king, she took a vow of eternal chastity and left Stanley's bed. Her magnificent effigy lies in much grander surroundings close to her son in Westminster Abbey. Lady Margaret had moved on and was laying claim to her true royal inheritance.

STAINDROP, St Mary's Church ***

East end of village on B688 Barnard Castle–Bishop Auckland road.

A large alabaster tomb-chest and effigies to Ralph Neville, 1st Earl of Westmorland (1354–1425) and his two wives, Margaret Stafford and **Joan Beaufort** (daughter of John of Gaunt by Katherine Swynford). Ralph Neville was a pillar of the Lancastrian dynasty, supporting Henry IV during his troubles with the Percys and others in the early 1400s as he struggled to secure his throne. Originally a retainer of John of Gaunt, he became councillor to all three Lancastrian kings and built up extensive estates in the north, based around four castles (Raby, Brancepeth, Middleham and Sheriff Hutton). By 1410, Neville was supreme in the north.

Ralph has special relevance for the Wars of the Roses because of his second marriage to Joan Beaufort in 1396 with her royal (but only recently legitimated) blood. Their eldest son was Richard Neville, Earl of Salisbury, and their grandson was another Richard Neville, Earl of Warwick. The 'Stafford' Nevilles were staunchly Lancastrian but of limited effectiveness, while the 'Beaufort' Nevilles take centre stage in our story as Yorkists. (For Joan Beaufort, see Lincoln)

Raby Castle, home of the Nevilles (senior branch) with view of Joan Beaufort's Tower.

While you are at Staindrop, do not miss the beautiful **Raby Castle** (1 mile north on A688), ancestral home of the Nevilles. Here was born **Cecily, Duchess of York** (née Neville), the youngest daughter of Ralph, above, and mother to Edward IV and Richard III. She was known as the 'Rose of Raby'. A walk in the park provides a great view of the castle exterior, in particular **Joan's (Beaufort) Tower** and the **Neville Gateway** in the south-west corner.

WARKWORTH, Castle ** £

Village centre on A1068 Ashington–Alnwick road. EH. 01665 711423.

The castle was favoured as the Earl of Northumberland's residence when in the county, whereas nearby Alnwick was the military fortress for border defence. The castle fell into Lancastrian hands in October 1462 when Queen Margaret and Pierre de Brézé invaded Northumberland and took control of most of it. However, the Yorkists quickly recaptured Warkworth as the Kingmaker marched north (in Edward IV's absence with measles at Durham) with a huge host. Warwick selected Warkworth as his HQ, and Lords Wenlock, Grey and Codnor and Cromwell were based there. Warwick managed the autumn campaign to besiege the Lancastrian-held castles of Alnwick, Bamburgh and Dunstanburgh through a daily round on horseback from Warkworth. By early January 1463, all three had surrendered and were

in Yorkist hands – an outstanding achievement by the Kingmaker.

The **tower** in the south-west corner was built in the late fifteenth century by **John Neville Lord Montagu**, the Kingmaker's youngest brother, and is named after him. It is the only surviving memorial to this unsung Yorkist commander. Montagu was made Earl of Northumberland in 1464 by Edward IV as the Percy lands were attainted, but famously had them taken back by Edward in 1470. Montagu occupied Warkworth until that time.

WETHERAL, Holy Trinity Church *

South side of village green, ¼ mile off B6263, down steep dead-end lane. June–August Sundays. KAL

By the **north door** there are two battered effigies and a tomb-chest for Sir Richard Salkeld (1500) and his wife, Jane Vaux ('SS' collar). They lived at nearby Corby Castle and were Neville retainers. In 1462 Sir Richard was rewarded by Edward IV for capturing in this area James Butler, Earl of Wiltshire, in flight after Towton, and for afterwards taking Carlisle with Lord Montagu, the Kingmaker's brother. He gained dispossessed Percy lands and was made Constable of Carlisle Castle. During the 1460s he helped the Kingmaker protect the West March. In 1469/70 he supported the Nevilles against Edward IV and was involved in a small-scale rising near Carlisle. He was pardoned in September 1470 by

The battered effigies of Sir Richard Salkeld and wife, Wetheral church.

Edward. Like so many other northerners, he became a retainer of **Richard III**, esquire of the body and councillor.

WILMSLOW, St Bartholomew's Church **
North end of town by River Bollin. Turn off A34 Congleton–Manchester under railway arches on A538 for Wilmslow. Church is ahead after ⅓ mile. 01625 520309.

At the Battle of Blore Heath in September 1459, the Lancastrian force under James Touchet, Lord Audley contained large contingents of Cheshire men. Audley's death and the ensuing defeat led to heavy casualties among these troops. On the floor of the **Prescott Chapel** (beneath the carpet) is one of the few remaining memorials to such men – a brass to Sir Robert del Bouthe (d. 1459) and his wife, Douce (d. 1453). Sir Robert was killed in the battle, or died from wounds later. Queen Margaret of Anjou had specially recruited this force of Cheshiremen under the banner of the Prince of Wales in order to begin the process of building up his prestige and support. She is said to have taken this defeat at the hands of Richard Neville, Earl of Salisbury particularly badly.

WINWICK, St Oswald's Church *
West side of village, ¾ mile north of junction 9 of M62, at fork of A573 Golborne road. KAL.

In the **Legh Chapel** there is a very interesting brass of Sir Piers Legh (1455–1527) and his wife, Ellen Savage (d. 1497), daughter of the Sir John Savage (I) and Katherine Stanley buried at Macclesfield. Sir Piers was a retainer of Thomas, Lord Stanley (note the family connection), who fought in Scotland with Richard, Duke of Gloucester and was made a knight banneret. He also received an annuity of £10 from Richard as king in 1483. He was present at the Battle of Bosworth, having linked up with Henry Tudor at the last moment on 19 August 1485 with a 'sizeable company'. He may also have been present at the Battle of Stoke Field (1487). He attended Henry VII's funeral in 1509.

His wife died in 1497. Unusually, he did not marry again and, in fact, in 1511 he moved away to Lyme Hall near Disley, Cheshire and entered a monastery. He qualified as an ordained priest and then financed the building of a chantry chapel at **Disley**, Cheshire (now the parish church, where he and Ellen are celebrated in **glass**).

BIBLIOGRAPHY

Baldwin, David, *Elizabeth Woodville: Mother of the Princes in the Tower*, Sutton Publishing, 2002

Bennett, Michael, *The Battle of Bosworth*, Sutton Publishing, 1985

Boardman, A.W., *The Battle of Towton*, Sutton Publishing, 1994

Brooks, Chris and Cherry, Martin, 'The Prince and the Parker', *The Journal of Stained Glass*, vol. XXVI (1992)

Carpenter, Christine, *The Wars of the Roses*, Cambridge University Press, 1997

Castor, Helen, *The King, the Crown and the Duchy of Lancaster*, Oxford University Press, 2000

Chrimes, S.B., *Henry VII*, Eyre Methuen, 1972

Clive, Mary, *This Sun of York*, Macmillan, 1973

Cokayne, George, *The Complete Peerage*, St Catherine's Press, 1910–59

Evans, H.T., *Wales and the Wars of the Roses*, Cambridge University Press, 1915; reissued Sutton Publishing, 1995

Gill, Louise, *Richard III and Buckingham's Rebellion*, Sutton Publishing, 1999

Gillingham, John, *The Wars of the Roses: Peace and Conflict in Fifteenth Century England*, 1981

Given-Wilson, Chris, *The English Nobility in the Late Middle Ages: The Fourteenth-Century Political Community*, Routledge & Kegan Paul, 1987

Goodman, Anthony, *The Wars of the Roses*, Routledge & Kegan Paul, 1981

——, *The Wars of the Roses – the Soldiers' Experience*, Tempus, 2005

Griffiths, R.A., *The Reign of Henry VI*, Benn, 1981; reissued Sutton Publishing, 1998

Griffiths, Ralph and Roger Thomas, *The Making of the Tudor Dynasty*, Sutton Publishing, 1985

Haigh, Philip A., *The Military Campaigns of the Wars of the Roses*, Sutton Publishing, 1995

——, *The Battle of Wakefield 1460*, Sutton Publishing, 1996

——, *From Wakefield to Towton*, Pen and Sword, 2002

Hammond, P.W., *The Battles of Barnet and Tewkesbury*, Sutton Publishing, 1990

Hampton, W.E., *Memorials of the Wars of the Roses: A Biographical Guide*, Richard III Society, 1979

Hicks, Michael, *Who's Who in Late Medieval England*, Shepheard-Walwyn, 1991

——, *False, Fleeting, Perjur'd Clarence*, Sutton Publishing, 1992

——, *Warwick the Kingmaker*, Blackwell, 1998

——, *Richard III*, Tempus, 2000

——, *Edward IV*, Arnold, 2004

Hodges, Geoffrey, *Ludford Bridge and Mortimer's Cross*, Logaston Press, 1989

Johnson, P.A., *Duke Richard of York 1411–60*, Oxford University Press, 1988

Jones, Michael K., *Bosworth 1485*, Tempus, 2002

Jones, Michael K. and Malcolm G. Underwood, *The King's Mother: Lady Margaret Beaufort, Countess of Richmond and Derby*, Cambridge University Press, 1992

Kinross, John, *Discovering Battlefields of England and Scotland*, Shire, 2004

Marks, Richard and Paul Williamson (eds), *Gothic Art for England 1400–1547*, Victoria and Albert Museum, 2003

Mee, Arthur, The King's England series, Hodder & Stoughton, 1936–

Pevsner, Nikolaus, The Buildings of England Series, from 1950s

Pollard, A.J, *Richard III and the Princes in the Tower*, Sutton Publishing, 1991

——, *The Wars of the Roses*, Macmillan, 2001

Ross, Charles, *Edward IV*, Yale University Press, 1974

——, *Richard III*, Yale University Press, 1981

Seward, Desmond, *Richard III*, Franklin Watts, 1982

——, *The Wars of the Roses*, Viking Penguin, 1995

Smurthwaite, David, *Ordnance Survey Battlefields of Britain*, Webb and Bower, 1984

Storey, R.L., *The End of the House of Lancaster*, Barrie and Rockliff, 1966; reissued Sutton Publishing, 1986

Watts, John, *Henry VI and the Politics of Kingship*, Cambridge University Press, 1996

Wedgwood, J.C., *History of Parliament – biographies of the Members of the House of Commons 1439–1509*, HMSO, 1936

Weir, Alison, *Britain's Royal Families*, Bodley Head, 1989

——, *The Princes in the Tower*, Bodley Head, 1992

——, *Lancaster and York*, Jonathan Cape, 1995

Wolffe, Bertram, *Henry VI*, Yale University Press, 1981

INDEX OF PEOPLE FEATURED IN THE GUIDE

Bold indicates location of biographical detail of a major participant. <u>Underline</u> means this is the site of a memorial or building associated with this person.

INDEX OF PRIMARY AND SECONDARY SITES